STRING QUARTETS

A Most Intimate Medium

A Listener's Guide to the Genre from 1800

JOHN HOOD

Second Edition – Version 2.0
Copyright © 2018

Dedicated to the memory
of a brother in Christ

Ken Hood [1948-2017]

The Lord is my shepherd,
I shall not want…
Surely goodness and mercy
shall follow me
all the days of my life…
And I shall dwell in the house
of the Lord forever

[Extracted from Psalm 23]

Table of Contents

i

ii

iv

v

vi

Preface to the Second Edition

This edition contains a few changes in the form and content from that which was first published in August 2017. It really doesn't seem that long ago.

I have managed to include discussions of approximately 240 composers and over 360 string quartet works this time. A lot of the new entries are from the twentieth century, or even more contemporary, but I am always on the lookout for interesting and/or neglected composers from any era. I expect to continue publishing regularly, although the gaps between books may be longer in future. They will also likely contain string quartet composers that people have not heard of – in fact, I probably haven't heard of most of them myself yet either – I am still searching.

You will find some images of CD covers, string quartet ensembles and sometimes sepia toned photos of old composers scattered throughout this book. Many thanks to all of the CD companies and string quartets who have freely given me permission to use these images, which are credited, where applicable. Apologies to any quartet that I couldn't fit in. Very rarely, I will use an image of a CD on an obscure label that I was not able to contact. I mention this fact with the image.

There are also a small number of discussions of string quintets and sextets contained herein – these ensembles are both closely related to string quartets and are normally augmented by a combination of an extra cello, viola or double bass. Although their repertoire is relatively limited, there are some wonderful works available, and I am sure they will be of interest to regular string quartet listeners. I'm going to keep up with this approach in the future.

Further, I have been working closely with Kai Christiansen from earsense, whose magnificent chamber music blog, located at www.earsense.org is organised in a more user-friendly style than YouTube and often includes multiple performances of a discussed work. Kai is a computer professional and has developed a fully functional database search engine, which allows you to go straight to a composer or work. We have a reciprocal arrangement and both reference each other as a source. I must confess that I find the vagaries of YouTube's search function to be very frustrating as it is not well implemented for this purpose, often returning too many irrelevant results. Similarly with Spotify, music can be quite hard to locate although it is possible to stumble upon some gems, as I have occasionally.

John Hood – September 2018

Updated Introduction

It has often been said that string quartets represent a composer's most intimate and personal works, and innermost thoughts – a statement with which I wholeheartedly agree. This humble assembly of two violins, viola and cello seems to be able to express the whole range of human emotional expression. I have many string quartets and have been listening to the genre for over 25 years, mostly in awe and with a sense of wonder. To my knowledge, there is to date no other listener's guide resembling this book, therefore, I thought it would be a useful addition to the string quartet literature.

Although my background is that of a musician, I am not classically trained, therefore this book is never really technical. Particularly, it is not an academic treatise. Rather, the discussions are about my personal reactions to the emotional sound of the music – these are the thoughts of just one, albeit impassioned listener. I am sure many would see these works from a different perspective, especially people with an academic or technical background.

For me, music is a place, and string quartets have taken me to some beautiful, fascinating and abstract places. My personal preference is for European quartets, from the first half of the twentieth century. However, there are quartets from many periods and countries contained within these pages. Basically restricting myself to only music composed after 1800, you will find some Classical but it will be *Late Classical.*

Just a note on my use of the word *abstract.* My online dictionary defines it as *Existing only in the mind; separated from embodiment.* I believe that music is the most abstract form of the arts, you can't see it and you can't touch it – only experience it. I also believe that we all hear music differently. The string quartet repertoire, particularly in the twentieth century, makes extensive use of abstract sound spaces that are *non-representational* or *intangible.* I have always been drawn to these musical spaces and thus the word is commonly used in this book. I just love that mysterious introspective feeling…

I do use some basic musical terms. These are underlined the first time I use a term in a discussion and descriptions can be found in the Glossary in Appendix 1, which contains Common Composer Markings and Other Relevant Musical Terms. I have also put up a PDF document of the glossary on my website, so that if you wish, you can download it and keep the PDF or a printed copy handy. This document's internet location can be found in Appendix 1. In any event, I am sure you will soon become familiar with my standard musical vocabulary. For what it's worth, YouTube and earsense references are also underlined as they are linked to available, listenable recordings in the Kindle eBook version.

I have devised my own selection of musical categories which you will encounter at the beginning of each composer's section. These can be found in the Categories and Style Descriptors located in Appendix 2. Although they are capitalised in their definition, sometimes that convention is discarded, in particular, when using the terms *modern* and *contemporary*, which tend to have very broad meanings. Apologies in advance to syntactical pedants on this issue.

The basics of the popular string quartet repertoire are mostly covered, but there will surely be some readers that feel I have not included some particular composer, possibly their favourite. It may be that the composer wasn't to my taste, or, that they are still on my 'short-list', which is constantly growing. My personal feeling is that most musicians, including quite a few string quartet ensembles that I have spoken to, have relatively little knowledge of quartets that are not in the standard touring repertoire. There seems to be about a 'top 50', then they rapidly thin out. I believe I have included most of this mythical list, although there are some notable exceptions, such as Brahms, who apparently composed three magnificent quartets, but I just cannot seem to make an emotional connection with them.

I have however, discussed many other, obscure, but fascinating composers that I have come across in my musical journey. You would be unlikely to hear their works when a string quartet comes to town, but for me, there is a wealth of wonderful music out there to be enjoyed. I would encourage you to seek out some of these works and listen for yourself, to determine your own taste and personal likes. After a life of owning record shops, playing music professionally and years of intense listening, I have always been of the opinion that we all hear and respond to music in different ways. But I suppose this question is ultimately one for the philosophers and I realise that these thoughts may be just the result of my own relatively strong attitudes and formative musical experiences.

Mostly, you will be able to hear this music on Spotify, earsense or YouTube and I indicate when this is the case.

Each quartet, or set of quartets, has an assigned *Listenability rating*. This is not about the quality of the music or performance, but more about the level of intensity of the piece. Some people may find certain modern quartets a little confronting, whereas I rather enjoy a little dissonance or chaos now and again, but not noise. I hope the rating will especially be of assistance to the novice listener.

It's worth mentioning that I often use the term *New and Used* when talking about availability from Amazon. This usually means that the item can no longer be obtained through Amazon, but that copies are held by Amazon resellers. I have attempted to include only quartets that are still available on CD, however, given the state of the music business, this may be a little problematic. Occasionally I do discuss a CD that is only available as a digital download, and we are definitely moving into a new era where recorded music is often more readily available by this method. A study of retail music sales data confirms my observation. Given this conclusion, I'd simply say – get in while you can.

Most of the material contained in this book originated in a string quartet blog, but has been extensively rewritten for the book. The blog is still very active

– details can be found in Appendix 3, Blog and Website. In the future, I intend to update the blog with my revisions when I get a chance.

John Hood – September 2018

COMPOSERS

Hans Abrahamsen
to
William Zinn

Hans Abrahamsen [born 1952]

Nationality: Danish
Quartets: At least four
Style: Contemporary

New Simplicity
String Quartets Nos. 2 & 3

The term *New Simplicity* is mentioned on the Wikipedia page for the composer. I realise now that I have discussed much music in the past that could be classed as such. It appears to be a term for a reaction against the advances, and sometimes excesses of Modernism.

The Second Quartet, written in 1981, is in four movements. It opens with a sense of minimalism, as brief episodes of an ostinato alternate with periods of short violin statements. This is soon discarded however, and the violins assume control in a slightly microtonal phase. Now a pensive violin is heard, quite confronting, as the second violin and viola construct a dissonant wall of sound. The violins segue into a soft, propulsive section with a rhythmic motif before a solo violin makes a statement featuring string sound effects which take us to the end.

The next movement, which is quite short, and dominated by chordal sounds, commences with sharp, spiky chords – it has no constant rhythm. Gradually, harmonised lines appear within the chords, making for a melodic effect. A return to the opening, at a lower volume leads into a totally abstract, random passage of violins before fading on a gentle chord.

The third movement opens with flute-like sounds, I really don't know how this is achieved, but it does emanate from violins. The mood is visceral, and develops into a sparse violin duet - wonderfully quiet melodies are heard. Now a sustained chord interrupts the mood, which soon returns, this time a little more assertive but still very gentle. Passive violins hold sustained tones into a soft conclusion.

The final movement begins with an atonal flourish, leading into a dissonant passage which begins aggressively but soon turns into a mood similar to that of the previous movement. A marvellous soundscape unfolds as the intensity is reduced and chordal backing underpins atonal violin musings. This effect is sustained for some minutes and is beautiful in its abstraction. A violin line slowly comes to the surface, before a sustained chord gives way to propulsion. The final passage is one of rapidly increasing dynamics and tension, as the work concludes on a chaotic crescendo moving into some final sharp chords. This is a fascinating movement, one that I have found very difficult to describe. Overall – a wonderful work.

The Third Quartet, also in four movements was composed in 2008, making it one of the more contemporary works that I have encountered. The first movement is extremely brief and is not of its time. The sound is almost like gentle Baroque flutes that express a short melody before fading out.

The next movement commences on a sustained chord, with no melodic development for some time. Eventually the violins begin to evince long tones – this is another fascinating soundscape. Now the violins construct a rhythmic pattern which doesn't last as a return to the sparsity ensues. The rhythmic pattern resumes, again not for long as the violins become more expressive. The music pauses, then continues with this magical mood to a conclusion.

The third movement is also very short and again not of its time. It starts with a very major scale sounding, ascending violin phrase, before being joined by the second violin, which offers up supporting harmonies. Again, the sound is flute-like and the music is allowed to briefly exist before a fadeout.

The final movement opens with a sustained, mildly dissonant chordal mood – there is very little musical movement here. Occasional pauses show indications of a background sound effect which I can neither recognise nor define. The piece continues with a feeling of stasis until the conclusion.

Just a note on the other quartets on this CD. The First, titled *10 Preludes* from 1973 is a collection of ten short pieces, in many contrasting styles. I have seen this recorded elsewhere as a one movement work. The Fourth, while on the surface appears to be a more challenging piece, is really a continuation of the style of those previously discussed. One, relatively long movement (for Abrahamsen) consists of a solo cello, with occasional interjections, for its entirety.

The review CD is titled *String Quartets Nos.1-4,* performed by the Arditti String Quartet, released on the WDR label. For me, it is one of their more approachable efforts, I usually find them quite confronting. This disc is available on Amazon US and UK.

It can also be found on Spotify, YouTube and earsense.

Listenability: Fascinating Contemporary works, filled with contrast.

Bruce Adolphe [born 1955]

Nationality: American
Quartets: At least four
Style: Contemporary

Two Named Quartets -
String Quartets Nos. 1 & 2

String Quartet No. 1, titled *By a Grace of Sense Surrounded*, is a one movement work. Opening with a mildly atonal mood, which is rather alluring, it then moves into a gentle melodic figure for a time before drifting into tempo with a slightly abstract tinge. The tempo never really seems to get going at this stage and there are lots of deep melodic episodes. The music develops into a series of many brief moments, variously melodic, atonal, solo, ensemble, and some minimalist parts. By my reckoning the longest continuous section is about two minutes. There is a beautiful solo cello statement, with the other players adding interest around the fringes, before it is the turn of the violin to engage in some brooding melodies. There is a quivering violin near the end which leads back into more solo-based playing and, finally, a conclusion. It only runs for about 14 minutes.

This is slightly modern music that sits on the conservative end of the genre. It contains gentle chaos and a large number of different atmospheres. It is a splendid piece of writing.

String Quartet No. 2 is titled *Turning, Returning* and contains four named movements. They are all short – again it runs for about 14 minutes.

At Night has an ostinato that continues virtually right throughout this brief movement. Melodies come and go in a similar manner to the previous piece, with the exception being the constant undercurrent of rhythm.

From My Childhood begins in a slow tempo with sustained notes leading to a melancholy feeling. There is a pulse here and the melodies drift across it. The pulse occasionally ceases for a while, leaving silence, before picking up again.

Fantasia is more insistent. It opens with a flourish of slightly dark melodies. The phrases grow longer and an ostinato is introduced. The quartet descends into chaos before working itself back into silence, and then a quiet violin statement to close.

At Night is similar to the former movements in that it is a constant series of different moods. It is more aggressive melodically and somewhat chaotic at times.

These works follows a consistent modern style. I enjoyed them immensely, although I would have preferred to have heard more. The two quartets don't quite make it to 30 minutes in total. However, there is a saving grace – there are also two piano pieces on the CD.

I preferred *In Memories Of* which is a 15-minute work with piano accompanied by the string quartet – and a very fine piece. The piano and quartet are constantly interacting, and there are also many introspective parts. I really like it. It's modern, much more than the quartets on the disc. The second piece *And All is Always Now* is for piano and violin. I didn't find it as attractive – it was a bit 'out there'.

Overall this disc is rather appealing. Titled *Turning, Returning,* and performed by the Brentano Quartet on New World Records, it is available on Amazon as an MP3 download. The circumstances keep changing, sometimes the CD is available and at other times it isn't. It's also on Spotify and YouTube, while the two quartets can be heard on earsense.

Listenability: Mildly modern.

— ooOoo —

Theodor Adorno [1903–1969]

Nationality: German
Quartets: One
Style: Early Modern

String Quartet Works

Adorno's one string quartet is complemented by a number of incidental works in the genre. There is a detailed article on Wikipedia which gives a firm impression that Adorno was a twelve-tone, serialist composer, drawing his influences from Schoenberg's methodologies. He also studied under Alban Berg – these two events taken together would be an indicator of his musical direction.

The *String Quartet* was written in 1921 and is in four movements, which are mostly quite brief. The work opens in an expansive atonal mood, with broad melodic violin brush strokes, featuring wide intervallic leaps. The sense of abstraction is perfect in this miniature setting. Sliding into a rhythmic passage, the violins are rather haunting before they eventually dissolve into nothing.

The second movement, twice as long, reveals its Early Modern conception. Slow, enticing violin melodies paint a sparse picture and a very measured dissonance prevails. Some of the writing is reminiscent of Charles Ives as the violins construct overlapping lines, which sometimes developing harmonies and a descending solo violin phrase cuts through the mood, leading into a tempo momentarily, before the violins adopt a more rhapsodic approach. Again the end is one of petering out.

The next movement is also brief, this time at a brisk tempo. Swirling violin lines lead to a passage with strong cello to be heard. The tempo now abates and the violins are more thoughtful in their musings. The same sense of abstraction

4

as previously heard dominates this movement with the violins contributing a flourish, and the cello carries the music to the end.

The final movement, the longest of the work, begins with a sparse passage of extremely disjointed melodies. The mood is that of a quiet dissonant lament which, supported by the ensemble gradually rises in intensity. This doesn't last and a gentle period transforms into some spirited violin utterances. The cello constantly probes as the violins continue on their entropic path with vague harmonies developing, to create another moving soundscape which again just fades into nothing.

The second work under consideration is *Two Pieces for String Quartet*. It begins in a slightly tempestuous manner with vague, sporadic violin and cello activity. Dissonant harmonies paint a striking landscape. The violins are very active, in an atonal manner, with a strange duet that lingers for a time. There is plenty of forward movement, but the music doesn't appear to be in any particular tempo. Now, the tempestuous feeling returns, although you could mount an argument that all of the discussed works are in this mood, albeit sometimes quietly. This particular movement has a sense of strength, as it forges its way to an abrupt conclusion.

The second of the two pieces opens with a solo violin, soon to be joined by the ensemble – the mood is mysterious. Recurring cello statements provide a brief moment of texture before a feeling of stasis develops. The violins continue in a very controlled manner, with economical phrasing. Gradually the intensity rises, with overlapping violin and cello melodic lines. A sense of tension evolves as the violins maintain their atonal musings. Finally, a solo cello passage terminates the piece.

The review CD also contains *Six Studies for String Quartet*, from 1920, which are cut from the same musical cloth, musically taut and progressive.

The Adorno works are paired with two pieces by Hans Eisler, who was a contemporary of Adorno. These are *String Quartet* from 1938 and *Prelude and Fugue on B–A–C–H* for string trio. Eisler was a more populist composer, apparently much to the chagrin of Schoenberg.

This CD, *Adorno, Eisler: Works for String Quartet*, performed by the Leipzig Quartet, and released on the CPO label, is available on Amazon US and UK.

The three Adorno pieces from this disc can be sampled on YouTube and earsense. Both sites also have the Eisler works.

Listenability: Thoughtful, mildly provocative early twentieth century music.

Eugen d'Albert [1864–1932]

Nationality: Scottish-German
Quartets: Two
Style: Romantic

String Quartet No. 2

This Second Quartet, in E-flat major, Opus 11, is made up of four movements. The work commences with a lush background of strings. Sensitive harmonised violin lines set the mood, allowing the cello to step forward to be the predominant instrument. It first complements the violins, then gives way to them as a slightly sparser sound emerges. New melodies are formed and harmonised in an almost empathic way – such is the unity of the violins. Now they are set free and the intensity soars, with the cello underpinning dynamic violins. A crescendo gives way to another melodic cello passage, and some harmonic thrusts interrupt the melodic flow. A recapitulation of the opening melodies is the beginning of the end for this movement, and it concludes on a sustained chord. Interestingly, the cello has been particularly prominent.

The following movement, marked allegro, has a slight abstraction in the opening, featuring a whirring viola, that is, in a constant rhythmic pattern. This rhythm is taken up by the violins as they pursue each other until the mood settles with a pizzicato interlude. A change comes over the piece with the emergence of the cello as it expresses freely, and the violins move into a skipping passage with strong cello lines in the background. The cello repeats a violin melody to initiate another change where violins fashion new melodies and the music comes to life again. The former whirring can still be heard and the cello ignores this, creating warm motifs that complement the violins. Nearing the end, it is set free again and leads the ensemble into a chord to finish.

The third movement is an adagio and a violin and cello fashion the opening feeling. The cello plays long tones for a time, then drops back into single notes. The next section has the cello pizzicato and walking, jazz-like, as the violins contemplate a soulful mood. The composer certainly has a feeling for the cello as it constantly adds to the conversation. Out of nowhere, a forceful, loud passage ensues with strong rhythmic thrusts, leading into a slightly rhapsodic feeling with the thrusts repeated. The cello underpins this feeling as it builds to a brief crescendo. Now we have the sweetest moment of the piece thus far, with the violins dancing lightly upon a warm cello carpet. A series of descending melodic lines changes the mood and the cello has the last say as it leads to a gentle close.

The final movement leaps into life with twin violins surging. They give way to the cello momentarily and dance harmonically around the mood. A pause brings some reflection with both violins intertwined. This movement now becomes energised as the violins swoop over the driving cello, which mimics their melodic movement. There are many sections of violin and cello harmonised melodies. Now it is time for the cello to introduce a melody and it steps forward with authority, before being subsumed back into the ensemble. A peaceful passage follows with the occasional cello statement leading the violins. The violins race and an extended harmonised violin melodic line leads to a magnificent conclusion.

The review CD, titled *d'Albert: String Quartets Nos. 1 & 2* by the Reinhold Quartett on the CPO label is freely available on Amazon US and UK, as is another promising looking version by the Sarastro Quartet. Both versions are on Spotify, YouTube and earsense.

Listenability: A fine Romantic quartet – features terrific cello.

— ooOoo —

William Alwyn [1905–1985]
Nationality: British
Quartets: Three
Style: Contemporary Modern

Spring Waters
String Quartet No. 2

According to Wikipedia, Alwyn '*relished dissonance, and devised his own alternative to twelve-tone serialism.*' Sounds like my kind of guy. His Second Quartet was written in 1975 and has three movements. It is titled *Spring Waters.*

The first movement opens in a picturesque mood as befits the title. A melody quickly develops and it soon becomes rowdy with violins swallow-diving over and around the ambience. The movement pauses and we have a recapitulation of the opening theme – the violins are very active here. The mood is enhanced with a solo cello statement, mostly at a low volume, with the melodies delightful at this level. A mournful first violin reaches out and there is an occasional response from the second violin. Now the volume increases for a brief interlude until the violins return with their dialogue. It extends for about three minutes to the end, and a fine three minutes it is, with very precious music and playing.

The next movement starts with a slightly serious motif-based theme. A brief period of pizzicato follows and then a recapitulation of the opening theme ensues, this time it is developed more extensively. A second theme is heard, then a third. Slowly it develops into a morose soundscape as a solo cello moves the music forward. Notwithstanding the occasional spikey interjection, the impression is slightly intangible. There are motifs and melodies in abundance, and much dialogue, but all the while measured. After a time, the ensemble returns in full with an energised, serious feeling. Then we have more tranquil violin dialogues, moving to a conclusion.

The final movement features some ever so soft string sound effects. The cello makes a brief statement and the quiet violins return, followed by a slow, gentle passage which makes for some fine introspection. Suddenly, the volume returns and there is a sense of urgency, before moving into a solo cello statement. The previous introspective impression returns, and the cello has more to say. Towards the end, the volume increases and there is some busy music until it finishes with the obligatory flourish.

The work has grown on me the past couple of days. It definitely sounds British, not particularly modern, but with some quietly mild atonality and dissonance, which is how I like it.

String Quartets 1-3 by the Maggini Quartet is available on the Naxos label at Amazon US and UK. It is also on Spotify and some of the quartets are available on YouTube. Many of Alwyn's quartets are on earsense, which also features the two string quartets of his wife, Doreen Carwithen.

Listenability: Quality British workmanship.

String Quartets Nos. 10 & 12

I have always been fascinated by the concept of bird migration so I have chosen to discuss String Quartet No. 10, titled *En Voyage*, together with another named quartet, No. 12, *Fantasia*.

Firstly *En Voyage*, which is in four named movements.

Departure – The work commences with a solo violin, which is soon joined by the ensemble. A cello introduces a constant rhythmic pattern and the first violin develops some strong melodies. There is definitely a feeling of leaving here as the first violin expresses over what is now an ensemble ostinato. The dynamics soar, only to subside again to a cello motif, as the first violin, repeating a phrase which has been heard before, is the dominant musical fragment in the movement. Soon it goes solo, with occasional interjections – it is very fine. A sweeping cello line leads a solo violin to conclude.

Seabirds – A repeated viola phrase underpins the opening, which is very aggressive, with the violin dynamics particularly strong. There is plenty of forward movement here, while the ensemble diminishes in power, and exchange phrases among themselves. The music is still hectic, just not so loud. This chaotic episode gradually recedes and individual instruments dialogue in a sparse manner. The opening melody returns for a moment, then the dynamics and tempo increase, leading to a powerful end.

The Lonely Waters – A violin and viola ostinato set up a mood for the cello to make a considered melodic statement. It wanders freely with the music again sounding like its title. This feeling goes on for some time until a slightly dour, full section ensues. It doesn't last however, and we are now in a most gentle mood with the solo cello expressing a simple major key melody. The ensemble ostinato resumes, in a gentle manner, and the movement fades out.

Trade Winds – This short movement opens with forceful, bird-like sounds, and a positively dynamic cello. A pizzicato section follows, where both violin and cello express in a measured way. The tempo and intensity return, and each instrument flails away until a more mellow passage ensues. As in the third movement, there are various simple major key melodies here. Another hectic passage of dialogue leads to an ending on a cello note.

This is a charming piece of program music, evoking sounds and moods associated with bird migration.

Now on to *Fantasia*.

This relatively brief work commences with an extremely prominent violin, over a distant background. Soon another violin steps forward and we have a section where both violins engage in combative mode. A brief pause allows for a drawing of breath. The violins are quiet here, and there are some wonderful, melancholy harmonised passages. A repeated major melody occurs, and the ensemble drifts around it. A quivering violin leads to a more chaotic section, which eventually peters out.

Now a violin repeats a slightly dissonant phrase, and it is joined by the ensemble. This is a most abstract section which lasts for some time before it slowly subsides into a cello moment and the violins become progressively softer. A solo viola background brings forth a flurry of animated violins before a strummed cello leads to an intense arco solo cello passage. The ensemble now produces a gentle, almost modal mood – there is no harmony to be found here. Nearing the end, strings begin to quiver excitedly in the background and a violin motif builds in intensity, only to fade to a conclusion.

In my previous discussion of Alwyn's Second String Quartet, *Spring Waters*, I found it to be a charming work and commented about '*quietly mild atonality and dissonance*'. The later quartets definitely show his development in these approaches.

The review CD, titled *String Quartets 10-13*, performed by the Tippett Quartet on Somm Recordings, is available on Amazon US and UK, and the disc is on Spotify. There are also many quartets on YouTube. As previously mentioned, earsense gives him a good coverage.

Listenability: Fine Contemporary British works.

[Image courtesy SOMM Recordings]

— ooOoo —

Volkmar Andreae [1879–1962]

Nationality: Swiss
Quartets: Two
Style: Late Romantic

String Quartet No. 2

The Second Quartet is in four movements and I found the inner movements – the second and third – to be quite intriguing.

The work opens with a flourish which leads immediately into a gentle passage. The flourish is then repeated, however this time the music moves into a more assertive phase, which is extended. This is a fascinating section as a violin leads the music into some interesting ambient and rhythmic moods. The feeling is sometimes influenced by brief forays into a minor tonality. The rhythmic sections tend to predominate, with the violin pushing the ensemble along. A folk-like theme is constantly re-examined and the cello sometimes makes solo statements, which are quite special. The ambient moods are usually in the minor tonality, and are quiet introspective. Nearing the end, the writing becomes orchestral and dramatic, producing a full sound.

The second movement commences with a slightly pulsing ensemble as a violin investigates a wispy melody. A minor texture unfolds and the violin continues to apply melodic variations – the mood strengthens as the cello comes into play. This music has a feeling that I can't quite fathom. It is mostly very sparse, but there is something intangible about it, as it works its way to a conclusion.

The next movement is the longest of the work. A throbbing viola and cello set up a harmonic background at a moderately slow tempo. The violin is majestic as it traverses this musical environment. A cello interjection only serves to deepen the feeling. Now a strong passage ensues and then fades to nothing as the opening pulsing returns and the violin is marvellous over a sparse pizzicato moment. Another change brings about an intensity that has thus far not been heard in the piece, again it is of an orchestral nature. A pause returns us to the opening sensitivity and the mood is very deep emotionally. The violin is now ever so quiet but beautifully melodic as it negotiates its way to the finish. This is a wonderful piece of writing.

The finale is energised as the ensemble provide a folk background, with positive melodies in abundance. This is pure Romanticism that has much impetus. The violins are jaunty until a slight mood change leads to a lessening of the dynamics. This is only brief and the ensemble comes back strongly with a firm conclusion to this short movement.

The review CD, titled *Volkmar Andreae - String Quartets*, performed by The Locrian Ensemble of London on Guild Music is available on Amazon UK and US. The disc is on Spotify and both quartets are on YouTube and earsense, which also lists an early quartet which is unknown to me.

Listenability: Very positive, rhythmic Romanticism.

George Antheil [1900–1959]

Nationality: American
Quartets: Three
Style: Early Modern

Early Minimalism?
String Quartet Works

An interesting thing about this composer's work is that the First Quartet shows the earliest examples of minimalist technique that I have heard. Antheil uses mechanically sounding ostinatos in this piece, and I believe that these are one of the pointers to the subsequent development of minimalism.

String Quartet No. 1, in one movement, was written in 1921. It commences with a basic ostinato motif that wouldn't be out of place in a Phillip Glass or Morton Feldman work. This motif is intertwined with other similar material which gives the introduction a strong rhythmic impetus. After a time, the mood moves into a beguiling quiet passage, then it is back to the motif. The music continues to oscillate between tranquil, abstract and the ostinato. Even the rhythmic sections have great melodic variety, while occasionally it drops the rhythm altogether and falls into rubato.

This piece is only 14 minutes long, but I found it to be wonderfully fulfilling. That basic motif to which I keep referring, is fascinating and seems to be so far ahead of its time.

String Quartet No. 2, written in 1927 is titled *For Sylvia Beach, With Love*, and is in four movements. No. 3 is also in four movements. These two quartets are mostly conservative, seemingly more folk-like, with simpler melodies and many pastoral moments. Each features a fine slow movement, and both are very beautiful. The review CD also contains two charming small suites, *Lithuanian Night* and *Six Little Pieces for String Quartet for Mary Louise Bok*. The former has another pleasing slow movement.

The particular recording under discussion is *The Complete String Quartets* by the Del Sol Quartet on the Naxos label. There is at least one other version but I've not heard it. There are several issues on Amazon US and UK and it can be found on Spotify. You can also sample several of Antheil's quartets on YouTube and earsense.

Listenability: Some delightful Modernism interspersed with the conservative - music to be savoured.

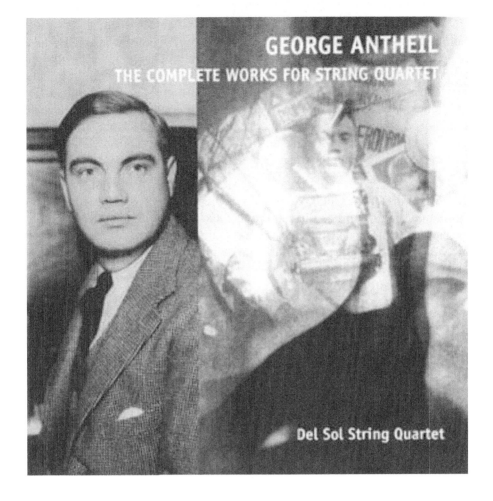

[Image courtesy Naxos Records]

— ooOoo —

Alfredo Aracil [born 1954]

Nationality: Spanish
Quartets: At least four
Style: Modern Contemporary

On the Edge
String Quartet No. 3

Alfredo Aracil's four string quartets are very modern in conception and bring to mind the phrase *'all music is sound, but not all sound is music.'* The composer stretches the boundaries of music with these works.

13

The Third Quartet, in one movement, runs for eighteen minutes. It begins as a solo cello statement, with atonal interjections from the other strings. The violins then pick up on the mood, and dialogue with the cello. Three minutes in, the cello still predominates, now dropping back to solo again. After around four minutes, the whole ensemble returns – it has now entered the world of sound and possibly left the world of music behind. The violins alternate between shimmering sections and occasional melodic lines. Now there is an exchange of dissonant lines from the whole ensemble until the violin soars alone, with the other instruments slowly rejoining the music.

After a time, some traditional harmony appears, but it does not last for long, reverting to dissonant violin, either solo or played over busy atonal backdrops. The shimmering returns as the cello probes the music with dissonant melodies. The violin now has a long episode of expressing a melody over the second violin and viola that delivers pure abstraction, with anxious moments as different instruments offer random interjections. The ending is a gradual coming down until all that is left is – nothing.

I have been listening to avante-garde jazz and classical music since 1970. I love abstract sounds and I find the piece beautiful. Emotionally it takes me somewhere I have never been before and I like that. Not once does it become either angry or aggressive. It is difficult to describe as it often does not use the traditional elements of music – for me it evokes images of a bleak landscape.

The review CD is titled *String Quartets*, performed by the Breton Quartet, on the Verso label (through Naxos) and can be found on Amazon US or UK. It's also on Spotify. If you want to try it, listen to String Quartet No. 3 which is the first piece – the others are a bit more difficult. You can hear the complete CD on earsense and some movements from Aracil's quartets are on YouTube.

Listenability: Quite avante-garde.

— ooOoo —

Anton Arensky [1861–1906]

Nationality: Russian
Quartets: Two
Style: Late Romantic

String Quartet No. 2

Of Arensky's two quartets, the first is positive and has much to recommend it, but I intend to discuss the second. It's a little more contemplative, which is how I like it. String Quartet No. 2 is in four movements, with two long and two short.

The work opens with a Russian-sounding, slow folk-like flavour as a sustained chordal backing gives rise to a hint of a melody. Soon, the ensemble breaks out and a graceful melody emerges from that hint. The melody is developed and leads the ensemble into a tempo – there is a conversation going on here. A recapitulation ensues, with the melody further developed into a full-blown passage. The music then moves into a static space for a while, before leading into a quiet but busy phase. Now it is racing, with the violins chasing one another. The tempo drops and breaks into a more dynamic episode. After a brief calm, the tempo returns with some fascinating melodic flourishes. We are still in folk territory and the tempo is moderate. The violins reignite the ensemble, before settling again and a lonely melody prevails until another tempo increase occurs – this is a stirring passage. As we near the end, the intensity drops back to the opening texture, it sounds very gentle here. The melody is a little funereal and gently fades out.

At just under three minutes, the second movement is short, opening with a stately violin melody backed with pizzicato strings. This is simple, but engaging. The violins overlap the melodic phrase and it slowly becomes a miniature piece all of its own.

The next movement opens at a brisk tempo and the violins converse over the backing for a short jaunty section. The atmosphere now changes with a familiar melody, causing the feeling to deepen. Another mood change sees the tempo increase into an almost playful feeling. That familiarity returns but it comes to an abrupt halt as the two violins pick up the piece again and carry it along nicely. The viola and cello enter now, creating a very lyrical moment. Suddenly there is movement as a new melody appears over a rhythmic tempo which eventually pauses, and the feeling is again folk-like, with a conspicuous violin. It is endearing and in a way, a highlight of the work – just a charming little fragment but such a beautiful melody. This extremely enticing mood is developed and as it moves toward the end, it is very sparse, and reminiscent of the first movement. What a delightful finish.

The final, short movement sounds almost like Beethoven for a time. It suggests a dirge-like feeling, and the violin melodies here are lamenting. Suddenly we are into a dance mode and the violins skip over the ensemble. The funereal feeling returns, with the cello being prominent. Then we are off to the dance again with an energising passage which concludes with a flourish.

The two quartets are available paired on several discs on Amazon. One CD, by the Lajtha Quartet on the Marco Polo label, also contains a fine *Piano Quintet* by the composer. There are many versions where No. 2 is coupled with another composer. The works are available on Spotify and a multitude of versions are on earsense – several performances can be found on YouTube.

Listenability: Not as introverted as I first thought. Well worth a listen.

Richard Arnell [1917–2009]

Nationality: British
Quartets: Six
Style: Late Romantic

String Quartets Nos. 3 & 4

Arnell wrote his six string quartets from 1940 to 1992. Interestingly, they all seem to me to be in a Late Romantic style.

The Third Quartet was completed in 1945, and was thus an early work. It opens with a stately theme, played by all instruments in simple harmony. The music then moves into tempo in a positive manner, with strong tonal melodies, before things relax a little as the first violin plays solo over a sparse accompaniment. After a time, the intensity increases and then drops into a charming melodic episode with all four instruments in conversation until a dashing passage follows with violin prominent again. Then the tempo eases a little and we have a charming pastoral section led by the violin. It continues with this feeling before a loud chordal rhythm prepares us for the end which comes quickly.

The second movement is marked lento and it opens with a slow, sparse melody in the violins. A most introspective fragment follows as the violin melody gives way to the whole ensemble having their say, eventually leading to a rich chordal phase and back again to a sparse section. This is the music I was born to listen to. It reminds me of another British composer, Daniel Jones, who is also in this book. Eventually, the music just fades into nothing – wonderful.

The third movement opens at a sprightly tempo with a very British dance-like theme. The tempo drops back and the ensemble plays with the melody as it progresses through various rhythmic scenarios. It is a dynamic movement. Nearing the end, it positively races to a conclusion.

After discussing so many composers who slip into modern mode every now and again, it's a pleasure to hear one that doesn't. This is Late Romanticism in 1945.

String Quartet No. 4 is a one movement work, written in 1951. Marked allegro, the opening is a busy theme with all instruments going full tilt. Around the one-minute mark, it drops back considerably into a beguiling atmosphere, where the cello is salient. It then begins to work its way back into a rhythm but is cut short with another slow, sparse passage. These sections are appealing and there is a constant duality here – first rhythmic, then sparse. We finally reach an extended tranquil section, with full chords and subtle lines from all instruments. There is some wonderful viola here, and a sense of movement leads to a swash-buckling conclusion. Instead, it drops back to two instruments with an elegant passage until it fades to the end.

16

These quartets are conservative, rewarding works. Just a note on some of the other quartets on the disc. No. 2 has a great slow movement while No. 5 contains seven movements, mostly short, but interesting.

Regarding availability, there is a CD, *String Quartets Nos. 1 to 5* by the Tippett Quartet, on the Dutton Epoch label at both Amazon US and UK. It is also on Presto Classical with some sound samples. I couldn't find any other listenable sources – what a shame.

Listenability: Charming very Late Romanticism.

[Tippett Quartet - Image courtesy TQ]

Malcolm Arnold [1921–2006]

Nationality: British
Quartets: Two
Style: Contemporary

String Quartet No. 2

Sir Malcolm Henry Arnold's Second Quartet, written in 1975, contains four movements.

The first, <u>allegro</u> movement opens with a frisky feeling of warmth, before a solo cello statement lowers the intensity. The violins suddenly turn a little modern, with a slightly <u>atonal</u> feeling. Now a pleasant, but frantic violin passage takes over and the intensity rises, but the music is <u>tonal</u>. The violins move on to an intertwining section, which is mild. Nearing the end, the violins express gracefully with sparse <u>harmonised</u> melodies before concluding quietly.

A solo violin introduces the second movement with a beauty that is difficult to describe. Using *double-stops* – playing two strings at once – the violin offers up a lonely, sparse passage. After a time the two violins take up a folk dance feeling. However, the accompaniment brings an intensity to the music which is quite overpowering in its rhythmic thrusts. The end is a measured folk-like flourish. This is a strange movement, with conflicting emotions being expressed freely.

An <u>andante</u> movement follows in a despondent feeling as a solo violin meanders with beautifully lamenting melodic lines. The second violin can occasionally be heard but the texture is very sparse. Both violins gradually begin to reach out, revealing a wonderful, mournful soundscape. A very slow tempo is initiated, with the slightest of pulses before the violins again become more expansive – it is mostly a duet here. The pulse returns and the ensemble gather to create a stronger sound. This is sustained for a time until a pause brings about a return to a solo violin, with sparse harmonies from the second violin leading to a quiet finish of a most affecting movement.

The final movement begins in a positive mood as a violin is supported by busy, but tender accompaniment. A slightly serious tone begins to develop, but it is short-lived. A return of the ensemble is also brief, and the violin again strikes out on its own with a slightly longing feeling before a sparse section unfolds and the violin continues its musings. Suddenly there is an energy as the ensemble provide complex interjections – the cello expresses powerfully and the ensemble is now in full flight. There is <u>pizzicato</u> and more double-stops and the music has a vitality about it. The mood is now quite assertive, and the violin builds the intensity before leading into a wonderful <u>pastoral</u> scene. There is another pause and three strong chords conclude the work.

This music is that of a unique composer. There are touches of Romanticism but also a nod to more modernist possibilities. The First Quartet is also wonderful and both feature appealing slow movements.

The review CD, *Arnold: String Quartets 1 & 2*, performed by the McCapra Quartet on the Naxos label is available on Amazon US and UK. There is also another version containing the two quartets on Naxos, by the Maggini Quartet.

Both discs are on Spotify - YouTube has an entirely different performance and the McCapra version is on earsense.

Listenability: Positive, appealing twentieth century work.

— ooOoo —

Juan de Arriaga [1806–1826]

Nationality: Spanish
Quartets: Three
Style: Late Classical

The Spanish Mozart
String Quartet No. 3

Arriaga was dubbed *'The Spanish Mozart'* due to his prodigious, youthful talent. They also shared the same birthday, January 27th. I have long enjoyed the energy of these works and I am going to discuss the Third Quartet. Set firmly in the Classical style, it is in four movements, and characterised by many instances of theme and variations.

The first movement commences with a lilting melody, which is both light and airy. There is a slight Spanish tinge to the opening and another terrific melody emerges. Both melodies are developed further and a change in tonality initiates a third melodic section. All of these moments are performed at a solid tempo. The composer now returns to the opening theme and there are several fine flourishes. A minor key section follows, which is very appealing. As the end approaches we have some wonderful descending patterns before it ends with one final uplifting flourish.

The next movement begins with a chordal statement, before the violins dialogue over a sustained chord. This is played out at a stately tempo, with the cello being salient until a tonal change brings forth a most enticing passage with shimmering violins and a measured violin melody. The next section is reminiscent of a ferris wheel as melodies follow each other around. A change from major to minor brings a sense of intensity to the music – the violins and cello are both passionate. The intensity rises up a notch further before a solo cello brings some serenity to the proceedings and the composer develops some marvellously attractive melodies. The sparsity is just beautiful, and the violins lead to a tranquil conclusion.

The third movement has a stronger Spanish flavour and the cello propels the music forward while the violins emote a feeling of anguish. A recapitulation follows, before a waltz time is introduced, with the violin sounding folk-like. Then there is a sweeping passage as the cello and violins dance with joy. A brief dialogue between a violin and cello ensues and the movement comes to a muted end.

The final movement opens with a positive, lively melodic section. After a few flourishes the violin reaches into the upper register and softens the ambience – there is a sense of longing here. Now the opening is repeated and this time, positivity is again achieved. The next section features the cello playing only on the second and fourth beats, leading to a folk rhythm. It is soon left behind as the violin drives the music forward, with a strong cello accompaniment. This is a most beautiful melody, although tempered, but still remains attractive. A repeat of a previous section occurs – the violin interplay is stunning as both violins reach for the sky. The work ends on a series of strong chords.

Arriaga died ten days before his twentieth birthday, apparently of a lung ailment, possibly tuberculosis. Many of his works have been lost but at least we are left with these three fine string quartets.

They are freely available on CD at Amazon US and UK. There appear to be at least ten versions. I've enjoyed Camerata Boccherini on the Naxos label and Quartet Sine Nomine on Claves Records. There are several versions on Spotify and all quartets are on YouTube and earsense.

Listenability: A brilliant Late Classical quartet.

— ooOoo —

Kurt Atterberg [1887–1974]

Nationality: Swedish

Quartets: Four
Style: Late Romantic

String Quartets Nos. 2 & 3

Apparently, Atterberg is a fine symphonist, and not unsurprisingly, his string quartets are quite orchestral, particularly the Second.

String Quartet No. 2, which is in three movements, opens with a charming, positive statement from the violins, with layered accompaniment. The tempo and intensity drop fairly quickly, but the sweet sense remains as two violins converse while the cello makes complementary statements. Now the work moves into a tempo and the tonality changes from major to minor. This features some lush writing for a solo violin, over a busy ensemble – now the second violin enters with pensive phrases. A brief pause again introduces a solo violin, soon to be joined by the second violin in a beautiful piece of writing, it is very tender. As the tempo resumes, it becomes quite stately. A deceleration leads to a solo violin, and a conclusion.

The next movement, marked andante, starts in a gentle manner as the violins work in the low register initially, but soon rise above a gentle accompaniment. The dynamics are low as the first violin crafts a fine, sparse melody. This is a beguiling section, far from the orchestral nature of the previous movement. The violin continues its journey as a quiet, but insistent tempo is initiated while the violin remains conspicuous, and the ensemble offer up pizzicato statements. The intensity slowly rises but the impression is maintained. The second violin now emerges and the violins make for a quietly calm ending.

The final movement features a powerful, chordal introduction which is rather serious. A series of dramatic ascending violin statements build tension as they move into a conversation. The violins are strong here and that ascending feeling returns. Now the first violin skips above the ensemble into a high register, only to return to a section with the violins pursuing each other. The violins continue, almost aggressively, and the work concludes with a flourish.

String Quartet No. 3 is in four movements, and is quite long. Again it features a slightly orchestral opening. The phrasing is delightful and the violins work in harmony as the tempo moves forward. A brief pause introduces a slow passage and the violins become flashy as they play with the mood and lead the ensemble through a prancing section. Now the first violin breaks free for a time and rises above the ensemble, followed by more prancing – this is a fine, mellow feeling. A pizzicato statement completes the movement with some strong, sustained violin tones.

The following movement features prominent violins and fine melodies as the rhythm is constant but measured. A quieter period ensues, which is basically just the two violins – it feels like an interlude. The melodies are gentle here, and a little melancholic. Finally, we have a tempo and the ensemble dance their way through a change into a minor tonality for a time. The end comes peacefully.

The third movement is a slow, melodic waltz. Violins lead the way, drifting over a subtle background. There is a sense of introspection at work here and the cello comes to the fore, with lamenting melodic lines. Now a more powerful force takes over and the tempo changes into a new, four-beat feeling. Intertwining violins take centre stage and the atmosphere becomes gentle again. The violins complete the scene with a faded duet.

The final movement is energised, with the violins adding a rhythmic impetus. This mellows and one violin takes the lead over a pleasing ensemble.

Now the violin engages in a call and response section with the ensemble before the intensity increases and the first violin soars playfully with the second violin offering great support. A light moment finds the violin playing some delightful melodies and, as the work builds, there are plenty of dynamic violin phrases. An extended, hectic violin statement leads to the conclusion.

The review CD, *Atterberg / Rangstrom: String Quartets*, performed by the Stenhammar Quartet on the CPO label, is filled out with a 13-minute string quartet work by another Swedish composer, Ture Rangstrom, who is marginally more modern than Atterberg. It is available on Amazon US and UK. The CD can be found on Spotify and YouTube, with several quartet versions on earsense.

Listenability: Wonderful Late Romantic quartets.

— ooOoo —

Milton Babbitt [1916–2011]

Nationality: American
Quartets: Six
Style: Modern Contemporary

A Devout Serialist
String Quartet No. 3

Babbitt's First Quartet was withdrawn and has never been published, played or recorded, leaving us with five extant works. He studied mathematics and then went on to examine the serial works of Schoenberg, Berg and Webern intensely, before constructing his own systems for creating music, based on serialism. These systems contain rules for melodic, rhythmic and textural methods of organising serial musical material – an approach which leads to highly abstract, unusual sounds. He has worked in both the Mathematics and Music faculties of various universities and I believe that this combination of disciplines has contributed to his unique approach to music. I intend to discuss the Third Quartet, written 1969–70 and in one movement, in my usual, non-technical manner. However, it just happens to be one of the most avante-garde pieces of music that I have enjoyed. Having said that, avant-garde is not really a style, but more a blanket term for new and experimental music.

The work commences in an apparently unstructured manner featuring some flute-like violin sounds, with prominent pizzicato accompaniment. This is followed by a passage of sparse, long tones, together with pizzicato interjections. A solo violin expresses a short interlude before the sporadic texture resumes – there is now a constant sense of pizzicato. The music has a high level of entropy as it edges forward with seemingly random assertions from all instruments.

Melodies jump to unusual intervals and there is a certain feeling of austerity projected, the composer doesn't give much away. Eventually a violin melodic line emerges with the second violin offering melodic support. There is some cooperation between instruments but no harmonic development.

This music has been suggested by some to contain elements of *pointillism*, which is a style of painting in small multi-coloured dots that merge when viewed from a distance.

The violins are now more assertive and occasionally move into a higher register, producing swooping phrases. Long tones appear in the violins and cello, and a sense of relaxed peace is initiated. This leads to a return of large melodic leaps which emphasise the abstract nature of the work and, some unusual articulation of notes also contributes to this feeling. There are many instrumental interjections, and various sections feature the sound of muted strings. Further constant changes in melodic, rhythmic and textural patterns finally bring the piece to an abrupt conclusion

This is not music to be understood, unless you have a comprehensive musical education – even then, I believe you would need access to the score. There is a brief analysis of this piece on Wikipedia here:

https://en.wikipedia.org/wiki/String_Quartet_No._3_(Babbitt)

I'm afraid I could not fathom its description of the structure, I just enjoy the total musical nature of the piece. Strangely, the dynamic level remains remarkably consistent throughout. I realise that my limited discussion will probably give you no idea as to the sound of the music. For that, you will have to experience it for yourself.

Babbitt's quartets are not readily available on CD. However, there is a recently recorded version of Quartets Nos. 2-6, by The Ars Combinatoria String Quartet which is available at a website here:

https://erikcarlson.bandcamp.com/album/milton-babbitt-string-quartets

There are recordings of all quartets for listening and the works can be purchased as downloads, both in MP3 and FLAC formats. The FLAC files are CD quality and can be burned to create audio CDs. I have been in contact with the Ars Combinatoria and was advised that they have no plans to release the works on CD.

Several quartets are on Spotify and YouTube, although not the reviewed work.

I shall leave you with a quote from Babbitt – *Listen, don't worry about whether or not the music sounds coherent to you the first time you hear it. What about the first time you hear a sentence in Hungarian? - assuming you're interested in listening to and learning Hungarian.*

Listenability: So abstract but, to me, beautiful.

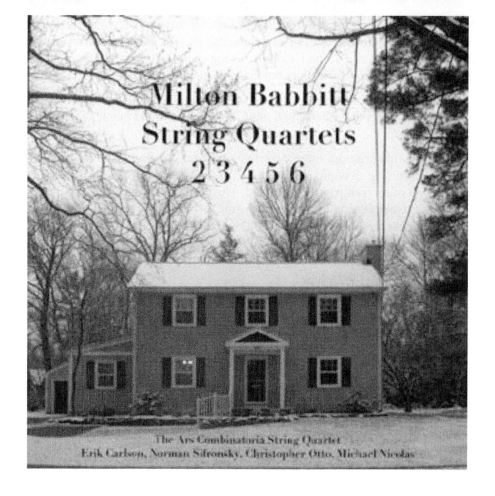

[Milton Babbitt's House]
[Photographer – Rosemary K. J. Davis]

Grazyna Bacewicz [1910–1969]

Nationality: Polish
Quartets: Seven
Style: Early Modern

The Progression of a Composer
String Quartets Nos. 1 & 4

Bacewicz was a Polish female composer, who wrote seven string quartets from 1938-1965. I thought I would discuss an early and a middle quartet, namely Nos. 1 and 4.

String Quartet No. 1 is in three movements, as are all of her early works. The first movement wanders through some simple phrases for a time before it breaks into an allegro tempo. It settles into this with some slightly atonal melodies. The tempo strengthens and new motifs are introduced – the music is moving forward and finds itself in an eminently satisfying passage. It backs off the dynamics but increases the tempo, becoming busy. After a pause, the opening returns until some pizzicato allows for variation in the thematic material. Towards the end of the movement, there are some attractive quiet periods, finishing with a sparkling flourish.

The next movement has a beautiful introductory statement. This is why I listen to string quartets – they can take me to places that no other music can. Such a winsome scene, which reminds me of earlier times. Shortly, a new melody is presented – it is very subtle. The tempo picks up again, the cello asserts a strong melody, and then the violins return. There is a hint of a plaintive melody as the movement winds down and fades out on a long note.

The final movement starts at a rollicking tempo and the violins skip across the ensemble, maintaining the positive sense. As with many European string quartets of the era, there are folk-like melodies to be found here. The two violins continue their conversation to a conclusion.

The Fourth Quartet opens in a sombre tone, with the cello taking the lead. The tempo quickens and the music becomes busy for a while before a recapitulation is followed by a new theme. A moderate tempo ensues and leads to a shift back to the opening, introducing a prolonged period of delicate ambience. It is a charming moment, definitely music of its time. The tempo takes over again, but not for long, as the introversion returns. The winding down to the conclusion is particularly felicitous – this is simple, thoughtful music. The volume never rises above moderate, yet there are incisive passages.

The second movement is again slow and alluring, with a tender forward pulse, containing small peaks in the melody. It sounds different, as the composer uses mesmeric notes rather than dissonance and a melodic theme emerges. A new section brings a new violin melody and it finally breaks into gentle introspection in a most engaging section. It finishes on a long violin note and a cello pop sound to conclude.

The final, short allegro movement is very rhythmic. A second theme is introduced and sustained by the violins. The movement turns into a cornucopia of folk themes that eventually race to the conclusion.

After Quartet No. 4, the composer becomes increasingly abstruse. There is still some fine music there but it seems to me to be a case of Modernity for its own sake. The change is not overbearing but should be noted by anyone interested in Bacewicz string quartets.

All of her quartets are freely available. There is a complete 2-CD set on the Chandos label, performed by the Silesian Quartet, at Amazon UK, which also has two separate Naxos CDs. It can be found on Spotify and pretty much all of the quartets are available on YouTube and earsense.

Listenability: Contrasting rhythms with some fine slow movements.

[Image courtesy Chandos Records]

Johann Sebastian Bach [1685–1750]

Nationality: German
Quartets: None
Style: Baroque

The Art of Fugue
Arranged for String Quartet

Bach was a Baroque master. In fact the Baroque era ends on the year of his passing, in deference to his stature. He never wrote music for the string quartet. Joseph Haydn, usually known as the *'father of the string quartet'*, wrote his first quartet in 1764, after Bach's death, and Bach may not have been particularly aware of the form.

Bach commenced composing *The Art of Fugue* in 1737, then after a break of ten years, went back to it in 1747. It was not completed when he died and the music just stops, in the middle of movement No. 20. Strangely, the music contains no tempo markings, no movement order and no mention of instrumentation required for the piece.

Given that most of Bach's music can be played by any ensemble – an amazing concept in itself, it is no surprise that this work has been arranged for many different combinations of instruments. There are several arrangements for string quartet. Composers of some of these arrangements have even 'completed' the piece but that does not occur in the version by the Keller Quartet that I will be discussing. It just stops dead.

As my definition of a <u>fugue</u> in the glossary is limited, I feel I should elaborate here. A fugue is based around a short musical phrase, known as the *subject*. The piece begins with one instrument playing the subject. At the completion a second instrument commences to play the same phrase, not necessarily with the same notes – it may start on a different pitch closely related to the subject, possibly an interval of a fourth or fifth, above or below. There is a continuation as other voices enter. By now, the voices are being constantly varied both rhythmically and harmonically. There is nothing trivial about Bach's fugues.

I must confess that after about thirty seconds I have usually forgotten the melodic concept of the subject and just listen in wonder to the brilliant dialogues between the four instruments.

I only intend to give sketches of some movements, and hope that they provide you with a flavour of the musical breadth of the work. Some of the music sounds almost orchestral and evokes Bach's *Brandenburg Concertos*, which are usually scored for moderately sized ensembles. Slower movements often have a plaintive feeling. Overall, I find that when the cello predominates, the music tends to be stately. When the violins take over, the music soars. Having said that, it is music for four equal voices – with all having a role to play.

No. 1 has a simple subject, taken at a rather slow pace. It rapidly develops into a myriad of overlapping voicings. The music is truly magnificent and for me, illustrates the genius of Bach.

No. 11 is particularly beautiful. One of the longer pieces, it commences with a joyous celebration before revealing a wonderful depth, particularly in the viola and cello parts. For me, the emotional content of this movement is overwhelming.

Movements 16-20 are marked as canons where only the cello and first violin are heard. Movement No. 18 has a very long slow subject, at least three bars in length, played by the cello. It then moves into a dialogue with the first violin.

The final movement, No. 20, is possibly the slowest of all. It runs for just over ten minutes and features wonderful changes in tempo which are usually accompanied by a significant change in the melodic material. Being unfinished it just stops in the middle of a phrase. How appropriate.

I don't think I ever fully appreciated the mysterious nature of this work until I listened to it intensely several times in preparation for my discussion. Its expressive scope within the limits of a string quartet is very broad. Or maybe I'm just underplaying the power and presence of a string quartet – heaven forbid.

As I mentioned, the version that I have is by the Keller Quartet, available on ECM – this disc comes with a marvellous essay. I know that the Emerson Quartet have also recorded it, but I've not heard their version. For a more detailed description there are many articles about fugues on the internet. My Google search for *The Art of Fugue* returned 420,000 pages.

Both the Keller and the Emerson are on Spotify and many fugues from the work on can be found on YouTube.

Listenability: A little intellectual but ultimately very satisfying, with an emotionally cleansing feeling – something different.

The Goldberg Variations
Arranged for String Quartet

Bach composed the Goldberg Variations for solo harpsichord. There is a quite interesting musical analysis of this piece on Wikipedia here:

https://en.wikipedia.org/wiki/Goldberg_Variations

This also contains many fascinating extra-musical anecdotes so I shall attempt to keep my introduction brief, and concern myself with the issues pertaining to this particular performance.

I came upon this string quartet arrangement only recently when I reviewed the companion piece on the CD, Glenn Gould's one string quartet. The work was arranged by members of the Catalyst Quartet, who are also the performers. I must confess to not being optimistic about this piece at the time. Clearly the brief nature of the arrangement would indicate that it was based on pianist Glenn Gould's 1955 recording which was itself a very shortened version, with very few of the marked repeats being performed. The movement lengths are very similar on both versions.

Technically the work is an aria followed by thirty variations on the eight notes of the aria bass part – these can be viewed variously as ten sets of three, three sets of ten and two sets of fifteen. The work concludes with a repeat of the aria. I won't bore you with the many discussions about the validity of Gould's version except to say that it changed the way that people thought about playing Bach on the piano.

This string quartet arrangement features many different combinations of instruments as it navigates the variations. When I first heard it, I was a little overwhelmed as the music seemed to fly past me very quickly. However, for this discussion, I listened to each variation individually and at a leisurely pace, sometimes more than once and was able to give each of them my full concentration. I haven't mentioned all of the movements, but it is a conscious selection.

The opening aria has to be one of Bach's most endearing melodies, and this is wonderfully expressed by the quartet. The movement is in two sections and the contrasting section, which just happens to be one of my favourite passages of Bach's solo piano pieces is filled with charm in its approach here. Unfortunately for me, it is the most significant instance where I really miss the repeats, as nominated by the composer. This precludes the joy of hearing the ebb and flow of these two marvellous melodic sections which I believe to be central to the work. Now on to the variations.

Variation 1 is a gorgeous romp for the first violin – there is such joy to be found here.

Variation 2 is another romp, this time a little more measured. I find it amazing that the quartet can capture the essence of this in 41 seconds – it is just so fulfilling.

Variation 3 is stunning, with two sections meshing beautifully with one another.

Variation 4 sparkles, despite its minimal length, and has a charm all of its own.

Variation 5 is a torrid workout for the two violins, which positively race against a more controlled viola and cello part.

Variation 6, a canon, features a sparkling violin, accompanied by a brilliant cameo from the cello. Interestingly, this last set of three variations just happens to be the shortest on the disc.

Variation 9, another canon even finds time in its 51 seconds duration to pause and restate the theme – again there is a fabulous cello part here.

Variation 11, a fugue, sustains interest with another sparkling cello role which sets up the fugal subject for all instruments to work with.

Variation 13 is taken at a slow tempo and evokes Bach's *Air on a G String*. This is a stunning piece for a moving solo violin over a gentle pizzicato cello. It runs over three sections and is one of the most pleasing pieces to be heard in this performance. Such sparse beauty.

Variation 14 is a tremendously moving soundscape, again for the violin and cello. It seems to be over as soon as it starts – such is its brevity.

Variation 15 takes up the mood from the previous piece and is a masterpiece of Baroque miniaturism. Featuring a pause mid-movement, the first violin and resonant arco cello paint a remarkable canvas.

Variation 16 is another masterful Baroque miniature, beginning with violin and cello in a slow tempo, before embarking on a spirited duet.

Variation 19 evokes a new, gentle mood with a smooth cello and a constant viola pizzicato supporting the first violin in its brief journey. This was recorded so softly that I had to boost it by eight decibels to appreciate its pleasures.

Variation 21, another canon, is a sombre, fascinating intertwining piece which sounds to me like all members of the quartet are involved.

Variation 23 is an energised collection of rapid ascending and descending violin lines, accompanied by the cello.

Variation 25 is a wonderfully lamenting piece that really speaks to me. I thought that I was familiar with The Goldbergs but this was a real treat – the solo violin lines are truly wonderful. Being the longest piece in this arrangement, it sustains its elegance for some considerable time and is mostly made up of two violin voices. Towards the end, the cello subtly drifts in, leading to a refined conclusion.

Variation 28 has a totally different feeling from the rest of the work. There is even a short section which is reminiscent of a miniature Bach *Brandenburg Concerto*.

Variation 30, and the last canon is a rich denouement with tremendous overlapping cello and violin lines.

The closing aria, slightly longer than the first, and a little slower, is a fascinating testament to the skill of Bach. The mood is sublime and the contrasting section is beautiful beyond belief. I marvel at the fact that Bach's works can apparently be successfully arranged for so many different musical ensembles.

This is a work that cries out for explanation of its many mysteries and for once, I believe that a little investigation into the form of the piece does help in its enjoyment. The previously mentioned Wikipedia article is a good start. There is also a great series of lectures by The Teaching Company (TTC) which really bring out the various concepts that define the mystery of the work.

The review CD, *Bach/Gould Project*, on the Azica label is performed by the Catalyst Quartet and is available on Amazon US and UK. As mentioned, it also contains Glenn Gould's one string quartet which is also in this book.

The CD can be heard on Spotify and YouTube.

Listenability: A transcendent experience – everyone should own a piano version as well.

Fugues from the
Well-Tempered-Clavier
Arranged for String Quartet

Bach wrote two sets of preludes and <u>fugues</u> for the piano, one in each of the 24 major and minor keys. At the beginning of Bach's career, pianos were tuned in such a way that restricted them to only be able to be played in a few keys. The modern piano tuning was developed during Bach's lifetime. This was achieved by using an approximate methodology. It is not absolutely mathematically nor musically accurate, but it enabled the piano to be played in all keys in a way that is satisfying to the ear. So the modern piano was born – the new method of tuning was known as *tempered*. Bach's two sets of preludes and fugues were named *Books 1 and 2 of The Well-Tempered Clavier*. They have come to be known by pianists as WTC or *The 48*.

Mozart arranged 12 of the pieces for string quartet. Later there were further arrangements written by A E Foster, who was himself a composer of over 50 string quartets. I have described the concept of fugue in the previous section, *The Art of Fugue*.

The notes in the CD booklet give a far more authoritative explanation than my offering. They also have some interesting anecdotal information that I won't go into here.

On to the task at hand. I'm going to discuss movements 1, 3, 5 and 10.

Track 1: *Book 1 – Fugue 1 in four voices* BWV 846
The piece has a jaunty subject and is played at a moderate pace. The cello is dominant and drives the music along. New melodic lines come faster than you can keep up with so just sit back and enjoy. There is a fabulous ending.

Track 3: *Book 1 – Fugue 12 in four voices* BWV 857
At a length of four minutes it represents one of the longer works. The subject is slow and introverted, and there is little pulse here. But it is very much alive, at times sounding like one of the *Brandenburg Concertos*, it is just so orchestral, and mostly in a call and response mode. The length allows Bach to thoroughly investigate the subject and many variations. Masterful writing and a majestic piece.

Track 5: *Book 1 – Fugue 16 in four voices* BWV 861
This is the shortest piece, well under two minutes. But at a swinging tempo, Bach tells a mini story which is very rewarding.

Track 10: *Book 1 – Fugue 24 in four voices* BWV 869
At a length of over six minutes this is the longest work. Such a lilting subject. It is given a gentle interpretation and the music unfolds at a restrained pace. A piece of immense beauty and transcendence, something that no one does better than Bach.

The above is not a random selection, they are indicative of the standard of the material. These are fine arrangements and this is a fabulous recording. I believe we have now exhausted all of the string quartet arrangements of Bach. There may be the occasional piece out there and I shall keep my eyes and ears open.

The music is from a CD by the Emerson Quartet titled simply *Bach Fugues* on Deutsche Grammophon. I don't always enjoy the Emersons – I sometimes find them too virtuosic and the music seems to get lost. Not here though, Bach keeps them in line. The CD is freely available on Amazon US, UK and Presto. The Emersons also recorded *The Art of Fugue*. Both versions are on Spotify and some of the fugues are on YouTube.

Listenability: Wonderful fugues from the master.

[Emerson String Quartet - Image courtesy ESQ]

Nicolas Bacri [born 1961]

Nationality: French
Quartets: At least nine
Style: Modern Contemporary

Homage to Beethoven
String Quartet No. 4

This work is in three movements and opens mysteriously as the cello and violin fade in and out. Slowly a melody begins to develop with the full ensemble. The viola repeats an ostinato phrase and the first violin meanders in a slightly dissonant manner. The other instruments lend support with long tones in a tempting section. The music doesn't seem to go anywhere, it's just a beautifully abstract feeling. Now the intensity increases and there are dissonant stabs. The cello comes to the fore with a strange entry, almost violent and not sounding really like a cello. Peace returns again for a time until the violins interject with furtive phrases. The level of dissonance increases, together with a sense of chaos. The violins finally settle on a taut passage and there is a rush to the finish line with a sudden stop. What a fascinating movement, introspective, but not over the top. There is not much melodic development but plenty of fine, musical flavours, which are to be savoured.

The next movement begins with total chaos. The viola hums like a bee and the violins fly like one. Then a ruthless section ensues with much forward propulsion, punctuated by rubato interludes. Suddenly we have a direct quote from the startling opening theme of Beethoven's *Grosse Fuge Opus 133*. The composer then employs a set of variations on this theme. The violins are virtuosic here in a forceful manner as the Beethoven quote is repeated before the music settles. A brief melodic interlude alternates with a dramatic section for a time. Scurrying violins set up another mysterious segment until the intensity returns and the violins duel in an extended passage to the end.

The final movement begins with long tones, separated by brief pauses. Not much melody here either, but it is an evocative scene. Melodies slowly begin to develop but they are simple, even child-like. After two minutes of stasis, the violins become more expressive and the pauses fall away. The music returns to the long tones and the desolate soundscape. The first violin is searching, longing, as it explores a naked melody. Another brief pause ensues, then we are back into the previous ambience. The violins sustain and the cello wanders through the murky depths of its lower register, leading to the work concluding with the cello.

I find this to be a wonderful piece, filled with many interesting, thoughtful spaces and places. It is a formidable tribute to Beethoven. Hats off to the Psophos Quartet too, they give a riveting performance.

Some parts of this work are quite modern, but there are some beautifully delicate adagios in there as well.

The review CD, titled *String Quartets Nos. 3, 4, 5, 6*, on AR RR-SE Records can be found on Amazon US and UK. This disc is also on Spotify, YouTube and earsense.

Listenability: Moderately challenging.

— ooOoo —

The Balanescu Quartet – Compilation

Nationality: N/A
Quartets: Four
Style: Contemporary

Something Different

The Balanescu Quartet formed in 1987 under leader and first violinist Alexander Balanescu and have toured extensively – I once saw them live. Their repertoire is mostly from contemporary composers and many recordings feature collaborations with rock musicians and modern quartet composers. They have recorded the string quartets of Michael Nyman, Kevin Volans and Gavin Bryars, and also made an album of arrangements of Kraftwerk songs, titled *Possessed*. The works on this CD, recorded in 1992, are not profound, but some days the Balanescu's approach just hits the spot. Beautiful for gentle listening, it features four entertaining, spirited works.

David Byrne – *High Life for Strings*. Byrne notes that on a visit to Africa he came to appreciate the many styles of the local musicians, especially the overlapping of the guitar parts. He then conceived a piece on the guitar and had it transcribed as a string quartet arrangement. It is a joyful work with the cello providing a constant rhythmic pattern, very African. There is some overdubbing as the score called for more than four parts. It bubbles along with the cello having a constant dialogue with the other instruments. Such a lilting, charming work.

Robert Moran – *Music from the Towers of the Moon*. This follows the standard four movement form. It begins with a joyous tone which is sustained until the gentle conclusion. The second movement is slow and thoughtful. It evokes memories of the final bars of the epic adagio of the Beethoven *String Quartet No. 15*. I get a similar feeling in the third movement – that Beethoven is just around the corner. Again it is slow and thoughtful. The last movement doesn't seem to fit with the others, it all seems just a little too much. What a shame.

John Lurie – *Stranger than Paradise*. Lurie was with the Lounge Lizards jazz group and wrote a soundtrack for a budget black and white movie. The six movements are quite short and are all named. Some movements contain improvisation. The opening *Bella by Barlight* is beautiful. After a few Morton Feldman moments, the violin takes over with an enchanting melody.

Improvisation I is dark and mysterious, what a great movement. *The Good and Happy Army* is indeed military-like, however not particularly inspiring. *The Sad Trees* is a short lament. *Eva and Willie's Room/Eva Unpacking* is a wonderful short eerie piece of abstraction, a solo piece for what sounds like the viola. *Improvisation II* tries to sustain a pensive mood but I don't find it very successful – there is no music in it. Having said that, I think that *Stranger than Paradise* is probably the most rewarding work on the CD.

Michael Torke – *Chalk*. The longest quartet on the CD, mostly has an insistent rhythm which pushes it along nicely. The opening minutes are a little angular, but it drops back a notch or two at times. There is a lot going on here.

The CD is very different from your normal contemporary string quartet recording. It has a bit of a 'pop' feel about it, which I find appealing. The cover doesn't have a title, just Balanescu Quartet, on the Argo label. On the spine it has *Byrne / Moran / Lurie / Torke*. The cover photo is distinctive, featuring a collage of a person made up by using parts of the faces of the four quartet members. It is readily available.

The CD is on Spotify and some of the Balanescu quartets are available for sampling on YouTube. You will have to scroll through the pages to find it – look for the four faces on the cover.

Listenability: Optimistic Contemporary works.

— ooOoo —

Ramón Barce [1928–2008]

Nationality: Spanish
Quartets: Eleven
Style: Modern Contemporary

String Quartets Nos. 1 and 2

Barce was so taken with the works of Schoenberg, Berg and Webern, aka *The Second Viennese School*, that he wrote a comprehensive treatise on Arnold Schoenberg's music. His style of composition has been described as *abstract expressionism* and his early string quartets were apparently influenced by Webern's development of Schoenberg's serial technique.

The First Quartet, written in 1958, is in three movements and opens with a sense of lilting abstraction. Atonal melodies are put forward but never reappear, nor are they developed. This is a characteristic of the serial nature of the composition. There appears to be no sense of structure, just a dialogue between the four players. A pizzicato cello supports the entropic melodies. The feeling changes for a time as the cello becomes more prominent and the texture is lighter, with the end almost perfunctory.

The next movement is definitely more structured. A very slow introduction features sustained violin tones leading to long melodies and a mysterious mood is developed as the cello underpins the violins. Some glissandos are heard as the music drifts along, almost aimlessly. Nearing the end, a sparsity emerges and subdued violins fade the movement out.

Quivering violins announce the final movement, which meanders until a brief pause occurs. The music which follows contains strangely harmonised melodic lines, with the abstraction palpable. Now an insistent cello goes solo and a violin picks up its melody in a fugue-like manner, a small concession to tonal music. Another pause introduces many glissandos with a pizzicato viola. This doesn't last and we have a change into a brief atonal flurry. The conclusion is a falling away of the instruments until there is nothing left.

By the time of the Second Quartet, written in 1965 and in two movements, Barce had developed his own take on serialism. The work commences with long, sustained, sparse violin tones, combined with frequent pauses. Some atonal harmony can be heard before a solo cello passage leads back into the opening mood with quiet sustained tones. The solo cello reappears and a violin spars with it. This leads to an extended passage of atonal interjections where entropy plays a significant role as the music becomes very disjointed – this is reminiscent of Elliott Carter's work although, not as rhythmically diverse. Another pause leads into several long notes from different instruments, interspersed with a throbbing cello. The attack from the violins is quite severe. Suddenly the work is energised and is quite random in nature before it ends sharply.

The final movement, which is very short, evokes Morton Feldman's style, opening with harmonised long tones. Slowly a rhythmic feeling evolves, however the music is still serial. A repeated violin tone allows for the other instruments to interject as they edge towards an evanescent conclusion.

This is classic serial music. I have heard this described as 'intellectual music', but I don't regard it as such. Having listened to the complete set of eleven quartets, I find them very emotionally expressive, albeit not in a conservative, tonal style. They have their own distinctive soundworld, the kind of musical spaces which I have enjoyed dipping into for many years.

The review CD, titled *Barce – String Quartets* by the Cuarteto Leonor on the Verso label, is a 3-CD set containing all eleven works. It is available on Amazon US and UK.

This set is on Spotify and all quartets can be found on YouTube and earsense.

Listenability: Fine, thoughtful, non-confronting works.

Incidental Images #1

String Quartet Walking

[Image courtesy Cypress String Quartet]
[Photographer – Basil Childers]

Zbigniew Bargielski [born 1937]

Nationality: Polish
Quartets: Six
Style: Contemporary Modern

String Quartets Nos. 2 & 4

Bargielski composes in a contemporary style and some of the quartets are quite modern. I have selected Nos. 2 & 4 which are both in one movement and relatively short. They are also some of his more conservative quartets.

String Quartet No. 2 is titled *Spring* and was written in 1980. It opens with a pensive solo violin which begins in the lower register. There are occasional interjections from the ensemble, becoming more frequent as the movement unfolds and the music moves into a slightly stilted tempo. The violins duet and descend into string sound effects at times and, eventually, into chaos. A pause brings a solo cello which is soon joined by a frantic violin which drifts in and out of the piece. The viola now complements the cello. Save for the violin, the passage is just so peaceful. The intensity gradually increases and the cello and viola pattern continues. A new section has a solo violin feeding small phrases to the ensemble which replies with a chord. Again, this is a quiet interlude as the violin becomes busier. Slowly a feeling of angst is attained as the ensemble support a sparse violin passage. The ensemble fall away and we are left with two atonal violins and some punctuating chords. The piece concludes with a solo violin statement.

I definitely wouldn't call it program music. There are very few parts that you could identify as being related to Spring. All the same, it is an interesting work.

String Quartet No. 4, written in 1994, titled *Burning Time,* takes a while to get going, with quiet, intermittent sustained violins being presented. A solo cello enters and throbs as the violins express sustained notes. Now the cello becomes more prominent and the violins move to fast, insistent phrases. One violin repeats a phrase and soon it is on its own, but for increasing ensemble thrusts. A change in harmony brings about a different texture with a quiet violin over string sound effects, which slowly disappear. They are replaced by a duet between the two violins – this is quite alluring and lasts for some time. The section then dissolves into chaos with more string sound effects. The cello begins its throbbing again, somewhat aggressively. The first violin spins out sparse melodies over a quivering second violin. A fadeout has the violin playing sparse phrases to the end.

These two quartets contain several elements of a certain modern style. These include: frantic playing; no recognisable melody; minimal/no development of melodic material; and silent openings, by which I mean that no real music is heard for 25-30 seconds. Arnold Schoenberg stated in the early 1900s that in 100 years we would all be whistling serial or 12-tone melodies. I doubt whether it will be these melodies. I continue to wonder at modern quartets because there are so many different styles, some of which take me to amazing musical places.

These works are available on a 2-CD set titled *String Quartets* by the Silesian String Quartet, on the CD Accord label. It is available on Amazon US and UK, although it looks slightly shaky as it is available on download as well. The set is on Spotify and several movements are on YouTube. All works can be heard on earsense.

Listenability: I wouldn't give it to my grandmother, but I find it interesting. It's Modern.

— ooOoo —

Béla Bartók [1881–1945]

Nationality: Hungarian
Quartets: Six
Style: Early Modern

String Quartet No. 1

Bela Bartók's six string quartets, together with those of Dmitri Shostakovich, are the most popular twentieth century string quartets by far. There are over 300 versions of his complete string quartets listed on Amazon UK. The First Quartet, written in 1909, and in three movements, is to be played without pauses between movements.

The opening to this work is one of my favourites. In my opinion, no composer has said so much, with so few notes, to begin a string quartet. Some of the melody apparently had already appeared in his *Violin Concerto No. 1*. Bartók's sparse, slightly dissonant introduction is just perfect. It opens with two violins and takes its time to bring in the viola and cello – there is such warmth and intangible character here. The cello begins to assert itself until we have several slight crescendos. After a time, the music cut back to the two violins. Then it is into powerful chords, first with one violin, followed by the second, answering the call. A new section quickly emerges, which is quite lyrical. Some more introspection follows before it moves into a recapitulation of the first theme, which is developed, all the time retaining the dissonance. A breathtaking episode of chords follows, before the music drops away to nothing.

The second movement begins in a sparse space. The violins are playful, but Bartók-playful, which is a little cheeky. A melody develops out of this formless interlude. Now the cello enters with thumping noises while the melodies continue. The feeling becomes intense as a solo cello section brings the tone back to lyrical again. There are some crescendos but the composer keeps them in check. Again the solo cello thumps us back into the lyricism. A violin in the high register takes over and we are almost back in the first movement. It is joined by the second violin to conclude.

The final movement opens with a flourish, interspersed with solo cello and the violin leads into a brief pause. Things now become intensely rhythmic, and very dynamic leading to a self-mocking passage, which is strange, atonal music. A lyrical fragment briefly emerges, followed by some intense moments which slowly lower the dynamics. A further brief pause leads into an episode of a racing tempo with spiking interjections. The movement is proving to be quite a journey through many different emotions, some parts lasting only a few bars. An extended dance-like episode leads into a period of brief chaos and a set of crescendos, then more chaos. A lyrical passage follows, which is beautiful. It again descends into chaos one more time, as we move towards a noisy conclusion on some strong chords. This is a brilliant work.

The quartet is freely available. I have it by the Tokyo Quartet as a 3-CD set paired with Janacek's two quartets, on the RCA Victor Red Seal label – this features the works in chronological order, a feat that cannot be accomplished on a 2-CD set due to the lengths of the individual quartets. You can have No. 1 on many single CDs but as the complete sets are so reasonably priced I suggest you take a chance.

There are several versions on Spotify and many on YouTube as well a plethora on earsense.

Listenability: Stunning Early Modern quartet.

String Quartet No. 2

The Second String Quartet was composed from 1915-1917 and is in three movements.

The first movement is particularly poignant and beautiful. It opens with a whisper of abstraction, with few melodic phrases. There is one motif which is stated and restated and variations on the motif persist for some time. A melody slowly becomes evident and there is a flurry of activity which returns to the opening flavour. A soft section produces a change – the previously mentioned motif is now revisited and is extensively examined from many standpoints. Eventually there is a brief crescendo before the volume again drops to a whisper. There is some melodic development here and much beauty. After a time it moves into a brief period of chaos which transforms into a tempo with the cello prominent. A loud statement is followed by a moderate volume and tranquility returns. As the ending approaches, some strong statements from the violins are heard until the cello takes over and leads the violins to a conclusion.

This movement is filled with deep feeling; it takes you on a journey. I can only remember one motif and it appears that the music refers to it regularly.

The second movement opens with a violin stretched against a taut rhythm – it is very busy. There are several string sound effects on show as the music surges forward. The tension is palpable as the violins engage in a terse dialogue.

Eventually, a section of call and response occurs and the rhythm is dispensed with as a solo violin proceeds over a fluid background. After a time the rhythm returns and there is another calm section, but it won't settle. Vigorous chord interjections lead into a solo violin until the cello makes a strong statement. A quiet chaos ensues and the cello thunders in with a huge chord to finish.

The final movement, marked lento, begins with another stunning ambience – it is sheer atonal beauty. Without a tempo, the individual voices seem to hang in the air, creating a profound melancholy effect. A violin begins to exert itself among the voices and brings a structure to the movement. It leads the other instruments for a while until a new mood takes over. There is a similarity to the movement opening, just four voices, each treading their own path. Now a violin phrase is picked up by each instrument in turn before the sparsity returns, and the ensemble then dialogues with the first violin. The intensity rises for a moment and then recedes back into the soundscape – what a wonderful place to be. The cello is mournful as it interacts with the violins. A violin melody eventually emerges, but it's subdued. The violin is supported by the cello and eventually takes over and finishes on a note played twice.

The first time I heard Bartók I found him to be impenetrable, but now I can hear the beautiful craftsmanship at work. This quartet is a marvel, with many fascinating musical places and spaces.

The work is freely available, and the six quartets fit onto a 2-CD set. You can have No. 2 on a number of single CDs, but as previously noted, the complete sets are reasonably priced.

There are several versions on Spotify and many on both YouTube and earsense.

Listenability: An evocative, rewarding, Early Modern quartet.

String Quartet No. 6

The Sixth Quartet, Bartók's last, contains four movements. It is worth noting that all movements are marked *mesto* - pensive, but sad. The first three also have qualifiers, indicating differences within the movements.

The first movement, like all of the others, begins gently, with plenty of emotion. A solo violin laments a slightly dissonant melody for some time. After a pause, the ensemble enters with a series of strong chords. Then we have a lot of murmurings, with not much melodic development, but beautiful nonetheless. One of the violins interjects a charming melody which is soon overwhelmed, and quieted. Some more entropic material occurs, at a moderate intensity – this section also lasts for a time. A strong statement by the whole ensemble ensues, leading into more scurrying sounds. Strings overlap and produce a slightly chaotic, but quiet feeling. There is not really a tempo but plenty of musical interest as the violins thrust forward. These hurried violins produce a strong intellectual feeling, and some melodic development takes the movement to its conclusion.

Another slow, sparse atmosphere introduces the next movement. Quivering violins spin out a background to mournful melodies. Suddenly a motif appears and it is taken up by all of the instruments. Melodic variations abound, all played with the same rhythm, but with beautifully crafted harmonised lines. The motif is restated and the cello and a violin carry it forward. A second violin is more melodic and makes its own way. One last restatement of the motif leads to a pause. Now there is an almost banjo-like texture with string sound effects in abundance. A violin leads the way and eventually works into a recurring phrase. The motif returns, beginning in an almost stately manner but soon degenerates into a parody, with instruments criss-crossing each other. The motif is still audible but it is modified in many ways. A drop in the tempo, together with a chord change brings a new texture, still based on the motif. A short variation ends the movement.

The mesto feeling is again obvious in the third movement. This is a measured piece of abstraction, with a slight sense of ascension in the various melodies as a mild fanfare introduces a step-like motion. Bartók deconstructs the feeling before reintroducing it and a change of key leads to further development before the tempo ceases and two violins lead the ensemble into another abstruse section. This is the heart and soul of Bartók. Some strong pizzicato, together with string sound effects, lead to a mysterious passage. The mesto here is qualified with *burletta*, meaning little joke, which accounts for the slightly dismissive, quirky nature of the music. Sanity eventually prevails and strong chords are alternated with strange melodies to complete the movement.

As previously noted, the final movement is all mesto with an almost orchestral opening featuring long, lamenting melodic lines. A pause reintroduces the instruments one at a time, slowly bringing about an unusual other-worldly sound. This is interrupted by some harmonised melodic lines which linger as they investigate the new atmosphere. A pause leads to some more orchestral sounds, although they are much sparser than the opening. A violin becomes salient and the intensity rises for a time, but soon dissipates back into a minimal soundscape. Occasional violin interjections break the ambience with their dissonance, but a pure melody played over a pizzicato and a gentle cello, concludes the quartet.

This is a magnificent work, it defines Bartók for me. I remember when I first heard it, I didn't get it, but now it just seems so right, even though it still fills me with a sense of mystery and wonder. As previously noted, all of Bartók's quartets are freely available on Amazon US and UK, in many combinations

There are several versions on Spotify and YouTube. You can also hear the work played by ten different ensembles on earsense.

Listenability: A twentieth century masterpiece.

[Béla Bartók – 1927]
[Image – Wiki Commons]

— ooOoo —

Jon Bauman [1939–2009]

Nationality: American
Quartets: Four
Style: Contemporary

Serious Music
String Quartets Nos. 1 & 2

String Quartet No. 1 is in four movements and is relatively short, opening with a beautiful cello line, and minimal violin support. The violins move into the picture and a wonderfully sparse, slow, modern mood is established. This builds from one of stasis to a violin-led section. There is a hint of dissonance and the cello has a significant role in the proceedings. I wish it could go on for ever, it's just so touching – the end comes quietly.

The next movement is dramatic, with strong interjections over an intangible background. The intensity rises and ends with a beautiful violin phrase. It's all over at 1:36.

The third movement is even shorter, at 35 seconds. A flurry of violins deliver a slightly chaotic end to this miniature.

The final movement is again indefinite. Violins express vague, sensitive feelings with some chaos. The ending is intense, and goes out on a chord.

This work runs for only around ten minutes and is reminiscent of the miniaturistic nature of some of Anton Webern's later works.

The Second Quartet is also in four movements. A strong opening flourish leads a move into a repeated, slightly atonal phrase with some intensity. The music then ebbs and flows, as a quiet cello line is supported by strange, distant violin phrases, producing a feeling of pure bliss. The intensity is restored, but only for a short time – the violin phrases persist as the first violin drifts across the surface revealing a fabulous sense of space. A strong rhythmic punctuation leads to a hectic violin phase as atonal melodies unfold. This is deep music, spinning out long violin lines to great effect. A repeated instance of ascending violin notes leads to a final chord.

The next, brief movement is marked grave and the violins create a lamenting atmosphere throughout this static movement. It is a stunning piece of writing.

The third movement opens busily, with violin conversations and pizzicato. So far these are the first optimistic sounds that I have heard. That soon changes as a solo violin fashions a disconsolate melody. Long sustained notes are the order of the day and eventually a second violin joins the fray. Now the whole ensemble moves forward, yet still retains the ambience. After a time the opening busyness returns with some effective chromatic phrases and eventually, some forceful playing to the end.

The final movement opens with a cello motif, at moderate tempo, which is taken up by the violins. Then the tempo is quickened with the same phrase being used and a sombre interlude emerges with minimal action from the violins. The tempo returns and the violins flirt with atonality. A short pause leads to a brief recapitulation of the opening melody by the cello – the phrase is repeated with varying textures. A return of the sombre passage is most welcome, it's a little like some of Morton Feldman's work. This moves into a spiralling violin statement where the notes come to rest in the highest register. The gentlest of sounds concludes the quartet.

These are absolutely marvellous works, filled with serious moments and some fine contrasts.

The review CD, *String Quartets Nos. 1, 2, 3, 4* performed by the Moyzes Quartet, on the Diskant/Albany label is available on Amazon US at a reasonable price.

It is on Spotify and you can listen to the complete string quartets, Nos. 1-4 on YouTube and earsense.

Listenability: Wonderful, meaningful quartets.

— ooOoo —

Jeremy Beck [born 1960]

Nationality: American
Quartets: At least five
Style: Contemporary

Four String Quartets

Jeremy Beck has written five string quartets – let's hope there are some more. Nos. 1, 2, 4 and 5 are all on the one CD with each quartet normally running about 15 minutes.

String Quartet No. 1 is a three movement work. It commences with a grave feeling which soon moves into a forceful section. The rhythms are reasonably intense, but they soon move in to an episode of melodic stability. The angst returns for a time, but transforms into a pastoral flavour. The violins lead the work, and do a fine job. Finally, some reflective moments ease into the conclusion.

Movement two is an adagio, and long melodies define the opening. The cello marks out its space with a sombre line. The violins come over the top – they are plaintive and we soon have pure introspection, a feeling which is sustained for the bulk of the movement. A forceful passage destroys the ambience but it quickly mellows and reverts back to introspection. The violins define the music with call and response from the ensemble. It finishes with a whisper.

The third and final movement is marked presto. Starting with a conversational approach, there is little emphasis on rhythm. The quartet are in a playful joust as melodies come and go, with all instruments contributing to the atmosphere, which is sustained for the duration of this charming piece.

String Quartet No. 2 is titled *Fathers and Sons*. The first movement, *Fathers,* is the longest piece on the disc, just over 12 minutes. It is a beautiful adagio. Long drawn-out melodies eventually give way to a brief, playful fragment. The adagio returns in a magnificent passage. While not being an American, I believe I can garner a sense of the open plains and those eroded rock formations that are seen in the drier parts of the US. The music now comes to a halt and there are key changes which I hadn't noticed before. Now all four members play the same rhythmic motif before interplay is reintroduced, leading to a rollicking feeling. Another distinct change of atmosphere leads to a decrease in tempo, and while starting gently, a new rhythmic motif soon appears. When

45

the section is over, the composer returns to the cerebral adagio tempo to complete the piece. What a terrific ending, so delicate and captivating.

The second movement, *Sons*, opens with a folksy feeling. Music like this could only come out of America. I wouldn't call it pastoral but it is music of the country. It's not until it is halfway through its five minute length that things become gently abstruse. It ends on a long faded note.

The Fourth Quartet is in four movements, with the first movement marked allegro *furioso*. Well, it isn't. It's a joyful romp for all concerned. Besides that, it quickly transforms into a lilting phase. The opening returns briefly and all's well that ends well.

The second movement is a fine piece of melancholia. It only runs for two minutes. The first violin works at the top of its range for a time before being joined, gently, by the ensemble. All have a part to play here but the cello is especially prominent.

The third movement again opens with a beautiful peaceful feeling. Cello and violin dominate proceedings. After a while, things become a little raucous, but it doesn't interrupt the peace which soon returns and holds its own until the conclusion.

Movement four begins with a shimmering feeling from the violins which is truly wonderful. As the movement develops, I'm beginning to feel that it seems to be Beck's trademark to have violin and cello duets. They are marvellous together here as they fade out to the end.

String Quartet No. 5 is in three movements. The first has a sense of duality – two moods come and go. The first is sparse, the other, more lyrical. The latter eventually predominates and, for a while, the piece is built around it. Suddenly the cello appears, marking out a constant tempo. The other instruments drift freely in the space until the cello drops the rhythm and joins the conversation. Another fade takes it out.

The second movement opens gracefully, with sparse instrumentation. This builds until all of the members are communicating freely. After a short pause, the violin enters with a lament that continues to the completion of the piece, with a most attractive ending.

The final movement commences as a dialogue between the first violin and cello. It is over two minutes before all members of the quartet are involved. The dialogue eventually extends to all four players and continues to the end with a swoop.

There are several different ensembles on the review CD so I won't mention them – they all play beautifully. This CD, *Quartets*, on the Innova label, is available on Amazon US and UK at present but it's starting to look a little scarce.

You can hear most of the quartets on YouTube and earsense.

Listenability: A fine collection.

Incidental Images #2

The Legendary Budapest String Quartet

[Image courtesy Wiki Commons]

Undoubtedly the world's most famous string quartet in the first half of the twentieth century, their faultless playing, general demeanour and vast repertoire allowed them to tour the world stages for over 50 years. Formed in 1918, they managed to sustain personnel for long periods, including virtuoso cellist Mischa Schneider, who left the quartet for a time, before returning, but still managed to clock up 38 years with the ensemble.

There is a fascinating biography, titled *Con Brio*, which gives an amazing insight into their music, personalities and group dynamics. Highly recommended for string quartet obsessives like myself.

Ludwig van Beethoven [1770–1827]

Nationality: German
Quartets: Sixteen
Style: Romantic/Transcendent

The Late Quartets
String Quartet No. 12

Music historians have divided Beethoven's string quartets into three periods: early, middle and late. The Late Quartets, Nos. 12 to 16, have assumed legendary status in classical music. They are often described as representing the pinnacle of Western Art Music. The most praised, and designated as the jewel in the crown, is No. 14, Opus 131 in C-sharp minor. I personally prefer No. 15 in A minor, Opus 132 and No. 12 in E-flat major, Opus 127.

The last three years of Beethoven's life were almost exclusively dedicated to string quartets. By this time he had been completely deaf for several years, so he never heard that which he was composing, except in his imagination. To accomplish such a result in these circumstances is a remarkable achievement. These works are truly transcendent and seem to be of another time and place. In my opinion, in terms of personal expression they stand head and shoulders above all other quartets in the genre.

String Quartet No. 12 is quite orchestral in conception, especially the first movement. Beethoven uses the same three major chords that can be found in 'three-chord songs' to fashion a stunning introduction to the piece. The chords are played sustained, in an orchestral fashion, with powerful voicings, and their occurrences are interspersed with many lilting melodies. The first melodic theme starts slowly but develops a strong rhythm. Following another round of chords the first melodic section is repeated. These sections are played in and out of tempo and can sound melancholic until they lift themselves up. A return to the opening chordal passage occurs twice and each time it proceeds into some wistful melodies, together with strong rhythmic dynamics. There is a recapitulation of the first melody several times. From there it leads into some new melodic material. Melodies recur, to be reshaped and reharmonised. The ending comes gently. There is some beautiful writing to be found here.

The next movement, which is an adagio, forms the emotional heart of the quartet. My review version runs for sixteen minutes. It opens ever so gently and moves into a longing melody which is sustained for around four minutes. It is then developed into a new sound, while still remaining restrained. The piece moves slowly into a walking tempo and then comes to life. Playful melodies abound, sometimes with a hint of darker material – it is a process of constant development. Following this, the tempo pauses and we are transported back into a longing interlude which is splendid, melancholic music. A chord change introduces a new, optimistic feeling, with a rhythmic accompaniment from the viola and cello. An ascending phrase is established and the music slowly becomes louder. Now the feeling drops back into a sparse melodic fragment. It is quietly majestic for a while and then proceeds to a slightly measured joyful passage. There is a brief pause and the peace returns with a gentle cello motif to support the violins, as they lead the music to a tranquil conclusion. This is definitely one of the finest movements of the Late Quartets. It is very touching, filled with both drama and beauty.

The third movement begins in an upbeat manner, with a skittish theme. An underlying cello theme anchors the tempo. The violins are playful, with joyous exchanges and the music is dynamically vibrant. An extended melody is wonderful, constantly turning back on itself to repeat critical melodic themes. A change to a minor key leads into a whole new feeling and new melodies are formed and developed. Now the opening returns for a time before the cello initiates a conversation. Another minor chord change leads into a hurried ending. This is definitely very positive music.

The final movement opens with a strangely vague feeling, before eventually settling into a rollicking manner. A new section emerges, rhythmic, beginning strongly but retreating a little as it progresses. Now another melodic theme is presented and appropriate variations are developed. A further rhythmic episode restates some of the earlier material, at times in different ways. Things begin to get a bit excited as the violins dominate proceedings before a flurry of notes following some punctuating chords, leads to the conclusion. All in all, a wonderful melodic journey can be found here.

I will discuss availability in the conclusion of this section on Beethoven.

Listenability: A stunning Romantic work.

String Quartet No. 14

This work is formally known as String Quartet No. 14 in C-sharp minor, Opus 131 and is reputed to be Beethoven's favourite composition. He also implied that it was made up of a collection of musical scraps that he had worked on in the past. Don't let that put you off – genius has no limits. Beethoven was well known to have used many ideas from the early sketches of his symphonies in other pieces. The work is in seven movements, to be played without pauses. I have chosen an historical version by the Busch Quartet from 1951 to discuss.

The first movement is a stunning, slow fugue. Soon we are lost in the overlaying of the voices as the ensemble examines the theme subject, and relate to each other. This is achingly beautiful, so rarified. The movement develops slowly, and at around the halfway point there is a recapitulation, the development continues. It is indeed heavenly music and the end is just a few lonely notes from the cello.

The next movement is short and played at a moderate tempo. A breezy opening gives way to a set of variations, never too far from the opening theme. It is very precious and develops ever so slowly in volume before there is a brief pause and the opening returns – bringing such joy. Towards the end, there is some playful conversation as the voices rework the themes. It ends on two quiet notes.

These two notes are picked up at volume for the opening of the third movement. It is so short, at 46 seconds that it functions purely as an interlude. It's practically over before it starts.

The fourth movement is by far the longest of the work. It starts with a genteel grace that harks back to Mozart and Haydn. A most attractive theme is introduced and is carried by the violin and cello. This is developed and a slow fugal interlude ensues – more heavenly music here. The delicate nature is sublime and the influence of the previously mentioned masters is ever-present. There is a slight rise in intensity, leading to a stately passage. The former theme is reintroduced and the bliss continues as the cello and violin support the melody, examining it from various angles. A change brings with it a solo violin, soon to be supported by the other voices. The solo violin is present in an excited state until it moves to the conclusion. The stunning writing in this movement begs the question, how do you follow such a movement?

Beethoven's answer is with an up-tempo movement, again of great Classical beauty. Marvellous melodies abound in a frisky manner. There is some wonderful thematic material here and the first violin works furiously to navigate it, sometimes with little accompaniment. The movement finishes with a flourish.

The sixth movement is again short and is a lament, featuring long tones and an elegant melody. It is all over very quickly and moves straight into the final movement, which opens rhythmically but keeps dropping into slow melodic interludes. Beethoven works the rhythmic motif over several times between these interludes. There are some fine melodies to be found here as they alternate with the motif. Somehow the music seems endless, but the end does finally come with a moderate flourish.

This quartet is a musical journey to be savoured. It runs for 39 minutes in the Busch version. It did not gain its lofty reputation by accident. Like all of Beethoven's Late Quartets, it contains several transcendent, heavenly spaces. It is an incredible composition.

Listenability: A must-have masterpiece.

String Quartet No. 15

Known formally as String Quartet No. 15 in A minor, Opus 132, this work was the first string quartet that I ever really heard, in 1991. The titanic adagio movement was played on Australia's national broadcaster, the ABC, on a show *The Search for Meaning,* early one Sunday evening. The minute the show was over I went to a CD and book store that stayed open Sunday nights to enquire about the music. The sales assistant said 'Ah, you've been listening to *The Search for Meaning*!' Fortuitously, they had a copy. It was 27 years ago and I have no idea of the performers but it was the commencement of a long and rewarding infatuation with string quartets.

This work usually consists of five movements, although occasionally it is performed as four, by combining two movements. It begins with a dark solo cello statement, then moves through a virtuoso violin melody full of earnest vigour. It then changes to a light skipping scene. The whole movement disintegrates, with incredibly moving sections giving way to joy. There are a number of recurring themes, with one intense melody returning time and time again.

The second movement has two recurring themes and some other-worldly passages that link the occurrence of these themes. All of this in preparation for the emotional centrepiece of the work, the adagio third movement.

At the time, Beethoven had a severe intestinal problem and after his recuperation he commenced a most remarkable movement. Due to his recovery from the illness he prefaced it with the inscription *Song of Thanksgiving to the Deity from a Convalescent in the Lydian Mode*. I have seen several different translations of the original German but this one is pretty typical.

The movement runs for about 20 minutes and I don't expect to be able to relate its many virtues in one or two paragraphs. It begins with a mournful, tranquil melody. Beethoven constantly returns to the theme throughout the piece. Following two interjections of an incredibly stately melody it returns to a sombre nature. After about 13 minutes, the music is no longer of this world. It has become so achingly beautiful and prayer-like – for me, this is indeed spiritual music. After a time the opening theme is restated and developed in a transcendent manner that simply defies description. It finally drifts forward to a conclusion. This was the music I heard that set me on my voyage of discovery.

The fourth and fifth movements return to this world and are filled with light melodies and many recapitulations. Restatements of one of the themes from the deep third movement are completely reharmonised in an optimistic manner and there is a return to joyful music. Such is the way of a master. These movements sound as if they could have originated in Beethoven's early or middle quartets. The final movement ends with a flourish and it is all over. I shall leave you with the words of a friend '*It takes you there and brings you back again!*'

Briefly revisiting the Late Quartets as a whole, a host of books and words have been written on their manifold soundscapes and mysteries. Amazon UK returns 2,546 results for '*Beethoven Complete String Quartets*'. I actually find that figure mind boggling – there would be some duplicates in there but it means a lot of ensembles have tried their hand with Beethoven. Searching '*Beethoven Late Quartets*' returns 877 results which is also amazing. Personally, I have three complete sets and three late sets. The Late Quartets usually come in a 3-CD format, while complete sets are usually from 7-8 discs.

Obviously many fine recorded performances of all of Beethoven's string quartets can be obtained. My personal favourite of the Late Quartets is by the Quartetto Italiano. I can also recommend the Tokyo and the Takacs, but there must be many other superb performances. It is the kind of music that is worthwhile to have multiple sets. They would all have something different to say about these magnificent works.

All of Beethoven's Late String Quartets are available on Spotify and YouTube. They are also on earsense, including seven versions of No. 15. They would all be worth hearing.

Listenability: The most transcendent music that I have ever heard.

[Ludwig van Beethoven – Public domain]

Elizabeth Bell [born 1928]

Nationality: American
Quartets: One
Style: Modern Contemporary

A Breath of Fresh Air
String Quartet No. 1

Elizabeth Bell wrote one string quartet and one symphony, both of which appear on the CD that I am about to discuss. The quartet, in four movements was written in 1957.

The work opens with a lone violin, soon to be joined by a sparse cello and viola, which leads to an amazing sense of entropy. The instruments seem to be meandering and there is no noticeable melody, yet it is pure atmosphere. A change brings the cello to the fore momentarily, and then we are back into the former mood. A dialogue begins to evolve and then the cello slows it down again – the piece continues as a reverie. The violin then moves into the high register and as it reaches the conclusion there is a slight lift in dynamics until the ensemble drops out, one by one and the violin breathes its last note.

The second movement opens with three sharp, dissonant chords. The cello enters and the violin begins with an atonal melody. The dissonant chords recur a number of times with atonal violin melodies filling in the gaps – this is beautifully introspective music. Now a solo violin introduces a new melody, interrupted by more chords before the cello takes on the melodic function as the ensemble converses in the background. Eventually they all blend together into one sound. Then follows new chord interjections and new melodies. The cello rhythm and violin melody lead into the conclusion with two sharp, indeterminate chords.

The next movement is slow and opens gently with two violins playing long melodic lines, before the cello adds support and the violins continue with plaintive, sparse melodies. A slight period of abstraction and pizzicato follows and the cello makes a lonely statement. Now it is back to one violin until the ensemble returns. The violin fades out to conclude.

The final movement opens in a swirling manner – this is mildly chaotic. Several chordal interjections appear and the cello supports the two violins. The music is busy, and rhythmically incisive passages alternate freely. Atonal violin lines are enthralling as they sustain the various moods until a solo violin enters for a period before it is back to the quartet and more chaos. Then follows two rhythmic chords and a sustained chord to end the work.

This is a brief review and I feel I need to justify it. The piece runs for 23 minutes but each movement has a number of static periods. It's not uninteresting, in fact it is magnificent – unique in that I cannot think of any other work in this style. Mostly it is a beguiling, atonal romp.

The review CD is available, paired with the symphony, as *Music of Elizabeth Bell* on Amazon US. I couldn't find it anywhere else. The symphony is interesting, slightly Mahler-like.

Listenability: Marvellously mild Modernism.

— ooOoo —

Alban Berg [1884–1935]

Nationality: Austrian
Quartets: Two
Style: Early Modern

Lyric Suite
for String Quartet

Alban Berg wrote two works for string quartet. They were his *String Quartet*, Opus 3, and the work under consideration. The Lyric Suite was written using the twelve-tone methodology, developed by Arnold Schoenberg. Although I have some knowledge of the basic techniques of the method, I don't claim to understand the detailed workings of the system, so I am going to discuss it in my usual manner, concentrating on my emotional response to the piece. For me, it is a work of total abstraction and I love it. It is in six movements.

The work opens in a slightly optimistic manner as the first violin takes centre stage. A pizzicato section sets up a backdrop for the violins to make their musical statements. Melodies do occur, but they tend not to be developed – the end is a flourish. This is a brief movement, as are most of the others.

The second movement, marked andante, begins with a lamenting violin played above a sparse background – this is a marvellous musical space. Now a tempo is introduced and the instruments clash briefly before settling back into a supportive musical environment. A calm period ensues and there is some peaceful, subtle playing which is almost Romantic, and quite attractive. The energy returns with several instrumental flourishes, and moments of great peace occur with the end coming as a surprise.

The third movement features string sound effects for a sustained period. The ensemble fidget about for over a minute, before any recognisable music can be detected. The feeling is intense for a time and the sound effects return. It finishes as it started, totally unintelligible to me, but ultimately rewarding.

The next movement, an adagio, develops a sense of gentle abstraction from the start. It is a great place to be. Violins make random statements and an intensity develops with melodies to be found here. Now comes a serene moment, which gradually grows louder with cello interjections, before dropping back into

54

serenity. Again, it is an almost Romantic sound until Berg inserts some microtones for a dissonant effect. The movement ends gently.

The fifth movement is aggressive with dissonant violin thrusts, before it too drops into serenity as string sound effects abound. The aggression returns, and the violins seem to whirl in ever diminishing circles. More serenity follows – what a fabulous sound, with string harmonics adding to the atmosphere. Now we have a return to the previous intensity and the cello is powerful. A hurried episode takes us to the conclusion.

The final movement starts softly, I didn't hear any music for 25 seconds. Assorted scraping noises accompany the violin's languid melodic lines. Surprisingly, a female soprano voice enters, singing in German. The voice is that of Dawn Upshaw, made famous for her performance in Gorecki's *Symphony of Sorrowful Songs*. The vocal alternates with the ensemble, which offers sound effects as support. The piece becomes dynamic for a time, then recedes back to a sense of grace, with the violin featured. There is another short soprano statement, before the music recedes into the distance.

You probably have no idea of how the piece sounds. Many technical analyses are to be found, but unless you are classically trained, I doubt if you will be any the wiser. Apart from Wikipedia, which is a good place to start, there is quite a complex discussion here:

https://monashcomposers.wordpress.com/2010/04/29/berg-lyric-suite/

However, this is music to be experienced. Overall, I didn't find it confronting, but I do enjoy pure abstraction. It's worth noting that Berg also arranged this piece for orchestra.

The music is readily obtainable – Amazon UK has eight pages of current recordings. There is a version on Naxos, *Berg: String Quartet / Lyric Suite / Wolf: Italian Serenade*, performed by the New Zealand String Quartet, which is at a nice price. There are several versions on Spotify and YouTube, which has an extraordinary version by the Juilliard String Quartet from 1950. This is also featured on earsense.

Listenability: Not as difficult as we are led to believe. It makes me wonder what all the fuss was about.

[Alban Berg – Image – Wiki Commons]

Boris Blacher [1903–1975]

Nationality: Russian-German
Quartets: Five
Style: Early Modern

String Quartets Nos. 1 & 2

Boris Blacher was born in a Russian-speaking region of China, to Russian parents. In 1922, he moved to Berlin to study and, eventually teach. His career was interrupted by National Socialism, being accused of writing degenerate music and losing his teaching post at the Dresden Conservatory – thanks, Wiki.

His First Quartet was written in 1930 and comprises three movements. The work opens with a skittish musical statement, notes seem to be going everywhere. A transformation into something more tangible takes place as the violins dance around the accompaniment. It is essentially a dialogue between all four instruments with random themes presented, without being re-presented. However the music just will not settle, until it concludes. The movement sets the tone for the remaining pieces.

The next movement is slow and features an ostinato from the cello while the violins drift above – this will not settle either. The violins meander until the cello joins them and a calm is reached. There is some interplay within the ensemble and it fades to an end, leaving us none the wiser. It is light, but ultimately very rewarding music.

The final movement opens with a busy section – it positively dances. First the cello dominates for a time before the violins take the lead. There is a small amount of dialogue but it feels like the melodies are almost random, seemingly bearing no relationship to each other. Then it just stops.

The Second Quartet, written in 1940, is in three movements and begins incredibly slowly and gently. After a time a fanfare brings the movement to life. There is an abundance of energy and a sense of entropy within the melodies, just no cohesion.

The second movement opens with a quiet cello ostinato, a bit like Ravel's *Bolero* as an insistent violin is central to the music. The cello underpins the movement, leading to an enthralling sound. The violins seem a lot more focussed, and some admirable slow melodies appear here – there is finally some structure. The ending is beautiful.

The third movement is again agitated, with melodies created, but not given time to take root. It is also very mannered. There often seems to be no obvious relationship between the instruments.

What to make of all this? The music is uniquely stylised. It moves along without form, the violins constantly playing different melodies. There are two components. The violins dance above, almost randomly as cello and viola provide the basis of the accompaniment. There is little melodic development in these two quartets.

I must make mention of the larghetto movement of the Third Quartet, which is also on the review CD. It is a marvellous piece of writing, totally out of character with that which I have just described. The cello anchors the piece with a motif, and, now the violins seem more focussed. The melodies are stated in half-time, which makes them all the more obvious - no agitation here. A charming theme keeps recurring until it finally peters out.

There is a CD of the complete string quartets, titled *Blacher: String Quartets Nos.1-5*, on the EDA label, by the Petersen Quartet on Amazon US and UK. It is not available on Spotify but many Blacher quartets can be found on YouTube and all of the works are on earsense.

Listenability: Slightly strange but appealing works.

— ooOoo —

Easley Blackwood [born 1933]

Nationality: American
Quartets: Three
Style: Contemporary Modern

String Quartets Nos. 1-3

Easley Blackwood's four string quartets are quite modern and as such, will not appeal to all tastes. However, there are some modern string quartet listeners out there. You know who you are.

Quartet No. 1, marked largo, which usually means *slow and stately*, commences with a slow period that lasts all of 30 seconds. It is followed by a slightly frantic passage which then moves back into the opening largo tempo. This is atonal music which uses much dissonance but I find it stimulating. The piece has a slow, tranquil, atonal quality for a time before the chaos returns. It winds down beautifully leaving a solo cello statement to complete the movement. The second movement is taken up with a quiet, simple, violin theme statement which concludes on a cello melody with pizzicato from the other instruments – introspection reigns supreme. The third movement has a strong rhythmic pulse together with a disjointed melody, played in a conversational manner. It is modern, but not angry music, it's just different.

The Second Quartet begins with a series of introspective melodies, taken at a moderate tempo, setting up a beautiful sense of dissonance. The tempo picks up and the ensemble takes on a conversational approach with the quartet bouncing ideas off each other. The cello now dominates, with some subtle accompaniment from the violins, leading to a superb section. The second, short movement is a gentle footrace which features some spikey violin interjections. It does not distract from the abstract beauty of the music. The final movement, marked molto lento, is simply stunning. It begins slowly and softly before moving into a darker place, which suddenly stops, leading into a lament for the two violins. There is more action, then absolute peace, as the violins whisper over the cello. A stark chord concludes the piece.

Now, on to String Quartet No. 3. The first movement opens with a pastoral feeling (you better believe it), with plenty of lilting melodies that are sustained to the end, which is peaceful. The second movement is also completely of a pastoral nature. The third movement is the longest piece on the CD and is a fine adagio, with not a note out of place. The final movement is a jaunty affair – a continuous collection of spirited melodies.

So there we have it, two modern quartets and the third, conservative. I must admit I find the combination a little puzzling, but eminently pleasing.

The CD under consideration, *Easley Blackwood, String Quartets, 1 - 3*, on Cedille Records, by the Pacifica Quartet is freely available. The cover is a wonderful picture of four multi-coloured butterfly wings, which would go nicely with your CD rack.

The disc is on Spotify and there are some sound samples on Presto Classical.

Listenability: A Modern composer expressing himself in different ways.

[Image courtesy Cedille Records]

Ernest Bloch [1880–1959]

Nationality: Swiss
Quartets: Five
Style: Early Modern

Some Serious Music
String Quartet No. 2

Bloch's five string quartets were written over an extended period, from 1916 to 1956. The Second Quartet was composed in 1945.

A weeping solo violin commences the work and the second violin presents a counter melody as a duet harmony forms. The cello arrives to complement this languishing feeling and the violins respond to its presence. The cello is solo for a time, then the violins return. A pause ensues, then movement, as the instruments strike out towards their purpose, that is, to reach high while still showing restraint. Towards the end, there is an increase in dynamics but the mood is sustained. The cello delivers two phrases, and dialogues with the violins, which carry us to the end. This is a magnificent emotion-drenched piece of music.

The next movement opens with rhythmic thrusts and a deal of excitement. An ostinato develops and the rhythm becomes stiff and stilted. Finally, the violins prevail and express a short section together before moving on to an introspective passage. The plangent cello steps forward and its resonance produces a fine sound. Now there is movement, slightly frantic with a strong tempo. This train-like atmosphere fades and the solo cello reappears with gentle violin musings. The cello **is** the music here. An abstract phase begins to form with the violins varying their volume and slicing through the accompaniment. A short violin duet leads to a serious full ensemble sound to conclude.

A gentle pulse, with serene violins introduce the third, andante movement, so I am not expecting any rhythmic surprises. The twin violins lament at length, and slow to a sustained chord. The violins regather, but are more concerned with creating a funereal tempo than any melodic development. Another ostinato occurs and the violins are very expressive over the ensemble. Some rhythmic movement by the cello leads into a series of statements which are intertwined with the violins to produce a stunning sound. The intensity then drops away while the cello and violin continue, this time, with rubato intertwining, which is very different from the previous occasion. The end comes with a slow fade until nothing more can be heard.

The finale begins with a spectacular set of violin thrusts and pizzicato rhythms, over which the violins express dramatically. Now the full ensemble is evident and the mood is slightly random. A violin initiates an ascending motif, then develops it until it becomes fundamental to the music. The violins are now more intense and a slight crescendo leads into a harmonic change. There is almost joy – which is not one of the composer's defining traits – to be found here. Another motif-based ostinato develops before a series of duet violin lines lead to

59

another crescendo. A pause brings forth sweeping violin melodies that move with the cello into a passage full of unresolved tension. A quite frantic pizzicato accompaniment is overwhelmed by the violins, which repeat a melodic motif and then introduce a stasis. Long violin tones continue but there is no motion. The work finishes on a sustained cello tone.

As you have probably gathered, Bloch writes serious music. I've also noticed that he works in a limited dynamic range, with the crescendos quite controlled.

I'm particularly drawn to historical quartet ensembles, so my review CD was by the early Pro Arte Quartet on the Laurel label. I see it can still be obtained from ArkivMusic. More freely available however, is a 2-CD set by the Griller Quartet, on the Decca label, which contains Quartets Nos. 1-4. They are also quite early – I have heard their set and can recommend it.

The Griller is on Spotify. I was surprised to find several historical quartets playing Bloch on YouTube. All of the composer's works for string quartet, including several shorter pieces, are available on earsense.

Listenability: Music of an extremely grave nature.

— oo0oo —

Alexander Borodin [1833–1887]

Nationality: Russian
Quartets: Two
Style: Late Romantic

A Consummate Melodist
String Quartet No. 1

Within Borodin's two string quartets, there are five movements which contain some of the most glorious melodies in the genre. It begs the question, how does one differentiate such beauty? I guess by giving it a go. The Second Quartet is the most popular but I am going to discuss the First Quartet, which is also extremely fine.

The work opens with a splendid, slightly melancholy melody, played slowly. The composer brings that melody into an orchestral-like section. After a time the tempo quickens to be lively and the violins dance, as does the cello, leading into another enticing melody, which is then developed by the quartet. The tempo quickens further for a moment, before the intensity drops back into another melodic section that simply races. There is a sustained joy with the violins really taking off. After a pause, sparsity briefly emerges but the violins build a strong melody as the dynamics rise. A recapitulation of a previous theme is delightful. This is followed by another, more measured joyful section before the theme returns, with a different orchestration. As we approach the end, quotes from previous melodies appear. The ending is the sound of two violins way up in their high registers.

The second movement begins with a delightful violin duet, until the viola enters. There is then an assertive passage which brings forth another melodic section – the violins dominate as they soar above the ensemble. Now the cello starts another fine melody, sometimes leading the way itself. The cello takes over and creates a slight ambivalence. A fanfare livens up the proceedings, bringing with it an old melody made new again. The intensity rises for a time and brings a serious tone, with plenty of powerful flourishes. The cello predominates as we approach the conclusion.

A stirring rhythm leads the next movement. The violins chatter away above the ensemble and propel the music forward. After a pause there is a period of bell-like violin harmonics which is attractive. The violins then work their way back into tempo and the race is on again. A full-sounding passage is maintained until it finishes with a couple of lone violin strokes.

The last movement, after a brief ensemble chord, opens with a longing melody from the violins, before the chord is played again. The cello leads with a statement until a series of sharp chords signal a change. Now the violins bring the piece into a rapid tempo with strong accompaniment, yielding to a bright, light ensemble interlude. The violins are busy, then move into another calm section. The rhythm returns, leading into one of those alternating, fast now, slow now, sections which I have come across many times before. The finale is fast and ends with a shimmering effect before a closing chord.

Availability is discussed below.

Listenability: Brilliantly expressive Romanticism.

String Quartet No. 2

The Second Quartet commences in a most lyrical fashion – Borodin was surely a master melodist. A series of wonderful overlapping violin lines constantly refer back to themselves, with the cello also reminding us of earlier melodies. A brief section of pizzicato accompaniment leads into a more forceful section where the violins combine to wonderful effect. A pause allows the cello to allude to the first theme and the violins soar above it with great ease before an extended section has the violins again expressing lyrically before returning to a recapitulation of the main theme – this is stunning writing. The violins withdraw slightly, allowing the cello to exert a melodic presence. Now another pizzicato passage leads the violins into a slightly darker mood, although it never wanders far from the intrinsic beauty of the movement. Another series of positive overlapping violin melodic lines leads to a gentle finish.

The next, slightly shorter movement is marked *scherzo* – in a vigorous, light, or playful manner. Busy violins construct a rapid sequence of phrases before introducing one of the more memorable melodies in the string quartet repertoire, a lilting collection of phrases that conveys great beauty. A pause initiates a change, with gentle, but assertive violin lines in a quicker tempo before moving into a set of variations on the previously heard melody. This tempo is decelerated and the ensemble investigates a complete, harmonised version of the main melody. Nearing the end, a frantic tempo leads to a handful of cello notes to end.

The third movement opens with another stunning, almost melancholic melody – Borodin's ability to create beautiful melodies is a great gift. A violin now investigates this melody in a higher register leading to a feeling of Romantic bliss. A second melody is now initiated, before returning to the introductory statement. Overlapping violins harmonise freely, with the cello expressing complementary lines. This leads to a rhapsodic passage with the violins again investigating the harmonic possibilities of the theme – this is another extraordinarily beautiful soundscape. Borodin begins to dissect the theme and present it in several different ways, all of them wonderful. The end is a slow, sparse section with a series of gently fading tones.

The final movement begins with a questioning solo violin line and the cello responds. This section is repeated, but is now followed by a violin at ever-increasing tempo. Harmonised lines are added to this frantic violin part and a new, characteristic melody develops. A drop in the tempo brings a pause in the music before a solo cello phrase has the violin repeating its opening question. A tempo develops and the music hurries forward with a fine violin melody skating over the ensemble. Another pause brings about a harmonised violin and cello statement of the movement opening melody. The cello now accelerates, pizzicato style and the violins return with vigorous phrases and another very lyrical melody, this time at a brisk tempo. The conclusion is a frantic violin dash to three final chords.

This quartet contains several melodies that have made their way into popular culture by being regularly used in television commercials and appearing in movies. If you are able to listen to the work you will undoubtedly recognise some of these melodies. The two quartets are both beautiful pieces.

There are many pairings of Borodin's two quartets on Amazon US and UK – I'm guessing about a hundred. I have them by the Borodin Quartet on the Chandos label. They are also available on Spotify and YouTube. Seven different performances of the First Quartet can be found on earsense, including the Borodins.

Listenability: A fine work featuring charming melodies in abundance.

[The current Borodin String Quartet – image courtesy BSQ]

— oo0oo —

Andre Boucourechliev [1925–1997]

Nationality: French
Quartets: At least one
Style: Modern Contemporary

String Quartet Works

Boucourechliev appears to have written at least one numbered string quartet and several other named works for the genre. It was difficult to garner much information about these works and there seems to be just one CD containing string quartet pieces. I intend to discuss *Miroir II* from 1989 and *Quartet III*, from 1994. There is also an early work, from 1969 on the CD, *Archipel II*.

Miroir II, subtitled *Five Pieces for String Quartet*, consists mainly of a series of brief, introspective soundscapes, some of which are quite alluring.

One – A superb opening features sparse, atmospheric instrumental lines that portray a feeling of great emotional depth. Sensuous violins are joined by the cello, which increases the intensity somewhat. A more dramatic moment ensues, as a sense of dissonance moves to a turbulent end.

Two – Again, a sensitive passage leads to another atmospheric section. At a low volume, the slightly abstract musings of the violins are interrupted only by occasional string sound effects – eventually, these effects become the music. Now an intensity develops as microtones lead to a feeling of angst. This is extremely modern music, and sometimes quite confronting. Minimal snatches of music coexist with jagged interjections. The end is a perfunctory, throwaway line.

Three – A wonderful, sparse, introspective mood initiates this movement – I find great beauty here. A feeling of warmth builds with the cello providing a sonorous background to the atonal musings of the violins. After a brief pause, the opening mood is re-examined, with barely audible violin tones. Now an aggressive cello completely transforms the work into a series of grating rhythmic phrases until the previous mood is revisited to marvellous effect, leading to a quiet conclusion.

Four – A sense of total peace introduces this rather short movement. The sound of a drone-like effect allows a series of wonderful atonal violin lines to be presented. An increase in intensity brings the cello to the forefront before a brief aggressive interlude leads directly into the next movement.

Five – With the previous mood continued, a dramatic passage unfolds. Cello and violin dig deep into their lowest registers as again, a peace is restored. The introduction of a loud ostinato motif leads to another intense passage, which lasts for some time before a slow fade concludes the work.

The one movement Third Quartet is quite brief, at just under 12 minutes. Beginning with a very low and resonant solo cello, it gradually works its way into the upper register, evoking memories of John Tavener's *The Protecting Veil*. After nearly two minutes, a violin blends with the cello, creating a wonderful sense of unity. With a feeling of inevitability, this soon changes and string sound effects emerge for a time, before reverting back to the former duet character. This is followed by a striking passage of intermittent atonal melodic lines from all instruments, which gradually returns to silence.

Now two violins engage in a moderately atonal duet, with pizzicato cello interjections – the feeling is one of pure introversion. A return to string sound effects at a moderate dynamic level has the music oscillating between passages of sparse violin lines, contrasted with the more dramatic, previously mentioned atonal mood. A chaos emerges with one violin bowing intensely over a sustained tone played by the second violin. As the end approaches, the sound is that of a barely audible violin in its upper register – a very lonely feeling concludes the work.

A couple of comments seem in order. Firstly, some parts of this music are quite daunting, while other sections inspire a great sense of abstract beauty – such is the way of the Contemporary string quartet repertoire.

Secondly, in the piece *Archipel II*, which is the longest work, listening is made difficult due to long sections being almost inaudible. I had to remaster it to discover its secrets – I would say that it is the most confronting work on the disc, even though it also contains moments of great beauty.

The review CD is titled *Boucourechliev: Intégrale de la Musique Pour Quatuor à Cordes*, which seems to imply that it contains the composer's complete output for string quartet. Possibly, there are no Nos. 1 and 2, I can only speculate. The works are performed by the French Quatuor Ysaÿe on the Aeon label.

The CD is available as *New and Used* from Amazon US and UK resellers.

All three works can be found on YouTube and earsense.

Listenability: Very modern, but I personally find it to be fulfilling.

— oo0oo —

Brian Boydell [1917–2000]

Nationality: Irish
Quartets: Three
Style: Contemporary

String Quartet No. 1

Boydell's three string quartets each evoke a unique soundscape. For me, they are reminiscent of Welshman Daniel Jones.

The First Quartet, written in 1949, is in three movements. The work opens at a larghetto tempo with a short solo cello statement. A violin enters in the background and the first violin comes in over the top – all of which is in a minor key. This is the kind of introduction that makes the hairs on the back of my neck stand up. The first violin plays a long, lamenting melody before the ensemble enters, eventually reaching a brief crescendo. The two violins return to the opening, with sparse cello accompaniment. Now a change comes over the music, bringing with it a certain optimism in a major key.

The long violin lines persist and the cello drops into a two-note ostinato for a time. Then comes an intense section where the violins once again play at crescendo volume. It soon falls away however, before rising again. There are some angst-ridden chords as the crescendos come and go. Eventually, the first violin leads the music back to the opening again and the cello ostinato returns for a time. When it stops, the two violins become ever so sparse and the final notes are played on the cello.

The second movement begins in an agitated fashion with a triplet motif underpinning the development. After a brief pause a solo violin leads into a cacophony – it is very busy. The agitation returns before moving into a pastoral

65

feeling. A <u>pizzicato</u> phrase lifts the intensity, the triplets return and then it's all over. It is a short movement.

The final movement opens with a brief, powerful statement before dropping back to two passive violins. The introduction is repeated and we are back to two violins again, evoking the feeling of the first movement. After some slow stabbing chords as the piece becomes dance-like. It is stretching the boundaries of <u>tonality</u> as it resolutely moves forward. Now follows some perfect peace with the two violins intertwined for a time – this is a most charming moment, in a slow tempo, eventually building in intensity whilst still retaining the tempo. The mood is broken by another crescendo with further agitation which lasts for a considerable time before returning to the previous peaceful feeling. Now the music becomes sparse with soft interjections from all instruments. They eventually gather together and the two violins converse over a cello and viola ostinato again. Moving towards the end, the violins increase the intensity before falling away, bringing about a brief, decisive conclusion.

Despite the sporadic agitation, there is much appealing music to be found here. The first movement is wonderful. The Second (1957) and Third (1969) Quartets are both interesting as well. The Second has a marvellous slow movement and they are both more modern than the First.

The review CD is available as *The Complete String Quartets* on the Carducci Classics label, by the Carducci String Quartet from Amazon US and UK. This disc is on Spotify, and can be found on <u>YouTube</u> and <u>earsense</u>.

Listenability: Quiet, emotional, accessible works.

— ooOoo —

Walter Braunfels [1882–1954]

Nationality: German
Quartets: Three
Style: Early Modern

String Quartet No. 1

Strangely, the First Quartet was written in 1944 and the Third in 1947, leading to all three being composed while Braunfels was well into his sixties. I feel that they sometimes evoke a Late Romantic style, but they also have a twentieth century quality, especially as they progress – so much for labels. I am going to examine the First String Quartet, which is the most conservative.

A violin opens the work with a questioning melodic motif that is quickly taken up by the ensemble. A rapid descending run from the violin leads into an elegant conversational passage, with the cello prominent. Now a bubbling tempo is established and the violins prevail. A solo cello statement invokes a change, which is reminiscent of the opening. Slowly the music becomes tempestuous and a repeat of the earlier descending phrase adds to the drama. The cello drives the accompaniment as the music works through several harmonic changes and the mood is positive with a touch of pizzicato. A new, rhythmic feeling unfolds, slightly serious, leading to an end on a minor chord.

The second, slow movement, begins with a rich layer of chords, and a sombre melody. The violin laments over a sparse background, with interest being provided by the second violin occasionally interjecting a complementary phrase. The low intensity drops even further, bringing a wonderful feeling of sparsity. Solo cello initiates a new mood with the violin rising in intensity and the ensemble following. This is again slightly tempestuous, but it doesn't last as simple violin melodies intertwine and a measured cello has its say. The sparsity returns with the cello leading the music to a peaceful place, where the violin finishes on a shrill note.

The third movement also commences with a questioning motif which is repeated and developed by the ensemble at varying tempos. The music eventually settles into a lilting mood, with the questioning motif being passed around all instruments. This motif has dominated the movement thus far – it's as if every section alludes to it. An extended solo cello passage develops into a race with the violins really pushing the tempo. The feeling is then moderated and new melodies begin to emerge. A solo cello passage reinvokes the question again and variations are constantly refined, at various tempos. The mood continues to be positive but, for me, the repeated motif has outstayed its welcome. The cello-violin race is repeated and leads to the end which, you guessed it, is the motif one more time.

The final movement, marked allegro, has a bright quality which is rather attractive. Lyrical violins twist and turn as they pursue each other in a manner similar to children playing. A pause leads to a sense of urgency, and a rise in tempo as the violins develop variations on new melodies, sometimes bordering on the pensive. This extended passage features much interplay with the ensemble and is quite serious until the very end, which has a sense of warmth to it.

The review CD, titled *Braunfels: String Quartets Nos. 1 & 2*, performed by the Auryn Quartet on the WDR label is available from Amazon UK and Presto Classical. It is also on Amazon US as a download only.

The CD can be found on Spotify, YouTube and earsense.

Listenability: Charming, mid twentieth century work.

Martin Bresnick [born 1946]

Nationality: American
Quartets: At least three
Style: Contemporary Modern

String Quartet No. 3

As with most contemporary composers, and especially academics, of which Bresnick is one, he has written music in many styles. The Third Quartet is from 1992 and contains three movements.

The work begins with a brilliant slow movement, marked *Calmo Risoluto Teneramente* – make of that what you will. It translates from Italian as *Calm Resolute Tenderly*, which is surely a meaningful composer directive. A sparse section of sustained brass-like chords eases into the work, there is no melody here, just the most wonderful soundscape. Slowly, slight changes to the harmonies begin to unfold and eventually, there is a sense of melody over the chords. As stronger melodies take shape, the feeling is almost spiritual, with the violins probing, sometimes even in a modal fashion. The sustained chords have dissipated now and some sharp interjections against a walking, pizzicato cello line create a fine mood. Nearing the end, the feeling is so sweet and light as the violins investigate pleasing, sparse melodies which eventually fade to an end. I found this movement to be very special, with a rare quality of uniquity – simply marvellous.

This is followed by a movement marked *Feroce Cascando* – Google had a little trouble working out which language this was, but I think that 'fierce' is the operative term – although it may be a little strong for the music as I hear it. Powerful, harmonised violin lines compete and glissandos and other string sound effects abound in this propulsive opening. A sudden pause leads to a violin expressing seemingly random phrases, over a very quiet, slightly rhythmic accompaniment. The intensity of the prominent violin increases, almost to a breaking point, in a strong solo passage. A slight easing of the pressure leads to an unusually long violin tone, which fades out.

The final movement is marked *Pensieri Oscuri le Stelle*, which again, is slightly ambiguous – I'm going with *Dark Thought the Stars*. A lone lamenting violin leads into a tender, harmonised, very sparse section. Then follows an increased sense of activity as two violins engage in a moderately dissonant dialogue, which eventually moves into a rhythmic phase with ensemble accompaniment. A sudden increase in tempo causes the intensity to lighten, but not for long. There is a return to a violin duet, with powerful, harsh phrases a feature. Now a shrill solo violin crafts a beautiful melodic passage and the second violin contributes in a lower register. For a time, the music is barely audible with minimal violin phrases, eventually becoming a succession of long tones, which brings the work to a faded conclusion.

The review CD, *Martin Bresnick - Music for Strings*, on New World Records/Composers Recordings also contains the five named-movement String Quartet No. 2, written in 1984 and titled *Bucephalus* – the name of Alexander the Great's legendary horse, together with another fascinating work, *Wir Weben, Wir Weben* (We weave) for String Sextet. These three pieces are all performed by different ensembles.

Unfortunately, this disc is not freely available, except as a download from Amazon US and UK. However, I recently picked up a *New and Used* copy via Amazon US.

The CD is on Spotify, together with a version of the Second Quartet performed by the Flux Quartet. YouTube has versions of both Quartets Nos. 2 and 3 but I find the Third Quartet to be way too confronting – it is just so different from the review CD.

Listenability: Mildly confronting work with a stunning slow movement.

[Image New World Records – Could not be contacted]

Frank Bridge [1879–1941]

Nationality: British
Quartets: Four
Style: Early Modern

String Quartet No. 4

Bridge's quartets are distinguished by a marked stylistic progression from the First, written in 1906, to the vastly more modern Fourth, in 1937.

The Fourth Quartet commences in a robust fashion, with slightly dissonant melodies overlapping to bring about a mildly chaotic mood. A prominent cello line leads the music into a serene space and the violins are measured. Slowly they develop into another dissonant, but pleasing section, before they reach out and the level of intensity increases. Now a sparser mood prevails and the violins duet with short melodic phrases, leading to a sense of forward movement. The intensity rises again and the violins duel – this is a world away from the pastoral nature of the First Quartet, and displays traits of modernism. The duel persists with a turgid tone for a time before peace is restored, an alluring dialogue softening the sound. Nearing the end, a sense of drama unfolds as the cello leads into a powerful passage. Finally we have a reconciliation of all instruments and the violins ever so quietly move to a conclusion.

A probing, questioning violin opens the next movement, soon to be joined by a second violin and viola pizzicato thrusts. The energy rises and falls, seemingly not being able to settle. There is very little melodic development and no melodies to capture the listener's attention, just a serious, dissonant soundscape. The music drops in and out of a tempo as the violins compete for melodic prominence – there is a feeling of underlying tension here. A gentler mood now prevails and a mild flurry of violins makes for an eerie sound. A lilting violin passage brings the movement to a considered end.

The final movement opening is dominated by a majestic violin phrase, which soon recedes, all the while being accompanied by the ensemble in a subtle manner. A tempo begins to form and the texture is similar to that of elements of the previous movement. There is a lot of musical energy generated, and a good deal of abstraction can be heard here. Dissonant violin lines begin to swirl, making for a mysterious sound – the violins push hard and the intensity is high as a rhythmic cello underpins the violins' musings and the tempo begins to pick up. The work finishes on a violin flourish and a held chord.

The complete quartets can be found on two Naxos CDs, performed by the Maggini Quartet. There are also several other CDs on Amazon US and UK containing various individual and paired quartets.

One of the Naxos discs containing the work can be found on Spotify. I had to search for 'Bridge String Quartet 4' to find it. It is also on YouTube and earsense.

Listenability: A slightly chaotic, but approachable, early twentieth century quartet.

— oo0oo —

Benjamin Britten [1913–1976]

Nationality: British
Quartets: Three
Style: Early Modern

String Quartet No. 1

I must admit that I have never been drawn to Britten's quartets but somebody suggested him to me in an email. My thanks to that person. I obtained a version by the Takacs Quartet which made me change my mind about this music. They bring such life and character to his work. Britten's First Quartet was written in 1941 and consists of four movements.

The piece opens with a violin gently trilling over a cello pizzicato background. This is sustained for longer than I would have expected and it is very elegant. Next comes a strong rhythmic phase with the violins playing spirited melodies leading to cessation of the rhythm, and we are left with two violins. Gradually the music works its way back to the opening violin and cello sound, before the feeling changes, with the cello coming to the fore while a violin trills. There is a dialogue between the cello and the violin before it moves into tempo again. A return to the opening leads to the end which turns out to be one iteration of the earlier rhythmic phrase.

The second movement is brief and starts at a strutting tempo over an ostinato. The violins are playful until the cello begins to force the pace which brings an intensity and a chaotic sound emerges. The ostinato returns and the violins resume their busy roles. The atmosphere is occasionally interspersed with more chaos and it eventually fades to the end, which comes with a loud flourish.

The third movement, marked andante *calmo*, is the longest movement, and the most beautiful. The composer crafts an expansive opening at this slow tempo. A stunning violin melody rises out of the music – this is some fine writing. Finally a stately loud chord ensues and the cello dialogues with the ensemble for a time, before retreating to an accompanying role for a moment – it then completely breaks free for a sustained solo assertion. The opening returns with the violin being salient, but all the while bringing great peace. A strong bank of chords again brings out the cello until the violins lead to a faded conclusion. It is a truly wonderful movement.

The finale opens with a dance-like feeling, with the whole ensemble involved. Now the violin dialogues with the cello, all at a breakneck pace. A change in the feeling has a prominent cello featured, together with a skittish violin which evolves into another racing section. A brief rhythmic interlude leads to an abrupt, satisfying end.

Due to the Takacs, I am now sold on Britten. I also checked out on Spotify, the Brodsky Quartet, who bring a similar spirit to the piece. Their andante calmo movement is just so precious, somewhat reminiscent of Barber's *Adagio for Strings*. I spoiled myself and listened to it a few times – it's very moving.

Regarding availability, the Takacs have the three quartets on a single CD on the Hyperion label. The Brodskys, on Challenge Classics include three short works, making it into a 2-CD set. Both of these can be found on Amazon US and UK, along with a host of other versions, some containing early, student works. Not too many with the three string quartets on one CD, however.

Spotify has three CDs, including the Brodsky 2-CD set. Also a vast number of versions of No. 1 and Britten's other two quartets are on YouTube while earsense features a plethora of recordings of the first three quartets – it seems that the Fourth is somewhat under-recorded.

Listenability: A very charming and ultimately beautiful work.

— ooOoo —

Leo Brouwer [born 1939]

Nationality: Cuban
Quartets: At least four
Style: Contemporary Modern

String Quartets Nos. 1 & 3

Brouwer is probably better known for his guitar works, some of which I have, than his chamber music, but I will be discussing two of his string quartets, which are both very fine.

The First Quartet is titled *To the Memory of Bela Bartok*. Written in 1961, it contains four movements.

The first movement is brief and opens with a strong melodic motif, which is repeated, before moving into a slightly folk-like feeling. A solo cello statement goes into an intense violin phase. This gives way to a return of the opening motif which leads to the conclusion.

The next movement features two slightly melancholic violins as they work their way through some tender melodies. The cello enters with a prominent statement which begins in a rhythmical manner. Now a solo violin takes over and leads the ensemble through a densely textured section, fading to a lyrical melody which sees the end of this, again, relatively short movement.

The third movement, marked lento, is the emotional heart of the work. It commences with a longing melody over sustained notes, save for a restless cello melody – this is gentle music. The two violins strike out on their own for a time before the cello enters again with deep, melodic phrases. A pause leads to a busy violin pizzicato, which is punctuated by ensemble chords. The opening returns and a violin laments. An ensemble arpeggio thickens the texture, and the violin is persistent, while being ever so quiet. Nearing the end, the intensity lifts slightly before a violin fades out.

The final movement begins in a pulsating manner with strong violin and cello parts. The cello takes over and, in its lower register, crafts a melody which is joined by the violins. There is tension in the air as the rhythm drives the movement forward. This gives way to a lilting moment with some beautiful, winsome melodies. A change brings a slight dissonance to the now rhythmic nature and a torrid violin statement leads to an abrupt end.

For me, this quartet doesn't evoke Bartok but that's okay – it shouldn't have to. It's a rich work, filled with many interesting textures.

String Quartet No. 3 is made up of four named movements.

Ritual Voice for New Year's Eve – Gentle, ascending notes begin this movement and a motif is repeated several times, before an intense violin brings in a slight dissonance, before working into a tempo. A viola ostinato emerges and the violins drift ever so lightly across this feeling. Now there is some melodic development and the intensity rises with other instruments picking up on the ostinato motif. A sudden stop leads to a chaotic passage which eventually gives way to a final chord.

Through the Body of the Wind – This movement drifts into existence as the violins set up a brief sparsity. Now some positive, slightly frantic solo violin gives way to a gentle lone violin which soars into its high register, with random notes from elsewhere. Rhythmic interjections occur sporadically but the violins continue with their sparsity. A quiet, rumbling sound leads to a fade-out.

Impossible Dance – A repeated violin note introduces this, the third movement. After several flourishes, the other instruments enter. The intensity ebbs and flows and a familiar melody takes shape until a frantic violin phrase brings in a pulse with sparse violin over the top of a gentle rhythmic motif. Now the melody begins to develop and all instruments have their role to play. A frenzied violin phrase lifts the intensity only for it to fall away again. A brief passage is followed by a strong chordal rhythm which brings the conclusion.

The Rhythm of the Night Changed – A quivering cello lays a foundation for the final movement. Cross-rhythms abound until the piece settles into a new repeated motif, which is somewhat reminiscent of the music of Philip Glass. Now the violins take centre stage with the cello occasionally adding interest. A peace briefly returns but is soon overwhelmed by percussive violins. These develop in vigour until they hit the final chord.

This work feels a lot like program music as it constantly evokes images related to the respective movement titles. It probably contains references to Cuban melody and rhythm, of which I am unaware.

The CD under discussion, performed by the Havana String Quartet, on the Zoho label also contains String Quartet No. 2, which is in one movement and is a wild rhythmic ride. There is also a short, but beautiful string trio, written in 1959. This disc is available on Amazon US and UK and is also on Spotify. The disc can be heard on earsense and there are movements from several quartets on YouTube.

Listenability: Unique, and contains fine melodies and rhythms.

[Image courtesy Zoho Records]

Max Bruch [1838–1920]

Nationality: German
Quartets: Two
Style: Romantic

String Quartet No. 1

Max Christian Friedrich Bruch was mostly known for his violin concertos, which are still played and recorded today. In fact there are nearly three thousand hits for them on Amazon. His two string quartets were completed early, the second when he was just 23 years old.

String Quartet No. 1 is in four movements. The first, marked andante–allegro, starts with a solo violin and a gentle melody. The ensemble move in to support its lofty expression, and fashion answering statements. At around one minute, we are out of andante and into allegro. This is characterised by a racing violin with the ensemble trying to keep up. After a period of brisk forward movement, it returns to the andante tempo with a lush sense of Romantic expression. The first violin presents some poignant melodies and then, accelerates into a new phase of frantic violin and rhythmic interjections. A brief stagnant moment reverts back to an energised passage. A feature of this movement is its constant change of tempo. A particularly longing melody has fine cello support, as it steps forward with strong playing, leading into another dramatic phase. Now soft but busy flurries again lead into a dynamic section which of course, only lasts for a time. The next moderate passage lingers in a slightly introspective mood before the violins build to a crescendo and an ending of several repeated chords.

Although this may sound slightly complex, it works beautifully, bringing to mind Mendelssohn's *Octet for Strings* which was written many years later.

A particularly sonorous mood commences the next, adagio movement. I hear a hint of a melody that has probably been plagiarised by someone else, and it is truly wonderful. A gentle tempo takes over but the mood remains restrained. This is a joyous moment, and the violin leads the ensemble through several calm passages. The feeling is very precious, with the violin lyrical, and producing a wonderful tone. A quiet finish ensues.

The next movement has an optimistic dance-like feeling to open. The violins are in charge but the cello makes some telling statements. The intensity drops and changes in harmony are perfect. Wistful violins craft marvellous melodies against a sympathetic background and a short solo violin moment leads to a resumption of the opening energy. All instruments contribute to this feeling, which moves on to a slightly lamenting passage, dramatically changing into a flourish of chords to conclude.

The finale is a selection of quivering bows which develops into a serious moment. A change into a minor tonality leads to a restrained section, before moving into more energy. This is now measured and the violin melodies develop a slightly lamenting moment – however, it is soon overwhelmed by rhythmic thrusts. The tempo drops back slightly and a stately mood is briefly presented until the violins again evoke yet-to-be-written Mendelssohn. Perhaps there was a bit of influence involved. The finish is strong.

My review CD, *Bruch: String Quartets Op.9, Op.10*, performed by the Diogenes Quartett, on the Brilliant Classics label is still available on Amazon UK. There are several versions, sometimes paired with other composers' works.

Spotify has two CDs, and both quartets are on YouTube. A version by the Diogenes can be found on earsense.

Listenability: A classic Romantic chamber work.

— ooOoo —

Norbert Burgmuller [1810–1836]

Nationality: Czech
Quartets: Four
Style: Late Classical

A Life Cut Short
String Quartet No.1

Burgmuller's First Quartet was written at age fifteen, followed by the second and third at sixteen. By the final quartet he was twenty-five, and nearing death. Mozart wrote his First Quartet at age twelve but I think I prefer the Burgmuller. For me the music comes across with influences of Haydn, Mozart and early Beethoven, although I have no proof for that assertion – it just sounds like it. It is highly likely that he heard Beethoven. If he did it may have been the first six quartets, Opus 18, although I also hear similarities to the *Razumovsky Quartets, Opus 59, Nos. 1-3*. I am going to discuss the First Quartet, which I find quite mellifluous and energetic. For one who doesn't listen to many Classical era quartets, I found this one rather engaging.

The work opens with a flourish which leads into an attractive melody. The flourishes return and a violin melody is developed over a convivial ensemble. The intensity of the violin increases with many sweeping bow strokes, before a subtle change ensues with the cello having an important role. Two strong chords lead back into a melodic section where the violin stretches out and tells quite a story. An ascending melody gives way to tranquility and a solo cello interlude. Again the two chords lead into a new melodic phase, and the composer uses these chords to delineate instances of melodic development. The opening melody returns and is recast. The sound is somewhat like Haydn and early Beethoven. By this time the melody has been turned upside down and inside out – the development is very effective. Nearing the end it becomes slightly frantic, and the movement ends on a sustained chord.

The next movement, marked adagio, begins with some sustained chords and a smattering of a melody that hangs in the air – there is no tempo here. A pause introduces a more vigorous section where the violins spar in building to a peak which then returns to the slow tempo. Now things become busy again for a while, and a repeat of the first movement ascending melody is heard, developed over a short time before the end comes with a flowing line into a chord.

The finale opens with a dashing violin line that cuts through the ensemble as they attempt to keep up with it. It is lively but strangely, also somewhat stately. The violin pursues a wispy phrase until the ensemble asserts itself with some powerful ascending interjections. It is followed by a dual violin dialogue. Each time the ensemble re-enters, the music goes up harmonically, which gives a positive thrust. A cello interlude is interrupted by an interjection where the violin moves into its high register. One last interjection is repeated, reharmonised and maintained until the end of the work.

This is an enjoyable work, as are the later three quartets. They are available as two separate CDs on the MDG label, performed by the Mannheim String Quartet, on Amazon US and UK. They are not on my Spotify but all four quartets are on YouTube and earsense.

I shall conclude with a slightly cryptic quote from Romantic composer Robert Schumann:

After Franz Schubert's death no other death could cause more sorrow than Burgmuller's... His talent has such brilliantly excellent qualities that only a blind man could entertain doubts about its existence.

I'll take that mangled metaphor as a compliment.

Listenability: A fine Late Classical quartet.

— oo0oo —

Ferruccio Busoni [1866–1924]

Nationality: Italian
Quartets: Two
Style: Late Romantic

String Quartet No. 2

Busoni was renowned for his piano transcriptions of Bach works, many of which I own – they are masterly. I am going to discuss his Second Quartet, which is in four movements.

The work opens with a cello-led melody, in a bright tempo. Soon, the violins take over and the music has a Classical sound, with a series of violin flourishes leading to a change. The tempo slows and the cello makes several positive statements, before the violins return. There have been many tempo changes thus far but the feeling finally settles on a violin duet over a positive background. Now the violin soars and leads the passage into a brisk tempo again. After a time the dynamics recede and quiet phrases from the violins appear, which are most appealing. One violin flies while the other provides support. The dynamics now have an intensity about them. A change into a minor key leads to a busy violin duet which slowly subsides and the energy returns while the violins are playful. Then follows another measured feeling, but only for a time as the cello pushes the violins into a strong tempo. The end is gentle, until a final flourish.

The next movement, marked andante, is of a sparse minor key nature. The violins become busy and the cello has several statements to make, all of which are answered by the violins. A new feeling of optimism prevails and the cello and violin call and response continues. The intensity is limited and a lot of solo cello lines are featured. We are back to a slightly lamenting mood now, even with one busy violin. A lilting violin concludes.

The third movement, marked vivace, is unusual rhythmically – it is slightly stilted and the ensemble doesn't seem to be going anywhere. A pause initiates a new feeling as minor chords accompany a meandering violin that wanders freely against a subtle background. Suddenly we have movement as a violin lays down a positive phrase. The other violin is a bit more demonstrative now and the energy level increases leading to a final chord.

The finale begins in a sombre manner with the violins in their lowest registers. The cello takes over and leads the music into a spirited section, leaving the minor key far behind. It does eventually return and the tempo decreases as a result. The first violin develops a phrase, then repeats it in another key, leading to another minor chord, and the violins become tense, albeit still busy. There are various tempo changes and the violins rise in intensity which is sustained to the end of the work.

Several versions of the two quartets exist on CD. My review copy was by the Pellegrini Quartet on the CPO label. This disc is on Spotify and many quartet movements are on YouTube. There also several versions of both quartets on earsense.

Listenability: An engaging Late Romantic work.

Roffredo Caetani [1871-1961]

Nationality: Italian
Quartets: Two
Style: Late Romantic

String Quartet No. 2

Caetani came from a very famous Italian family, his ancestor Benedetto Caetani was elected to the papacy as Pope Boniface VIII in 1294. Roffredo was the last male member of the family.

The Second Quartet opens with a strong minor chord, reminiscent of Haydn's *Seven Last Words*. The feeling is orchestral-like with rich harmonies supporting expressive violin statements. A mellowing of the mood ensues, before constantly gaining in strength, becoming almost rhapsodic. The violins rise above the ensemble, creating a wonderful, full sound. Now a change comes over the piece, with a moderate pastoral feeling, leading to a very engaging passage, replete with sparse but powerful violin melodic lines. This rubato passage moves into a tempo for a time and the violins reach out with dramatic trills as the energy level constantly rises and falls. An extended slow passage reveals a sense of beauty before it regathers energy and moves into another powerful section. The final throes of the movement progress from the sublime to the intense, which then drops back to a gentle violin conclusion. The whole movement has been dominated by a strong minor tonality.

The next movement, marked *Molto lento* (very slowly), opens in a sublime, understated manner as haunting violin lines press forward gently, which evokes for me, a feeling of being in a church. A sombre pulse is present and the violin continues in this manner for some time. A slight crescendo leads to a short solo second violin line, which is harmonised by the first violin as they work together to craft a stunning mood. A cello line now becomes involved and its resonant tones are truly wonderful. Simple, but extremely moving violin lines move into a brief rhythmic passage where the violins investigate a motif. Now a further change features an arresting violin dialogue that carries the music forward in a way that would not be out of place in a late Beethoven quartet, particularly No. 12. This whole movement has great antecedents in string quartet history. The end comes with a long cello tone.

The final movement hints at the first movement, very minor sounding, but this time with a vibrant tempo. The forward movement is controlled but strong and a return to the opening fanfare develops, leading into a rhapsodic section of gypsy-like solo violin soaring over the ensemble. Now the cello has a melodic role before the violins return with a new feeling of measured melodic development, as they intertwine to great effect. This is a positive passage which again, I believe looks back to Bach and Vivaldi as the harmonies seem to flow in a Baroque manner. A rubato section emerges briefly, but the energetic Baroque feeling is soon resumed. A few solo cello notes invoke another new lamenting passage and the conclusion comes quickly, with a flourish.

Broadly, this music, written in the twentieth century, looks backward with a rather unique approach to a string quartet – sometimes orchestral, with a touch of Bach, Beethoven and Vivaldi. It is a fine work.

The review CD, *Caetani: The Two String Quartets*, performed by the Alauda Quartet, on the Brilliant Classics label, is available on Amazon US and UK, at a surprisingly reasonable price.

Both quartets are available on Spotify, YouTube and earsense.

Listenability: Unusually, a very modern sounding Late Romantic quartet.

[Image courtesy Brilliant Classics]

Jean Cartan [1906–1932]

Nationality: French
Quartets: Two
Style: Early Modern

The Two String Quartets

Both of Cartan's string quartets were written at the tender age of 21. He died at 25 from tuberculosis.

The First Quartet is in four movements, and rather short. It begins in a surprisingly modern mood for one so young, with atonal melodies in abundance. A sense of drama unfolds as the intensity builds before returning to a somewhat pastoral feeling. As is the composer's wont, this doesn't last for long and soon the violins are again expressing assertive atonal statements. Slow, introspective melodies evolve into a tempo and the violins seem to contradict each other, before moving to a final flourish.

The next movement opens in a strange harlequin-like manner with many rhythmic changes, moving into a slow, considered passage before returning to the opening mood. A hectic moment occurs as the violins hurry towards the finish, a chord with a prolonged cello tone that hangs in the air.

The third movement is much more controlled as a serious mood unfolds. All instruments project forward movement but the combination brings a sense of quiet. The overlapping of the various instrumental lines is simply wonderful with this feeling continuing to the end.

The final movement commences with an unrelenting pulse, which forms the basis of most of the movement. Violins rise and fall, occasionally expressing a sweetness until the pulse returns in a vigorous manner, with associated thrusting atonal violin melodic lines. Nearing the end, some harmony appears, and the music begins to sound very fresh. The conclusion is an exaggerated gesture by the ensemble.

The Second Quartet opens with a solo violin statement before being joined by the ensemble, in a feeling of ambiguous tonality. Gently dissonant, there is a tempo, with various instruments providing melodic statements. A pause changes the mood to a rubato character but this is soon discarded as the violins exchange phrases. Another pause brings a lamenting section, beautiful in its abstraction. The violins again engage in a dialogue and the cello provides a rhythm underneath the rubato musings of the violins. Now a viola pizzicato motif is heard, however the violins maintain their persistent atonal dialogue. The end comes with a sustained chord.

The next movement begins in a chaotic manner, very reminiscent of Schoenberg. The tempo is strong until a sustained tone introduces a litany of string sound effects. Now rhythmic melodic lines overlap for a time, before moving into a delightfully French feeling. There seem to be ever so many mood changes in this piece – now a cello ostinato serves as a springboard for expressive violin meanderings. The music surges forward, with all instruments creating a measured chaos, if such a thing is possible. A return to the sparkling French feeling leads to a terminating flourish.

The final movement, the longest by far, has a dramatic cello and violin introduction and is again conversational. A change brings with it sublime, lamenting harmonised violin lines. Gradually the tempo increases and another chaotic passage ensues. Syncopated rhythms follow, then a viola ostinato, however nothing seems to last for long as the music just won't settle. Now we have spare violin melodies, intertwining with the cello and viola for a pronounced unusual effect. A short passage of violin trills gives way to abstraction, replete with rhythmic interjections and a very strong attack with the bow on the first violin. Another sparse section consists of two atonal violins over a pizzicato viola, producing a remarkable introspective soundscape as a pulsing cello feeds the violins with ideas which gradually move to a conclusion.

These two quartets are profound in that they were composed at such a young age, and in the period of the 1920s, when modern music was not always fully accepted. They are wonderful works, filled with exciting melodic and rhythmic possibilities. The review CD also contains two further pieces, *Introduction and Allegro for Wind Quintet and Piano* and a simply vibrant and entertaining *Sonatina for Flute and Clarinet*.

This CD, titled *Jean Cartan: Chamber Music*, is performed by Quatuor Stanislas and an augmented Ensemble Stanislas, released on the Timpani label. It is available on Amazon US, but not Amazon UK. It can however, also be found at ArkivMusic, and Presto Classical.

Both quartets are available on Spotify, YouTube and earsense.

Listenability: A fine set of quartets from a young, adventurous composer.

Elliott Carter [1908–2012]

Nationality: American
Quartets: Five
Style: Modern Contemporary

As Modern As It Gets
String Quartet No. 1

Carter is probably the most radical composer in this book. I am going to discuss his First Quartet, written in 1951. Please be aware that this is modern, abstract, atonal music and all movements should be appreciated in this light.

The opening movement, marked *fantasia,* begins with a strong solo cello. Eventually some pizzicato accompaniment ensues, soon to be joined by melodies on the first violin. Now all of the ensemble are engaged, with the cello still being prominent – the feeling is quite disjointed. The intensity drops for a time and the music becomes beautiful in its modernity. Sparse sections are contrasted with intense melodic phrases. Some of the violin melodies are quite alluring, particularly in the violin duet moments. The energy level rises and falls as the movement unfolds. Also, there is a degree of dissonance to be heard – this is definitely not tonal music. A violin duet moves straight into the next movement.

The short second movement follows on with skittish violins before moving into a sparse phase which is slowly energised. A solo cello statement brings on a dissonance in the violins as they scurry about for a time in an agitated duet while the cello is used sparingly as interjections. Then the music just stops.

The even shorter third movement is also agitated. It settles into long tones, making for a wonderful, albeit brief, soundscape. It ends on a pizzicato flourish and one lonely cello note.

The cello carries over into the fourth movement. It plays alone for a time until a quiet solo violin ever so slowly comes into prominence. Then the solo cello returns, to be joined by the solo violin, as before. This is ever so delicate, and deeply moving. There are occasional cello interjections and finally we have the whole ensemble in play. The mournful violin is sustained but now other things are happening around it. The cello is outrageous in its projection, being quite agitated. A long atonal violin phrase brings us back to the sound of the solo violin again. Eventually the second violin adds its influence to create a wonderful introspective soundscape – the cello jauntily joins in. Carter dissects this, as individual instruments assert themselves. A pizzicato violin carries the movement to its conclusion as a violin and cello fade out.

The final movement, which is long, opens with a distant sounding violin in the high register, which is joined by the ensemble, causing it to drop back to a lower register. There is some gentle abstraction as instruments move in and out. Occasionally there is some hint of a tempo, but not very often. Now the violins are working overtime and the cello again features. The mood then drops back to indeterminate phrases and dialogue with some interesting feelings projected as Carter edges the piece forward. It really is a collection of random statements with no semblance of structure. Some extremely loud cello ensues, leading to further violin and viola dialogues. Occasionally there are some harmonised passages, but mostly it is every man for himself – this leads to some fascinating, serene sounds which are very evocative. As we near the end of the piece some attempts at chordal accompaniment are made, but they are soon abandoned, leaving a lone violin to conclude.

I really like this piece. However, a lot of people probably wouldn't consider it as music. For me, it doesn't cross the line into noise, as did many of Carter's contemporaries. I can't recall any composer who sounds like Carter, he definitely has a unique modern style.

String Quartet No. 1 is readily available on Amazon US and UK, as two complete 2-CD sets, each containing the five quartets. I have the Juilliard Quartet, who were personally associated with the composer for a long period of time. It is on the Sony Classical label and is very reasonably priced. The other complete set is by the more contemporary Pacifica Quartet on Naxos, which I haven't heard. Several individual CDs featuring this work are also available.

Some of the single CDs are on Spotify and a variety of quartets and movements exist on YouTube. There are several versions of most Carter quartets on earsense.

Listenability: Difficult music for some.

String Quartet No. 2

Elliott Cook Carter Jr.'s Second string quartet was written in 1959, and it achieved the composer a Pulitzer Prize. There is much discussion as to his fundamental style, with many opinions that he was a serial composer, a concept that Carter denied.

The structure of this work is unusual. It consists of four movements, which are bookended by an introduction and a conclusion. Also, the first three movements are followed by cadenzas for cello, viola and violin, respectively. A *cadenza* is a term for a solo instrumental passage, near or at the end of a composition where a soloist usually improvises in the style of the work. They are rarely found in chamber music, but are often associated with piano concertos. In this quartet, the cadenzas are not exclusively solo.

The short introduction commences with a probing violin, in an atonal mood. Other instruments drift in and out, leading to a moment of intensity, which is not sustained.

There is no pause between movements and we are straight into some moderate abstraction, mostly led by the first violin. The texture then thickens and Carter's innate sense of dialogue eventually prevails. This music has no apparent structure, it just burbles along. Some dramatic statements do occur, giving way to a period of angst which concludes the movement.

The first cadenza, for viola, is brief and sparse in its texture. The viola laments as numerous interjections occur although some solo passages are evident.

A new movement opens with string sound effects for a time, with plenty of pizzicato. The mood is measured, and a constant dialogue evolves, characterised by a sparse texture. An important part of Carter's style is attention to *timbre*, which is the textural sound of the instruments. Sometimes, there appear to be woodwinds in the ensemble. Again, there is no recognisable structure and the movement ends with a solo cello section.

The next cadenza is for cello, which gently probes a sparse mood. Slowly, the ensemble presents supporting tones. Ultimately, the cello dominates this section, however it is never really assertive, but maintains the sparsity.

The third movement, marked andante, begins in a very peaceful manner. Totally without tempo, it paints a mildly atonal soundscape. This is very moving music, while still maintaining a high level of abstraction. The harmonies are just so gentle, it is a fascinating space to be in – this is a marvellous movement.

The following violin cadenza is mostly solo violin. It wanders all over the fingerboard in a fascinating statement with many shrill passages. A long pause gives way to another very shrill violin sound and a hint of the other instruments, barely audible, to conclude.

The final movement has the two violins in an extended exchange. Another aspect of the composer's freedom in composition is that he treats rhythm like melody, making it subject to all kind of interesting variations – you can never feel a constant tempo in this work. There is very little of the viola or cello here until the violins lower the dynamics substantially and other voices become evident. Moving towards the end, the mood becomes quite chaotic, frantic even, for a short time.

We have now reached the conclusion, which is a typical Carter scenario, no structure and intermittent musings from all instruments. A lamenting violin appears, only to gradually fade into nothingness.

For me, Carter's quartets are an acquired taste. When I first came across them, over 25 years ago, I found them to be impenetrable. Now I am very fond of their expressive, abstract, atonal beauty.

My review 2-CD set is titled *Elliott Carter: The Five String Quartets* by the Juilliard Quartet, who had a long association with Carter and premiered all of his quartets both in performance, and on recordings. This version is freely available and there are also other complete sets – the Pacifica Quartet sounds promising. Naxos has also released a magnificent 3-CD, 1-DVD *100th Anniversary Release* set of the Pacifica Quartet recordings, together with other larger ensemble works and some interviews with Carter – only for the rich and famous.

These quartets can be sampled on Spotify, YouTube and earsense.

Listenability: An unconventional style, and he doesn't get any easier…

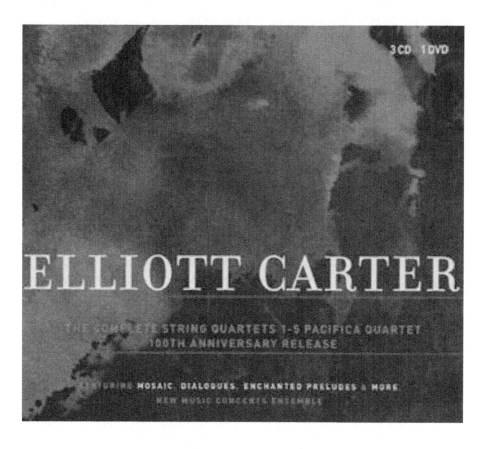

[The deluxe edition – courtesy Naxos Records]

Robert Casadesus [1899–1972]

Nationality: French
Quartets: Four
Style: Early Modern

Fine French String Quartets
String Quartets Nos. 3 & 4

Casadesus, besides being a composer in many styles, was also a renowned concert pianist. I have particularly enjoyed his playing of the mature Mozart Piano Concertos. His string quartets are not long, with all fitting on a single CD. I am going to discuss String Quartet No. 3, written in 1950, and String Quartet No. 4, from 1957.

A charming cello sound introduces the Third Quartet, which is in a conversational manner. The intensity rises and falls continuously before we have a change. The first violin then leads the second into the high register for a crescendo. Things are slightly chaotic for a time until a touch of the Romantic prevails to the finish.

The second movement is bouncy, and a little stilted. The violins are playful over a strong cello motif, which pauses and then moves into a more introverted, minor atmosphere. This is measured chaos, and a fabulous section. Now the composer takes us back to the beginning, and shortly after, to the end.

The next movement, marked adagio, is controlled both in volume and intensity, creating a beautiful soundscape. The violins are restrained and only eventually drift into the higher register with some splendid sounds. This feeling is sustained for the whole movement – there are only subtle changes. Nearing the conclusion the music is down to just the two violins. Slowly the cello returns for a short time until the movement winds down in a peaceful manner.

The final movement opens with the cello, which is played almost jazz style. The violins are conspicuous in this passage, particularly as the cello stops, leaving the two violins to continue on their own. The cello motif returns and we are back into the opening feeling, with busy violins. There is a strong rhythmic impetus, punctuated by chords, which then gives way to the cello motif again. The violins play harmonised lines and the intensity is high before another crescendo for the two violins concludes the work. This is truly some joyous music.

The Fourth Quartet begins slowly with a salient cello, which is wonderfully evocative. Interestingly, a mood similar to this is achieved in three of the four quartet opening movements, but it is played differently each time. The violins meander over the ensemble – this is a terrific place to be. There is no tempo, just a drifting consciousness. Now the intensity drops and we are left with much more space for a while, before returning to the opening theme. The violins

87

predominate, thickening the texture as we move towards a conclusion with the two violins gently fading together.

The next movement is carried by a cello motif which allows the violins to roam freely – it is a bustling introduction. A chord change, together with a pizzicato, lifts the intensity creating a very busy passage. A brief pause allows for a tempo change, back to moderato. Now the viola picks up the rhythm and a repeat of the chord change and pizzicato ensues, leading us back to where we were at the start of the movement. The violins end with a brief flourish.

The third, quite brief movement at 1:26, is another adagio. Due to its length, there is little music to describe except for a brief violin crescendo, which leads to the conclusion.

The final movement is again slow. It sounds like Early Music for a time until the whole ensemble comes into play. This is marvellous, with the instruments intertwining to produce the desired effect. Suddenly, it becomes more assertive with both violins in their high register before dropping back to two violins and we start the process of rebuilding the texture. The tempo increases and we are almost into chaos. The violins leap into the high register for a sharp ending to the work.

Two things. Firstly, I'd have to say that these pieces are reminiscent of the great tradition of French quartets of Debussy and Ravel. I can't think of any other composers, French or otherwise, about whom I could say the same. Casadesus gives more than just a nod to his masters, he sometimes evokes their moods and feelings as well. Secondly, all of the movements are fairly brief, some barely reaching five minutes. This is not a criticism, it's just that they are usually over quickly. At least it allows for all four quartets to be heard.

Regarding availability, there is a CD on Amazon UK, *Quators Nos. 1-4* by Quator Manfred, I believe on the Casadesus label. Interestingly it comes with a fascinating DVD. The CD is also available as *New and Used* and as an MP3 download. It appears that these quartets are neither on Spotify nor YouTube. What a shame.

Listenability: Classic, timeless Impressionistic quartets.

Jordi Cervello [born 1935]

Nationality: Catalan
Quartets: Four
Style: Contemporary

A Profound Discovery
Four Suites

Trawling through Spotify recently I came across a beguiling CD, titled simply *Quartets*. I had not heard of Cervello before so I experienced what turned out to be a long, rewarding first listen.

The music on the CD does not consist of numbered quartets but rather named suites, each with several movements. For instance, the first suite, *Remembrance*, contains four movements and runs to about 21 minutes. The first two movements are mostly taken at a slow tempo and they evoke a profound feeling of melancholy and introversion. Then the tempo quickens and you have a sense of the composer's Spanish background. There is some wonderful use of trills in the accompaniment, while the final movement produces a magnificent pensive feeling, slow and soft, but thankfully loud enough to be audible. I have a thing about recording and remastering engineers setting the volume way too low – even quiet music deserves to be heard.

Dos Movimentos begins in a similar manner. A solo cello lament introduces the piece and plays a significant part in this slow movement. It is thought-provoking writing. The second movement is more obviously Spanish, with an appropriate tempo.

The next, five-movement piece is titled *Etuden nach Kreutzer*, which appears to translate to *Research by Kreutzer* in German. This is the most energetic suite on the CD. However, as with the previous pieces, it also breaks into a sombre nature in places. The faster movements usually have a slightly Spanish feeling.

The final work is titled *A Bach* but I cannot readily find anything about Bach in it. For me, it continues with the flavour of the previous works, but please don't assume that it all sounds the same, it certainly doesn't. The composer finds many ways to express melancholia.

This CD is reminiscent of Haydn's *Seven Last Words*, (also in this book) in that it contains many tempo markings such as andante and lento, amongst others, all of which indicate slow or moderate tempos. I shall have to find some more synonyms for beautiful, abstract and melancholy because that is what this music is all about.

Given the above, this disc is ultimately introspective. My favourite movements in string quartets are slow, melancholy, inward-looking and sometimes angular, as opposed to the approach of some composers who deal in anger and aggression. This one really left a mark on me.

As far as I know, there is only one version of these works on the Columna Music label, by the Atrium Quartet. I have a feeling from Amazon US and UK that it is going to be harder to obtain soon. However after being in touch with the label, I can tell you that it is still available at their website here:

https://www.columnamusica.com/en/catalogue/cervello-quartets

Check it out on Spotify, it might just make your day. There are also some of the quartets on YouTube and all of these works are on earsense.

Listenability: Magnificent melancholy music.

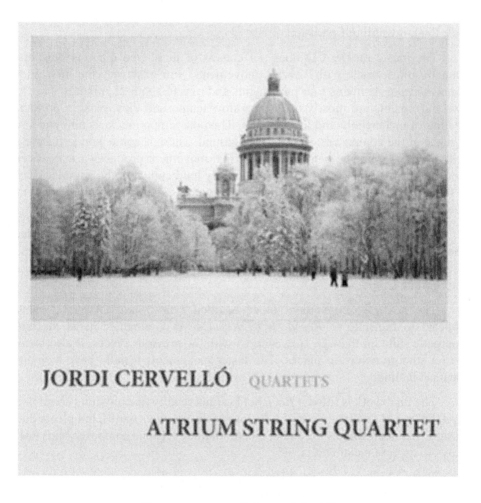

[Image courtesy Columna Music]

Ruperto Chapí [1851–1909]

Nationality: Spanish
Quartets: Four
Style: Romantic

A Spanish Romantic
String Quartet No. 2

Interestingly, all of Ruperto Chapí y Lorente's four string quartets were written over a four year period, just before he died. I am going to discuss String Quartet No. 2 in F Major, which was composed in 1904.

The Second Quartet opens with a Spanish-sounding, questioning melodic violin line, the length of which is eight bars, and is repeated once. The line is in a call and response manner, with silent bars delineating the conversation and on the second iteration it is the cello that responds. It is quite a masterful piece of orchestration with the accompaniment only playing on certain bars. The composer makes complex layers out of simple structure, which I believe is central to his style. I don't think I could explain it any better – you would have to hear it for yourself. The basic line is then reconstructed melodically, but with the same rhythm, and is harmonised. A short motif is now repeated rapidly, and leads to a march-like feeling, and eventually we are back into classic Romanticism. A pause brings a recapitulation of the complete opening and there are constant references to the opening melody as the music progresses. A sprightly passage has an excitable violin leading another march feeling before the dynamics begin to ebb and flow as the ensemble investigates harmonic and rhythmic variations on the main theme. A virtuoso violin melody occasionally interrupts proceedings but basically the rhythmic dominates the melodic in this movement. Nearing the end, the cello re-presents the main theme, basically solo. A brief, sparse passage gives way to more intensity and we hear the harmonised theme again, one more time. Not surprisingly, there is a rush to the end, which is a series of strong chords.

The next movement is mellower, and that is a relief. A series of almost Haydnesque moments unfold and lyricism prevails. Slowly a recognisable melody is heard, harmonised with lush chords. The texture thus far is sparse, with a flavour of early Beethoven being achieved. Rhythm takes a back seat here and Romantic harmonies are in order. Now a taut, descending ensemble line brings some tension, while the same melodic motif from the opening is still being presented, at different dynamic levels and textures. A violin rises into its high register and the ensemble brings about a sense of forward movement for the first time. A violin and cello dialogue is brief and the sparsity returns before the violin soars gently into its shrill zone and a gentle finish occurs.

Pizzicato strokes introduce the third movement and dominate the opening before an extended passage of soft violin tones unfolds. This is interrupted by a waltz-like section, without pizzicato, allowing the violins to craft further

Romantic melodies, although there is always a slight Spanish tinge to the music. With the return of rhythmic pizzicato, the violins continue to express in short, discrete phrases, a feeling which proceeds to the end. I have to say that this does become a little tedious – I presume the movement is meant to contrast with those around it.

The final movement is again rhythmically focussed, with quite varying levels in the dynamics. Wispy melodic sections, with some percussive pizzicato strokes are heard as the ensemble dissects the opening melodic lines. There are also some charming, harmonised melodic phases, which normally bring about more rhythmic tension. A dark, foreboding moment is a fabulous sound, totally different to anything heard so far. Now the music sweeps into classic Spanish melodies again but it is not long before the composer's rhythmic propensity propels the work to a dynamic conclusion.

This is music with nary a note out of place and I don't quite know what to make of that. Being written in Spain, over a hundred years ago, I suspect the country was quite insular then. It is definitely a Romantic work but it is also replete with Spanish flair, texture, excitement, and modal melodies. I enjoyed it but don't think I quite understood it, possibly due to lack of cultural awareness.

The review CD, *Ruperto Chapí: String Quartets Nos. 1 & 2* is on the Sono Luminus label, performed by Cuarteto Latinoamericano, an ensemble I seem to regularly encounter. This is available on Amazon US and UK. I couldn't locate any recordings of Quartets Nos. 3 and 4, although I do have copies of them, and prefer the later to the earlier, in this case. If they had been available I would have preferred to discuss them.

The CD is on Spotify and YouTube, while earsense has all four string quartets.

Listenability: Perfectly and strictly composed Spanish Romantic works.

— oo0oo —

Ernest Chausson [1855–1899]

Nationality: French
Quartets: One – FOSQC
Style: Late Romantic

String Quartet No. 1

I often wonder why so many popular French composers from the late 19th century and on, wrote only one string quartet? Were they taking a lead from Debussy and Ravel? Chausson was a member of the French One String Quartet Club. Others include Gabriel Faure, Cesar Franck, Henri Dutilleux, Albert

Roussel, Jean Cras and many more. You will see several others scattered throughout these pages.

Chausson's quartet, in three movements, opens at a slow tempo. All of the instruments take a turn at the lead melody and, when the tempo gets a bit confusing, they all revert back to the slow, measured opening. Suddenly we leave melancholia behind, the tempo lifts, and the violin sweeps above the ensemble. It becomes a pastoral scene, with the violin in command. The cello then takes over, leading the music into another slow passage. The tempo picks up, and the violin enters with its own story to tell. Gradually, the ensemble gathers force and the music is reminiscent of an earlier section as the performers then express themselves in a hectic manner, continuing for some time. The violin soars again in a positive mood, leading to a rich tapestry which gently brings the music back to the ground. Joy abounds here and it is full of romance before the piece again gathers impetus for a time until it slowly falls apart. In the penultimate bars it blatantly quotes the opening measures of Debussy's string quartet before it comes to a stop. This is magical.

The second movement also begins slowly, this time with an attractive melody, full of romance. It's so fine, the composer repeats it and builds to a climax, before dropping back and the cello enters with an aching solo and is absorbed back into the ensemble. Again the intensity drops and the violin sustains the atmosphere, which eventually lifts, leading to all instruments working together in harmony for the greater good. Now we are moving towards the end and the cello again takes precedence. The first hint of a real tempo change comes with the strings supporting the violin as it gently comes to rest, and it is over.

The final movement is bright and breezy, the violin leading over some fine ensemble work. This playful tone continues for some time before seguing into an extended gentle section. When it eventually changes, it introduces the only drama in the work. The serious tone is soon swept away by the first violin, which takes the music into a minor tonality, the first time this has been heard. After a short period of stasis, the mood rises again. It positively races for a time, then returns to a melancholia, before concluding the work with a fine flourish.

Interestingly, this quartet was incomplete when he died. His friend, Vincent d'Indy completed the third and final movement.

Most of these one string quartet pieces are highlights of the Late Romantic string quartet repertoire. The French certainly have shown a gift for romance in this genre.

There are many individual recordings of this piece available. I would go with a pairing with one of the other members of the FOSQC. I also quite fancy it paired with a piece for piano, violin and string quartet on Hyperion, by an augmented Chilingirian Quartet. The quartet is available to sample on Spotify, YouTube and earsense.

Listenability: Let's just say it has a certain 'je ne sais quoi'.

Carlos Chávez [1899–1978]

Nationality: Mexican
Quartets: Three
Style: Contemporary

String Quartets Nos. 1 & 3

The First Quartet consists of four, relatively short movements and opens with strong rhythmic possibilities, which seems to be a feature of the composer's work. Finely crafted melodies reach out to catch your attention – I hear a fleeting hint of Spanish influence here. A more measured period features much quivering of bows, bringing a tension to the surface. Now a calm gradually develops as the violins spin out sustained melodies. A solo cello phrase leads us into pastoral territory, where the movement ends.

An adagio movement follows, and is ever so tranquil and slightly introspective. The cello features with long melodic lines and has a powerful presence. When the violins return, it is with a sense of desolation and longing. There is some wonderful writing here, it's a fine adagio. The cello sustains long tones as the whispering violins fade out.

The third, short movement is energetic as it stays close to the sound of some long forgotten popular music. It is a bustling feeling, and the violins work relentlessly. Cello thrusts lead to pizzicato sounds and simple melodies bring this extremely brief movement to its conclusion.

The final movement is a slow, short lament – it is all about melancholia here. Various sustained tones mix with longing melodies. It clocks in at 2:22.

On to the Third Quartet. In three movements, it features a joyous opening, with delightful melodies. After a time, the intensity drops a little and the music takes on a different hue. It is still insistent however, and a strong rhythmic melody is supported by forceful ensemble playing. A violin asserts itself with a persistent note, before changing into a lonely mode, where two violins and the cello make fine statements. The melodic intensity returns and the movement finishes on a chord. This music also seems to have a folk-nature to its feeling.

The next movement is marked lento, and is very fine. A solo violin introduces proceedings but is soon supported by a poignant harmonic background. The violins develop wonderfully sweet melodies and the mood is attractive and emotional – it is a thoughtful section. Interweaving violins produce a most charming sound, seemingly of an early twentieth century nature, as it meanders to a finish.

The final movement opens with a sense of fanfare, and the violins engage in a spirited dialogue. A fine rhythmic fragment allows the violins to jab at the music. A change incorporates a stronger ensemble, particularly the cello before the violins go it alone, with the cello making intermittent statements. This is again joyous. I'm not familiar with Mexican folk music but the piece seems to contain folk elements. The sound is now more fractured and each instrument has a role to play within an almost chaotic soundscape. As we near the end, the violins regain control and develop fast-moving melodies. It really is relentless, but in a conservative manner, nothing dissonant here. The conclusion comes with a brilliant fanfare.

This CD, titled *String Quartets 1-3* is performed by Cuarteto Latinoamericano on the Urtext label. Unfortunately it's only available as a download on Amazon and Presto, however it can still be obtained from Naxos Direct. The three quartets are all on Spotify, YouTube and earsense.

Listenability: Very positive and easy on the ear, together with some wonderful slow movements.

[Chávez with Quartetto Latinoamericano]
[Image – Urtext label – could not be contacted]

The Cold Dancer – Compilation

Nationality: Scottish
Quartets: Four
Style: Contemporary

Contemporary String Quartets from Scotland

This is a fascinating compilation performed by the Edinburgh Quartet. I shall attempt to do it justice. There are works by four composers on the disc.

James Clapperton is featured with his *The Great Divorce for String Quartet,* a one movement work, running for about 16 minutes. It opens with wistful violins that set up a beautiful atmosphere, allowing the cello to provide seemingly random melodic statements. It is a fabulous piece of writing, very longing. Slight changes occur in the style of the violins which lead to a different mood and a dissonant note that hangs in the air, precipitating a more serious nature. The piece is minimal in its progress – things do not happen quickly. A sparsity moves into some melodic development, the violins are truly wonderful. Slowly, an emotional intensity is building with the cello thickening the harmonic texture. Suddenly, the music becomes a dance, but not for long and we are now drawn briefly back into sparsity. A lone violin makes intermittent melancholic statements and after a time, the other strings prance above and around this sadness. The juxtaposition of a longing, sparse violin, together with busier strings, makes for a compelling sound. The cello creates a plaintive statement, all the while accompanied by the sweeping violins. A solo violin concludes the piece. It is a stunning soundscape.

An unnamed string quartet by Judith Weir is in three movements. A slow but intense opening features effective use of microtones as it paints an abstract, slightly bleak atmosphere. A lift in intensity brings with it a rhythmic framework as the cello punches out phrases, while the violins continue with chromatic flurries and reach for the sky as the cello becomes more dissonant. The violins take over now, and the end comes with a note suspended in time.

The second movement begins with a stilted rhythmic motif played by the whole ensemble. The violins then begin to express themselves, while the motif can still be heard in the background. It's an engrossing, interesting sound. The cello now begins to become involved in the melodic development and a change leads to the opening motif reappearing, with the violins playing in a sparse fashion. The end is one iteration of the motif.

The final movement is short and starts with a violent flourish, which is soon overtaken by a prancing violin statement – light and airy, although tension develops as it moves forward. There is much dissonance here and it finishes when you least expect it, leaving you hanging there. This is a fine contemporary work.

Another one movement quartet, titled *The Cold Dancer*, is by Kenneth Dempster. It has a rhapsodic opening with many powerful twists and turns. This feeling gradually subsides and moves into another rhapsodic period where the violins are busy. The music gives way to a rhythmic passage, leading into a violin duet, which is dissonant and varies in intensity. A calm comes over the work as the cello sustains long notes and the violins become lyrical for a time. A further change invokes stabbing violin notes and a chaotic musical soundscape. I'm only halfway through and I've never come across a piece with so many mood changes. The violins pretend to fall away only to return with much vigour before a new prominent violin part ensues as the violins play with string sound effects and a chromatic feeling. With the ending approaching, a succession of high violin notes fade into the distance.

The fourth work on the CD is a three movement quartet by William Sweeney. I won't be discussing this at present, mostly because it runs for 36 minutes but it does sound promising.

I rather like some of these themed compilations. They are not like many CDs which have, stylistically, two totally unrelated string quartets on them. The works on this disc seem to share some sense of commonality of texture, even though they are all quite different.

This CD, on the Delphian label, performed by the Edinburgh Quartet is available at Amazon US and UK as *The Cold Dancer*. It can be heard on Spotify.

Listenability: A very interesting mixture of contemporary sounds.

— oo0oo —

Osvaldo Coluccino [born 1963]

Nationality: Italian
Quartets: Two
Style: Contemporary Modern

Aoin and Attimo – Two Works
for String Quartet

Aoin for String Quartet was composed in 2002 and is in two movements. The first movement opens with a slightly ambient feeling which continues throughout the work. A sustained chord is the first thing we hear; it then changes to a different sustained chord. A cello note signals the beginning of several random notes with a dash of pizzicato, before moving back to another sustained chord. Now there is melodic movement within the chord – sometimes it is single notes, other times modification of a chord tone. A pause brings a quivering of bows and pizzicato. There is minimal music here, although it is sparsity, not stasis, as violins drift in and out. Suddenly a solo cello leads to a brief, loud passage before the music returns to its former sound. A joyless violin works its way through string sound effects, and more sustained chords, to the end.

The second movement is significantly longer than the first. Scratchy violin tones are heard to begin the movement. This **is** stasis for a time, with only intermittent tones being played by the ensemble with a buffeted cello making for a strange sound. There are no melodies here, only fragments, but the intensity increases with string sound effects in abundance – I would love to see the score. Occasionally, simple chords are formed by the sound of two instruments, and they could be any member of the quartet participating. Small crescendos are developed and now the sound has more consistency. Sustained chords return for a time, but these are interrupted by an abstruse collection of various, almost random notes. Another strong sustained chord emerges, then after a pause, another. This becomes a pattern with brief periods of sustained chords alternating with pauses. The work concludes on one of these chords.

Attimo for String Quartet was composed in 2007 and is in one movement. It commences again in an ambient manner, as sparse single notes contribute to a fragmentary feeling. Slowly, you can hear the piece gathering forces and a sustained note allows the ensemble to move into a more assertive mode, although it is still rather stark. Sustained chords are slowly introduced, and the timbre of the instruments is a little raw at times. A low resonant cello joins the chords, which then stop, with a return to string sound effects and no formal melodies. Essentially, this music defies description as it meanders through a labyrinth of assorted sounds. The cello, when it appears, is particularly salient. A phrase starts to develop, but is not sustained. Some further chords do gather in between silences, similar to the previous work and the texture of these chords is modified by the instruments playing sparse phrases. The chords slowly increase in texture and intensity, while remaining totally abstract in nature. A sustained chord that contains melodic movement finally appears and is complemented with groans from the ensemble. The same chord gains melodic momentum as it nears the end and gently concludes.

Is this the most avant-garde composer that I have discussed? I don't know, but I would put him up there with Elliott Carter and Morton Feldman. Coluccino's minimal approach is nothing like the intensity of Carter, and, although I can hear brief allusions to Morton Feldman's style, they are really quite different. These works have a sense of abstraction all of their own. Only by listening to them, will they reveal their secrets.

The review CD, *Osvaldo Coluccino: String Quartets* on the Neos label, is performed by Quartetto d'Archi del Teatro La Fenice. There are two other pieces on the disc, *Eco Immobile – for piano quartet* and *Talea – for violin and cello*. These are both fine, introspective works in the style of the quartets.

The CD can be found at Presto, Amazon US, and Amazon UK as a download. You can sample the works on Spotify, YouTube or earsense.

Listenability: Quite Modern, but not noisy.

[Image courtesy Neos Records]

— ooOoo —

Dinos Constantinides [1929–2012]

Nationality: Greek
Quartets: Three
Style: Contemporary

String Quartets Nos. 1 & 2

Constantinides' three string quartets are all short works. There is a dearth of information about him on the internet, he doesn't even appear on Wikipedia. I can tell you that they were composed in 1950, 1957 and 1987, respectively.

The First Quartet is in three movements. It opens in a quietly introspective manner before moving into a tempo. The violins quiver while the cello is strong and there are many interjections. Suddenly a rushing passage takes off, littered with string sound effects – there are a lot of glissandos. The introspection

99

continues with much melodic action, and some orchestral-like harmonised lines, before ending on a slightly dissonant chord.

The next movement follows with a lamenting scene as the violins play long, quivering notes and a sense of melancholy prevails. The violins edge forward as the cello offers up some glissandos of its own, yet there is no real forward movement, just sound. It is sometimes slightly harsh, but offers up a sparsity that is beguiling. The cello dialogues with the violins and the mood is again introspective before a sustained chord fades to the end.

The final movement is energised and there is a sense of ostinato as the violins are quite animated, expressing long melodies. Now the rhythm dissipates and we are left with ensemble thrusts which propel the violins into the stratosphere. Returning to the ground, the violins are strong and conclude this very brief movement.

The Second Quartet, titled *Mutability*, is in four movements. Again, it starts with a lament and becomes almost orchestral in its sound – for me, it evokes Arvo Pärt with constant sweeping violin statements over a sparse background. This is heavenly, beautiful writing. A fluttering of strong violins leads to a repeated motif which acts as a springboard for the violins. Following a brief period of stasis, the motif returns – this time, not for so long. When the rhythm subsides, the cello echoes a violin melody and soon the introductory orchestral texture returns. The cello is magnificent here and the violins are so understated. The end is a delicate, slow passage on this mood.

Now we have another abstract beginning with random groupings of notes and shifting textures. The composer seems to revel in these beautiful, unpretentious soundscapes. The feeling gently pans out into an extended passage as the violins are very expressive. Towards the end the music becomes ever so sparse and just fades away.

The third movement is animated, with a propulsive viola motif and much activity, which doesn't last and the previous stasis returns. The cello pulsates as the violins again reach skyward with glissandos aplenty. A tempo ensues and there is agitation from all instruments before an orchestral sweep from the violins checks the tempo and the cello repeats a long, rhythmic phrase. This is very effective as the violins hold a sustained chord until the cello ceases and the music finishes with two violins on a chord.

The final movement is slightly rhapsodic, interspersed with interjections. String sound effects are in abundance as the music becomes hymn-like, repeating a lamenting phrase. I believe the Greek influence can be heard in the melodies, evoking images of a countryside with the use of simple melodies. This leads to a period of agitation although the sparsity is still evident. Some energy is felt before the cello tempers this with long tones. A funereal melodic statement from the violins is very Greek. Paradoxically, this creates a sense of optimism as it gently fades. Now a period of intense activity comes and goes, all the while being broken up intermittently by the previous melody, eventually leading to a slowly faded ending.

I won't be discussing the one movement Third Quartet, but I can tell you that it is very much a soundscape filled with spaces and sparse instrumental interjections. There are also several other short pieces for string quartet on the disc.

So what to make of this strange, possibly unique music? I believe the composer uses ethnic sounds from his country and shapes them into his own world. They could be called one-dimensional but I am quite taken by the way he presents this ambient abstract music. Oh, and he pretty much always writes in minor keys.

The review CD, titled *Dinos Constantinides: String Quartets*, on Centaur Records and performed by various string quartet ensembles is available from Amazon US but not UK, but it is on Presto Classical. The full CD can be heard on Spotify, YouTube and earsense.

Listenability: Wonderfully mild and melancholy soundscapes.

— ooOoo —

Diego Conti [born 1958]

Nationality: Italian
Quartets: At least six
Style: Modern Contemporary

The First and Last Quartets

Conti is relatively obscure – I couldn't find him on Wikipedia, or glean much from Google. Thanks to Kai from earsense for tracking down his nationality for me. I am going to discuss String Quartets Nos. 1 and 6.

The First Quartet, which is quite brief in its three movements, opens with a dissonant chordal thrust. This is quite typical of the composer. Most of the movements within his quartets start in a confronting manner, before quickly settling into a more conservative mood. In this piece there is an ever intensifying dissonant violin section which flows into a beautiful solo violin melody. This is quickly joined by pizzicato accompaniment and later, some seemingly random statements – all the while the violin continues with its haunting melody, as the second violin complements it. There are some sweet harmonies negotiated here, expressing a great feeling of wonder. Now a somewhat aggressive phase is introduced and the violins briefly dash frantically to a conclusion.

Eerie violins sounds announce the next movement, slowly leading into a rhapsodic passage where the whole ensemble is in full voice. The mood subsequently mellows to reveal an expressive, expansive soundscape, before a return to the opening statements, which lead to a quiet ending. I'd have to say that this short movement does not contain much music.

The final movement, marked lento, just happens to be the longest in the work. As usual, there is a dramatic introductory phrase, which is repeated and interspersed with gentle atonal musings. A strongly rhythmic passage ensues before a solo cello statement brings peace to the mood – this turns out to be most alluring. The violins create an ascending series of motifs, with ever-increasing intensity. A pause leads to a hint of the opening and strong harmonised violin lines are very effective, combined with a sparse cello accompaniment. The violins, slightly lamenting, express an introspective mood, with sustained notes – the end is abrupt.

The Sixth Quartet is twice as long as the First, but is in one movement. Again, a jagged introductory phrase leads into a quivering of violins that gradually increase in dynamics. A sombre passage begins to unfold, with plenty of space between the sections. A lone violin expresses a sparse line, with some glissandos, before the ensemble moves in behind it with probing statements. This feeling is sustained for some time, in a very thoughtful passage. I should note that a lot of this movement is scarcely audible, I remastered the track to gain a better understanding of its many subtle changes. Again the violins present an eerie tone, with slowly developing harmonised, sparse melodies. A change brings about a gentle but dissonant violin duet that uses microtones to great effect – this is a most mesmeric passage. Now the music is stripped to the bare essentials as both violins evoke string sound effects and slowly move the music forward, in a most measured manner. The effects eventually give way to a more melodic approach, which is very evocative and lamenting, in a most precious, atmospheric feeling. The second half of this piece is a magnificent, abstract soundscape, which continues to a gently fading conclusion.

For me, these are simply marvellous quartets – I'm glad that there are six of them – all different but having a shared emotional space. Be prepared to strain your ears, some of the music is recorded very softly.

The review 2-CD set, *Diego Conti: String Quartets*, released on the Italian Tactus Records label and performed by Officina Musicale, contains quartets Nos. 1-6 and is available on Amazon US and UK.

This set can be found on Spotify and all six quartets are on YouTube and earsense.

Listenability: Modern, with moments of great emotional depth.

Incidental Images #3

The Future of the String Quartet

[The Nightingale String Quartet]
[Image courtesy NSQ website]

This young Danish all female quartet have had great success in chamber music competitions and with their absolutely marvellous complete Rued Langaard 3-CD set, which has received high praise in the media.

Paul Cooper [1926–1996]

Nationality: American
Quartets: Six
Style: Contemporary

String Quartet No. 5

Cooper wrote his six string quartets between 1952 and 1977. Only Nos. 5 and 6 are available on CD. As I am fond of slow movements, and it consists of four slow movements, I shall discuss the Fifth. This quartet is titled *Umbrae* which means *'A region of complete shadow resulting from total obstruction of light'*, according to my online dictionary.

The first movement begins with a drone – a sustained chord with the cello being prominent. A melody begins to form but it is unclear. The drone fades away leaving the four instruments to exchange dialogue with each other in a mildly chaotic manner. A return of the drone leading to a loud chord initiates a faded ending. This may not sound like much, but it is beguiling.

There seems to be a modern technique, I've encountered it before, where all of the instruments seem to busily play independently of each other. It is chaotic, but if not played too loudly, it does establish a musical substance. I expect there is more to come.

Movement two is slow. The aforementioned technique comes into play again but at this tempo, makes for a different effect. Atonal chords begin to form and the music briefly drops into a rhythm before resuming the drone with the violins playing sweeping melodies. There are microtones being used here so the dissonance level is high. After a time, a viola ostinato underpins the violins. Again there seems to be no connection between the instruments, but it works. Several loud chords lead back into a tempo which fades to a solo violin hovering in the high register. The feeling descends into one of almost complete entropy before fading out.

There is not much variation in these first two movements, but they still take me to some interesting, introverted, musical spaces.

The third movement begins with some string instrument sound effects, mostly plucked – it is a gentle pizzicato. After some sweet melodies, the plucking returns for a while, then it's back into the music. This contrast continues, plucked, then bowed, and back again. Eventually there is a peaceful ending.

The final movement begins with one violin note played for about 30 seconds before the other instruments make their entry. Their atonality soon overwhelms the violin. The music stops and then moves through some dissonant chords before settling on a sustained chord with a violin melody. This appears to be a recapitulation of the first movement opening. A phrase develops and the violin soars into the high register again, way above the ensemble, reminiscent of John Tavener's *The Protecting Veil*. The violin ceases and it is all over.

I think that this piece could have done with a bit more music. The movements are not long and it feels that the composer missed an opportunity even to just sustain some sections. That would have made it all the more powerful. However, there is some great music in here.

I shall discuss availability later.

Listenability: Intriguing, slightly academic.

String Quartet No. 6

This work opens ever so quietly with inauspicious string sound effects. However they do get louder before they pause, and immediately start up again. There is a hint of a melody from the violins and the cello is prominent but there is no tempo. Then follows some stabbing atonal chords before a return to sound effects – quite powerful really. A pause leads to a fine abstract scene with plenty of spaces. A violin brings forth the first real melody and the ensemble paints an introspective background. This doesn't last long and a more abstruse atmosphere follows. The violins pursue a dialogue with occasional atonal flourishes. After a time the introspection returns with sparse melodic violin phrases, mostly in the high register. It is sustained until a fade into the end of the movement. This is some fine writing, leading to a variety of textures, some of which are quite dense.

The next movement again begins with mild atonal string sound effects, coupled with a cello phrase. There is an attempt by the viola to establish an ostinato but the composer settles for another, inward looking space. The music is random here – it's an interesting entropic soundscape. The violins increase the intensity with atonal sparring before dropping into a brooding feeling. Nearing the end of the movement the violins gently present melodic ideas over a tranquil background.

The short final movement has a sparse atonal opening. The ensemble pulsates while the first violin sketches a long melody. A deeply resonant solo cello has a role before the violin becomes very loud. As this dissipates a violin repeats a phrase over an ostinato until it fades into the distance. It's over.

As you will have noted, there is a bit of atonality here, but this leads to some wonderful soundscapes. I rather wish that more than two quartets of Cooper were available. Perhaps they will come in the future.

This piece is on the same CD as the previously mentioned String Quartet No. 5. Titled *Cooper: Chamber Works, String Quartet No. 5 & 6* on Composers Recordings, performed by the Shepherd Quartet – it also contains a number of shorter works.

This disc is currently available on Amazon US as a CD, and Amazon UK as an MP3 download. It is also on Spotify and there is one quartet on both YouTube and earsense.

Listenability: Again, intriguing, and slightly academic.

Roland Corp [born 1951]

Nationality: British
Quartets: At least two
Style: Contemporary

String Quartet No. 1

After a slightly stuttering opening, featuring minor chords, the work takes flight with medium tempo rhythmic ideas and the passage moves along nicely. An ascending motif is prominent, then the intensity rises. There are plenty of rhythmic motifs played by the whole ensemble although every now and again it reverts back to two violins. The movement finishes on a five note motif.

The next movement starts softly, with a slightly anguished theme, which is repeated. Changes in harmony, together with a rise in intensity, lead to a loud crescendo. When it can't rise any further, it just disintegrates. The opening theme returns and then introduces a tranquil section, featuring long violin melodies. Eventually it is just violins but soon switches to the full ensemble with the second violin and viola shimmering, as the first violin spins out melodies. Finally a change comes in the form of a cello ostinato building to a crescendo which persists for a short time, then drops back to a lead violin, expressing an ethnic sounding melody, before the cello initiates another ostinato. The passage again rises in intensity, but not for so long this time. A pause allows a cello and violin to duet and a short period of dissonance leads to an end.

The third movement commences with a slight feeling of abstraction. The tempo is brisk and the violins are chaotic and intense, with a hint of a melody in spite of the overpowering rhythm. With no sign of the tempo abating we are left with the violins which just stop. It is a short movement, a little over three minutes.

A dissonant character opens the fourth movement which soon moves into a tempo and the violins converse. The cello interjects with an ascending motif as the dialogue continues. This mood lasts for a while until a more majestic feeling takes over. Now we have a brisk pulse and the violins duel, rather than converse. The pulse stops for a solo cello and then the ensemble returns. There is a short, chaotic episode before the movement finishes.

This CD is available performed by the Maggini Quartet on the Naxos label, on Amazon UK and US. It can be heard on Spotify, YouTube and earsense.

Listenability: Hmmm – a satisfying, slightly abstract experience.

Eleanor Cory [born 1944]

Nationality: American
Quartets: At least three
Style: Contemporary Modern

String Quartets Nos. 2 & 3

Cory's music is quite contemporary, but it does contain some poignant soundscapes. These are short works, together they run about 30 minutes.

String Quartet No. 2 was written in 2000. The first movement is challenging at times. Opening in a dissonant manner with no recognisable pulse, the violins are rhythmically intense and wander about in an atonal manner. It slowly develops into a feeling of abstract beauty with the violins sparse and measured, even though the note selection is dissonant. The intensity rises ever so slowly, with violins playing on top of each other. There is some rhythmic punctuation but the violins continue the feeling to a conclusion.

The second movement begins with a slow, lamenting chordal interlude. Out of this comes a short solo violin statement before it returns to the opening ambience. This pattern is repeated until the ensemble joins the violin. The sound is ever so peaceful with the first violin offering up dissonant but satisfying melodies. Now a pause returns to the opening, with the cello becoming prominent. A mild chaos ensues but the violin cuts through to calm proceedings. Chord patterns emerge, only to dissipate and the violin ends the movement.

The final movement is short and unsettled from the start. The violins gently spin out atonal melodies, and, eventually, the music moves into a rhythm as the violins contribute some stabbing chords which remain to the end of the movement. Like I said, these are short works.

String Quartet No. 3, written in 2009, opens with a mournful solo violin that reaches skyward for its melodic inspiration. A short solo cello statement is complemented by the violins, before it also moves into its upper register. Now a rhythmic motif is established by the violins and the cello returns. A pause brings back the two violins for an extended period, occasionally interrupted by cello interjections. The cello now finds its own motif and, together with the violins, takes the movement out.

The second movement begins with a sparse cello and violin passage. The second violin enters, adding texture, before string sound effects come into play for a delicate section. The cello and violin return to create a most interesting soundscape. The texture thickens again and the intensity lifts as the violins push forward. More gentle string sound effects are now heard, and the movement ends.

The final movement opens with a train-like ostinato as the violins scatter random notes about. The motif changes key and the cello starts to express itself with vigour. Now the key changes occur more often before the music suddenly pauses. A period of string sound effects, together with the cello part, create a skittish mood and the ostinato returns, with many more key changes. The cello joins in with the motif, the intensity rises and the violin is left on its own to express the final moments. The rhythm stops dead and that's it.

Having just heard these pieces for a second time, they certainly don't seem as difficult as I first thought. In fact, they are mostly harmless atonal romps with many instances of fine abstract beauty.

As to availability, these two quartets have both been recorded – unfortunately they are on different CDs. No. 2 is on a CD titled *Chasing Time* on the Albany label featuring the Atlantic Quartet while No. 3 is on a Naxos release, *Cory: Things Are & String Quartet No. 3* played by the Momenta Quartet. As I listened to the pieces on Spotify I only checked out a small sample of the other works – they generally seemed quite contemporary. Both of the discs are on Amazon US and UK.

They can be sampled on Spotify, YouTube and earsense.

Listenability: Shame about the two CDs, but thoroughly interesting works individually.

[Image courtesy Naxos Records]

Jean Cras [1879–1932]

Nationality: French
Quartets: One – FOSQC
Style: Late Romantic

String Quartet No. 1

The Cras quartet, written in 1909, contains four movements. It commences with a deep cello melody before the violins go solo – this is slow and splendidly moving. A brief pause ensues before a violin leads with a new melody, and plenty of space for the other instruments before the melody becomes orchestral as the violins skate across the ensemble's musings. Another brief pause and a new very gentle melody emerges, and the violins converse, then the cello has its say. The orchestral tone returns and a sweeping downward violin phrase brings impetus. Then a slow tempo emerges, the cello abounds and we are back in quartet territory. The violins repeat the descending phrase several times and the ending comes as a fine piece of miniaturisation – a fabulous, tiny self-contained fragment.

The next movement opens with a strikingly beautiful melody. It meanders along until a little more orchestral writing occurs, which is truly wonderful. It gently floats back to the two violins and the dialogue continues for two minutes before it ends peacefully.

The third movement begins with a cello and then a simple folk melody appears. A brief orchestral phase gives way to a recapitulation of the opening theme, leading to a shimmering effect which invokes a new theme, developed slowly into a period of great sensitivity. The cello returns to pizzicato accompaniment, then the violins take over. Again, it sounds slightly orchestral as a major tonality changes to minor, leading to an increased intensity which is sustained to the conclusion.

The final movement opens with a shimmering flourish, which, after a slight pause, is repeated. The piece moves into a moderate tempo and then into a stately passage, as new phrases are explored and the intensity recedes. Now some longer melodies evoke Edvard Grieg. Finally, Cras returns as the introductory nature resumes. The next section is wonderful, full of optimism as the violins dominate. With the end in sight, an increase in intensity leads to an orchestral-like chord.

You will have to excuse my use of the word, and concept, of *orchestral*. It's represented here by strong writing, with full sounding sections that are so reminiscent of an orchestra. Also, I hope it is pretty obvious that I really like this piece.

This work is freely available on Amazon US or UK. There are many different pairings, some with other members of the FOSQC. I like the look of a version paired with a piano quintet on Timpani Classics, performed by Quatour Louvigny. The work is on Spotify and several versions can be found on YouTube and earsense.

Listenability: Fabulous French Late Romantic quartet.

[Image courtesy Timpani Classics]

— oo0oo —

Robert Crawford [1925-2012]

Nationality: Scottish
Quartets: Four
Style: Early Modern

The First String Quartet

It was quite difficult to obtain any information on Robert Caldwell Crawford until I eventually came across a small PDF, announcing his death, which can be viewed here:

www.wrightmusic.net/pdfs/robert-crawford.pdf

This document contains interesting comments on his string quartets, and I found it to be quite rewarding. I am going to discuss the First Quartet, which was composed in 1949.

The work opens in a moderate tempo as the first violin expresses with great emotion from its entrance, gaining wonderful support from the ensemble. After a slightly hesitant melodic moment, a brief rhythmic passage leads into another beautiful violin section with a gentle level of introspection being provided by the accompaniment, which ever so slowly diminishes in intensity. This leads into a brief, impassioned section, which builds into a climax. Various moods unfold, with the first violin being the constant point of reference, and the cello often creating a musical space all of its own. The ending is slightly ambivalent as if the violin has somewhere else to go, but doesn't manage to make it, as it just drifts away. The duality in this movement is startling, with the mood constantly moving between the tender and the impassioned, sometimes even alluding to the abstract. This has a certain forward looking presence that is unusual for a piece from 1949.

An adagio cantabile (slowly, in a singing style) tempo introduces the second movement. Shimmering, singing, hymnal lines make for a marvellous entrance. Long melodic lines are harmonised to perfection and for me, this is classic British music. A walking cello extends this mood as it becomes almost extreme in its pastoral nature – these are two words I wouldn't normally put together. The violin is most enticing and imparts a unique texture to the music. Nearing the end, it becomes frantic, frenzied even, and stops abruptly.

The next movement features a restless violin line to open, which is developed at some length by the composer. Again this is music of a measured, abstract nature. A brief rhythmical, highly charged passage gives way to the previously heard solemn walking cello lines with the violin constructing self-referential melodies. Now the restless feeling is heard and the music evokes the sound of bats emerging from a cave with frantic, virtuosic harmonised violin lines which eventually taper off to a quiet conclusion that flows straight into the next movement.

The finale, with its held over note is marked *mesto*, which is very Bartok, and drifts in a labyrinthine manner evoking dark spaces. A second violin adds a harmonised line to this walking jazz-style melody. Now string sound effects emerge from the background to briefly support this marvellous soundscape. The two violins seem to be using micro-tones as there is a slight degree of dissonance in their expression. The appearance of the cello is most interesting as it mimics the strange violin lines, all of which is played out in a ¾ time signature. A return to busy, strongly harmonised violins is brief and the sense of mystery is continued to a sedate conclusion.

I found the three works on the review CD to be totally fascinating, with the composer drawing me into the unique vision that was his musical world.

This disc, titled *Robert Crawford: String Quartets Nos. 1-3*, is on the Delphian label, performed by the Edinburgh Quartet. If this was the only music they ever recorded, it would be enough – this is a superb effort. The CD is available on Amazon UK and Presto Classical – Amazon US has it as a download only.

Unfortunately the disc can only be heard on Spotify, as far as I am aware.

Listenability: A transcendent Early Modern work.

[Image courtesy Delphian label]

Carl Czerny [1791–1857]

Nationality: Austrian
Quartets: At least twenty
Style: Late Classical

String Quartet in E minor

Of Czerny's many string quartets, I believe most of them were never published, and, to my knowledge, only six have been recorded. I'm also not sure as to when this quartet was composed, along with many in the music academic fraternity – he is a bit of a mystery man. The work is in four movements and is set firmly in a Classical style.

The first movement, marked allegro, opens with its minor key tonality obvious. It has a surging quality as the ensemble moves forward. A prominent violin espouses an appealing melody, before an interlude of a series of harmonised melodic lines occurs. The violin returns with variations and the ensemble ebbs and flows with it. A recapitulation of the opening solidifies the mood before strong phrases bring some vigour to the piece. However, the overriding sense is of the violin melodies, which are attractive. I hear a hint of the feeling of Beethoven's *Razumovsky Quartets, Opus 59* at work here. The music continues but now the intensity of the minor key is gone. Another strong passage leads to an underlying feeling of tension, and the minor tonality is reinvoked, if only briefly. Peaceful moods alternate with vigorous passages, and the minor tonality comes and goes. There is an almost cadenza-like feeling, with the solo violin leading the way. The end is a series of thrusts, followed by a strong final chord.

The andante second movement begins with a slow ascending minor melody that is very satisfying. The cello steps out for a solo statement as the violins fill in the gaps in the cello's melodic phrases. A stately mood ensues with a very gentle violin skating across the music. In the background, the viola fashions a subtle rhythmic motif, which supports the violin. Now the viola steps out, crafting a melody over shimmering violins. A pizzicato appears, but the ensemble pushes on with their melodic development, and intensity. A beautiful cello melody is once again to the fore, before it moves into quivering mode, then walking. All the while, a measured ensemble is preparing the way for a conclusion, which comes quietly.

The next movement is marked vivace, and a violin leads the ensemble, slowly increasing the intensity. There is much happening here with a pulsating tempo and brief pauses are utilised to delineate vigorous sections. Now a slow, Mozart-like sound develops, with subtle violin and measured accompaniment. The intensity eventually returns with an energy that continues to the end.

The finale commences at a moderate tempo, with the violins leading a path through various chord changes, resulting in a very positive phase. There is also a relief occasionally where the tempo drops back – mostly however, the ensemble continues in a robust manner. The chord changes reappear and are negotiated with ease by the violins. One last robust passage leads to a short, quiet statement before the mood becomes overwhelming and concludes in a striking manner.

Sometimes this work sounds a little like the Romantic period, but at other times, pure Classicism reigns. It is a fine piece.

The review 2-CD set, titled *Czerny: String Quartets,* on the Capriccio label and performed by the Sheridan Ensemble, is available on Amazon UK and US. There is another, 3-CD set *Czerny: Rediscovered Genius* performed by the St. Lawrence String Quartet which contains some string quartets, including the E minor and other material, with all of the music recorded live. It's very pricey. Strangely, I didn't notice any single CDs containing the work, but there may be some.

The Sheridan Ensemble CD is on Spotify and YouTube. There are two versions on earsense.

Listenability: A nice blend of the major and the minor tonalities make this work very enjoyable.

[Image courtesy Capriccio via Naxos Classics]

Roland Dahinden [born 1962]

Nationality: Swiss
Quartets: Five
Style: Contemporary

Mr Minimalism
String Quartets Nos. 2-5

Dahinden, a Swiss trombonist and composer, appears to have written five string quartets, four of which make up the review CD *Flying White*. I am also going to briefly examine another CD, *Silberen*.

I believe Dahinden has been listening to a lot of Morton Feldman. It took me a little while to get over that, but after a few listens I have found these quartets to be strikingly peaceful. I thought long and hard about discussing this work, given that it may be too esoteric, but it is fine music. The four quartets on *Flying White* are all named, one movement works – most of them are short. You can hear a slight development of style as you progress through the pieces.

String Quartet No. 2 – *Mind Rock*. This work is made up mostly of strange chords, usually lasting 2-3 seconds. When a chord is played, there is either little or no melodic movement within that chord. I wouldn't call them melodies but some consecutive chords contain notes that might be construed as melodic development. This piece runs to a little over fourteen minutes.

String Quartet No. 3 – *Mond See*. Similar to *Mind Rock* but slightly more melodic, and is the same length. This movement has more entropy with varying lengths of gaps between the chords. It is a lot more spacious than No. 2.

String Quartet No. 4 – *Flying White*. Basically, more of the same. However, there is a lot more obvious melodic development in the chords. There are also a few string quartet sound effects thrown in. It runs for twelve minutes.

String Quartet No. 5 – *Poids de'Lombre* (*Shadow Weight*). Similar again, but definite melodies appear here. This one clocks in at over twenty-five minutes (and it really rocks.)

Now onto *Silberen* (*Silvery*). This CD contains a 45 minute piece entitled *Piano and String Quartet*. The pianist is Hildegard Kleeb, Dahinden's wife. It also features the Arditti Quartet, who I normally tend to find quite confronting. They play beautifully here, very measured and sparse. The work is reminiscent of Morton Feldman's *Piano and String Quartet*. But then again, it isn't. It just uses the same instrumentation, and possibly, form. Interestingly, you never hear people complain about who wrote the 100,000[th] composition in sonata form. This piece, which runs for 45 minutes, is sparse, with the quartet and piano entering at varying times, sometimes alone, sometimes together. There is no tempo, no harmony and no melodic development. It's just a piece of pure abstraction – I couldn't begin to analyse it. It is what it is, whatever that is. You have to hear it for yourself. I'd venture an opinion that some people would not like it. However,

I'm pretty comfortable with the Morton Feldman approach and I could definitely listen to it again. This style of music is great to have on while you are doing something, it gives you space to think.

There is a total absence of forward movement in these works. I remember enjoying Quartets Nos. 2 & 3 when I first heard them, but I now find Nos. 4 and 5 to be similarly appealing. The *Piano and String Quartet* is just a unique piece and I really like it, just as I enjoy Feldman's soundscapes.

It reminds me of a slightly pompous Arnold Schoenberg quote – *'If it's art, it's not for the people. If it's for the people, it's not art.'*

Make of that what you will.

The *Flying White* CD is on Mode Records, performed by Klangforum Wien String Quartet. It is freely available on Amazon US and UK, as is the *Silberen* CD, also on Mode. Both CDs are on Spotify and most of Dahinden's quartets are available on YouTube with Nos. 2-5 on earsense.

Listenability: Extreme but beguiling minimalism.

[Image courtesy Mode Records]

Richard Danielpour [born 1956]

Nationality: American
Quartets: At least seven
Style: Contemporary

String Quartet No. 2

The Second Quartet is titled *Shadow Dances*, and consists of four named movements. Don't be put off by the movement titles, in most cases, they don't reflect the music, which is absolutely magnificent.

The first movement, titled *Stomping Ground* begins with a string fanfare before moving into a rhythmic section. A repeat of the fanfare leads to a sprightly, slightly atonal passage. There is a constant undercurrent of rhythm and we are treated to the fanfare again. The rhythm persists but there is a sense of sparsity until the violins begin to become more expressive. This doesn't last and a peace emerges as the violins trade attractive melodies. Now we have a return to the rhythmic action, but this doesn't last either as some sensitive violin melodies emerge, eventually leading to a final flourish.

The next movement, *The Little Dicta,* opens with a sound of shimmering strings. This evolves into a cello-led rhythmic phase, with some quite dynamic chordal interludes. A return to the opening strings moves into a particularly charming short passage, which soon returns to the previous rhythmic feeling. Bowed, short, sharp notes provide the accompaniment to various melodic lines from a variety of instruments. A tender passage ensues, with occasional resolute motifs, before a fade to end.

For me, *My Father's Song*, is the highlight of the quartet. A shrill violin sits beautifully with the second violin in a lower register, producing an aching feeling of beauty with no tempo. The lower violin steps forward and is ethnic-sounding, and almost transcendent – this is a stunning passage. A pause introduces a new blend of sounds from the ensemble, as the violins produce a yearning that you could reach out and touch. Now the cello steps forward as the violins favour string sound effects. I can distinguish glissando and harmonics, but there is some other texture as well. For the first time, the use of rhythmic motifs gives the piece some forward movement. Then follows a feeling of angst from the violins as they express with strong tones, and the mood is tense. A surging violin phrase propels the music forward to a greater intensity before a pause brings about a lush atmosphere, as a quivering violin and cello duel. The violins return with their own duet, which is very intense, although it gradually softens and takes me to a place that I've not been before. The mood is again angst-ridden as the violins craft overlapping melodies. A soft, quivering violin leads to another faded passage.

The final movement, titled *The Trickster*, begins in a positive, propulsive manner which soon settles into an atonal feeling. Intermittent pulsating interjections are quite frantic as atonal violin lines criss-cross in a firm manner.

117

The intensity now recedes a little rhythmically but the violins are still strong. The cello is powerful here and the feeling, dynamic. There is a constancy about this passage which finally abates, leaving a solo violin to craft a short melody. A return to the rhythm seemed inevitable and a powerful harmonised violin flourish concludes the work.

I must confess to being quite excited by all of the composer's quartets. I probably tend towards the earlier works but the later ones have some brilliantly captivating slower movements and are still very fine.

The review CD, *Richard Danielpour - String Quartets Nos. 2, 3, & 4*, on Arabesque Records and performed by the American String Quartet, is available on Amazon US and UK. There is a further disc *String Quartets Nos. 5-7*, on the Naxos label, which is also freely available. I should mention that one track on each CD contains a vocalist. They certainly don't detract from the music in any way, in fact the string writing behind the vocals is stunning.

Both discs can be found on Spotify and YouTube. All quartets are also on earsense.

Listenability: Wonderful melodic work, with a touch of Modernism.

[The American String Quartet – Photographer: Peter Schaaf]

Claude Debussy [1862–1918]

Nationality: French
Quartets: One – FOSQC
Style: Early Modern

The String Quartet

Claude Debussy's one quartet is in four movements. Beginning with a measured rhythm, a strong melody is then established on top of a busy accompaniment. Now there is a gentle period which slowly develops in intensity and a violin plays a lamenting line before the opening is repeated. The two violins take control and instigate some marvellous melodies, as well as a recapitulation of the first theme. It then darkens as the composer reharmonises the main melody. The ending is a busy long phrase, which goes out on a flourish.

The second movement opens with pizzicato. Eventually a violin and cello emerge with a melodic statement. The opening chords return several times but the melody is persistent and won't yield until a solo cello introduces a new flavour. The violins float across the top of the music beautifully. The pizzicato returns, then an old melody is made new again. The movement concludes with cello and a violin.

The next movement features a solo cello with interjections from the other strings followed by an extremely calm and graceful period for the violins. Eventually the cello and viola enter, all the time playing in a measured way. It is very precious music – the violins are oh, so gentle. A new melody takes over, together with a chord change and slowly builds into a new space for the whole ensemble. There is a hint of a previous melody before it breaks into a full orchestral sounding passage. It now drops back to nothing, just a few autumn leaves of melodic ideas. We have a chord change as two violins wander over the other strings, which are sustained. The leaves are gently blown away, leaving nothing.

The final movement opens with a cello in the lower register, making for a quiet, sparse opening. A hint of a melody emerges from the cello and it really moves – the whole quartet is pushing hard. A violin comes to the fore and we are back into standard string quartet fare. There are hints of previous melodies, judiciously worked into the form. Now comes agitation and melodies recur at a crescendo level. These taper off, then are reinvigorated for the final chord. Thank you, Claude Debussy.

Many people have asked me about similar sounding music, usually enquiring about Debussy and Maurice Ravel, but I haven't come up with any. The nearest I can manage is fellow Frenchman Robert Casadesus who wrote four beautiful quartets – they are also in this book.

There is a plethora of fine recordings available – Amazon US has at least sixteen hundred listings. I have the Quartetto Italiano on the Australian

Eloquence label, paired with the Ravel. They were made for each other, and made in heaven, at that.

The Debussy Quartet is on Spotify and can be sampled on YouTube. There is also a classic version by the Danish String Quartet along with many other ensembles on earsense.

Listenability: Beautiful Impressionism with an Early Modern feeling.

— ooOoo —

Lex van Delden [1919–1988]

Nationality: Dutch
Quartets: Three
Style: Contemporary

String Quartets Nos. 1 & 3

The First Quartet, written in 1954, opens with a prominent cello which underpins the violin's melodic development. The mood is one of gentle agitation, and abstraction in the violin melodies. It doesn't last and we are soon into a rubato phase with intermittent musings. The feeling of the introduction returns and quite animated discussions take place. The solo violin soars for a while, before returning to the ensemble, where a lamenting passage is introduced by the cello, but the status quo is soon resumed, this time becoming slightly more energised. It ends in this fashion.

The next movement features a very resonant cello before the violins duet, again in a rubato fashion. There are some shimmering sounds in the background and a harmonised cello leads into another sparse space. Very high harmonics from a violin make for a short interlude. Now some pizzicato emerges and the music adopts a more serious tone. A new mood has just the violins, before the cello gently eases in, way down in its lower register. Quivering violins allow the cello to craft a lamenting melody, which fades out.

The third movement is a pizzicato romp which leads into a slow passage – it's barely moving. A very mild sense of introspection ensues, it seems to be the composer's modus operandi. Now the violins make a short statement leading to the end, which is a pizzicato flourish.

A presto tempo opens the final movement which leads to the most chaos yet encountered. Again, it doesn't last and we are back into a lamenting phase where the violins exchange sometimes ethnic-sounding lines. Now it is about rhythm for a time and this segues into a nervous viola pattern with scant violin melodies evident. The dynamics and intensity rise, but again it is only for a time. The ensemble delivers up an ostinato, allowing the violins to ramble freely. Different sections come and go regularly, finally leading into one which finishes on a strong chord.

This is the music I was born to listen to. I just love its intangible, introspective soundscapes.

On to the Third Quartet. Titled *Willink tetraptych* and written in 1979, it was inspired by a work of *fantastic realist* Dutch artist Albert Carel Willink. A *tetraptych* is a group of four paintings or pieces of art placed together, or next to each other and displayed as one. The quartet consists of four named movements, likely corresponding to the set of four paintings.

Anteaters – This short movement opens with a strong, slightly dissonant melody before moving into some pizzicato statements and scurrying sounds. The violin returns and is followed by the ensemble with some longing melodies over a calm background. There is a passage of dissonant shimmering violins, which leads to some rhythmic statements with a serene violin in its highest register, sustaining a very quiet wispy note. The ensemble stops, leaving the violin to continue with the note to the end.

The Superfluous Witness – A busy introduction to this movement soon subsides to a whisper, before picking up the dynamics again. After some dissonant action there is a series of long pauses, interspersed with ensemble interjections. Now the cello goes into pizzicato and another short pause ensues. I just realised that these pauses are not silences, they are inaudible musical spaces – it sounds like the recording engineers used the full capabilities of digital recording to achieve this rather annoying result. Some quivering violins form a melodic phrase and rhythmic interjections follow. Again we are back with that sustained note from the previous movement, to conclude.

Mrs Fopma – A very measured section introduces this movement. Fascinating harmonised melodies form, bringing a wonderful mood, with touches of mild dissonance. The cello makes melodic statements and finally, goes solo. Now the violins return, similar to the opening section and the dynamics slowly increase with the melodic statements becoming more assertive. A solo violin soars over this passage before it returns to the opening mood again. This quiet is sustained, with the cello being prominent near the end, which is two soft cello notes.

The Eternal Scream – The finale is not as frantic as its title may suggest. It is busy however, and dissonant motifs overlay a sparse violin melody. The cello leads for a short time until the mood dissipates, leading into an almost rubato section. Another pause introduces a charming, mildly dissonant harmonised violin line. Now that solo note recurs and is ended by more interjections, these are softer now. This is reminiscent of the previous movement and ends in a similar manner.

Van Delden has certainly worked out his style – there is so much measured abstraction in these works, but they are sublime. Another characteristic is never standing still, the music is always moving on.

The review CD titled *Delden: Complete String Quartets*, on the MDG label, is performed by the Utrecht String Quartet and is available on Amazon UK. The three quartets are all on YouTube and earsense.

Listenability: Fascinating controlled, gently abstract works. Very entertaining.

— ooOoo —

Frederick Delius [1862–1934]

Nationality: British
Quartets: One
Style: Late Romantic

String Quartet No. 1

Frederick Theodore Albert Delius was a giant of British musical circles at the beginning of the twentieth century. He wrote his one string quartet in 1916.

The work opens in a wonderfully lilting manner with attractive violin melodies intertwining. A brief pizzicato relief returns to the opening feeling – this is luxuriant music. Another pizzicato interlude leads the violins to follow the viola. The music surges now, and the ensemble are as one as they move into a persistent phrase before the intensity drops, with hints of that phrase returning. A recapitulation of the opening melody follows, but it soon moves into variations. The melodies are less expansive now and a brief pause brings the music back to life. The sound is vigorous and the violins rise above the ensemble with much energy. A brief, joyful violin statement leads to a sedate conclusion to the movement.

The second movement is brief and features a dominant violin at tempo. There are episodes of call and response before the violin again takes charge. The viola has a melodic section to express itself until it is absorbed back into the ensemble – the melodies just seem so British. Now the first violin leads another call and response before finishing on a bright motif.

The next movement, titled *Late Swallows* by Delius, is the longest in the work. It is slow, but still optimistic. The cello echoes the violin's opening melody and the ensemble works this melody through a set of attractive variations. Now, a hint of sadness is revealed, even though the previous melody is still being developed, while a minor tonality is at work here. A brief pause introduces a new mood which is sparse and features a recurring melody, delicately harmonised by the ensemble. The sparsity leads to a deep, slightly lamenting feeling, which continues for some time before a solo violin wafts over a quiet ensemble to conclude the section. What follows is even more delicate, not much can be heard but for the violin. The status quo is resumed as violin and ensemble combine for a short statement. We are still in a lament, however, and the cello has some

122

statements to make. The music becomes measured again, it is very precious with the end coming on a sustained, faded violin tone.

The final movement opens with some rhythmic chords, but soon drops into a melodic passage before a brisk tempo ensues and melody gives way to rhythm. The previous, scant melody resumes and there is much rhythmic variation. Now the violin takes its rightful place and leads the ensemble in a considered manner as the earlier brisk tempo returns, with the cello being particularly busy. As the end approaches, some strong chordal phrases are heard and the work concludes.

Delius being British, I went straight to Amazon UK and found over one hundred versions, mostly reasonably priced. My review copy was the Brodsky Quartet on the ASV label, coupled with Edward Elgar's String Quartet. This CD also serves as the basis for my later discussion of the Elgar.

There are several versions, including the Brodskys on Spotify, and YouTube. If you wish to hear it beautifully played by the British Fitzwilliam Quartet, it's on earsense.

Listenability: A charming Late Romantic work.

— ooOoo —

David Diamond [1915–2005]

Nationality: American
Quartets: Eleven
Style: Contemporary

String Quartets Nos. 1 & 6

David Diamond wrote eleven symphonies together with his eleven string quartets. The quartets were written between 1940 and the early 2000s. Quite a substantial timeframe really.

String Quartet No. 1 is in one movement with three tempo markings, adagio - allegro - andante, so basically it should be pretty slow, but it doesn't turn out that way. The opening notes remind me of Mahler, it just sounds so symphonic. It's also a little like Charles Ives – very American. The stately opening moves through a pastoral section until we begin to experience some jagged edges and a swirling of notes. The music takes on a serious tone in the allegro tempo – there is also plenty of forward movement here. It finally settles as a Mahler-like mood returns, the tempo disappears and we are back into the opening. There is a distinct pause in the proceedings, as if needed to gather one's thoughts. This whole middle period is all about moving towards the final andante. It doesn't get more pastoral than this, an early American soundscape, the beauty of which is remarkable. Then, the tempo lifts and the music is on the move again. The rural sound remains but it is on a more positive note as flurries are everywhere and the energy is infectious. As we move toward the end, the rhythm dissipates but returns for one final closing flourish. This is a fine first string quartet.

String Quartet No. 5 is also on this CD but I won't be discussing it. It was written in 1960 and, to my ears, it sounds more modern than No. 6, even rather angry at times.

String Quartet No. 6 is in two movements and was written in 1962. The first movement shows a lot of progression from the first quartet. It begins with a slow, atonal lament. This is the music for which I paid my money. Mysterious and unsettling, it has a sense of agitation that is not intense, but you can feel it. Slowly, a period of chaos emerges, all the while retaining the low intensity before the volume comes up and we proceed with some angular, slight aggression. This relents and moves back into the abstraction of a formless movement, wandering freely through several spatial soundscapes.

The opening of the second movement, marked adagio, is reminiscent of Bela Bartok's First String Quartet with its sparse melodies. It quickly and quietly moves into a tempo. After a time, this dissipates, leaving the melody to wander freely around some long forgotten scene. The movement continues to alternate between slow, atonal assertions and jumpy melodic sections. One of these is pure pizzicato. As it moves inexorably to its conclusion, it still manages to continue with alterations in texture and approach.

Wikipedia refers to Diamond as '*a tonal, sometimes modal composer whose work was overtaken by the dominance of the atonal movement*'. In my opinion, his quartets contain large slabs of atonality and dissonance. His work however, is always kept in check, both technically and emotionally.

The review CD is Volume 3 of a set of Diamond's *Complete Quartets* on the Albany Records label, performed by the Potomac String Quartet. The set is freely available on Amazon US.

Two volumes of the set are on my Spotify and many of Diamond's quartets are also available on YouTube and earsense.

Listenability: Satisfying, mostly measured works.

Ernst Dohnanyi [1877–1960]

Nationality: Hungarian
Quartets: Three
Style: Early Modern

String Quartet No. 3

Besides his many compositions, Dohnanyi was also a conductor and fine pianist. Wikipedia cites two quotes – Dohnanyi as a *'victim of Nazism'*, and *'was a forgotten hero of the Holocaust resistance'*. He stayed in Europe during the war, but emigrated to the US in 1946, where he took up various musical posts.

The Third String Quartet was written in 1926 and contains three movements. It opens in a charming manner, as the violins search for a melody. A violin expresses lyrically in a low register and the piece moves into a tempo, with alluring violin lines. Melodic development persists and there is a dash of Impressionism here – it sounds quite French. Suddenly the mood becomes more rhythmic, and more serious. The violins excel here as brief, random fragments lead into a probing violin section. The propulsion returns and the violins dominate as they exchange phrases, with not much input from the other players, in a virtuosic performance from the violins. Occasionally they release the tension for a time and drop back into an Impressionistic feeling – this is a most attractive passage. The intensity gradually increases as the ensemble achieves a powerful rhythmic impetus. The virtuoso violins return for a time and quickly move to the conclusion, a sharp sweeping chordal effect.

An andante tempo introduces the middle movement, with a touch of elegance – it is almost Classical in style. Gentle and fetching melodies dominate, the cello being supportive in its strong statements. A pause brings with it a dancing tempo and the violins are joyous. The cello is still prominent as the violins negotiate enticing melodies and another brief pause introduces a serious tone where the violins construct harmonised melodies over a rhythmic viola motif. There are tonal changes and the intensity rises and falls – again, the violins dominate. Now it becomes pastoral and the melodies less serious, but with a strong sense of purpose. This music displays great emotion, and a brief cello interlude lowers the intensity even further. The melodies become sparse and wistful, and remain so to the end. It is a marvellous piece of writing.

The final movement begins with a galloping tempo and the music becomes very busy although it still maintains that Classical feeling. The galloping dissipates and the feeling becomes more modern, and slightly burlesque for a time. Now we have a recapitulation of the opening theme, which is energised. A playful period ensues as the tempo rises to the ridiculously fast, and the piece is concluded with several strong chords.

This is a relatively early modern work, however it shows no sign of dissonance, but does look back into the past for some of the forms used. It specifically hints at Debussy, Ravel and Haydn for me, but doesn't really sound like European music from 1926. It also features great rhythmic possibilities and an endless supply of melodic ideas.

The CD review copy is on Naxos, titled *String Quartets Nos. 1 and 3*, performed by the Aviv Quartet. This version and several other combinations of two quartets are available on Amazon US and UK.

Several versions exist on Spotify and all of the three quartets are on YouTube and earsense.

Listenability: A melodic Early Modern work.

— oo0oo —

Gaetano Donizetti [1797–1848]

Nationality: Italian
Quartets: Nineteen
Style: Late Classical

String Quartet No. 10

Donizetti's String Quartet No. 10 would have to be one of the earliest quartets I've discussed, but a promise is a promise – string quartets from 1800 on. The work is in four movements and, importantly, is in the key of G minor, which gives it a serious sound. It also contains two slow movements, which is probably why I was drawn to it.

The quartet commences with a string of evenly spaced minor chords before a slow melody begins to unfold, following the harmonies of the opening chords. Now a rhythmic pattern is set up in the accompaniment and a new melody is developed. A solo violin phrase terminates the rhythmic patterns and another melody is developed over a sumptuous layer of chords. The opening melody returns and is embellished, as a background of gentle accompaniment ensues. A solo violin phrase moves into a repeated note which brings the movement slowly to an end. Being from the early 1800s, this music is definitely of the Classical era, and is extremely fine writing.

The next movement opens with a minor chord flourish and soon moves into a tempo with the first violin leading the way. It works through various melodies, always with a complementary accompaniment. This has a charming ambience, featuring differing rhythmic patterns as the music unfolds. Now two violins work in tandem to develop the melodic material and lilting melodies give way to a little more intensity which leads to a brief melodic statement, concluding on a flourish.

The third movement, marked larghetto, is stately in a minor key with the melodies sorrowful and heartfelt. After a time a tempo emerges with the first violin contributing long, sweeping phrases as the ensemble drift along in the background. The first violin continues to dominate as the ensemble slowly increases in volume. Now it drops away and the first violin ends on a long, sustained note.

The brief final movement is firmly in the Classical style. This music could be from the 18th century. Its dance form has all instruments contributing to the melodic diversity and development. A steady accompaniment takes us to the conclusion.

Most of Donizetti's string quartets, excepting the six early works, are available on CD. This one, *Donizetti: String Quartets 10-12,* on the CPO label and performed by the Revolutionary Drawing Room, is freely obtainable on Amazon US and UK.

It can be heard on Spotify and YouTube and there are many Donizetti quartets on earsense.

Listenability: A work of great craftsmanship and feeling.

[Image courtesy CPO Records]

Lucien Durosoir [1878–1955]

Nationality: French
Quartets: Three
Style: Early Modern

String Quartet No. 3

I came across Durosoir while browsing an online book in PDF format, *A Guide to Forgotten String Quartets* by Lyle Chan (page 38) which can be Googled. Much of his music was not performed during his lifetime and the quartets were discovered by his son, Luc, after his death. One of the great thrills in writing is in the discovery of an obscure composer, whose work really touches me. Such is the case with Durosoir.

String Quartet No. 3 was written in 1933-34 and is in three movements. The work opens with a steady cello and brilliantly positive violin melodies – it is so French you can smell the croissants and coffee. A somewhat subdued passage is overtaken by the sound of charming melodies and a hint of pizzicato, with the violins having a slight Gypsy nature – this extended opening section is a beautiful piece of writing. Suddenly the work bursts into life, probably not unlike Paris traffic. The opening melodies then return, alternating for a time with the livelier parts. A pause brings about a thoughtful moment when the violin produces a longing melody, which is occasionally interrupted by the previous lively section. The longing violin does persist however, and the effect is wonderful. Now a new melody takes shape, bright and uninhibited, constantly probing. This feeling continues for some time, before a strong flourish leads to a lone violin playing the last note.

The next movement begins with a sparse, but elegant feeling. The cello anchors a wistful violin melody that promotes calm and a measured sense of abstraction. A slight rise in intensity doesn't last and the music drifts back into serenity. There is a tranquility as the violin meanders, seemingly searching for a melody. A change now comes over the piece and violin melodies drift skyward and bring a rhythmic intensity for the first time. The composer won't be pinned down as he constantly changes the atmosphere, leading to a light and airy feeling. The violins float as a moderately serious texture is quickly dealt with, and a longing melody takes over, with an intangible feeling. The violins begin to build but as usual, it doesn't last. A poignancy shapes the conclusion.

The final movement has a steady pulse and is of a marginally serious nature, and again, a little chaotic. There is a violin phrase that returns often and, as before, there are many moods, most of them are also revisited. Eventually it gives way to a pleasant violin interlude, before reintroducing the pulse and the chaos. There is a hint of melodic development of the earlier phrase by a strange sounding violin, it's almost a strangled tone. The opening feeling returns and is developed for a time. Now a completely new feeling is introduced which is sparse and introspective – the cello laments as the violins continue to drift with thin melodies. It is the most melancholic moment in the whole quartet and is sustained until the end, leaving us with a feeling of sadness.

This quartet, along with the two earlier works, show Durosoir as being very French, to the extent of evoking memories of Debussy and Ravel. Having said that, his quartets are also unique, both in the use of form and harmony. Despite his influences, the composer is definitely his own man. Added to this, all three quartets are quite different in character. Listening to No. 1 while writing, I can tell that it has a harder edge to it than No. 3.

The review CD is available as *Durosoir: Quatuors a cordes* or *String Quartets 1-3*, on the Alpha label, performed by Quatuor Diotima, on Amazon US and Presto Classical. This CD is on Spotify but I couldn't find it anywhere else.

Listenability: A terrific recording of three fine works by an individualistic composer, paradoxically, steeped in the French tradition.

— ooOoo —

Pascal Dusapin [born 1955]

Nationality: French
Quartets: At least seven
Style: Modern Contemporary

With Orchestra
String Quartet No. 6

According to Wikipedia on Dusapin, '*His music is marked by its microtonality, tension, and energy*'. I don't know about the microtonality, but the other two attributes are definitely evident in this work. String Quartet No. 6 was written for String Quartet and Orchestra, and titled *The Hinterland*. On my review CD, no longer available, it is in one movement. Strangely, the orchestra is not particularly prominent in this piece.

The work opens with a propulsive, machine-like rhythm, together with string sound effects which are at times reminiscent of bird calls or flutes – there are plenty of glissandos here. The orchestra can barely be heard, although it may be that they provide some of the persistent rhythm. It is quite a dense passage and it is a little difficult to distinguish individual instruments. The intensity rises, with cello phrases interjecting. Next, double basses enter, leading to a brief quiet passage, however the rhythm soon returns. I hear the orchestra now, in the background, purely textural, playing sustained chords. The dynamics fluctuate regularly and some of the violin flourishes reappear as bird calls. A chaos now comes over the piece, turning it into a cacophony – it's very intense. Sounds of the orchestra reappear, with the double basses being prominent.

A brief pause brings a meditative feeling to the work as two violins play sparse, emotive melodies. A cello makes an extended solo statement, replete with string sound effects, leading to the return of the rhythm and further chaos. The violins break free and concoct a passage of an almost frenzied nature. A rhythm again ensues, this time it is more orchestral. The two violins return and, for a moment, there is absolute silence. The quartet then continue to play in a chaotic, but not frenetic manner. Another violin dominated phase unfolds but it is soon joined by the ensemble in a long section. Presently, some orchestral rumblings can be heard and we have a return to the opening feeling, which this time is pure rhythm, featuring mostly string quartet.

Another pause brings in a sweeping orchestral section, which doesn't last. It reminds me of a *mellotron,* which is a keyboard instrument containing tape recordings of orchestral string sounds. The string quartet returns, filled with extreme energy – the texture is reminiscent of some of Elliott Carter's later quartets, with an extended section of dissonance. Orchestral interjections bring incredible tension to the music, but this soon dissipates. The end comes with soft flute-like violin sounds, together with other abstract murmurings before the very last note sounds, like a flute, but it may be a violin.

This piece is a journey, a wild ride, and very modern. It is filled with musical notes, but that doesn't necessarily make it music – it is more a rhythmic soundscape where the rules of music do not apply.

The only available version, on the Aeon label, performed by the Arditti String Quartet, and the Orchestre Philharmonique de Radio France, is in five movements, and runs the same length as mine. It also contains String Quartet No. 7, which runs for almost 39 minutes – this too appears to be more sound than music, featuring many silences, together with seemingly random interjections. It has no tempo.

This CD is available at Amazon UK and *Hinterland* can be found on YouTube along with several other early quartets. All of the composer's quartets are on earsense.

Listenability: Difficult for some – a very Modern Contemporary work.

Henri Dutilleux [1916–2013]

Nationality: French
Quartets: One – FOSQC
Style: Modern Contemporary

Ainsi la Nuit
String Quartet No. 1

Dutilleux was much later than most of the members of the FOSQC. His quartet, titled *Ainsi la nuit*, which I believe translates to *Thus the night*, was written from 1973-76. Apparently, before it was composed, Dutilleux studied intensely the quartets of Beethoven, Bartok and particularly, Webern's *Six Bagatelles* – thanks, Wiki.

I must confess to being somewhat ambivalent about this work in the past; some parts seemed to grate with me. I can never work out why it is so popular, especially among the theorists. However, somebody suggested it via email so I thought I would try it. The version that I will review is in seven named (all in French) movements, performed by the Juilliard Quartet, who premiered the work. I've noticed that several other versions have an extra five short movements inserted. I believe they all contain the same music, they just seem to be bridging passages. The Orpheus String Quartet compress it into just two movements.

Nocturne opens with a slightly dissonant chord, followed by some string sound effects, before the two violins play short motifs. Several violin swoops are heard and one violin forms a melody. There is a lot of sound in the background – it may be a pizzicato, an effect or a violin melody. A repeated motif forms and is picked up by the ensemble, which leads to the end.

Miroir d'espace has a string sound effect introduction, before random notes appear from each instrument. It doesn't last long and the movement is basically all string sound effects, with the occasional violin interjection.

Litanies starts with a solo violin. There is a strong rhythmic motif presented with string effects spread around it. The motif ceases and the first violin plays some melodic material, with more effects, particularly pizzicato. It seems to stop on a random note.

Litanies 2 is the longest movement in the work at just under four minutes. The start is reminiscent of some of Morton Feldman's *String Quartet II*. It has a longing melody, swapped between the two violins. Recurring motifs are supported by abstruse interludes from the ensemble – I really like the level of abstraction in this movement.

Constellations starts frantically, before settling into a passage of further string sound effects. Violin and cello melodies coexist, with a sense of birdsong, to end.

Nocturne 2 is the shortest movement at 51 seconds duration. A bird sounding violin acts like a bird too, with deliberate swoops. The other violin offers supportive phrases before the movement degenerates into pure string sound effects.

Temps suspendu has another Feldman-like introduction with subtle violin melodies. There are some scurrying sounds but mostly it is two violins with effects in the background – this is quite engaging really. The violins continue to assert themselves for the duration.

You can probably tell by now that it is not a tonal work. I don't know about Beethoven or Bartok, but I do hear a lot of Webern, particularly his penchant for miniature movements, and the serial style in general, in this piece. It's definitely more abstract than the Berg that I have previously discussed. For me, it is basically a dissonant soundscape, but I did enjoy it.

There is a saying *'all music is sound, but not all sound is music'*. This particular piece is music to me. I believe that some late 20th century composers crossed the line from sound into noise, for its own sake. This however, is just an opinion, and we all hear and relate to music differently, and that's admirable. End of sermon.

As to availability, there are several versions at Amazon US and UK. Being only around 18 minutes long, it will always be paired with another one or two quartets. Some CDs have it together with the Debussy and Ravel quartets. I am always ready to recommend the Juilliard String Quartet – their version of the above three quartets is on Sony Classical.

The Dutilleux is on Spotify and YouTube, with three versions to be found on earsense.

Listenability: Not for the faint-hearted. Would suit closet Modernist. However the combination with the Debussy and Ravel is attractive.

— oo0oo —

Antonin Dvorak [1841–1904]

Nationality: Czech
Quartets: Fourteen
Style: Romantic

The Essence
String Quartet No. 10

I regard Antonin Dvorak as one of the giants of the Romantic era. I constantly find myself review referring to a Dvorak influence when discussing another composer's work. He is one of my favourite quartet composers, just so distinctive.

The Tenth Quartet is in four movements and opens with a strong cello part leading to a charming melody. A quick chord change brings about a rhythm, and the violins dance as an exciting new melody develops. It is typical Dvorak, folk melodies with his splendid, distinctive accompanying harmonised lines. The music rambles through the harmonies at will, sometimes with rhythmic changes. Then follows a recapitulation and the opening cello pattern returns, with the opening melodies also restated and redeveloped. Again a key change brings variations to the piece and a fresh feeling is introduced, with new melodies and harmonic backgrounds. The violins swoop in a bird like fashion and propel the piece forward. After a time, earlier melodies are again revisited, all with the composer's characteristic folksy harmony. There is a long phase that darts here and there, all the time moving forward – this is brilliant writing. The composer has several melodic sections to work with and is able to sustain interest for some time. The initial theme returns to take us to the end of the movement, with a high violin melody and a gentle chord.

The next movement begins with a delicate melody over strummed cello chords – I think this melody is one of the composer's finest. It is first developed, and then restated before another gorgeous melody arises out of the first, as the violin accelerates for a brief period. A recapitulation ensues and then we have a splendid moment in tempo, with the violins so playful. There is plenty of melodic development here, along with many tempo changes. The slow opening is hinted at, and then reharmonised as a light, airy interlude concludes the movement.

The third movement is again slow, opening with a subdued ensemble. The feeling is simply longing and a violin melody is answered by the ensemble twice, before moving into a swirling fragment until the call and response resumes. A high solo melody transforms into a rich ensemble sound as descending chords bring a new melody to light. There is a sense of majesty as the violins probe new feelings. A long section takes shape at a moderate tempo, and there remains a lingering poignancy with the cello salient. The violins carry the music forward now and it ends on a sustained chord.

A rapid violin leads the final movement and is sustained for some time. Brief, slow interludes are regularly swept aside as the violin constantly returns. These contrasting phases go on for some time until the quick tempo eventually abates and a new theme is introduced. A fine harmonised line for the two violins comes and goes, and there is now a final energised fragment as a violin states the melody in three separate tempos, the last of which is at breakneck pace. We are left with a flourish to end.

I believe this work, Opus 51, marks the beginning of the mature stage of the composer's string quartet development. You can hear in this and the later works, the key elements of the composer's style. These include: modal and pentatonic scales; folk-like chords, melodies and rhythms; the highly personal nature of his harmonised melodic lines; the wonderful use of trills as an effect; and his unusually prominent use of the cello as a melodic device. I've always considered Dvorak as one of the most influential composers in the first half of the twentieth century – even Schoenberg drew from Dvorak in his 1896 quartet. In particular, his influence permeates throughout the European string quartet repertoire, at least until 1950 when the whole genre started to diffuse into many disparate, sometimes highly personal styles.

As to availability, over 160 versions exist on Amazon US and UK, and it's not even his most popular quartet. I suggest a pairing with one of the later quartets, especially Nos. 12, 13 or 14.

There are several versions of this work on Spotify, many on YouTube and seven performances can be found on earsense – enjoy!

Listenability: Classic Dvorak, with all his bells and whistles.

String Quartet No. 12

Dvorak spent three years in America in the early 1890s. He took up the position of Director at the National Conservatory of Music in New York. During this time he spent a summer holiday in Spillville, a small Czech community in Iowa. While there, he completed his Symphony No. 9 and wrote a string quartet and a string quintet. This String Quartet No. 12, Opus 96 was titled *The American*, as was the lesser known string quintet, Opus 97.

The distinctive sound of this piece comes mainly from the use of pentatonic scales. These only have five notes as compared to the seven notes in a normal Western music scale. The composer also found inspiration in African-American spirituals, native American-Indian music and American folksong.

The opening movement sets an atmosphere that continues throughout this piece with the use of pentatonics, giving the music a clear 'open' sound. The incisive opening theme is stated on the cello and then picked up by the violin, with a magnificent trilled background. For me, it is one of the most striking melodies to be found in the repertoire and is truly powerful music. Now the violins craft a gentle melody before we have a recapitulation of the opening theme. Several chord changes impinge on the development of this theme. The intensity rises, all the while reworking the opening melodic material. Now it returns at a leisurely tempo and a change to a minor key brings new, interesting melodic ideas. Further variations are played out before a slow period ensues, evoking an earlier sub-theme. Three restatements of the opening phrase, at volume, conclude the movement – this is a fabulous piece of writing.

The second movement is a slow lament which this time uses a minor pentatonic scale, giving it a graceful, mesmeric quality. It is marked lento and opens with a slow cello phrase before the violin enters with an attractive melody. It is melancholy, and the longing melody is developed over a subtle background until a chord change brings a little optimism to the piece. The sadness returns and again, another chord change brings with it a slightly more positive feeling. Remaining on the edge of melancholy, the composer develops some wonderful melodies and violin follows violin in a stunning, gentle passage. The feeling drops back to one violin with subtle accompaniment. The violin is again longing, in a most passionate way. The cello enters and repeats a violin phrase twice, in different registers, and the violin returns for a faded end.

The next movement starts in a positive manner which promotes a sprightly mood. A slow section quickly gives way to more joyful music and a quote from the first movement is reworked. Shimmering violins lead to a rhythm section and there is much ado with the violins expressing positive melodies. Now we have further repeats of earlier themes, which lead to a conclusion.

The finale has a folk character with the cello playing on the two and the four beat, which enhances this feeling. A period of descending tonalities follows, and the intensity briefly rises. Not for long however, and we move into an ever so slow passage. A violin gently struts before the intensity rises again and we have a recapitulation of the opening melody. A moderate tempo ensues as the violins investigate the melody. Now there is a sweeping feeling which builds to a crescendo, finishing the work on a strong flourish.

It is a magnificent, magical quartet and strengthens my feeling that Dvorak is one of the finest Romantic composers.

There is some discussion as to the extent of the influence of folk themes in the work. It has been suggested that there are direct links to extant folk themes but, to my knowledge no one has ever come up with an example. I believe the themes acted more as inspiration, rather than influence. The composer was already familiar with pentatonic scales as they are found in folk music all over the world, and European composers have used them extensively.

Opus 96 has become one of the most popular quartets in the idiom and hence, can be found on many recordings. My recommendation is the Janacek String Quartet which is coupled with the String Quintet, Opus 97 that was also written on the summer holiday, played by members of the Vienna Octet. It is still available on the Decca label. However, as noted below, there is a marvellous two-CD version of the above performances coupled with two earlier works, a string quintet and a string sextet. This set is on the Australian budget label Eloquence. You may have to seek these out but they are well worth it.

Many versions of this quartet are available on Spotify, YouTube and earsense.

I shall leave you with a quote from Dvorak – *'I know that I would never have written my quartet if I had never seen America'.*

Listenability: A magnificent example of the genre.

The Last Quartets
String Quartets Nos. 13 & 14

Dvorak's last two quartets were No. 13 in G major, Opus 106, and No. 14 in A major, Opus 105. The numbers are out of order as Opus 105 was started before Opus 106 but not finished until after the latter.

Opus 106 is in four movements. It is a substantial work, clocking in at just over 31 minutes on my review CD. The first movement opens with a typical flourish and a charming melody is introduced, and then another, followed by a return to the former. Now a new, plaintive melody ensues, with harmonies from the ensemble. After eight minutes, the composer is still working with melodies and phrases from the first two minutes. He hurries to the end with great vigour. The strength of the writing gives this movement an orchestral flavour.

Movement two is marked adagio and so be it. The tempo is slow and I believe I can hear evidence of the composer's American sojourn here. The melodies are not so obvious until about the three minute mark, when he moves into a pentatonic scale. A brief pause signals a change with solo cello prevailing. Major turns to minor and the movement edges forward, bringing with it a deeply felt sense of the pastoral. The adagio tempo dominates the movement to the end.

The third movement begins with a pure folk melody. It settles in gently and then returns to an earlier theme with a sweeping sense of forward movement on display here. A false ending carries on into a slightly orchestral sound and Dvorak forges his way to the conclusion with wonderful recapitulations of the many melodies he has introduced thus far. This is a very memorable movement.

The finale, marked andante opens quietly before moving into a dance. Rhythmic sections constantly alternate with slow interludes, and melodies from earlier movements are frequently revisited. I find this movement a little long but hey, it's a wild ride.

Now on to Quartet No 14. The first movement, marked adagio – allegro, has the stamp of Beethoven on its opening bars. There is a tremendous sense of longing in this section – a truly special place to be. It quickly moves into more positive territory with hectic rhythms before it returns to the opening melody, with variations. There is movement from major to minor keys which gives the passage further interest. Dvorak is a very conversational composer, his work is scattered with instances of call and response. The energy finally dissipates and leads to another charming melody. After a time, it takes off again and the rhythm predominates, before returning to an earlier melodic theme, with a different treatment. The conclusion is peaceful with the instruments conversing with each other.

Movement two opens with prancing melodies. It then moves into a peace, which is developed using pentatonic scales before the key changes and the tempo returns. The composer has such a distinctive style it is difficult to imagine anyone else composing this music. A brief pause leads back into a positive melody, which is developed in various tempos, mostly of a strident nature. The conclusion is a measured variant of the original melody.

The third movement begins slowly with an enticing long melody that recalls String Quartet No. 12, the one written in America. These last three, twelve through fourteen, do in fact form a set – they share many properties. Now the melody lingers for a while until a rhythmic tempo is established, the cello carrying the other instruments. Then it is back to Czechoslovakia for a time with a simple melody. The use of contrast between major and minor is enchanting and the conclusion is a variation on a previously used theme.

The final movement, marked allegro, starts in the cello, picking up on a melody used earlier before moving into a galloping style for a time. The melody returns, with a further major to minor change. Melodic development abounds and two quotes from Beethoven's Late Quartets can be found here. The cello leads the ensemble into a new melody, as old material is constantly reworked and another brief Beethoven quote is heard. The end is frenetic and final.

Strangely, to find both String Quartets Nos. 13 and 14 on one disc is difficult, unless you have 1200 British pounds to spare. The same disc is also available used, for four British pounds. They can be obtained on separate discs, very easily. Please refer to the comments on versions in the previous works. There is also a terrific *Dvorak: The Essential String Quartets* by the Panocha Quartet on the Supraphon label, containing the composer's last five quartets, Nos. 10-14, which are all fine works. It is a 3-CD set at a reasonable price.

Spotify has these two works, but you may have to specify the number 13 (or 14) to find them. Many of Dvorak's quartets, including Nos. 13 & 14 are available on YouTube. You can also hear String Quartet No. 14 performed by the Stamitz Quartet and many other fine ensembles at earsense.

Listenability: Two magnificent, mature quartets.

String Quintet in E-flat Major

Aside from Dvorak's fourteen string quartets, he also composed several very attractive works for augmented string ensembles. In this instance, his Opus 97, the quintet instrumentation is two violins, two violas and a cello. Written while Dvorak was in America, it came immediately after his wonderful String Quartet No. 12, *The American*, and shares that work's title, as well as the prominent use of pentatonic scales in its strong melodic construction. The quintet is in four movements and quite substantial in length.

The opening is very considered and proceeds forward with superbly crafted melodies over a sombre cello background. A brief rhythmic foray creates a stronger melodic section. For me, the melodies presented here are transcendent in their beauty. Pentatonic phrases abound and the piece gathers a strong rhythmic impetus. A return to the opening theme coexists with a period of descending harmonies that are often revisited during the movement, and, throughout the work. Persistent changes into a minor tonality are extremely attractive and a stately passage simply sparkles with life before the descending harmonies temper the mood. Earlier melodic phrases are repeated, before leading into a sparse passage with gentle evocations of the principal theme that moves to a quiet termination. This brief look into Dvorak's world is most noble, and very satisfying.

The next movement, marked allegro, is a gentle romp that gathers intensity with pentatonic melodies in abundance over a rhythmic accompaniment. Again, it is not particularly dynamic and occupies a middle ground of energy. A change comes over the work as a lone violin laments over a pizzicato background. We then have a further return to a tempo, although the music could still be described as light and airy. The composer seems to be exercising a sense of control until there is a final flourish.

A larghetto movement follows, one that reveals Dvorak at his finest, invoking a melancholy feeling with the gentlest of melodies edging forward. A hint of the earlier descending harmonies is not developed, instead another period of transcendence unfolds. The mood finally gives way to a measured tempo and a wonderful, flowing melodic line before a return to the opening character, this time with some rhythmic development. Violins move into the high register in a delightful manner, before falling back into the sombre mood. Slowly, the composer begins to develop a new section with a fluttering of bows, leading to an unusual approach to constructing a melody. After a pause, a dynamic passage ensues, with new melodies to be found. The tempo dissipates but the melodies survive, moving through several different backgrounds and a return to the descending harmonic motif is heard twice before a series of translucent chords conclude.

The finale opens in a very positive mood, replete with hints of folk melodies and firm but measured rhythms. After a recapitulation of the first theme, the music becomes thoughtful and those descending harmonies recur, this time in a different context. The rhythm soon picks up again and a subtle change in harmony leads to a wonderfully cheerful passage, which includes references to some earlier motifs. With several mood swings between minor and major tonalities, the music constantly reinvents itself, and moves into a section of strong melodic chords, one of which is sustained to complete the work.

My review copy contains the Quintet Opus 97 paired with the String Quartet No. 12 Opus 96 on the Decca label, which is now a little scarce. Fortunately the Australian budget label Eloquence has issued the contents on a delightful 2-CD set, *Dvorak: String Quartet, Quintets, and Sextet*. This issue is available on Amazon US with fine performances at a very nice price. There are hundreds of other pairings of Opus 97 on a single CD – my suggestion would be the Keller Quartet with String Quartet No. 12, which is also on Amazon US.

I am very fond of Dvorak's string chamber music and intend to discuss at least a couple of his other augmented ensembles in the future.

There are several performances on Spotify, YouTube and a marvellous version by the Vienna Philharmonia Quintet on earsense.

Listenability: Essential listening for those predisposed to Dvorak's wonderful chamber music.

[Image courtesy Supraphon label]

— oo0oo —

Edward Elgar [1857–1934]

Nationality: British
Quartets: One
Style: Late Romantic

String Quartet No. 1

Elgar's string quartet opens with scything violins and great depth of feeling. A powerful passage unfolds with fine melodies and plangent support from the cello. Harmonised lines abound until the mood turns thoughtful. This peaceful passage gradually increases in intensity and the violins positively resonate with energy. A pause brings about another thoughtful section, but this too, has an underlying feeling of intensity. Now breaking free, the violins become rhapsodic and generate an undercurrent of momentum in an emotionally charged section. Strong, harmonised lines gradually diminish and lead to a gentler melodic mood with powerful violin interplay, before the music moves into another introspective moment. A prominent cello part supports the violins as they rise to the occasion. Tonally, the violins have a rich sound and their further harmonised lines slowly decrease in intensity to finish.

The next movement is pastoral, gentle even, as the ensemble presents a wonderfully melodic mood – this is finely crafted British writing. The rich sonority of the ensemble is stunning as they create numerous melodic lines before a slight ensemble pulse begins to emerge, but it too is gentle. Overlapping violin lines are most lyrical and the feeling moves into a minimal section for two violins, which doesn't last. Now a violin strikes out with a forceful melody and carries the ensemble along with it until this is eventually tempered, and we have another subtle, pastoral moment. A prolonged peaceful passage unfolds and the beauty is refined. One violin reaches skyward, then descends to rejoin the other as both move into a subtle musical space, leading to a most satisfying ending.

The finale opens with strong violins, many flourishes and some rhythmic punctuation. The music becomes energised and swirling violins contribute evocative, harmonised lines. This is followed by a sensitive section where the violins express gently until they move into a tempo and push hard, while all the time retaining the beauty, albeit powerfully. The cello presents some sonorous lines and the violins respond in kind. Now the cello reaches out and for a time, leads the violins. A rhythmic violin, reminiscent of the first movement opening, leads to a return of the energised, harmonised flourishes. Some racing virtuoso lines move to a fine conclusion.

This is music that keeps you wondering will the composer ever run out of melodic ideas – he doesn't. The playing on this performance by the Brodsky Quartet is superb as they really present this music in a most favourable light.

The review CD by the Brodskys, on the ASV label, comes paired with the only string quartet of Elgar's contemporary Frederick Delius. I reviewed this recently and already it has been assigned to the available as *New and Used* category on Amazon US and UK. The UK site has it as an MP3 download, although sixty-six other recordings of the work can be found there, with many different pairings.

Several performances of the work, including the Brodskys, can be found on Spotify and there are a host of clips on YouTube as well as eight versions on earsense.

Listenability: A Late Romantic masterpiece.

[Elgar in 1931 – Wiki Commons]

— oo0oo —

Catharinus Elling [1858–1942]

Nationality: Norwegian
Quartets: Two
Style: Romantic

The String Quartets

Elling's string quartets are not numbered but are referred to as the D major, from 1897 and the A minor, from 1903. Quoting Wikipedia – *Elling is principally known for his extensive work on collecting and recording Norwegian folk music* – this influence can definitely be heard in the quartets.

The D Major Quartet, in four movements, opens in a lively manner with obvious folk-derived melodies. These are beautifully crafted and evoke a most optimistic mood. After a time, they seem to become slightly withdrawn before returning to the opening character. A sense of peace comes over the work but this soon leads to a frenetic violin passage. Then follows a brief respite from the

141

insistent tempo, but the joyful utterances are resumed. Sweeping violin phrases lead to a dramatic section which ends on a strong chord.

The next, andante movement is in a minor key and the feeling is one of expressive violins over a strong harmonic background. A pause brings about a stately mood, with powerful harmonised melodic lines – this is a moment of great beauty and wonder. To me, it evokes the best of Dvorak, with the folk idiom again being used as a musical basis of this slow movement. Nearing the end, the music subsides into rich, long, sustained chords.

A brief allegretto movement follows and this time, the composer looks back to the Classical era, with the courtly, measured feeling of a Mozart or Haydn. A pause leads to a jumpy tempo, and slightly frantic violin lines before a return to the opening mood, which is this time accompanied by the sound of pizzicato. I have to say that this melody reminds me of the main theme from *Jesus Christ, Superstar* – both melodically and rhythmically, which of course came over one hundred years later. It is certainly not unusual to find classical themes appearing in popular music.

The final movement is again stately, this time with a tempo marking of lento, producing a gorgeous opening melody. A pause leads to a lift in tempo and dynamics as a recurrent theme is continuously harmonised with an increased intensity. This section reveals the composer to be an exceptional melodist of great imagination, the music is bursting with interesting melodic ideas. As the movement progresses, the rhythmic impetus is stunning and leads to a powerful flourish to conclude.

The later, A minor Quartet, in three movements is substantially shorter than its precursor and opens cautiously with the minor key evident. A leading violin expresses several fine melodies, closely related to the minor tonality. There is even an air of Gypsy music at times until a return to traditional harmonies and a rhythmic character, which continues to a hectic ending.

The next movement, marked andante, is the longest of the work. A rich harmonic carpet introduces a simple, plaintive melody which gradually becomes a little torrid. The simplicity is resumed and the ensemble trade attractive melodic lines with an ostinato viola passage in the background. Now the torrid feeling reappears for a short section before the opening is revisited. Again, overlapping melodic lines evoke a feeling of simplicity and beauty as the cello offers fine support with resonant harmonies and the violins continue their storytelling. The ending is almost transparent as a shrill violin and sombre chord are heard.

The final movement shifts into a major tonality and another simple, melodic passage is developed. A change in harmony brings about a new section with the violins in a close dialogue. Questions are asked with responses presented and, as the intensity rises, free-flowing melodies abound, together with further evidence of a dialogue. The end comes as a surprise with a scattered handful of notes. This has been a brief movement.

The review CD, titled *Catharinus Elling: Quartets*, on the Cimax Classics label, is performed by the Engegård Quartet. The disc contains both quartets together with a dramatic, substantial piano quartet and is available on Amazon US and UK.

This disc is on Spotify and YouTube while both string quartets can be heard on earsense.

Listenability: Belies the Romantic label, creating works of melodic and rhythmic delight.

— oo0oo —

George Enescu [1881–1955]

Nationality: Romanian
Quartets: Two
Style: Early Modern

String Quartet No. 2

Of Enescu's two string quartets, I have selected the second as it has a more abstract flavour than the first. It was written in 1952 and contains four movements.

The work opens with a solo violin which is soon joined by the second violin, and a slightly abstruse melody meanders through the opening. Support comes from the cello and viola as the melody becomes busy, with several violin sound effects leading into a skittish manner. The violin then dominates to create a beguiling atmosphere. Now the cello moves the music into a tempo and the first violin continues its meandering. Towards the end, there is a hint of darkness and the melody becomes more pronounced. It is all very calm, with the cello taking the movement out, ever so peacefully.

The next movement commences with solo cello, the violins eventually appearing as accompaniment. The cello continues to feature with subtle violin tones in the background, before it drops out and we are left with a slow violin melody, similar to the first movement, which produces a beautifully introspective sound. There is a brief cello return, but it departs leaving the violins to create a most wonderful soundscape. The whole quartet is involved, but only for a short while as the music returns to a violin and intermittent cello. Suddenly the intensity rises and some chord interjections occur. Now it returns to a precious moment – the tempo has gone and all things are sparse. A long pause leads back to the solo cello and a violin joins in to fade to a finish. This is a most intangible, enchanting movement.

The third movement begins with cello again but it is soon overtaken by violins expressing various string sound effects. There are agitated melodies while

143

the cello remains as a pulse – then there is a lot more melodic action. The intensity drops again and we are left with a wonderful, sparse feeling. The cello takes over and ringing violin tones fade to the end.

A loud flourish opens the last movement. The violins are dance-like and well pleased with themselves. The cello and viola join in, thickening the sound, before leading to a sense of sparsity, together with a longing melody. The opening feeling returns for a time, until the ensemble comes back in – now a little chaos and abstraction emerge from the violins. This sustains the feeling for quite a while, the texture is now dense as the quartet plays with aggression. The music is full of flourishes and energetic violin lines. The end is accomplished with a flourish.

This is a quietly intense quartet that employs several hints of modern traits. I found it to be quite satisfying. Many versions of this pairing are on Amazon US and UK. My review copy is the CD on Naxos, *String Quartets 1 & 2,* performed by the Ad Libitum Quartet.

A complete performance, and various single movements, can be found on YouTube. They are also on Spotify and earsense.

Listenability: Interesting – brooding, but not too dark.

— ooOoo —

Robert Erickson [1917–1997]

Nationality: American
Quartets: Four
Style: Contemporary

Corfu and
String Quartet No. 1

Of Erickson's four quartets, two are numbered; 1 and 2, and two are named, *Corfu* and *Solstice*. Quartet No. 2 and both of the named works are in one movement. I am going to discuss String Quartet No. 1 and *Corfu*.

The First Quartet is in three movements and opens with a sprightly abstract feeling as notes seem to fly about the room. There is no obvious melody, the two violins seem to just converse. After a time there is a pause and the music is stripped back to one violin, before the cello joins in and we are back to the opening. It is intangible but pleasing. The intensity rises as it progresses and there is even some harmony to be found. Near the ending, the music becomes a little richer and then goes out with a flourish. I wouldn't call it memorable but that's possibly because very little gets repeated – it's just a piece of mild abstraction. I like it.

144

The next movement begins with a longing solo violin melody, soon to be joined by another violin. Again, there doesn't seem to be any firm relationship between the two instruments. The cello eventually enters, then the viola, and we have another piece of abstraction. The cello rumbles about as if on the sea bottom while violins swim above. It is much slower than the first movement but inhabits a similar soundscape. Winding down, the violins are left to bring about a faded conclusion.

The final movement begins with an energised violin and, as before, the other instruments wander in, seemingly at random. A connection does seem to develop between the two violins here as they occupy the same register. A change ensues and the tempo has gone – this section is quite poignant as the two violins exchange slow melodies. The entrance of the cello slows the tempo even further for a time, but normal service is resumed as the violins parry. I think the word here is entropy, there is no apparent structure. The ending comes with the two violins gradually receding into the distance.

This work is nonrepresentational and definitely not program music. I am drawn to mild abstraction and I like it a lot.

I shall now consider *Corfu*, which as I mentioned previously, is in one movement. The opening is one dissonant chord which fades out fairly quickly, leading to a violin expressing the three notes of a major chord; not normally enough for a memorable melody, but it works here. Interestingly, the opening notes of Mozart's First Symphony are the very same triad. A second violin enters and there is a hint of microtones in the playing. A brief pause ensues before a sustained cello introduces a simple melody in the violin. Now the cello sustains and there are long notes from the violins which do not really define a melody. This gradually gains in intensity and a melody does start to unfold. A violin phrase appears in the high register, and the two violins go it alone in harmony. Sustained violin notes herald a cello melody – the cello is prominent here, with an occasional use of microtones. A violin returns for a sweeping passage as it constantly changes register, becoming shrill and using harmonics for effect.

Suddenly a loud chord is heard and the violins introduce further microtonal melodies. They duet for a time until the cello enters in support and the shrill notes return leading to another poignant interlude. There is a drone present which leads to a modal feeling, and a high degree of entropy as the violins wander through the scales. A solo violin leads into a sustained microtonal phrase. If it sounds bleak, it probably is.

The first violin now ventures into shrill territory with subtle harmonics from the second violin. The cello returns and anchors the piece for a time until it begins to assert itself before the violins take control again. The sparsity of this music is rewarding – it leaves time for contemplation. As the end draws near, there is an interruption by a brief, slightly dissonant chord. The last minute features the two violins working their way to a consonant conclusion.

Whilst mildly abstruse, this piece is essentially meditative – again, I like it. When I first heard this music about six months ago, I didn't get it but it feels so right now. Regarding the other two pieces, *Solstice* is again meditative and the Second Quartet more abstract. Apart from String Quartet No. 1, all of the pieces are quite long.

This music is nominally modern but it doesn't contain the negative traits that have been associated with this genre in the past. We are now in an era where, unlike 200 years ago, not everybody writes in the same style. In fact I don't believe there is a common twenty-first century style. *Vive la différence*.

These quartets come on a 2-CD set entitled *Robert Erickson – The Complete String Quartets* on the New World Records label, by the Del Sol Quartet. It is quite pricey on Amazon UK, much cheaper on Amazon US.

The set is on Spotify and all of the works can be heard on YouTube and earsense.

Listenability: Very listenable, and unique stylistically in the sound world that it inhabits. It ticks all of my boxes.

[Image – New World Records – not able to be contacted]

Gabriel Faure [1845–1924]

Nationality: French
Quartets: One – FOSQC
Style: Late Romantic

The String Quartet

Faure wrote his only string quartet in 1924, the last year of his life. The work commences in a rubato manner with the cello featured, in a minor key, until the quartet eventually breaks into tempo in a positive manner. The music now returns to the opening, this time with a lot more support for the cello. Ascending melodic lines give a feeling of immense exhilaration before a recapitulation of the opening melody. A new interlude takes shape, very beautifully. Gently moving forward, it lays out a carpet for the violins to ply their trade. Melodies abound in this measured phase and the cello returns to lead the ensemble through a tranquility to the end.

The opening of the second movement reveals deep feeling. The tempo starts to be obvious as the ensemble supports the first violin in a charming passage – you can feel the intensity rise and fall as the violin leads the way. Now, a positivity emerges and then the music drops back to a lament. The constant tempo gives the movement substance, leading to a broad, expansive phase as the violins express freely, with a slight crescendo, before moving back into a minor key. The cello returns to lead the ensemble until the violins feel a need to take control. This movement is wonderful, so gentle and melodic. It's music that takes you somewhere warm and comfortable.

Solo cello opens the third, and final movement, before resuming a supporting role. The section is mostly positive, occasionally with a touch of angst – the minor key adds to this feeling. A cello return again implements a change, which brings with it an air of mild tension. The violin then sketches out a poignant melody, this is very charming. The tension rises ever so slightly as Faure works this mood for several minutes. I gradually realised that this mood **is** the movement. As is common, the music ends with a brief flourish.

There are 44 versions of this work to be found on Amazon UK, usually paired with some other quartet or, maybe even a chamber work. I quite fancy a pairing with Ravel on the Naxos label, performed by the Ad Libitum Quartet.

This piece is available to sample on Spotify and YouTube. Eight versions of the work can be heard on earsense.

Listenability: Another fine Late Romantic French quartet.

Morton Feldman [1926–1987]

Nationality: American
Quartets: Two
Style: Modern Contemporary

String Quartet II

Feldman referred to this work as String Quartet II, so I shall use that nomenclature. This must be one of the most unusual string quartets ever written. It has a precedent in his First Quartet, which points the way to the six-hour Second Quartet, which has a structural approach that is unique in the repertoire. I like to refer to it as a minimalist work, even though that word has never been absolutely defined, not to my satisfaction at least. Also, most of the composers who have been classified as minimalists such as Reich, Glass et al are now trying to shake off the tag. In all fairness, it doesn't apply to all of their work.

Technically the structure underpinning this work is straight-forward. The piece is made up of many motifs or musical phrases. Each motif is repeated a predetermined number of times before moving on to the next motif, which is again repeated. The number of repeats can vary considerably, from a small number such as two or three or up to ten times – I've never counted them, but I have seen the score. Occasionally, some motifs return at different points, which gives a satisfying sensation. Most however, appear only once.

I recall the first time I heard the piece. I was working in a basement office of a CD store when I came across it. For me, it really hit the spot – strange and mysterious, but beautiful. I listened to the whole piece over four discs and distinctly recall the moment when it ended. No flourish, it just stopped.

I think I have run out of words for this one. You really need to hear it to decide for yourself whether it is a musical experience that you would enjoy. There are two recorded versions, by the Ives Ensemble and the Flux String Quartet. I prefer the Ives Ensemble as I find the dynamic range of the Flux too broad. At a moderate volume sometimes you can't hear the music. Maybe that's how Feldman wanted it...

If the above has piqued your interest, try listening to the Ives' on Spotify. It is a little difficult to find as all of the CD covers displayed look similar, with red text on a white background. But it is there, as String Quartet II.

I feel it is important for me to reiterate – don't buy it until you have sampled it and know what you are getting into. For me, it is a unique and beautiful experience. Having said that, I don't listen to it very often and, if I do, it's usually only one disc.

Both versions of the work are available. The Ives Quartet 4-CD set is on the Hat Hut label, the Flux Quartet 5-CD or 1-DVD sets are on Mode Records.

You might also like to sample the First String Quartet which exists as a fine version on a single Naxos CD. It is also on Spotify.

Snippets of String Quartet II can be found on YouTube and the complete work can be heard on earsense.

Listenability: Caution, may induce psychosis.

String Quartet and Orchestra

I am forever searching for string quartet and orchestra compositions and arrangements but generally find them disappointing. In fact, some of them are downright terrible. The worst have probably been the Beethoven Late Quartets and Janacek's Kreutzer Sonata. Only Feldman has got it right, in my opinion. He seems to get the balance just perfect, the string quartet does not get drowned out. Importantly, he is not writing a string orchestra arrangement of a string quartet, but a work for string quartet and orchestra. It is a conversational piece, a dialogue between the quartet and orchestra which runs for nearly 26 minutes.

The quartet opens the piece, going it alone with a probing melody. Then the orchestra comes in gently, with a little muffled percussion which is a nice touch. The quartet comes back into prominence with the orchestral strings complementing them. Occasionally the orchestra plays solo but the quartet is never far away. For somebody who adores abstract, hanging chords, this is heaven – there is plenty of Feldman space here. A piano plays a chord and the quartet returns, followed by a moderately loud, sharp, chord cluster from the orchestra. The opening melody returns with the quartet again prominent. The orchestra just plays so softly, and sometimes it is difficult to differentiate the two entities, it is so well balanced. The orchestra keeps feeding the quartet those long hanging chords, and a rumble of low pitched sounds. The quartet now plays a recapitulation of the first theme before moving into phrases reminiscent of Feldman's String Quartet II. A lone piano chord leads to a brief silence – the orchestra comes back with a response and the piano again plays just one chord. We are now at the halfway mark.

An extended orchestral section ensues. Occasionally the piano will play one chord. The quartet resumes, beginning with that theme again, then blending with the orchestra. The chord voicings are so subtle, sometimes you can't tell what you are listening to. The orchestra takes over again, with a rumbling sound that lasts over a minute, which is a long time for Feldman. Now we have true dialogue, with quartet and orchestra alternating more frequently. The quartet breaks into a new melodic phase while the orchestra offers up accompaniment in a measured way. A further low rumbling sound introduces a new section with the quartet prevailing. There is some pizzicato from the quartet going on here. The orchestra returns with those hanging chords and you can still hear the pizzicato. With one minute to go, the quartet expresses its final recapitulation and it's all over.

I have just listened to the piece twice as I have been writing. I'm sure that if I listened again, I would have different words to say. This is an absolutely wonderful piece, probably my favourite Feldman composition, after String Quartet II. The beauty is in the writing and the inability, sometimes, to be able to differentiate between quartet and orchestral playing. The orchestra rarely rises

149

above the level of the quartet. And then of course, there is some profound abstraction here.

Congratulations to the sound engineers, who performed the recording, mixing and mastering. Nobody has ever done a better job in balancing such a delicate work.

The review CD is titled *Atlantis* by the Radio-Sinfonie-Orchester Frankfurt on the Hat Hut label. As far as I am aware there are no other CDs containing the piece. There is however, a live recording, which I have heard on the internet. There are two other fine pieces on the CD, *Oboe and Orchestra* (16:38) and *Atlantis* (11:41).

The CD is on Spotify and you can listen to this piece on YouTube and earsense.

Listenability: An incredible view into Feldman's world.

[The inimitable Morton Feldman]
[Image courtesy Neu Records]

Incidental Images #4

Three x 3 String Quartet Composers

[Benjamin Britten – images courtesy Wiki Commons]

[Camille Saint-Saens – images courtesy Wiki Commons]

[Dmitri Shostakovich – images courtesy Wiki Commons]

John Fernstrom [1897–1961]

Nationality: Swedish
Quartets: Eight
Style: Contemporary

String Quartets Nos. 6 & 8

String Quartet No. 6 is in four movements. Strangely, it opens with a slight middle-eastern tinge. This continues for some time, before moving into a more Western sound. A sparkling violin line inserts a passionate feeling into the section before it drops back to a minimal instrumentation. The opening melodies return but they don't sound so ethnic now, possibly due to the use of Western harmonies. The movement ends abruptly.

The next movement, marked lento, begins with sparse violins investigating their upper registers in a subdued manner, with interest created by the cello, playing a melodic role. The violins continue their musings and there is a brief period of intensity which subsides into a pause. When the music returns, it is powerful with slightly harsh violin lines. Again, this fades to a solo violin before the second violin and cello return in a pensive manner. It fades out with solo violin – this is delicate music.

The third movement is short and hurried as the two violins engage with the occasional cello assertion. Quivering violins are set against a pizzicato, then the opening theme returns. The end comes quickly.

The final movement has a slight tango feeling as the violins spin out ethnic melodies. The harmonic background softens the ambience. Now a solo violin takes flight and a flourish reintroduces the ensemble while an insistent first violin sustains the ethnic flavour – it's almost Gypsy-like, not what you would expect from a Swede. The flourish returns and the ensemble is energised. Syncopated interjections drive the violin melody forward and it concludes on a sweeping phrase.

The range of sounds in this work were a pleasant surprise.

String Quartet No. 8, again, is in four movements. The first movement is marked andante and is quite short. The opening melodic statements are modal and have a stately sound. It is a gentle mood, evoking music from a previous age. The finish is a no-frills sustained violin note.

The second movement is even shorter and again, not of its time. It opens with a prancing feeling and the violins express positive melodies at a brisk pace. This is all about the interplay between the violins, the cello is only heard sparingly. The two violins give a flourish and then finish on four held notes. It is a likeable movement.

Movement three features the two violins, one in an extremely high register, creating a particularly delicate feeling. The cello makes a melodic contribution and then supports the violins in their endeavours. It briefly comes to the fore as the music again takes on a modal feeling and a quiet violin concludes. Once more, I feel that it is music not of its time.

The final movement is in a jaunty waltz-time. The violins weave their way through several appealing melodies before the music briefly moves into double-time. A pause brings the cello into play, and it supports the violins. Now the tempo is back in double-time and sweeping violins express strong melodies. The violins resolve on a chord to complete the work.

I'm not sure why, but I was actually expecting something avante-garde from Fernstrom – maybe I had him confused with Ferneyhough, but I was so wrong. His music has a timeless quality, I wouldn't try to put a label on it. I found it to be terrifically positive and uplifting.

This music is available on at least two discs. My review copy is on Naxos, by the Vlach Quartet, containing quartets 3, 6 and 8, at a reasonable price. Another disc, by the Lysell Quartet contains quartets 4, 6, 7 and 8 – this is quite pricey. The Vlach is on Spotify and there are some individual movements on YouTube. Most of Fernstrom's quartets are on earsense.

Listenability: Non-confronting, melodic music that would fit into any collection.

— oo0oo —

Zdeněk Fibich [1850–1900]

Nationality: Czech
Quartets: Two
Style: Romantic

String Quartet No. 1

Fibich's First Quartet is in four movements. An allegro tempo opens the work, with lyrical, floating melodies being the focus. The tempo is gentle as the violins duet around a charming melodic motif. I hear a hint of the Classical here, possibly Mozart. A tender harmonic background supports the violins as they continue with their melodic development in a stately manner. A recurring theme sounds familiar, but I can't quite place it. A change in mood is sparse, although the violins are still sweet, while the cello and viola adopt a Classical-style approach to the harmony. Nearing the end, there is a brief dramatic interlude, with pulsing violins, but this soon returns to the predominant feeling of the movement. A melancholy moment ensues before the violins contribute a final flourish.

The next, andante movement features a lush chordal background as the violins weave delicate melodies, freed from a tempo. There are some slightly virtuosic violin phrases which introduce a moment of dynamic intensity – this is answered by a sparse ensemble, which makes for an interesting, contrasting passage. The violins carry the music forward with ever-evolving melodies, supported by gentle ensemble pulses. Now the violins move up a register and their wistful playing evokes a feeling of great peace. A solo cello phrase leads to an attractive ending.

The third movement is march-like, as the violins again lead the ensemble, this time in a structured manner. Pizzicato can be heard in the background and the violins become rhythmically active, with assured phrasing. A new mood increases the intensity for a time, but this soon returns to the previous lighter feeling. The end is a very controlled variation on an earlier theme.

The finale is in a brisk tempo, with a highly charged violin passage. There is some melodic development before the mood changes into a slow, stately section with strong violin phrases, which are often echoed by the cello. What follows is a combination of the two previous moods, with the hectic violin punctuated by slower ensemble responses. Eventually, just when you think the tempo has won out, the stately feeling returns. All instruments have a strong role to play here and another powerful passage emerges – this time the cello is the frantic voice. A fine series of harmonised melodies leads to an almost surprising conclusion.

The review CD, *Fibich: String Quartets*, on the Orfeo label and performed by the Kocian Quartet contains both Nos. 1 and 2, together with a 12-minute piece, *Variations for String Quartet*. This disc is available on Amazon US, UK and Presto Classical. There are several other versions of the First Quartet, one of which has it paired with the two fine quartets of Smetana.

Some of these versions, including the Kocian, can be found on Spotify and there are several quartets on YouTube. The three pieces on the review CD are also on earsense, this time performed by the Panocha Quartet, which is on the Supraphon label.

Listenability: An appealing Romantic work.

Graham Fitkin [born 1963]

Nationality: British
Quartets: At least six
Style: Contemporary

Modern Minimalist Works

Fitkin seems to compose string quartets exclusively as named, one movement works – there are six on the review CD. He is also a self-proclaimed minimalist composer who juggles that style with melodic development. You can read an interview from 2017 where he discusses this disc from Presto Classical here:

www.prestoclassical.co.uk/classical/articles/1971--interview-graham-fitkin-on-the-string-quartet

I don't know how long it will be available but there you have it.

For me, *Inside*, the longest track on the album, is superb. The opening has a brass-like sound as it forms a drone. A sparse, long, three-note melodic violin phrase takes over – the length is about four bars, at a very slow tempo. Sometimes, distant second violin musings are heard. A brief pause leads back to a stronger evocation of the phrase, this time harmonised by the second violin. There is a certain spirituality about this, and is somewhat reminiscent of Morton Feldman's work. After a time an ostinato motif begins to develop before leading into three sharp chords. The former mood is now resumed until the ostinato returns before another brief pause leads into a section for a dancing violin, which transforms into some serious undertones from the ensemble. Again, this is very sparse with occasional hints of another ostinato motif. Eventually the motif prevails and a tension comes into the music as the violins express dissonance.

A succession of loud, sharp chords lead into an intense passage of minimalism with the violins continuing their dissonance over another strong rhythmic motif. Then a violin flourish ensues for a brief period, before the ostinato returns. There are many variations here as the piece constantly evolves with different motifs – sometimes they are simple, at other times, complex. A rhythmic chordal passage is heard, and the music returns to its insistent pulsing with the violins regularly coming up with new patterns. Dropping back to a subtle motif, the music starts to build again as the violins engage. Eventually, all movement stops and the two violins hint at the opening melodic phrase – this is stasis. Now the phrase is heard in its entirety as the opening feeling is repeated. The violins drift into a new mood, with slightly dissonant harmonies presented by the duo. A quiet period of two sustained violins ends the work.

What a fascinating piece. The interaction of the minimalism with the melodic passages has the balance just right. Some of the other pieces are more rhythmic, while two short pieces, *A Small Quartet* and *Another Small Quartet*, which both sound very similar, are exercises in introspection, no rhythm here.

The review CD *Graham Fitkin – String Quartets*, on the Signum Classics label, and performed by the Sacconi Quartet, is available from Amazon UK and Presto Classical. Strangely, considering it has just been released, it is only on Amazon US as a download.

The complete disc can be heard on Spotify, YouTube, and earsense.

Listenability: Fine, accessible Contemporary works.

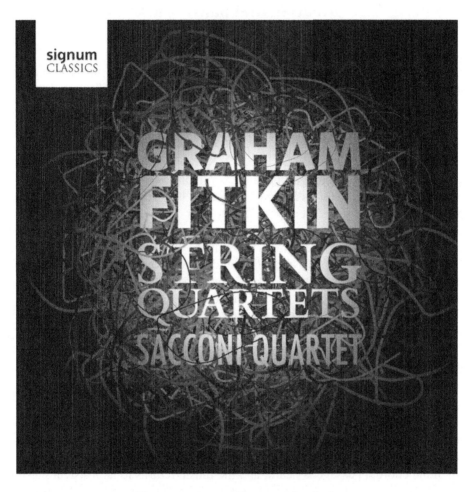

[Image courtesy Signum Classics]

Joseph Foerster [1859–1951]

Nationality: Czech
Quartets: Five
Style: Romantic

String Quartets Nos. 2 & 4

The Second Quartet, in three movements, opens in a delicate manner. It almost sounds like a church organ chord played extremely softly, which paints a most sombre mood, very sparse. Eventually we have movement, in waltz time, which is sustained until the violin dominates, before the cello takes over, leading the ensemble into new territory. Slowly at first, it builds as the violin takes control again and introduces a new melody, with subsequent variations. Nearing the end, the chord changes and the dynamics increase. After a solo cello interjection we have a very interesting brief interlude that concludes with a fine example of miniaturism.

The second movement again begins with a longing feeling. After a time, it moves into a tempo but the longing persists. Now the mood totally changes as a repeated chord leads into a solo violin passage. Slowly the ensemble re-enters and the music starts to move forward but the longing remains. This is the centrepiece of the movement – it is sustained for some time. It concludes by going back to solo violin but then returns to the previous style. The cello ends the movement, which has maintained a soulful character for its entirety.

The final movement, by far the longest, opens in a wonderful, delicate setting. The solo violin is salient and there are multiple short fugue-like sections at work here. Now a rhythm takes over – it's a march really. The music returns to delicate for a time until the tempo lifts. This seems to be a case of alternating sections – delicate, then rhythmic. Out of this comes a new mood which doesn't last and I feel the composer is playing with me here. Another uplifting interlude is heard, but again, it slows right down and develops a serious nature. Just when you least expect it, a stunning piece of solo violin leads into a brief turmoil. It is redeveloped and sustained for a time. We are then back into a floating mood which takes on a slightly serious nature with a change from major to minor. As the end approaches the violin is very precious and it's all over.

The Fourth Quartet begins with a solo violin which persists as all of the other players gradually enter. The opening theme is mellow in the extreme. Slightly rustic, it has a delicate, measured charm about it, with some fine melodic writing and interplay between the violins. Suddenly there is a slight change in the air as the piece becomes more thoughtful with less interplay. Now a sweeping descending violin creates a sombre feeling. Eventually the solo violin returns – this is a wonderful place to be. A recapitulation of the opening theme allows for an ending on a note that hangs in the air. Beautiful.

The second movement is slow as it edges forward with a violin being accompanied by a slightly rhythmic phrase, and is very stately. The melody changes slightly, and the ensemble follows. This continues, with some variation, but always refers back to the basic phrase. Now the cello has a melodic role and, after a brief pause, we are into folk territory as the violins dance above the ensemble. The cello brings about a change in the tempo, returning to slow. You can feel that the ending is imminent as the cello comes to the fore. The melody is engrossing as it winds down with a fade.

The final movement is an allegro and is set as a fugue which gives everyone a chance to feature. There are manifold variations here but the fugal subject persists. After a brief pause, the music regathers momentum and a solo violin is answered by the ensemble. The fugue subject is swept away and the piece finishes on a hanging chord.

For anybody who likes Romantic string quartets these are fine works. There is a 2-CD set titled *The Complete String Quartets* by the Stamic Quartet on the Supraphon label. It is available on both Amazon US and UK.

Spotify also has the complete 2-CD set. There are several quartets on YouTube and the Fourth Quartet can be heard on earsense.

Listenability: A beautiful set of classic Late Romanticism.

[Image courtesy Supraphon label]

Lukas Foss [1922–2009]

Nationality: German-American
Quartets: Five
Style: Contemporary

Modern Minimalism
String Quartet No. 3

Of Foss's five string quartets, several have been recorded, but only No. 3 is still available. It was composed in 1975.

The Third Quartet is in one movement and opens with a violin expressing a rising and falling glissando motif. The second violin joins in, out of sync and, as the piece unfolds, all instruments experiment with this slightly dissonant motif. Eventually they all conform to a rhythmic pattern and come together, albeit with several deviations. Just as this mood has settled, it changes and an abstract scene evolves, leading to a fascinating feeling. There are string sound effects aplenty, and little structure, but I am drawn into its mystery. A further change is introduced with loud glissando swoops which lead into a pulsing ostinato, and all rhythm. Slowly, subtle changes occur – this is classic minimalism. The violins introduce slight variations and the tonality changes along with a slight diminution in tempo.

Now the violins become more expressive and an intense passage follows. For me, the music falls just short of agitation as the violins continually thrust forward. The ostinato motif slowly succumbs to change, leading to a more assertive section by the violins. I keep waiting for the tension to break, but the composer sustains the strong momentum for a considerable time.

Eventually the ostinato ceases and sporadic violin sounds lead into another brilliant soundspace, occasionally interrupted by one repetition of the previous ostinato. We are down to one violin which makes gentle, seemingly random statements – the music is almost inaudible at this point. Slowly the solo violin quietly makes its own rhythmic motif. The dynamics are so low at this point that it masks any development that may be occurring. By turning the volume up, I can hear two violins duelling in a mild manner. Finally the volume increases slightly with an Ives-like canvas of string sounds.

Suddenly the loud ostinato returns and we are back into further intense minimalism with strong propulsion. There is some musical development from the violins but it is basically a wall of sound. The conclusion is abrupt.

Even given the above, this is not a demanding work, although it has an intense quality that I tend not to discuss very often.

The work is only available on a CD titled *Lukas Foss: Curriculum Vitae*, on the New World Records label, performed by the Columbia Quartet. Interestingly the Product Description on Amazon US quotes an un-named source – '*it's been characterized as a minimalist Grosse Fugue.*' This allusion to Beethoven's famous substituted quartet finale movement is probably a little overstated but it gives one person's impression of the quartet.

There are three other works for small ensembles on the CD. I particularly liked *For Six*, a work for melodic percussion instruments which evokes Terry Riley's iconic *In C*. The two other pieces feature a bandoneon.

As stated this CD is available on Amazon US and UK. It is also on Spotify and the Third Quartet can be found on YouTube and earsense.

Listenability: Slightly avante-garde – intense propulsive minimalism.

— oo0oo —

César Franck [1822–1890]

Nationality: French
Quartets: One – FOSQC
Style: Late Romantic

String Quartet No. 1

César-Auguste-Jean-Guillaume-Hubert Franck's one quartet is very long, at forty-four minutes. The work is in four movements and I am going to discuss a classic performance by the Juilliard String Quartet.

The work opens with a delicate violin melody, and strong chordal accompaniment. The melody is slowly developed, things are peaceful. A cello statement enters, with a reiteration of the opening melody and then begins to construct some variations of its own. The violin returns and picks up the tempo a little, and the music moves forward. A pause brings about a change, with slight hints of a minor tonality – it is positively sumptuous. The cello steps forward again, with delicate, sustained notes and a return to a tempo is gentle, but some increase in dynamics is forthcoming. The cello enters again and delivers a strong melody, before combining with the violins in a positive moment. A violin now exhibits some yearning and the ensemble adjusts to this. It's only mild, but sounding very much of the Romantic era.

The cello comes to the fore again, and duets with a violin. Now things become slightly tempestuous, with the cello and violin going at it. This soon returns to a peace and some harmonic movement allows the cello and violin to craft strong melodies. Now we have the violins supporting a cello line with rhythmically intense, but gentle backing. The cello remains conspicuous, mostly leading the violins for a time. A recapitulation of the opening melody is heard, until the first violin breaks free and eventually duets with the cello. A slow, soft chordal interlude concludes. The dynamics stay in a small range for the whole of this movement. It is a lovely introduction and also, the longest movement of the work.

There is a mysterious, busy start to the second movement. A minor sound allows the ensemble, particularly the cello, to develop a tempo, but at a soft dynamic. Now the cello is almost solo as it creates a longing feeling, with a measured accompaniment – the violin is strong here. A harmonic change occurs and the movement ends on four plucked cello notes.

The next movement opens in a slightly longing, stately manner and again, the music is measured. The cello enters for its almost obligatory solo statement. It doesn't work out that way, although it is a strong voice in the ensemble. A new melody is presented, still melancholy but rich in texture. The cello is again prominent, and contributes further to the melancholic nature. The violins return to take over – they are just so sparse. Now some tension is provided but it doesn't last for more than a few bars, before we are almost back to a stasis. As the end approaches, a lone violin fades.

The finale begins with a flourish but then settles into what has been the default feeling of the whole piece. The flurry is repeated several times and the music begins to blossom. These are the most positive sounds that I have heard so far. A tempo is developed and some attractive melodies occur, with various new rhythmic ideas to complement them. We now return to the peace and violins meander through a series of gentle melodies. Franck can certainly craft a fine melody, they just keep coming. The lamenting has receded and there is some melodic and chordal material presented. Occasionally the composer reverts to the earlier action and builds new melodies around the feeling. This is sustained for a time, until gentle chords emerge. The promise of propulsion is always there, but rarely comes to fruition. A succession of slow melodies leads into a final flourish and the work concludes.

This is beautiful, conservative music. Franck certainly knows how to write for the cello and many enticing cello interludes are to be found throughout the work. It's amazing that the whole quartet is in such a limited dynamic range. The loudest note is probably the last one.

The review CD, by the Juilliard Quartet on Sony Classical, also contains Smetana's String Quartet No. 1. It is on Amazon UK but not US. However, hundreds of other versions exist on both sites, all paired with various other works.

The Juilliard disc is on Spotify and several versions of the quartet are on YouTube, with eight versions on earsense.

Listenability: Magnificent, epic early Romantic quartet.

Benjamin Frankel [1906–1973]

Nationality: British
Quartets: Five
Style: Contemporary

String Quartets Nos. 1 & 3

I am not usually effusive in my praise for many string quartets because I don't find all string quartets to be profound – it's just a fact of life. However in this case, I shall make an exception. I find Frankel's work to be wonderful. But that's just me, and I might change my mind tomorrow. Such is the string quartet experience.

The First Quartet, in four movements, commences with a slow, sparse violin duet that takes me straight to where I like to go. This elegiac feeling persists, with occasional increases in dynamics and intensity. The cello is brilliant as it adds touches of colour to this heavenly sound. The violins eventually fade out.

A fanfare introduces the next movement and strong melodies ring out. After a time, the violins set up a dynamic quivering phase which draws strong statements from the cello. The music is tending towards fever pitch as the quivering returns. The ending is almost perfunctory as the two violins play seemingly random pitches.

The third movement is again slow and lamenting, although it is slightly darker than the first movement. Violins explore beautiful, dissonant melodies, and the cello makes a strong contribution. Suddenly, there is a lift in intensity and the piece becomes more assertive. The violins generate some powerful chords, before introducing a new, slow tempo, which eventually leads to the violins petering out.

The final movement begins slowly, but soon moves into a brisk tempo. Violin thrusts are answered by the cello and the intensity drops slightly, before the violins again break into song. This leads to a bright and breezy end to the work.

The Third Quartet is in five movements, and opens with a hectic urgency, where every instrument displays a high level of intensity. There are many rhythmic thrusts, all based around a strong motif. The piece moves into a tempo, while retaining the intensity – it's powerful. The opening theme returns and the movement concludes on a high.

The next movement, which is rather short, contains a grand opening statement before it moves into an exciting, vigorous phase. This is serious music, it positively overwhelms me. The end is a fade on some scattered violin phrases.

The third movement is a brilliant soundscape. A viola trills as the cello inserts single notes – the violins engage in pizzicato and slowly develop the ambience. The level of abstraction is high but it is in no way noisy music. The

162

violins sweeten in texture, and a pizzicato sustains a fabulous atmosphere which eventually moves to a faded conclusion.

The fourth movement is marked lento, and is a beautiful sound canvas that features sensitive violin lines over a slightly dark background. The cello has a strong part to play as it merges with the violins for a special feeling. It is again, a magnificent soundscape that really speaks to me. Its ever so gentle sound is sustained until a tranquil conclusion.

The finale is short, just under two minutes. It is reminiscent of the first movement and very dynamic. The energy is propulsive and it ends with a flourish.

I realise that I have written less than I normally do, in describing these quartets. There is just something about this music that sustains my interest, but is also a little indefinable. I can tell you that they are fine pieces. I loved the preponderance of slow movements in the First Quartet.

This 2-CD set, *Frankel: Complete String Quartets,* on the CPO label, performed by the Nomos Quartet, is available on Amazon US and UK. The full set is on Spotify and several quartets exist on YouTube. Both of the discussed works are on earsense.

Listenability: Magnificent, personal music.

[Image courtesy CPO Records]

Peter Fricker [1920–1990]

Nationality: British
Quartets: Three
Style: Contemporary

British Modernism
String Quartet No. 3

Fricker's Third Quartet was composed during 1975-1976 and is in five movements. The work commences in a strange soundspace. A violin plays slow dissonant lines over a background of string sound effects and various random interjections from the ensemble. There is an intermittent strummed cello along with the use of glissandos – this atmosphere continues for some time. Eventually we have some slightly jaunty, but intense, harmonised and seemingly random violin melodies as the second violin comes into play. The ensemble is now definitely more measured, with a lot less dissonance. It is still a passive mood, however. The first violin leads the ensemble with some strange melodic lines and at times the cello repeats an ostinato motif in support. The first violin is now very prominent over a deliberate ensemble. Ever changing, but always passive, the movement fades with a sparse solo violin. This is indeed strange music.

The second, short movement, at just under two minutes, begins with a rhythmically punctuated chordal texture. A violin has a sweeping statement to make, over a supportive ensemble, before the opening rhythmic passage returns. It now moves into a short period of chaos, and concludes with a return to the opening feeling.

An adagio tempo opens the third movement in a call and response pattern, with sparse ascending solo violin lines being answered by the ensemble, which is in a much lower register. Eventually the ensemble steps forward to create a stunning mood. Now we are into pure rubato and the violin soars over intermittent ensemble passages. The feeling is constant – and pure abstract beauty.

The next movement, again very brief, features some incisive rhythmic statements before the violins move into a skittish feeling as they dance above the ensemble for a time. A hint of the opening is recalled – this is very dynamic and there are some dramatic statements here. It feels like I am experiencing the longest two minutes of my life. The two violins conclude by moving straight into the next movement.

The finale features the two violins from the previous movement, as they rebuild the musical intensity. A solo cello statement ensues and some rather sharp ensemble interjections lead into a period of stasis. All instruments wander freely in this space. Now a tempo and a dynamic set in – it is quite vigorous. Then we are back into occasional statements from the cello and the violins. The mood constantly changes, but all the while being animated and very modern as the different sections come and go, usually with great intensity. Becoming positively

164

frantic, dynamic statements persist until the conclusion which has maintained the intensity and is very loud.

This is quite confronting music, containing some challenging passages. Strangely, the first two quartets are much more approachable, temperate even.

The review CD, titled *Fricker: The String Quartets*, on the Naxos label, is performed by the Villiers Quartet. It also contains String Quartets Nos. 1 and 2, and some minor pieces. It is available at Amazon US and UK.

This disc is on Spotify and all three quartets are on YouTube and earsense.

Listenability: This is quite Modern music, but the first two quartets are more conservative – a nice blend.

— ooOoo —

Jefferson Friedman [born 1974]

Nationality: American
Quartets: At least three
Style: Modern Contemporary

String Quartet No. 3

Friedman's Third Quartet was written in 2005, and is in three movements. The work begins calmly, in fact I couldn't hear any music until about ten seconds into the piece. A slightly bleak sustained chord finds its way to the surface and increases in volume for around 30 seconds – the dynamics become almost excruciating as a violin takes over with intense, rapid phrases. The tonality changes frequently and there are many string sound effects. The volume suddenly drops, leaving one violin to offer up a sparse phrase which leads into a brief chordal moment, then more rapid violin phrases, until it stops abruptly. This movement is brief, clocking in at 2:34. Interestingly, it bears no obvious relationship to the rest of the piece.

The second movement is long, at eighteen minutes. It opens with a solo violin, a sparse atonal melody, and lots of space between the notes. The ensemble enters, but they are way in the background. The violin is featured in a long, drawn-out melody. Now murmurings begin to appear and a deep, resonant solo cello comes into play with a strong melodic statement. After a time, a solo violin returns, still ever so gently, for a quiet period and a brief interlude of a galloping motif gives way to a racing violin, supported with string sound effects. The galloping motif returns, followed by another racing moment – this has become a pattern as rapid sections flow into one another, all the while maintaining the brisk tempo. The harmony changes constantly and many and varied sound effects can be heard as the piece progresses through various moods.

There are periods where the violins soar, and at other times, just the pulsating motif is heard. An almost silent passage ensues, with an incredibly soft violin. A fabulous feeling is achieved, as the ensemble edges its way into the music. This is repeated, but in a more conservative manner, featuring some stunning, enticing violin. The music is reminiscent of parts of the fourth movement, the adagio, of Beethoven's *String Quartet No. 15* – high praise indeed. The solo violin is absolutely beautiful, teasing out long lines, with gentle ensemble work. The violin soars into its high register and melodic movement begins to appear in the background.

Now we are back to solo violin, working a motif through different harmonies. A second violin is frenzied in its rhythmic manner. The tension builds, almost unbearably, before cutting back to nothingness, then starting again. A brief return to the previously mentioned motif brings on an increase in dynamics and leads to an abrupt stop.

The final movement emulates the second in that no music is heard for a time. A low drone eventually ensues, with the cello making up most of the sound, even though the violins are present. A change in tonality introduces an intangible violin melody that floats over the drone. This section has a spiritual quality, similar to John Tavener, with the violin entrancing as it follows the occasional changes in tonality. A substantially long fade leads to the conclusion of the work.

This is a wonderful piece of writing. I would classify the style as characterised by an extreme range in dynamics, periods of silence, frenetic rhythms and deeply moving sections. I think it is an illustration of the many different styles that Modern Contemporary composition has produced. It's a fabulous piece of music. String Quartet No. 2, also on the disc, is similar, but has more of the rhythmic material and less of the peaceful.

It's also worth mentioning that two tracks on the CD follow the popular modern trend of techno remixes. They are extensively deconstructed versions of some of Friedman's works, presumably string quartets. It wasn't obvious to me as to which string quartets were used as the source for these tracks, based on one listening.

This CD, titled *Jefferson Friedman: Quartets*, on the Naxos label, performed by the Chiara String Quartet is on Amazon US and UK, but only as a download on Presto, and you know what that means. Although, having said that, Naxos have been remarkably resilient in keep things available from their own website distribution outlet.

The CD is also available for listening on Spotify and YouTube while the Third Quartet can be heard on earsense.

Listenability: Fascinating Contemporary work.

Incidental Images #5

A Prized Instrument

[Orpheus String Quartet violinist with a 1709 Stradivarius Violin]
[Image courtesy Orpheus String Quartet]
[Photographer – Josep Molinari]

Friedrich Theodor Fröhlich [1803–1836]

Nationality: Swiss
Quartets: Four
Style: Romantic

String Quartet in G Minor

I haven't been able to establish a chronology for these works so I shall refer to it as String Quartet in G Minor, which is in four movements and apparently dates from 1826.

The first, <u>andante</u> movement opens in a stately manner, coloured significantly by its minor <u>tonality</u>. The sound is rich with a slow melody and classic Romantic <u>harmony</u>. As the first violin expresses its slightly lamenting melody the ensemble bathes it in a sensitive accompaniment. A change ensues and the violin becomes folk-like, at tempo, although the stately feeling is maintained. Gradually the violin is more dynamic and expressive as it spreads its wings. We now have a return to the opening character and the harmony is very strong here, it overshadows the melody with a wonderful sensitivity. Charming, attractive <u>harmonies</u> are developed and great passion is felt. A new passage brings the first violin back into focus and the intensity rises as the phrasing becomes more complex for a time. Eventually, the peaceful sound of the opening is heard, but it does not last as the violin again displays great expression and asserts itself within the music. This wonderful passage is further developed, leading to a shrill note from the violin, which pauses for a moment, allowing the ensemble to go it alone until the first violin returns for a soft ending.

The next movement is a brief *scherzo*, variously a vigorous, light, or playful mood. Prancing violins express at tempo, before moving into a strong virtuosic passage. The first violinist is all over the fingerboard, with delightfully skittish melodies, leading to a final flourish.

Now follows a <u>largo</u> movement, again stately and delightfully Romantic in style, somewhat reminiscent of Mozart and Haydn. The ensemble embark on a rhythmic passage, with flowing melodic lines, to a very sympathetic accompaniment – the cello here is particularly fine. The music works through several different moods, mostly determined by the leading violin. One particular section has the ensemble projecting a delicate rhythm, which serves as a carpet for the first violin. Wonderful harmonies are in abundance as the music gently drifts towards a conclusion.

The <u>allegro</u> finale is introduced by a cello motif, constantly recurring and always answered by the violins. Now the violins take the lead and develop a slightly sombre section before being set free to express a positive conversation with the ensemble. Long violin phrases give way to shorter motifs that are answered by the cello. For me, there is a sense of the music attempting to break out of its Romantic nature, but this never happens – the composer is always in control. A walking cello underpins an alluring violin duet, which concludes the work.

While I am not naturally drawn emotionally to the Romantic style, I always enjoy it when I discuss a quartet from this era as it seems to reveal the deep traditions within the string quartet repertoire. This is very fine music.

The review CD, titled *Fröhlich: String Quartets,* on the Musiques Suisse label, performed by The Beethoven Quartet, contains three quartets on one disc and is available on Amazon US and UK. There is also a 2-CD set by the Rasumowsky Quartett, *Fröhlich: Complete String Quartets*, on the CPO label, which has all four works.

Both versions are on Spotify, while the Rasumowsky complete version can be heard on YouTube and earsense.

Listenability: Charming, early Romantic works.

[Image courtesy CPO label]

Kenneth Fuchs [born 1956]

Nationality: American
Quartets: At least five
Style: Contemporary

String Quartet No. 2

The Second Quartet is titled *Where Have You Been* and contains five named movements.

Heart of Darkness opens with a solo cello and occasional interjections from the ensemble. There is a loud flourish and a period of rhythm which leads into a solo violin. Then follows a period of dissonance before the solo violin returns. It's busy until it drops back to a pizzicato cello, and a fade to the end.

The Other Side commences with a rather timid rhythmic phrase. A pastoral melody emerges from the violin and the key changes. The violin continues on its way into the upper register together with the second violin – the viola and cello join in, maintaining the pastoral feeling. The cello has a solo statement until, after a time, interjections occur. Now the tempo ceases and the violin returns to its high register as a gentle accompaniment concludes the movement.

The Marriage opens in a serious tone before the violins take over with an exciting duet, which eventually recalls the serious opening. This passage is a little confronting and concludes the movement. It only runs for just under three minutes.

They Are Not Heard at All starts with a solo violin. The music covers the whole tonal range of the instrument. I keep wondering when the other instruments will enter. At about two minutes a few murmurings are heard, but the solo violin continues. Eventually, some accompaniment occurs but the violin continues to dominate. It is turning into a solo violin piece with occasional sparse statements from the other members. Taken as a whole, the violin investigates many moods as it journeys through the movement.

Where Have You Been has a rhythmic pulse from the start. An exquisite violin melody occurs but is soon discarded for a conversation between the violin and noisy interjections from the ensemble. Nearing the end we have a positive change as the piece makes for a hurried exit.

Two things worth mentioning about this work as a whole. Firstly, it contains so much violin to so little ensemble playing. Secondly, many of what I would call interjections seem to turn up at random, usually totally destroying the nature of the violin statements. Taken together, these two features leave me feeling a little dissatisfied.

This work is still interesting and the composer is definitely worth persevering with. Some listeners might find the interjections angry. Personally, I feel they are just a little miffed.

Regarding availability, Quartets Nos. 2, 3 & 4 can be found on the Albany label, performed by the American String Quartet on Amazon US and UK. There is also a 2-CD set, *Fuchs – Complete String Quartets*, by the Minguet Quartet on the MDG label, which can sometimes be found in two separate volumes.

The work can be heard on Spotify. There are many of Kenneth Fuchs' quartets on YouTube, but unfortunately not No. 2.

Listenability: Interesting, if a little unsatisfying.

— oo0oo —

Hans Gál [1890–1987]

Nationality: Austrian-British
Quartets: Four
Style: Early Modern

The Last String Quartet – No. 4

The Fourth Quartet opens in a typical Gál style, one which permeates all of his string quartets. The sound is one of brilliantly expressive, other-worldly melodies over a sumptuous string background. Suddenly, a tempo brings life to the piece and dissonant phrases are scattered freely throughout this quite tempestuous section. The mood now reverts back to the sparse nature of the beginning, and is possibly even more measured. Two violins, in different registers, create long, mysterious melodic lines that have an unusual sense of strength in their abstract nature. The cello steps forward and mingles with its own, similar melodic lines and we have three pitch registers making up the sound. A change brings about a more expansive passage, however the violins and cello continue to express positive statements, with an occasional pizzicato background. The dynamics increase in intensity and a particularly strong section ensues. A sense of moderate, but constant abstraction is most beguiling – sometimes it seems almost rhapsodic. Now, a controlled passage with another sense of sparsity unfolds. Nearing the end, the cello incites the ensemble into a short, torrid passage with a final flourish.

The next, brief movement features a dance-like tempo, with positive violin melodies – this is much lighter in texture than that which has gone before. The characteristic constant violin phrases bring a fullness to the sound. A sustained chord signals the end.

This time, for the third movement, there is a definite change of texture, at least for a time. A pulsing cello leads the violins into sombre territory, with tightly controlled lamenting melodic lines. A sustained ensemble chord frees the first violin for a brief solo passage but the status quo is soon resumed, although there is a little more use of harmony here, something that I hadn't noticed before with the constancy of the melodic development. A new sense of sparsity evokes the first movement, albeit at a slower tempo. Some harmonised melodic lines are heard for the first time in the work – these bring about a new texture, which is somewhat mournful. A scattering of pizzicato strokes lead to a gentle finish.

Strong, somewhat light-hearted violins introduce the final movement. This feeling is definitely more optimistic, and has a distinctively British quality. Melodically, this is quite a contrast to the first three movements with not a hint of introversion to be heard. A brief, slightly pensive passage quickly moves into a sweeping section with the violins in full flight. The end comes with a positively orchestral sound that concludes very strongly.

I think it is worth noting that the four quartets were composed in 1916, 1929, 1969 and 1970 respectively. In other words they are in two pairs, with a forty year gap. I recently heard the Second Quartet and recall it to be very similar in style to the much later work under discussion. Gál's style is certainly unique, in that he constantly works with the same textures, that is, a constant stream of non-harmonised melodies with occasional diversions into other moods.

Wikipedia has this to say on Gál's consistency of style: *Gál's style is rooted in the Austro-German musical tradition, but from the early 1920s he had developed his own musical language, to which he remained true throughout his long career. He never followed prevailing fashions, nor abandoned his belief in the importance of tonality.*

All of the composer's quartets are available but I selected *Hans Gál: String Quartets, Vol. 1*, performed by the Edinburgh Quartet on the Meridian label for review as it appears to be the most reasonably priced. Volume 2 is rather expensive and only available from Amazon UK Resellers – there is also a 2-CD complete set which contains the four quartets together with other pieces for string quartet.

The complete set is on Spotify, YouTube and earsense.

Listenability: I found all of Gál's quartets to be rather interesting – he is a unique stylist.

Steven Gerber [1948–2015]

Nationality: American
Quartets: Six
Style: Contemporary Modern

String Quartets Nos. 4-6

The three quartets that are available on my review CD are relatively short so I intend to discuss them all.

Quartet No. 4, in three movements, commences with a lyrical melodic and chordal passage. The ensemble then begins to ask questions in a firm manner. It is followed by a rich pastoral theme which is dense in texture. Now the violins erupt into a furious passage before again dropping back into a pastoral scene – this is reminiscent of the opening and leads to a tender ending.

The next movement begins with a solo violin and a wonderful, wailing melody – rather marvellous really. A hint of pizzicato is heard and brings a tempo into play, which disappears as quickly as it started. The violin raises its intensity – it is powerful and the cello sets up an ostinato for a time, followed by some interjections, before dropping back into the ostinato. The violin continues on its dissonant journey until the end comes with a solo cello note. I don't believe the second violin or viola were evident in this movement.

A loud fanfare introduces the final movement. The cello makes assertive statements against a background of pulsating violins. Active violins now deliver a sense of urgency, and the ensemble projects a dense texture. There is little melody, but plenty of almost random material presented. Towards the end, an epic passage terminates the quartet.

The Fifth Quartet, in two movements, starts with a dissonant chordal phase featuring strong abstraction. A change brings about a collection of harmonised melodies that are initially powerful, but gradually drop in intensity. An interlude emerges that is filled with sensitive melodies and viola pizzicato accompaniment. Suddenly there is more space as a violin asserts itself over ensemble movement. A pause brings in a violin drifting across various textures, until the violin stabs viciously and then returns to the previous feeling, which is now mellow and positive. More violin interjections lead back to a dissonant sound and a powerful conclusion.

The second movement has a dissonant opening which doesn't last as the violins lead the music through several periods of entropy before returning to the sound of the introduction, again, only for a short time. The abstraction returns with string sound effects. Now a slightly conservative tone emerges, before drifting back into the previous nebulosity. Some melodies can be heard for a time, but it then returns to pure abstraction. I can't quite pin this movement down. It keeps returning to two different moods which are developed and redeveloped each time.

Quartet No. 6 is in three movements. Strangely, it starts with heavy melodies played over a beautiful trill before the violin converses with a strong ensemble. A pause returns to the trill and a texture of great intensity. Sometimes, there is a brief quiet interlude and then the intensity returns. It's almost as if the violin is an accompaniment to the machinations of the ensemble. It all ends with a flourish.

The second movement is short at 1:23 and features a strong cello phrase, with an almost industrial sound. It persists with this machine-like feeling, dropping slightly in intensity to conclude.

The final movement opens uncharacteristically softly, and slightly mournful. A tempo sets in and a sparse section takes over. Violins investigate rhythmic possibilities and sparse melodies. A powerful, rearing cello heightens the intensity until the feeling cuts back to the violins. An engaging chordal mood takes us to the end.

This is a composer with a unique approach. It's modern and it seems that one trait of modernity is to be unencumbered by tradition in a quest for a personal expression – this is definitely the case with Gerber. He is never aggressive but his attention to detail within abstract textures is very satisfying.

The disc also contains a three movement work, *Fantasy, Fugue & Chaconne for Violin and Cello.*

This CD, titled *Steven R. Gerber: String Quartets*, on the Albany label, performed by the Amernet String Quartet, is obtainable from Amazon US and UK. It is able to be heard on Spotify, earsense and YouTube.

Listenability: Modern, but not avante-garde.

— oo0oo —

Roberto Gerhard [1896–1970]

Nationality: Catalonian
Quartets: Two
Style: Modern Contemporary

String Quartets Nos. 1 & 2

Apart from the two known quartets, apparently there are three earlier works, which are considered lost. The third was later modified as the *Concertino for Strings.*

String Quartet No. 1, in four movements, opens with an expansive chord, slightly dissonant, which increases in volume. A strong cello underpins some atonal melodic development – this has a very 1950s modern feeling. Some string sound effects accompany a rather raw toned violin which eventually moves into a busy phase, until the cello returns and the violins construct atonal melodies around it. There is prominent pizzicato that adds to this mysterious feeling, and a tension which develops as the individual instruments dialogue and push the music forward. Eventually the tension dissipates, but the underlying feeling remains – very abstract. The dynamics rise and fall, all the while continuing with an almost random note selection. There is a little rhythmic emphasis nearing the end and a scurrying passage of two violins leads to a final chord.

The following movement is rather brief and commences in a sparse manner. Soon the feeling is similar to the first movement, with small sections of interesting moods for two violins. They follow the same melodic line, with each applying variations. The end is another scurrying passage, milder this time that just stops.

The third movement begins with a slightly screeching chord, but it's not loud. There is a definite change from the first two movements in that things occur rather slowly. There are many long chords, played by overlapping instruments – also many string sound effects. Atonal sounds abound as the chords reach out for something intangible and a deep resonant cello adds to this soundscape. Long notes form sustained chords, evoking a mystifying section that ends on one long violin note. I should mention that this movement is extremely quiet, I had to increase the volume considerably to hear its nuances.

The final movement opens sharply but soon develops into an agitated section of atonality and random pizzicato interjections. This is another abstruse soundscape, however, it is in no way aggressive, just filled with scurrying violin sounds and seemingly random cello intrusions. There are some rhythmic punctuations, especially nearing the end. A very pulsating cello appears, with a tone indicating that it is being struck very powerfully. This brings on a short, loud passage which quickly gives way to a soft violin dialogue that staggers to a conclusion.

String Quartet No. 2 is in seven movements, generally very brief, so I am going to consider it mostly as a whole. A long violin tone introduces the work – there is very little input from the ensemble here. Slowly the second violin drifts in and there is a powerful cello interjection. A loud chord is heard and some string sound effects from the cello lead into several dissonant chords. Now pizzicato takes over and wispy violin statements follow. A quiet passage has the two violins in a dialogue as pizzicato jabs permeate their conversation.

The fourth movement, by far the longest, evokes the First Quartet in that sustained solo violin tones are the prominent feature. This music is very sparse and there is little interplay – sometimes there are silences, but the violin always returns. Occasional atonal chords are heard but it is basically another case of a desolate soundscape.

Dominant string sound effects are now evident, before a section with a short, rhythmic violin motif. There is some skipping cello and various pizzicato explorations which lead into an agitated mood. This becomes tempered but the sound overall is still quite dissonant. Pulsing violins create a rhythmic ostinato, with various atonal thrusts leading to the conclusion, which is one cello note.

I would characterise this music as being very modern, although the two works were composed in 1950 and 1961 respectively. They both contain a high level of abstraction, dissonance and entropy. As previously mentioned, I enjoy this type of music, except when it becomes overwhelmingly aggressive or dark. This is not the case with Gerhard.

The review CD, titled *Gerhard, R: String Quartets Nos. 1 and 2*, on the Metier label and performed by the Kreutzer Quartet is available on Amazon UK. An alternate version, by the Arditti Quartet is available from Presto Classical and as a download from Amazon US – they also have some *New and Used*.

Several versions are available for listening on Spotify, YouTube and earsense.

Listenability: Difficult for some.

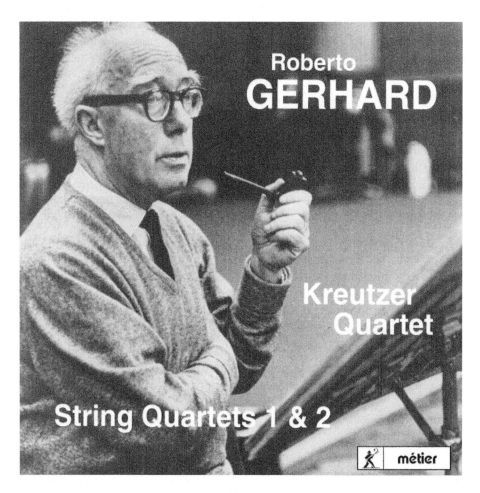

[Image courtesy Metier/Divine Art]

Philip Glass [born 1937]

Nationality: American
Quartets: At least seven
Style: Contemporary

Minimalism or Music?
String Quartets Nos. 3 & 4

Glass has developed quite a following with his constant nods to minimalism, scattered among his many works. He has composed a host of movie soundtracks and his influence is far-reaching.

The Third Quartet, titled *Mishima*, was written in 1985 and consists of six named movements. These movements were originally composed as part of a soundtrack to a film, *Mishima – A Life in Four Chapters*, which was in turn based upon a book by prolific Japanese author and playwright Yukio Mishima.

1957: Award Montage – Opens with a collection of harmonised rhythmic motifs that vary in dynamics, but never in tempo. Occasionally there can be heard a hint of what might be described as melody but I don't think I would see it that way. The interest in this movement is basically the varying dynamics, with the concept being repeated to the end, which consists of six delayed notes – the last of which is allowed to fade out.

November 25: Ichigaya – This very brief movement consists of a slow, metric ostinato, with intermittent two-note melodic phrases inserted. It is all over very quickly.

Grandmother and Kimitake – Strong, rhythmic chords are heard before the music settles into a series of punctuating harmonised chords over a constant viola motif. A brief pause brings about an increase in dynamics and the motif slowly begins to take precedence as the intensity overall reduces. The end is a sustained chord.

1962: Body Building – A slight cello introductory note opens this brief movement, which leads into another ostinato. This is joined by further constant rhythmic interjections. The mood suddenly changes, bringing a return to the sense of the first movement, finally stopping surprisingly on an upstroke.

Blood Oath – With another motif-based beginning, the overarching nature of the piece is resumed. Some moving cello sounds are heard and a change, mid-movement, has all instruments in a higher register, with constantly shifting harmonies. A return to a motif similar to the opening is heard before we again have a sharp stop.

Mishima/Closing – The movement begins with a two-chord motif over an ostinato and the first melody heard so far, played by a sparse violin, is briefly expressed. After another ostinato period, the melodic violin returns, sometimes even responding to the shifting harmonies. The end is pared down to one instrument, slowly leading to a fade.

Now on to the Fourth Quartet, titled *Buczak*, written in 1989 and containing three movements.

Opening with strong ensemble chords, it evokes the introduction to Beethoven's *String Quartet No. 12*. This segues into the characteristic style of the previous work, with harmonised, rhythmic motifs prevailing. Now sporadic violin notes are heard – I'm not sure that they could be called a melody, but they do change with the harmonies. For a time the violin part drops out, only to return later. A not so brief pause leads back to the introductory chords, in a powerful manner. This passage is followed by more insistent motifs, and further dynamic variations between instruments which change the sound of the passage. The end is unexpected, maybe.

The next movement begins with a solo violin floating over a slightly rhythmic, thoughtful harmonic background – this is a fascinating passage, the solo violin being almost flutelike in its texture, creating a mysterious emotional space. A change to a sparse violin line, over a slightly more insistent two-chord rhythmic motif, has the violin following the changes in the accompanying harmony. This continues for some time until the seeming obligatory, perfunctory finish.

The final movement again opens in a chordal manner, leading to yet another ostinato. This whole section is repeated, but when the ostinato begins, it signals the introduction of a sweeping solo violin melody. Now a rise in dynamics gives way to an emphasised pulse. Another, not so brief pause commences a passage with the solo violin again expressing a melody over a constant harmonic underpinning. The propulsive emphasis returns for a time, only to lead back to the introductory section, with the violin this time a little more rhythmic and the cello providing some melodic interest. Various motif-based passages unfold, usually returning to the opening chordal section. Nearing the end, the violin predominates one more time before the work concludes at the end of one instance of a motif.

For over 200 years, music has usually been defined as having three major elements – *melody, harmony and rhythm*. Over time, further characteristics including *dynamics, texture* and *form*, amongst others are now routinely used. So do these works represent music? I'm not particularly familiar with the other works of Glass, but I believe they do. Contemporary composers have come up with new musical languages – in Glass's works, I would class them as Minimalism, which often places little, or no emphasis, on melody.

Interestingly, I have experienced the Phillip Glass Ensemble live, and the music presented was so loud and distorted that I doubt that even the most ardent fan of Glass could have defended it. The sound was nothing like the measured, pristine nature of his recordings, but more a cacophony of noise and definitely not enjoyable. *Caveat emptor* – let the buyer (concert-goer) beware!

The review CD, titled *Glass: String Quartets Nos.1-4*, on the Naxos label and performed admirably by the Carducci Quartet is freely available at a nice price. Several other versions can be found on Amazon US and UK, including

Kronos Quartet and the Smith Quartet. Brooklyn Rider have recorded the comparatively new Quartets Nos. 6 and 7.

All of the above-mentioned CDs can be found on Spotify, and there are many performances on YouTube, with Quartets 1 to 5 on earsense.

Listenability: Not to everybody's taste, but he does seem to have a large following.

— ooOoo —

Alexander Glazunov [1865–1936]

Nationality: Russian
Quartets: Seven
Style: Late Romantic

String Quartets Nos. 3 & 4

Of Glazunov's seven string quartets, I have selected Nos. 3 and 4, both in four movements, for their Late Romantic beauty, charm and zest.

String Quartet No. 3, titled *Slavonic*, opens gently as a violin develops pastoral melodies, to a wonderfully subtle accompaniment. There is a hint of Tchaikovsky here, as a gentle nature is maintained. A new melody introduces a slightly more vigorous tone – the cello rumbles in the background. Now the violins dominate, but still in a subtle manner, if that is possible. A pizzicato interlude is delicate, introducing a new melody which leads to the conclusion. This is sweet, measured music.

A solo cello line introduces the following movement, which is then picked up by the violins. Slowly, they develop the melody with wonderful harmonies, leading to a tender sound, rich in the Romantic tradition. The violins continue to form beautiful lines, with variations provided by the ensemble. Nearing the end, the music becomes almost choral as it concludes peacefully.

The third movement features a gentle rhythmic folk music phrase, which underpins the development. It is taken up by the ensemble, contributing to a rich harmonic background. A pause initiates another strong melody as the violins double the tempo in a dance-like fashion. This subsides and the previous melody is revisited. It has a pulsating feeling, but remains gentle, with occasional rhythmic forays occurring. The solo violin is featured prominently, and the music is very precious. Now the dance feeling returns, and the movement ends on a flourish.

The final movement is another energised dance. After a time, the intensity is reduced but the propulsion is still there. A recapitulation follows and a new section brings a searing violin into play, and several changes in dynamics occur.

179

The dance tempo returns, and a solo cello leads to a brief pause before a lyrical violin leads into a slightly lamenting sound. Ascending violins reintroduce a vigorous tempo and dance above the ensemble while another lament gives way to a rhythmic violin, swirling to a Russian sound from the ensemble. A jaunty feeling develops with a short period of melodic development and again we have a brief lament followed by another hectic passage. This music won't settle. A stately mood doesn't last long, but is repeated before a race to the finish line, and a final ensemble flourish.

The Fourth Quartet commences in a wonderfully lush chordal manner, interspersed with a several instances of a marvellous violin line. The chords continue for some time until they finally break out into a brisk pace, the violins flowing, with the cello offering great support. This melody is reworked and the tempo drops back a little, with violin and cello offering a call and response phase before the violins move on, again at a moderate tempo. Pizzicato provides a variation to the accompaniment as the sound now becomes gentle for a time, then we have an evocation of an earlier melody. The chordal sounds are charming and the violins create sensitive melodies. The closing moments have a conspicuous cello adding to fine folk-sounding melodies. There is another spirited race to the end.

The next movement is again contemplative, with longing melodic lines probing a subtle background, which continues for some time, until slowly the second violin and viola come into play. A slight forward movement is present, and a lyricism develops – this is beguiling, and very pleasant. Now the first violin becomes more expansive and leads the ensemble with increased momentum into an extended passage. The end is graceful.

A propulsive flavour opens the third movement. The tempo is brisk and the violins respond to each other with great enthusiasm. This movement is essentially a cornucopia of rhythmically charged melodic lines, and continues with great vigour to a conclusion.

The final movement starts with a poignant layered texture, which is most endearing. It soon breaks into tempo and the violins dance in a positive manner. This is Glazunov's voice, a light flowing sense of melody and an almost orchestral concept – he also develops melodies over a long time frame. In this instance there is a rhapsodic feeling for a time, and a sense of the lyrical continues. A change in the intensity comes about with shimmering violins and rapid lines. The ending is a series of orchestral thrusts and a final chord.

I've realised that Glazunov's music is nearly always gentle, even when tempos are high. It certainly makes for peaceful listening.

Both quartets are available on a single CD on the Praga Digitals label at Amazon UK, performed by the Zemlinsky Quartet. There is also an added piece for string quartet and horn on this version. Amazon US has a set of five individual CDs on the MDG label, performed by the Utrecht Quartet. I haven't heard them but I would expect them to be of a high standard as I find this quartet to be a fine ensemble.

There are several CDs on Spotify and also some individual quartets on YouTube and earsense, which has a fine version by the Utrecht Quartet.

Listenability: Delightful Late Romantic works.

[Image courtesy Praga Digitals]

Glenn Gould [1932–1982]

Nationality: Canadian
Quartets: One
Style: Early Modern

The String Quartet

I have long been a fan of Glenn Gould as a pianist – his Bach playing introduced me to the world of classical piano and particularly, twentieth century composers such as Schoenberg, Krenek and Hindemith, all of which shed some light on this quartet. Unfortunately, some of his other playing reminds me of a song about a little girl that I learned as a child – Gould's Beethoven Sonatas are bad and his Mozart is horrid! He desperately wanted to be a composer but only created a handful of completed works. The string quartet is Opus No. 1. His brilliant pianism and his eccentric personality made him one of the more interesting musicians of the last 60 years. I have read at least five Gould biographies – such a fascinating life.

The work under discussion opens with a droning chord sustained by the ensemble, as a lone violin expresses a continuous long tone, creating a feeling that to me, strangely enough, sounds quite like a British Early Modern style, while creating a fabulous soundspace. The drone ceases and a sustained second violin is left to support the lamenting first violin. The ensemble now comes into play with a series of strong dissonant chords before leading into a powerful cello passage with various voices supporting it – this is a serious mood. The cello continues to dominate, even in the background as various, sometimes dissonant lines are expressed by the violins, while occasional viola pizzicato statements can be heard. Now the music moves into a lilting passage that features a melody that I recognise, but just can't place at present, it may be from Robert Schumann. Moving from this section a Romantic passage unfolds and the cello is especially prominent here, with its raw tone cutting through the ensemble.

This Romantic feeling is maintained for a time, gradually becoming more modern as the violins drift in and out of dissonance, evoking both Krenek and Hindemith in style. The mood is strong, with a sense of chaos prevalent. The intensity continues to increase and the sound is very powerful until a change leads into a milder, melodically driven passage. Now a new, conservative melody emerges, with the violins musing over sensitive ensemble harmonies. This doesn't last for long and a solo cello moment signals a return to a slow, sensitive feeling. The cello however, is persistent and again is heard solo for a time until a very measured slightly dissonant passage unfolds, with great feeling. Sustained tones are now the focus, especially from a deep cello which leads into a sparse feeling of abstraction, slowly introducing the violins, which become more dominant as they develop a rich harmonic canvas.

The music is now firmly in the Early Modern mould of Hindemith, Krenek and Schoenberg as dissonant sections are constantly presented, to varying effect. The intensity increases and the texture becomes quite dense. Surging violins create a wall of dissonance which eventually abates, leading to a measured section with attractive melodies and finally back to a solo cello. Out of this arises a strutting passage, again, slightly abstract and I hear a hint of that Schumann-like melody before the music becomes dense and dissonant again. The composer seems to be searching for a purpose here and finally settles on a quiet, mellow passage. This is replaced by a series of strongly harmonised cello and violin lines, at a skipping tempo.

Nearing the end, for the first time I am getting the feeling that the composer is running out of ideas. More quiet passages are presented, before again moving on to a more powerful section which leads into a dominant cello passage, with ensemble murmurings in the background. The violins eventually become more expressive but the background feeling persists. Another solo cello moment occurs and the music is beginning to sound a bit aimless to the point of stalling. Now the violins explode into action with strong lines before two dissonant flourishes and a strong chord conclude the work.

Interestingly, Gould does not sustain moods for long, he always seems to be moving forward. Also, he never seems to return to develop previous themes. Moreover, he doesn't seem to be able to make up his mind about a coherent style, constantly oscillating between Late Romantic musings and modernist episodes. Apparently it took Gould three years of working on this piece, before he released it for publication. While it has many interesting moments, especially if you are fond of Early Modernism as I am, it seems to lack coherency and/or structural unity. Having said that, it is definitely interesting enough to be worth a listen, especially for Gould obsessives, of which there are many, including myself.

The other work on the review CD is a string quartet arrangement of Bach's *Goldberg Variations*, a piece which will always be associated with Gould as it was his first commercial recording, the success of which instantly launched him onto the world's concert stages. This arrangement appears to be based on Gould's 1955 recording, which is an extremely short and almost frenzied rendition of the work.

This CD, titled *Bach/Gould Project*, on the Azica label and performed by the Catalyst Quartet is available on Amazon US and UK.

It is available to be heard on Spotify and YouTube. There are also four versions on earsense.

Listenability: Coupled with the Goldbergs, I just had to have it.

Edvard Grieg [1843–1907]

Nationality: Norwegian
Quartets: Two
Style: Late Romantic

String Quartet No. 1

Grieg wrote two string quartets, with the second remaining unfinished. His First Quartet, in G minor, is of epic proportions, and was written during 1877-1878. It contains four movements.

The work commences with a minor key fanfare, before leading into a rhythmically charged passage which passes through many harmonic changes and several dark moments. A pause leads to a totally contrasting, lyrical period, which develops into another brisk tempo, this time in a major tonality, with playful violin lines. Small crescendos are built, and the melodies are folksy. A powerful chordal sequence returns the music into a minor tonality, with more melodic development. Again, lyrical melodies abound. Another rhythmically powerful episode leads into a subdued moment – it's almost a murmur. Now the tempo returns and a strong melody drives the music forward and some descending violin phrases lead into another chordal statement. A false ending brings a new subdued melodic section, interspersed with occasional rhythmic interjections. The violin leaps into a high register, then descends into its lowest. This is followed by a thoughtful interlude, which transforms into a beautiful phase – almost funereal. It is particularly subtle, and out of it rises a most enticing melody. A quiet period of shimmering violins concludes this movement, which has been quite a journey.

The second movement opens with a longing theme, but not too dark. A melody rises up and grows in stature as time passes. Now we have a tempo, and the sound becomes almost Gypsy-like with stirring violin phrases. The tempo recedes and the violins converse in an elegant manner. A new tempo ensues and the ensemble builds a most lyrical sound with the tone of the first violin wonderful. Brief frantic interjections occur, but they don't last – the lyrical feeling remains until the end of this terrific, melodic movement.

The next movement begins in a rhythmic and dramatic manner. This alternates with more tranquil, melodic sections. The violins take it upon themselves to express in an attractive mood before the drama returns. Now we have movement, and melodic development. A brief pause leads into a simple folk phase, where the violins display wonderful lyricism. Brief dramatic interjections don't affect the persistent melodic nature and a stirring melodic line leads to a flourish to conclude.

The final movement starts in the minor tonality and the opening is sparse until a rhythmic episode develops, with stirring violin lines. A new tempo, almost dance-like, also produces fine melodies before a brief, but powerful minor passage, which leads into further fine melodies at tempo. An optimistic tone emerges and exciting melodies dominate proceedings. A fascinating descending violin line is a feature of the movement – it keeps popping up everywhere. The optimism continues, and, as we near the end, many pulsing interjections spar with the melodies. A minor chord concludes the movement.

This quartet is very melodic, which is a feature of Grieg's style. The first classical record I ever purchased was his *Peer Gynt Suites 1 & 2,* and I can still remember the contrasting longing, and optimistic melodies.

Many versions of this quartet are available. I fancy Grieg – *String Quartets*, on the Hyperion label, performed by the Chilingirian String Quartet. Spotify features three versions and several are on YouTube. There is also a wonderful performance by the Guarneri Quartet on earsense.

Listenability: A fine, Late Romantic work from a melodic master.

— ooOoo —

Jesús Guridi [1886–1961]

Nationality: Spanish-Basque
Quartets: Two
Style: Late Romantic

String Quartet No. 1

Jesús Guridi Bidaola's First Quartet was written in 1934, and consists of four movements. The piece has a beautifully haunting opening – two harmonised violins are at work here. This melody is developed and soon moves into a high register. A recapitulation of the opening is brief and leads to a pause, followed by a stately mood, filled with great emotion. Another pause introduces a strong harmonised chordal section which in turn gives way to an alluring passage as the violins sketch out a folk-sounding melody. A solo cello statement introduces another brief chordal section. The music now becomes more expansive, with a cello ostinato, while the violins continue with their sumptuous melodies. Another pause brings about a sparse violin duet that again evokes deep feeling. The violins dominate this movement as a further restatement of the opening melody is heard. The ending is very precious.

The second movement, marked vivace, features a singing solo violin introduction. Occasional ensemble sounds are heard as the violin continues with its mood and a strong cello line appears to complement the general character. A period of two violins leads into a slow passage – this is quite wonderful in its sparsity as the violins overlap with a moving, minor key melody. A fluttering cello passage completely changes the mood for a time, adding energy, but the violins conclude the movement on a wispy chord.

The third, adagio movement features the two violins in a lament, the cello and viola add support. This is a sombre mood, with a slight pulse. The violins reach out with a sustained period of great emotional depth – the sound is almost orchestral, the cello again being prominent and the feeling is achingly beautiful. A slight change in the mood is positive and the violins drift towards a faded ending, followed by a closing chord. What a wonderful movement.

The final movement sparkles as the violins duet with the cello in a dance-like manner. There are brief episodes of drama as the violins move forward at a bright tempo. A melodic motif is passed between the violins and cello as the viola provides rhythmic pizzicato interjections, leading to an optimistic mood. Some chordal passages are developed and a rhythmic impetus carries the work to a conclusion, which is a violin flourish.

The review CD, *Guridi: Complete String Quartets*, performed by the Breton Quartet, on the Naxos label is available on Amazon US and UK.

Samples can be heard on Spotify, YouTube and earsense.

Listenability: Slightly Spanish-sounding, melodic Late Romantic quartet.

— oo0oo —

Pavel Haas [1899–1944]

Nationality: Czech
Quartets: Three
Style: Early Modern

From Monkey Mountains
String Quartet No. 2

Haas was one of the musicians ostracized by Hitler's Nazi movement, as a purported proponent of *Entartete* (degenerate) music. He was killed in the Holocaust. Influenced by Janacek, under whom he studied, this work, *From Monkey Mountains,* ranges from agitation to wonderful brooding soundscapes, and many places in between. It is in four named movements.

Landscape – This first movement of String Quartet No. 2 is one of my favourites in the genre. It opens with a strikingly soulful, lamenting, repeated motif. I wouldn't call it an ostinato, as the tempo is so slow, but it does have impetus. A solo violin floats over this motif, which occasionally changes chords, leading to melodic development in the violin, even to the extent of sounding modal or ethnic. The motif gradually becomes louder, and the violin is ever so sparse now. A pause leads to a new harmonic background, which surges into a tempo. It's all background for a time. The violin reappears, this time over another motif. I feel that this motif **is** the music, even though we have violins drifting

186

across the surface. Now the motif becomes ever so slow and a wonderful harmonic change brings with it a new feeling. The cello steps to the forefront and it negotiates the previously mentioned change in harmony. The first violin returns to lament over a sombre background, interrupted by a flashy, descending phrase, which occurs a number of times. Now both violins are ascendant, one being busy in the high register and the second, playing soft, long, low tones, almost as part of the ensemble. The intensity eventually rises, and the opening motif reappears. The end is a long chord.

I feel as if I haven't done justice to the magnificence of this movement, but it would probably take several more pages to do so. I believe the background could stand on its own. It's a marvellous piece of writing.

Coach, Coachman and Horse – This relatively short movement opens with low string sound effects, and many glissandos. A phrase from the first movement is hinted at before the music is whipped into a frenzy. There is a persistent pulse, which gradually dissolves back into the opening. That first movement quote returns, it seems the composer is playing with us here. More quotes follow, then it absolutely races to the end.

The Moon and I – Returning to the longing nature of the first movement, a lamenting violin melody is supported with a sombre accompaniment. There is no tempo here, it is pure stasis. The second violin rises to the surface and the duet effect is wonderful – this is a most personal statement from the composer. It's like the first movement without the accompaniment. Now the cello comes into play and converses with the violins as a tempo forms. This mysterious, but lovely phase persists for some time until it peaks, then dissolves back into stasis. That wonderful harmonic change from the first movement is repeated, but under different rhythmic circumstances. A violin slowly emerges out of the space and makes a moving statement. Further harmonies from the first movement are repeated. You could reach out and touch this music, it is just so precious. It goes out with a whisper.

Wild Night – The final movement begins with a stilted violin played over a background of violin trills. Then a strong tempo is enforced, you can almost hear the jackboots. A pizzicato motif of a few bars leads into a slightly frenzied episode where a violin soars over powerful interjections. This **is** degenerate music. The hostile feeling gives way to a racing violin passage. The next section is almost burlesque in nature – it is so out of context, it mocks itself. Now the aggression returns, but only briefly and we are back into a most longing, peaceful atmosphere. The two violins lead the music, which is almost pathos. There are again distant references to the first movement. This is music of hope. A solo violin reaches skyward before the jackboots return to bring about a severe ending.

This is a fascinating, evocative work, with so much beauty, and, at times, not a little anger.

My review copy, titled *Haas-Krasa-String Quartets* performed by the Hawthorne String Quartet, in the Decca *Entartete Musik* series, seems to be no longer available. The problem with finding this composer's works is that there exists a Pavel Haas Quartet, who always come up in the searches. They have recorded No. 2, paired with Janacek's *Intimate Letters* on the Supraphon label. This sounds like a fine coupling, with plenty of passion. There is also a chamber orchestra version recorded by the Australian Chamber Orchestra, which I svery fine.

The Supraphon disc is on Spotify. The work is also on YouTube and both of the mentioned versions are on earsense.

Listenability: Early Modern – slightly abstract – ultimately brilliant.

[Image courtesy Supraphon Records]

Incidental Images #6

A Further Three x 3 String Quartet Composers

[Pyotr Ilyich Tchaikovsky - images courtesy Wiki Commons]

[Sergey Prokofiev - images courtesy Wiki Commons]

[Gabriel Faure - images courtesy Wiki Commons]

Alois Haba [1893–1973]

Nationality: Czech
Quartets: Sixteen
Style: Modern Contemporary

The Notes Between the Notes
String Quartets Nos. 5 & 7

There are several things worth mentioning about Haba. Firstly, he created his own system for dealing with microtones and also worked out a method of notation for his unique music. Secondly, he wrote the quartets in two time blocks. Nos. 1 to 5 were written from 1919 to 1923, while Nos. 6 to 16 were written from 1950 to 1967 – quite a gap really. The first five were fairly long, from 1950 they are all short. I'm going to discuss No. 5, the last one of the first block, and No. 7 which I happen to really like. It is also the first of three consecutive works that he wrote without using the microtone system.

The Fifth Quartet, which is in three movements, begins in a busy manner, full of interesting melodies and harmonies. I hear the cello accompaniment as sounding slightly dissonant due to the microtones – the violin is also dissonant. The music is not very structured, it's a bit of a free-for-all, with little melodic development. There is an ever so slight change and the ensemble weighs in behind the violin. Following are some violin duet lines, and the rhythm eventually stops, leading to a sense of freedom for a while. Now the cello picks up the pace and carries the music in a resolute manner. The violins are spirited as they play a long unison phrase that concludes the movement.

The second, andante movement, opens with a mournful passage where you can really notice the dissonance. A solo violin meanders over the ensemble and creates a long melodic line. The viola leads before the violins take over again – the dissonance is striking even though it is technically slight. The viola and cello rumble about while the violins muse in the foreground. The cello returns and the dissonance is becoming more powerful – this is modern music. The cello comes to the fore for a time as the other strings play sustained tones in the background. Now the violins reassert themselves and break into a harmonised line. The conclusion is a slow grind with the violin and cello fading out.

The final movement has a train-like rhythm. The cello is the engine and the violins are the crew. A beguiling violin melody is joined by the viola and the cello moves into a different feeling. There is a flourish, and another, before the cello ostinato returns to solidify the tempo. Now the cello leads while the others follow – even train-like string sound effects can be heard. A change in the rhythm brings some sweeping melodic statements but we are soon back to the cello ostinato which continues while the violins slow down, creating an interesting effect. The work finishes with a flourish. I didn't notice any microtones in this final movement.

String Quartet No. 7 from 1951, is again in three movements. The opening is quite orchestral, with a strong melody which abandons its slightly harsh edge and becomes more folk-like. It is now a touch serious, and the violins spar for a time before introducing a new melody. Things are busy, dramatic even. It doesn't last. The ensemble re-enters with the opening melody and ends on a chord.

The second movement opens with a tranquil, contemplative melody. A chordal period ensues and the violins rise above the ensemble, creating a fine impression. Now a second violin brings movement, gently expressing itself behind the first violin, but in a totally different way. There exists two moods at once, if that makes any sense. A tempo begins to develop with a violin phrase, and the second violin picks up on it – no cello or viola to be heard here. Now the whole ensemble regathers for a quiet closing chord.

The third movement is dance-like and is filled with a measured joyous energy, which turns folksy again with several attractive descending arpeggios to be heard as the violins flirt with each other. The cello enters to strengthen the rhythm and the movement ends with a fade and a flourish. As previously noted, no dissonance here.

I have long been fascinated by Haba and his uniquity in the use of quarter-tone and sixth-tone scales. The difference between his microtonal and regular tonal pieces is significant. He tends more to the modern.

I was a bit concerned about availability but a new set has now appeared so it is fair game.

Haba's quartets are only available as complete 4-CD sets. The one I have, on the Beyer Records label, by the Stamitz Quartet may not be available for much longer. When you spend a bit of time on Amazon, you notice ominous signs. The new set is by the Haba Quartett, on Neos Music, but I haven't heard it.

However you can, as it is on Spotify. There are also many quartets on earsense and YouTube.

Listenability: Fascinating Modern music in a unique style.

[Image courtesy NEOS label]

— ooOoo —

John Harbison [born 1938]

Nationality: American
Quartets: Five
Style: Contemporary Modern

String Quartet No. 2

John Harris Harbison appears to have been influenced by the American 1950-1960s school, which included Feldman and Cage et al, but seems to have broken free from that approach to create his own unique style. I intend to discuss String Quartet No. 2, which is in five movements. The composer markings for this quartet also make sense as movement names, so I shall use them.

Fantasia opens the work with the two violins carrying a sparse melancholy melody. One flies high, the other acts as support. Now the cello enters and the sound becomes one of slight chaos which continues with assertive violins. I wouldn't say it reaches breaking point, but it is powerful. Suddenly there is a change to a more structured melody, but it is still intense. This soon drops back to the opening theme, played with more conviction this time before a strong chordal moment comes out of nowhere and the movement is over.

Concerto is brief, and again features two violins, this time at tempo, with one violin pizzicato. Essentially, this movement is a bit of a romp with driving violin melodies. There is a drop in intensity and the end moves straight into the next movement.

Recitative and Aria, the longest movement, is slow and a violin plays long notes over a measured, sombre backdrop. There is no tempo, but some interplay starts to appear. The violins become agitated for a time with a flurry of short phrases as the intensity slowly diminishes and the piece assumes more form. This involves a solo violin, with occasional melancholic prompts from the ensemble. As the violin increases in intensity, the texture of the backdrop is thickened. After a time, the cello becomes prominent with its own melody, which cuts through the violins. It is a wonderful, intangible soundscape as the cello begins to soar and the ensemble rises with it – what a beautiful cacophony. Now the violins duel with piercing, jagged phrases. A brief pause brings about a gentle mood, with both violins engaging in melodic statements, similar to the opening feeling. However, the violins won't be subjugated, and they begin to move into their high register and continue their duel. Frequent statements from the cello occur, until the movement just fades away.

Sonata begins with gentle abstraction. The violins work this feeling with occasional interjections from the cello and it becomes more structured as the violins continue their third movement duel, and are quite animated. Now they settle, before starting to rebuild their dialogue again. This time it is even more mellow, with some harmonised melodic lines occurring. There is still a degree of abstraction, but nothing too noisy. Some string sound effects are heard and the ending is preceded by a rhythmic violin phrase, which carries over into the next movement.

Chorale Fantasia continues the phrase, until a violin totally deconstructs it, before resuming its previous dialogue. A pizzicato backdrop allows the violin and cello to make strong, ascending melodic statements. This transforms into a state of semi-chaos which continues for some time, and the full ensemble engages in a hectic episode. Further harmonised ascending melodic lines occur, building to a crescendo which concludes the piece.

This is a busy work, albeit with some pleasing slow moments. The review copy contains three other worthy quartets – I am especially fond of the third, which is in one movement. It features close harmony – that is, the music is in a fairly restricted tonal range, giving it a taut sound.

This disc, titled *First Four String Quartets*, on the Centaur label and performed by the Lydian String Quartet, is available on Amazon US and Presto.

It is also on Spotify and there are several quartet movements on YouTube. Many complete quartets can be found on earsense.

Listenability: Enjoyable, measured Contemporary Modernism.

— oo0oo —

Joseph Haydn [1732–1809]

Nationality: Austrian
Quartets: Sixty-eight
Style: Classical

Opus 33 – Rebirth of the String Quartet

I know I specified string quartets from 1800 but this one deserves a special mention. Before his first quartet, Haydn wrote several *divertimenti*, which is an 18th-century musical genre of a light and entertaining nature usually consisting of several movements for strings, winds, or both. Haydn's pieces were for two violins, viola and cello – a string quartet.

Haydn did not use the title *String Quartet* until his Opus 33, although all the early quartet ensemble works are now generally referred to as string quartets. Before we get to Opus 33, I would like to mention No. 1 of Opus 1. Its style is simple, static and neither rhythmically nor harmonically complex. It consists of a solo violin being accompanied by a violin, viola and cello. These latter three instruments share the same phrasing throughout the piece, only changing harmonically. They are never heard by themselves. The piece is basically a divertimento.

On to Opus 33, written in 1779 and known as *The Russian Quartets*. I have a quote from a website – foghornclassics.com:

When he published these quartets, Haydn described them as having been written "in a quite new, special manner," and the quartets - Haydn's first in eight years - represent a rethinking of the form. Gone are all traces of the old divertimento-style quartet, and in its place is an increasingly subtle approach to the possibilities of the form: a new clarity of texture, greater use of all four voices (particularly of the viola and cello), full exploitation of the motivic possibilities within themes, polished contrapuntal writing, and the replacement of the minuet movements with scherzos.

These changes in style were radical and they form the basis of the string quartet repertoire which followed. Although new forms have evolved and new ways of composing have been developed, these concepts are still embedded in modern string quartet composition, over 200 years on.

Haydn named String Quartet No. 1 of Opus 33 a *string quartet* and it contains many examples of the quoted concepts. It is in four movements.

The opening is a simple melody, in a call and response mode. Some of the accompaniment is in the old divertimento style but many other instances can be found where the ensemble breaks into individual, overlapping voices. There is a variation on the opening theme before we have an exposition repeat. Various themes are developed within the movement but it is simple, stylised music. A series of flourishes lead us into the conclusion.

The next movement is short, again it features call and response. It illustrates the creative use of overlapping instruments and counterpoint, which give the movement substance. Nearing the end, the violins converse, with a complex intertwining episode.

The third movement is a simple andante waltz, with a definite motif which runs, slightly modified, virtually through the whole movement. The cello has several solo moments during the opening melody before the violin takes over. After a time the cello has another solo statement before the ensemble returns and there is a recapitulation of the opening melody, which is fairly static, based on the ¾ waltz time. As it develops, the opening violin melody is extensively reharmonised. A change to a minor key brings about some melodic action and multiple voices abound. The cello comes to the fore once again until the first violin re-emerges to lead to a conclusion.

The final movement is in a frisky mood with the violins fairly racing. After a brief moderate section the virtuoso violins return and then converse. Changing harmonies allow for variation before the beginning reappears. The piece ends on a flourish.

This quartet is so different from Opus 1 – it's like radio compared with black and white TV. Hearing this style led Mozart to compose six quartets dedicated to Haydn and the pupil was able to outshine the master in invoking these new concepts. Beethoven took it a step further and gave us colour TV.

The six quartets that make up Opus 33 are all readily available. The whole set takes up two CDs but many single CDs exist, each containing up to three quartets. There is a version on Naxos by the Kodaly Quartet that contains the reviewed work. If you are going to invest in Haydn I suggest you start with Opus 33 or higher. Opus Nos. 64 and 76 are especially fine.

Most of Haydn's quartets are on Spotify and Opus 33 can be found here on YouTube. There are several pages of many Haydn quartets on earsense.

Listenability: He's not called the *father of the string quartet* for nothing. Pure Classical quartets.

Opus 51 – The Seven Last Words of Jesus Christ on the Cross

Opus 51 by Haydn was composed as an orchestral piece and was first performed for a Good Friday service in 1783. It was subsequently arranged for string quartet, as an oratorio, and was also published as a piano arrangement. It exists under many names – I have seen examples ranging from *The Seven Words* to *The Seven Last Words of Our Saviour on the Cross* and other variations.

Haydn was a devout Catholic and the string quartet arrangement is a tranquil, meditative piece with its mood truly reflecting the sombre nature of the title. The most striking aspect of the work is that all movements, with the exception of the last, are taken at slow tempos. The score is littered with tempo markings of *adagio*, *lento*, *largo* and *grave* – all related to slow and meaningful tempos. This gives the work a prayer-like quality and allows Haydn the opportunity to craft some transcendent melodies. There is some wonderful music here. The last movement is a satisfying forceful and almost symphonic finale.

Ultimately it is a spiritual and thought provoking quartet. I have not heard anything else like it.

I have fine performances by the Amadeus Quartet on Deutsche Grammophon and the Rosamunde Quartet on ECM. I can also recommend the version by the Kodaly Quartet on Naxos. There are several versions of the quartet on Spotify and YouTube, while earsense has ten versions of the work, including the superb Amadeus recording.

Listenability: A wonderfully spiritual quartet from the Classical master.

— oo0oo —

Gustav Helsted [1857–1924]

Nationality: Danish
Quartets: Five
Style: Late Romantic

String Quartet No. 5

I am going to discuss Helsted's last quartet, which is officially known as String Quartet in F minor, Opus. 33, written in 1922 and containing four movements.

The work opens with a melodic motif that repeatedly asks a question. A move to variations on this motif makes for a satisfying mood. There is plenty of rhythmic intensity for a time, until the opening question is revisited – more variations occur. A graceful period of melodic development ensues, this is somewhat pastoral. A new section is joyful and the questioning motif can occasionally be heard in the background. Pizzicato is introduced and the mood becomes quite intense as the violins are strong. This eventually subsides and some soft violin melodies finally give way to a strong chordal flourish.

The next movement, a presto, has a powerful introduction with much rhythmic impetus, before it gives way to a more relaxed violin duet passage, still at tempo. A change to a quieter section brings attractive melodies that are carried by two violins – this is a most romantic feeling. The intensity drops back to almost nothing and a new mood is slightly rhapsodic as the intensity gradually returns. The violins are again very fine as they drift in and out of various registers. Further pizzicato leads to another dynamic concluding flourish.

An andante movement commences at a dirge-like tempo, with all instruments in a low register. The cello throbs a pulsing motif as the violins intertwine in a serious manner. A lamenting passage slowly develops and the violins begin to become more forceful. A change returns to the opening character, this time the violins are wonderfully pure in their tone and melodic development, making for a marvellous feeling. Now a solo violin is heard, briefly, soon to be joined by its partner. The rhythm has gone and the violins express an alluring duet. The cello makes an entrance with long tones and the violins become more assertive before developing a rich chordal texture to finish.

The final movement begins in an assertive manner with much activity. The whole ensemble engages and moves into another pastoral phase with some delightful melodies passed around between the violins. The feeling remains strong for some time and rhythmic punctuation adds to the impetus, while the violins ebb and flow. This movement is a feature for the violins and they make for a delightful atmosphere. Nearing the end, they are positively dynamic as they make a dash to the concluding chord.

The review CD has this quartet paired with a fine decet (tentet) of curious instrumentation.

It is available as *Gustav Helsted - Decet & String Quartet* on the DaCapo label, performed by members of the Danish Sinfonietta, at Amazon US and UK.

The work can be heard on Spotify, YouTube and earsense.

Listenability: Classic Late Romanticism – a very fine melodic work.

Jacques Hétu [1938–2010]

Nationality: Canadian
Quartets: At least two
Style: Contemporary

String Quartets Nos. 1 and 2

The First Quartet, composed in 1972, and in four movements is considerably more energised than the Second and begins with some rhythmically probing violin lines. These phrases are cut short in an unusual staccato manner, almost clipped. The intensity is moderate as the violins spin out atonal lines, interspersed with strong rhythmic thrusts. A succession of short passages vary between rhythmic and more spacious melodic phrases – leading to an air of mystery and soon, a strange ending.

The following movement is mysterious from the start with long, atonal melodies reaching out to something unknown. Some mildly jagged chordal sounds in the low register are very evocative. A sense of vigour is now apparent, but it soon descends to the emotional depths of the previous passage. A solo violin wails over a solemn background and features a strong attack with the bow, leading to some piercing notes. This doesn't last and the violin retreats into the depths of the accompaniment, with long foreboding tones which conclude the movement.

The third movement is brief and opens in a furious manner. Violin stabs are accompanied by an ostinato until a mood similar to some of the previous movement begins to unfold. This a followed by a return to the frantic, before a short period of atonal pizzicato races furiously to the end.

The final movement has a strange, disjointed nature as two violins construct seemingly random lines. Now they combine in an unusual harmony as they edge their way forward. This entropic passage has the violins scurrying, sometimes with intensity. A new mood ensues as the violins return to an atonal approach, definitely an impalpable feeling here. Different passages reappear with some of the earlier frantic activity being present. The end is a sustained dissonant chord from the two violins.

On to the Second Quartet, in three movements, which was written in 1991.

An adagio movement commences the work, with a sparse, lamenting violin line and a measured accompaniment. Gradually the solo violin breaks free for a time, and is then joined by a sympathetic second violin. This section features a gentle atonality – the mood is quite superb. A solo cello is heard and it is absorbed into the music, almost effortlessly. A quivering of bows form a shimmering background as the violin again becomes the dominant voice. A brief pause leads to the return of the second violin and they drift forward, almost trance-like, eventually leading to a faded ending.

The next movement begins in an energised manner as a tension is developed by all instruments. This soon peters out, leaving an atonal conversation between the violins with occasional cello and violin interjections. Now more energy is heard and the violins spar with pizzicato mutterings from the viola and cello. Again, the energy dissipates and the violins muse, before adopting an animated discussion – the end is sharp.

The final movement features a resonant timbre, at a tempo that is virtually rubato and formless. The violins express a gentle rhythmic pulse and the cello weaves in and around this passage with a great degree of feeling, until it is temporarily overwhelmed by the violins, although they are still quite circumspect. This evokes a marvellous sense of atonal, peaceful beauty. A pause brings about a gentle, sensitive moment of sparse wonder before long, sustained chords conclude the work.

The review CD, *Hétu: Complete Chamber Works for Strings*, on the Naxos label, performed by the New Orford String Quartet also contains two enhanced ensemble pieces, a *Sextet* and *Serenade*, together with some other incidental pieces for string quartet. It is available at a nice price on Amazon US, but is quite expensive on Amazon UK.

This disc can be found on Spotify and there is an alternative version of String Quartet No. 2, by the Saint John String Quartet on earsense.

Listenability: Mildly confronting modernist quartets.

— ooOoo —

Hidden Treasures – Compilation

Nationality: Various
Quartets: N/A
Style: Mostly 20th Century

A Contemplative Compilation

This disc is a themed compilation of mostly introspective works for string quartet. I intend to discuss three composers' contributions.

Alisdair MacClean's String Quartet No. 2 is in two movements, both of which are marked lento and lento-allegro, respectively. This work seems to set the mood for the whole CD. A solo violin initiates the movement with long tones, eventually backed by mild pizzicato statements. String sound effects abound and a deep solo cello statement is heard. An air of palpable tension evolves as cello lines are paraphrased by first one, then two violins and a sense of forward propulsion is felt. The sound of the strings is now very rich and mournful as the long tones return. Out of this feeling arises a strong but serious melodic line with the cello and pizzicato viola providing abstract support. A plucked viola accompanies a solo violin line to the end.

Again, a solo violin opens the second movement, with droning ensemble sounds that morph first into arrhythmic interjections before moving on to an ensemble dialogue with folk-like melodies. A pulse is created and the violin, and then cello, express longing statements to the sound of a chordal rhythm. This passage is of a pastoral nature but there are also some serious melodic statements interspersed within the mood. The violins now reach higher and the cello responds with a powerful passage which calls the violins to heel. A brief reprise leads to a solo violin being answered by the ensemble, leading to a brief flourish to conclude.

John Ireland's *The Holy Boy*, whilst being extremely short has come to be seen as a classic of British string quartet composition. Its length belies its beauty as the sweetest of harmonised violin melodies unfold. It feels like a tone-poem in miniature, with simple, but wonderfully expressive melodies being at its heart. The end is pure.

The longest work on the CD is Srul Glick's *From Out of the Depths*, which is in six named movements. This piece can be seen as a summing up of the emotional tone of the whole disc. All of the movements pertain to contemplation and reflection on things of the past.

Mourning Music features a pensive ensemble, with deep emotional expression and no change in dynamics. The reflective tone is sustained for the whole of its short duration.

These I Remember is not much longer, but while having a gentle rhythmic pulse which edges the music forward, it is bereft of melodic development. Suddenly, a soaring violin rises above the ensemble with a fine melodic statement which transforms the movement – the end comes quickly.

Lament is again brief and features a violin duet over a drone background. The melodies are achingly beautiful, in a way evoking Arvo Pärt, before the drone fades to a conclusion.

I Believe opens in a lush, lyrical manner, seemingly much more contemporary than its predecessors. Quivering bows support an attractive melody, before a change to a gently throbbing passage brings all instruments to bear on the feeling. The volume increases although not for long, as the music briefly pauses before returning to the opening mood. It finishes on a strong chordal sweep.

So Many Times is another lamenting piece, with two overlapping violins expressing powerfully over an understated ensemble. A new theme evokes something familiar, possibly the opening of Debussy's *Prelude to the Afternoon of a Faun*, before moving into another heartfelt passage to conclude.

Remembrance contains another inspirational melody, very simple in nature, which develops into a gentle rhapsody, before finishing the work.

The music on this CD is remarkable for its consistent interpretations of profound, contemplative soundscapes.

The other composers represented on the disc are Joaquin Turina, Ernest MacMillan, Healey Willan, Frank Bridge and Ernest Bloch, some of which can be found elsewhere in this book. I must admit to concentrating on the melancholy as there is also some more positive music here, but certainly not much.

The review CD, titled *Hidden Treasures*, on the Naxos label and performed by the Saint John String Quartet, is available on Amazon US and UK.

It can also be sampled in full on Spotify and YouTube.

Listenability: Charming, but deeply involving twentieth century works.

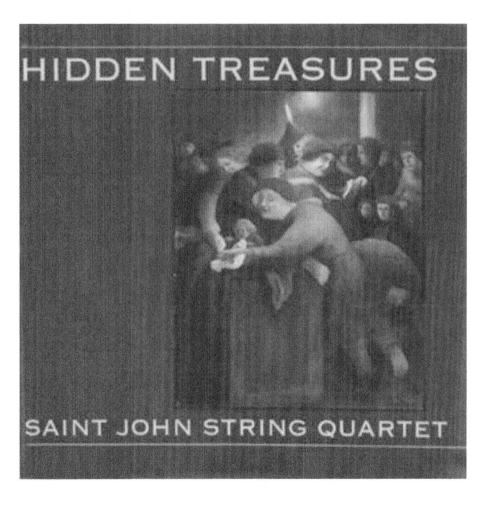

[Image courtesy Naxos label]

Paul Hindemith [1895–1963]

Nationality: German
Quartets: Seven
Style: Early Modern

The Lost Quartet
String Quartet No. 1

Hindemith's Opus 2 – String Quartet No. 1, sometimes called No. 0, was only discovered in 1994. My complete set of the composer's quartets by the Kocian Quartet was unfortunately recorded before this date and therefore does not feature the piece, which is disappointing. I shall be discussing it from a different, single CD. It is a four movement work, quite long at just over 40 minutes.

It has one of the finest openings in the chamber music repertoire. For me, it is up there with the opening of the Felix Mendelssohn *String Octet* in terms of its vigour and pure joy. It has such a forward propulsion and an, oh, so positive melody as you will find. Hindemith works with this melody for about two minutes before he introduces a new theme. There is a persuasive motif that the composer feels bears repeating. Moving into another phase features a recapitulation of the opening – it is wonderful to hear it again in a long restatement. A new theme develops and we are treated to another set of variations on the opening theme. New melodic lines fly by, recapitulations occur and the momentum is sustained until a quiet passage brings with it introspection. All the while you can sense the opening theme as the composer applies multiple sets of variations to the melodic material. The brisk tempo mostly continues throughout the whole movement. Another recapitulation occurs – I can never get enough of it.

A slow period brings forth a particularly brilliant melody. The tempo lessens for a short while and the change produces another new melody. A previous theme is reintroduced, and again there is hint of the opening. Hindemith is determined to sustain the tempo and introduces multiple sets of variations. The final moments are reflective as he leads the movement to a satisfying end. I just love this movement. I think it is one of the finest in the string quartet repertoire. What a wonderful discovery it must have been in 1994.

The second movement, marked adagio, features a quiet and beguiling theme. The cello and the first violin dominate over an extended melody. Eventually the theme builds and breaks into a moderate tempo with a new melodic line – this is a charming section. I can hear hints of melodies from the first movement, but they are never resolved. A slow passage unfolds, with the solo cello reaching the bottom of its range. The violin returns with a wonderful melody that just seems to go on and on. The ensemble builds a feeling of great strength, they are resolute. Then the movement drops away, leaving the violin to sketch out a sombre melody, backed by the cello. As the theme develops, the ensemble returns and fills out the music, giving it a grand feeling, as the violin soars and works at subthemes from the first movement. With the movement winding down, there is another return to material from the first theme as it quietly fades away. I had never noticed it before but these first two movements are inextricably linked.

Movement three opens with a skittish phase, led by the violin. The dynamics change to a lower level, but the feeling is sustained. The cello enters and dialogues with the violin, becoming chaotic in a pleasant manner. This gives way to a slow passage, where the violin and cello are predominant. It is a fascinating interlude, with a lot of intertwining of lines. The opening feeling returns, as the violin struts its stuff, with interjections from the ensemble. Then it stops, just like that.

The fourth and final movement begins in a jovial manner, very playful. The violin sets a breakneck pace as the ensemble attempts to keep up. After a while, the intensity drops but the feeling continues – this is a celebration. The first violin prevails and I notice a theme from the first movement in the cello, very subtly before a violin quotes openly from the same movement. It continues to dominate, almost in a frantic but not frenzied manner, constantly moving the music forward. More recapitulation occurs – Hindemith certainly gets value from his melodic material. The violin leads the movement to a graceful conclusion.

This is a terrific string quartet. My review copy, *Paul Hindemith: String Quartets, Vol. 3*, on the Naxos label and performed by the Amar Quartet also contains String Quartet No. 4, arguably Hindemith's most popular quartet.

This CD is on Spotify. The first movement of No. 1 can be heard on YouTube, together with many others – earsense has three versions of the work.

Listenability: One of my favourite string quartets. Long and worth every second.

String Quartet No. 4

This work is in five movements and opens with a solo lamenting violin, soon to be joined by the viola. I would describe the feeling as gently atonal. The cello enters and the intensity rises for a short time, only to briefly revert back to the original mood. Now comes an aggressive, agitated passage followed by a fade and a brief pause before a violin meanders wistfully with a walking cello line in support. It is a beautiful piece of writing. The viola returns to add to the ambience – this lasts for a few minutes and is rather attractive. Now a sense of foreboding comes over the work as the violins and viola become slightly darker. The faded ending is very precious.

The next movement opens with a loud dynamic. The violin engages with the ensemble before the piece drops back to a lower volume with a slightly agitated feeling. A pause allows for a solo cello statement, which leads the music into a forceful rhythm. The violin again engages in a duel with the ensemble, then gradually moves the music back into a peaceful space. As the end approaches there is a short burst of intensity and the ensemble finishes on a strong chord.

The third movement opens with a cello ostinato which varies its harmony as it develops. This has a slightly stately feeling, along with a sense of atonality. The ostinato returns briefly before a pause brings the violins together over a walking cello line. A fascinating section follows as the violins develop a conversational rapport. The ostinato is reintroduced, and the writing for the violins is expressive. Slowly the intensity rises, only to fall again when the cello goes into half-time, leading to much more space. Now it's just one violin and the cello, leading to a fade out.

The next, short movement opens with a strong cello, soon to be joined by the violins. A brief pause leads to the cello conversing with the violins for a few moments and then it's all over. It is a strange movement, not seeming to sit comfortably with the rest of the music.

The final movement is again violin and cello meandering in a slightly atonal interlude. Things become busy and loud. I believe that at the halfway point, we have still only heard violin and cello. Now the viola enters and a frantic atmosphere ensues. Nearing the end, it drops back again to violin and cello. A loud flourish concludes the piece.

Apparently, this is one of Hindemith's most popular quartets. Although it has many peaceful moods, there are also some aggressive passages.

No. 4 is paired with the marvellous No. 1 on Naxos so it represents a good introduction to Hindemith. Besides more single CDs, several complete 2-CD sets can be found on Amazon. I think I would lean towards the Danish Quartet on CPO, as it also contains the lost quartet.

The Naxos release is on Spotify and No. 4 can be found on YouTube. Again, earsense excels, with seven different recordings of the work.

Listenability: A strange mixture of intangible beauty interspersed with agitation.

— ooOoo —

Vagn Holmboe [1909–1996]

Nationality: Danish
Quartets: Twenty
Style: Contemporary

String Quartets Nos. 3 & 7

Vagn Gylding Holmboe wrote 20 string quartets, which is likely to be more than any other serious composer from the twentieth-century. As one of a number of various Nordic composers that I have heard, I believe they share a common sound, and work within the same emotional areas. Of course, this is a generalisation but common traits often do occur.

I am going to discuss a peaceful String Quartet No. 3, which is in four movements and opens in a bleak and introspective manner. A violin attempts to set up a melody to get the piece moving but it remains static. After a brief cello statement the violin brilliantly paints a longing soundscape which is maintained until the texture thickens and the violin jousts with the other voices. It is not sustained and we return to the violin, supported by murky interjections. Finally the violin soars above the ensemble for a moment before concluding the movement as a solo voice.

The next movement is busy and the sound is one of four equal voices scurrying about, creating mildly abstract lines and a tempo to match them. Things start to develop as the intensity drops with the texture becoming lighter. The constant movement still prevails as each voice makes its contribution. There is a flurry near the end, the ambience dissipates and the violin fades out to conclude.

The third movement opens with a gentle atonal fugue and, another evocative soundspace. The composer seems to revel in wandering melodies and so far has not provided anything resembling a tempo. In Holmboe's world, all voices are equal, with the occasional spirited violin phrase being the exception to the rule.

The final movement begins with a short motif, repeated a few times before launching into a passage which is bordering on chaos. Again, the equal voices propel the movement forward. Now many short segments change incrementally, but the overall sound doesn't vary substantially. A pause signals a slight variation as the ensemble work together for a time before it is back to the jousting, leading to a flourish, and the violin ends with two chords.

This is a fabulous, slightly introspective atonal work. It is very rewarding.

String Quartet No. 7 is much more dynamic. The work was written in 1964-65 and is in three movements. It offers up a completely different soundscape from that of the Third. It opens in an aggressive fashion with the cello salient and slowly, the other instruments respond to its call. The violin is shrill and this softens the mood to become almost pastoral as the violins converse. This leads into another cello-driven aggressive mood which does not last long as the violin dialogue returns. It is also brief, and we have a repeat of the cello-led section. The violin dialogue resumes – it's bitter-sweet. Finally, nearing the end, the cello returns and the movement concludes as it began. This is some dramatic music.

The next movement begins with a pizzicato phase which sets up the violin to flit about as it likes. There is a sense of something scurrying about this, and the voices hint at atonality. Now there is a change and we have a gently peaceful passage for a while – it doesn't last and the chaos returns. A resumption of the pizzicato proceeds to the end of the movement.

The final movement opens with a longing section, and a sparse melody. It's beautiful if you are drawn to the introspective. The violins move forward and the cello provides support. A soft brief motif is introduced and the violin returns solo, bringing the motif with it, somewhat louder this time. Slowly a chaos takes over, but after a time it fades back into a sparsity again. The violin predominates for a short while until it is joined by the ensemble, and it jumps into a furious tempo which is then terminated by a conspicuous cello, leading to a solo violin lament until the other voices add a measured support. It is another extraordinary section, taut but eminently rewarding. As the end becomes near, all join in for a final flourish to conclude the movement. This is a fine, vigorous work.

Holmboe's complete quartets have been recorded on the DaCapo label by the Kontra Quartet on seven CDs. No. 3 is on Volume 1, and No. 7 on Volume 3. They are also available in a complete box set. As some of the CDs are becoming deleted, you can buy the box set on Amazon UK for less than the price of a single CD. If he appeals to you, go for the box now. You can be sure it won't be around for long and it's reasonably priced both on Amazon US and UK.

Surprisingly, the complete box set is on Spotify, and many quartets are on earsense and YouTube.

Listenability: Fascinating mood-driven Nordic works.

— ooOoo —

Arthur Honegger [1892–1955]

Nationality: Swiss
Quartets: Three
Style: Early Modern

Moving With Modernity
String Quartets Nos. 1 & 3

Honegger wrote three string quartets between 1917 and 1937. In these two, three movement works, you can hear the composer's development as he becomes aware of things going on around him.

String Quartet No. 1 was written in 1917. The first movement is marked appassionato which sounds promising. Passionate it is, as the ensemble attacks some strong melodies with vigour. The music softens and becomes lilting until the fire returns. Then follows a moment where the composer, and the ensemble, pause for breath. When they resume, the movement alternates between passion, with slightly atonal melodies, and periods of a more conservative selection of notes. The energy persists until it is time to dawdle to a conclusion.

The second movement is the emotional centrepiece of this work. It is marked adagio and runs for thirteen minutes, about half the length of the quartet. This features a stunning opening, played with great feeling. The cello then goes it alone until the ensemble inevitably enters – it is slow and calm. There seem to be no melodies for a time, just a soundscape – my kind of music. When the melodies do arrive, they are just so intangible, you are not sure whether they are melodies or a soundscape. After a short while, some form begins to emerge. There is some wonderful writing here, somewhat reminiscent of a tone poem, it is just so focussed on the delicate ambience. The feeling becomes more expansive for a time but soon returns to the tranquility, which persists until it totally subsides. I don't believe I have heard a softer slow movement of this length.

The third and final movement starts off in an emphatic manner, producing quite a contrast. I am finding the first part of the movement dull, there just doesn't seem to be any musical progress – I keep waiting for something to happen. Approaching the end, there is a bit of a flourish which then transforms into a gentle pastoral flavour which remains until the end of the movement.

There was a long gap before the Second Quartet was written in 1936. I am going to leave this one as the Third was written just a year later, in 1937.

The Third Quartet opens with some atonal musings, signalling the difference in style to the first – it is considerably more modern. I'd like to call it a secretive allegro as it takes time to reveal its intentions, eventually working its way into a vigorous, mildly atonal frolic. Near the conclusion it reverts to secretive again, and goes out with further furtive atonal musings.

The second movement is another adagio which again is a lot more modern than that of the First Quartet. A gentle atonality pervades the opening – the melodies are measured and it has a special kind of peace. The movement is more than half over before it begins to assert itself, only to return to the previous mood. Near the conclusion it barely rises above a whisper as it peters out. It is a fascinating, mesmeric movement.

The final movement opens with a walking cello while ornaments are provided by the ensemble. This changes into a rhythm, which bubbles along with slightly abstract playing from the violins. It settles into a tranquil cello interlude, leading to particularly positive ensemble work. When the impetus returns, it is sustained until the conclusion.

These pieces reveal Honegger to be open to the progress that the string quartet idiom was going through in his time. His was a measured response, but there is a definite change in emphasis from the First to the Third Quartet.

All three quartets are freely available on Amazon US and UK, including a version on Surround Sounds, performed by the Erato Quartet. Spotify has Quartets Nos. 1 and 2 and you can listen to them on YouTube. All three quartets can be found on earsense.

Listenability: Late Romantic moving forwards.

Katherine Hoover [born 1937]

Nationality: American
Quartets: Two
Style: Contemporary

String Quartet No. 1

This four movement work opens in a serious manner with sparse atonal violins. Then a viola ostinato takes over, in a strange, hesitant rhythm. I counted it out as five-and-a-half beats to the bar, and I'm reliably informed that this can be described as an 11/8 time signature. It's subtle, but you can feel a sense of rhythmic uncertainty here. The violins eventually drift in with their soft contributions and a melody forms. The sound cuts back to the viola with a throbbing cello for a time before the violins return and a violin flurry leads to a tempestuous violin duet where atonal phrases are freely exchanged. This gives way to a quiet phase, which is tonal, and quite fetching. The violins slowly become more serious and proceed to a fluttering ending.

The next movement features a brief flourish before moving into a tempo. The viola and cello lay down a rhythmic pattern and the violins drift casually across, and around it. Staccato bowed strikes add to the effect. A slightly entropic episode ensues as the violins persist, but the tempo disappears and the cello adds melodic jabs. Now we have a dialogue between a violin and the cello, which again, displays no obvious tempo. This short movement ends on a violin thrust.

The third movement opens with an eerie, questioning violin, evoking a response from the ensemble. The texture is sparse but a melody eventually emerges – it's modal and engaging. Gradually a warmth develops and the melody is complemented by the second violin, leading to a fascinating atmosphere. The melodies are more expansive now, and brief violin flutters begin to appear. The violins sustain the atmosphere to the conclusion.

The final movement features some dynamic violin thrusts as the violins play off each other – it is atonal and intense. The level of abstraction rises for a time, then drifts into a texture of string sound effects. Now a viola pizzicato provides a background for the violins' musings. A series of vigorous interjections leads to a strong rhythmic pattern which eventually gives way to a probing section, where melodies are teased out against a backdrop of rhythm. As the end nears, the violins drift into the high register and we are left with a final cello note.

This is a terrific contemporary work with a moderate dash of modernistic traits. String Quartet No. 2, which is also on the disc, is more modern, but still appealing. As a bonus there is also a string trio included.

This CD, titled *Hoover: String Quartets Nos. 1 & 2 – Trio*, performed by the Colorado Quartet, on the Parnassus label, is available on Amazon US and Presto.

It is also on Spotify and all tracks on the CD are on <u>YouTube</u>. The two quartets are on <u>earsense</u>.

Listenability: Serious, but ultimately rewarding.

— oo0oo —

Christian Horneman [1840–1906]

Nationality: Danish
Quartets: Two
Style: Romantic

String Quartets Nos. 1 and 2

Horneman's two string quartets, written in 1859 and 1861 respectively, are both conservative Romantic works. Each consists of four movements, including one slow movement, which was the standard form for string quartets of the composer's time.

The First Quartet opens in a stirring fashion with sweeping, pulsating violin melodies. Several solo cello interludes make for a fine contrast with the expressive nature of the violins, which constantly push the music forward. Rhythmic melodic lines abound and the cello is very prominent, often repeating violin phrases – this is uplifting music. A hint of a minor <u>tonality</u> deepens the texture as the violins continue to intertwine with strong, positive melodies. A swirling passage leads to a final chord.

An <u>andante</u> movement follows, with a poignant violin melody being supported by appropriately measured ensemble playing. A pause leads into a fine, almost enchanting passage where the first violin crafts expansive melodies, set against a gently rhythmic background. Now the cello has a part to play and dialogues with the solo violin, in a dance-like manner. Slowly, a new mood forms with an enthused violin part and an active ensemble. This eventually becomes understated and the violin is very melancholy here. Suddenly, a strong passage again leads into a final chord.

The brief third movement is set at a jaunty tempo in a classic Romantic style – shades of the past here. A rhythmic change leads to a charming section of violin melodies developed over ensemble thrusts. The sound is so sweet for a time, until an energy returns to the music, with flurries of violin strokes contributing to a joyful nature, which continues until the end.

The final movement opens in a virtuosic manner, with the first violin positively racing. There is a strong interplay with the ensemble here and the cello appears to mimic the violin, even to the extent of using forceful trills. Now the music begins again, as the first violin fashions a new mood, one of fast, but <u>lyrical</u>

lines and several virtuosic flourishes. A prominent descending violin line is repeated and the energy level is high. There is a strong final flourish to conclude.

The Second Quartet also opens in a positive manner, before giving way to a more serious tone with the first violin leading the ensemble through various harmonic backgrounds. An increase in tempo continues the serious sound with the first violin simply dazzling for a time. The backing is inherently busy, but still manages to respond to the melodic musings of the first violin. Nearing the end, a change of rhythm and harmony evoke Mendelssohn's *Octet for Strings* – high praise indeed. The conclusion lets the listener down easy.

The second, adagio movement is a stately exposition of a harmonised theme. This sumptuous, slightly serious melody is surrounded by a great deal of space. The music simply aches, belying its simplicity and is wonderfully executed. The cello part is simply outstanding, its rich tone blending with the violin. Now a gently pulsing ensemble rhythm is introduced – the violin is wistful at this time, as the ensemble ebbs gently. The tempo recedes and a rubato passage ensues, leading to a great depth of feeling. A new tempo is established but the violin is understated in its expression. The end comes ever so quietly.

The third, brief movement commences with a moderate tempo, accented by ensemble interjections. A pause leads to another rubato passage and then into an alluring rising melodic line, developing into a hint of some familiar phrase that I can't quite place. A recapitulation of the opening follows to conclude.

The finale is energised and features delightful harmonised melodic lines at tempo. There is a feeling of the Classical era here – Mozart and Haydn. Now a dominant violin melody ensues, as the ensemble seem to struggle to keep up. Strong cello lines emerge and lead to a duet with the violin, evoking a feeling of great energy. This duet continues to evolve and undergoes several changes of harmony. With the return of the ensemble, the cello is no less evident and the violin positively races to a final flourish.

The review CD also contains a short, one movement work by another Danish composer, Asger Hamerik who was a little later than Horneman. The CD, titled *Horneman - Hamerik: String Quartets*, performed by the Arild String Quartet and on the DaCapo label, is available on Amazon US and UK.

It can be sampled on Spotify, YouTube and earsense.

Listenability: Fine, melodic Romantic works of great depth and melodic invention.

Incidental Images #7

Portrait of Woman with Cello

[Messages String Quartet cellist Urbanek-Kalinowska]
[Image courtesy MSQ website]

Joseph Horovitz [born 1926]

Nationality: Austrian–British
Quartets: At least five
Style: Early Modern

String Quartets Nos. 4 & 5

Although I have classified Horovitz as Early Modern, there is also a sense of Romanticism to be found in his music. I am going to discuss String Quartets Nos. 4 and 5.

The Fourth Quartet, in three movements, features a tempo marking of grave *maestoso* (stately or majestic), and opens in this manner. A rich, deep solo cello line is harmonised by violins, making for a most expressive introduction. The violins work their way into a strong section, briefly pause and then become slightly wistful as they dialogue, leaving the cello to walk in a jazz-like pizzicato. Now a feeling of drama unfolds and the violins become more animated, in a prancing manner. A return to the sound of a solo cello, again walking, leads to an alluring violin passage where harmonised lines approach, but never quite realise, a sense of dissonance. There is a passion in this music, before a violin concludes with a line that floats over a sustained ensemble chord.

The next movement, marked allegro-molto, liberates the piece and suggests a slightly perfunctory character, with a measured section of lilting violins. A brief pause ensues and now the violins come again with more authority, again mildly dissonant. A pulsing cello phrase brings energy and a return to the opening character. The end is a slightly self-mocking pizzicato over a strong cello phrase.

The final lento movement is especially beautiful as gentle melodies move in waves over a sparse accompaniment – this is music of the heavens. A solo violin first expresses lyrically, then moves into a trilling pattern, which leads the ensemble to return with distant, evocative sounds. A new section features sparse intertwining melodic lines, with the cello being prominent. A brief moment of tension soon dissipates and the end is rather casual.

The Fifth Quartet, in one movement, is again majestic in its beauty. Several lamenting violin lines are heard before a tempo is established. There is some tonal ambiguity here as the music becomes a little introspective. A chaos ensues, with rhythmic violin punctuations creating tension. Now serenity returns as the violins move in a slow, expressive manner – they just manage to keep the music alive. This is a magnificent mood, with a divine feeling not often favoured by Contemporary composers.

A shift to a strongly rhythmic passage leads to the two violins conversing at a rapid pace, with occasional ensemble interspersions. The feeling turns almost chaotic as the violins constantly criss-cross each other's slightly dissonant melodic lines. The intensity eventually gives way to pensive violins over a persistent viola motif. Another brief pause initiates a sumptuous passage, where the cello provides a rich harmonic and rhythmic environment.

212

A further pause brings a return to chaos, with the dynamics varying widely as the passage unfolds. A brief pizzicato moment slows the pace and lowers the intensity, back to an almost complete stasis – this is particularly moving as the violins evoke a sense of wonder, which is continued to a most satisfying conclusion.

These two works are most exhilarating, and contain many fine moments.

The review CD, *Joseph Horovitz - Fantasia & Quartets*, performed by the Carducci Quartet on their label, Carducci Classics, also contains two other significant works – a fine *Fantasia on a Theme of Couperin* by the presumably augmented Carducci Ensemble and a stunning *Oboe Quartet*, featuring one Nicholas Daniel on oboe. The CD is available on Amazon US and UK.

This music can be heard on Spotify, YouTube and earsense.

Listenability: Charming, captivating string quartet works.

— ooOoo —

Jacques Ibert [1890–1962]

Nationality: French
Quartets: One – FOSQC
Style: Early Modern

The String Quartet

The work opens in a snappy manner, with the violins expressing lines that seem to envelop themselves, somewhat akin to circular motion. This continues for some time until a solo cello line appears, leading into an answering solo violin phrase. Soon the tempo abates and a rubato passage becomes serious. Some sparse melodic phrases create a magical moment, but a sense of tempo soon returns, slightly less dynamic than the opening section. Now we have another change, into a short rubato, then the cello pushes out statements as the violins scurry about in response. A return to the opening flavour is a delightful mood which finally ends on a high violin and cello note.

The next, andante movement, commences with a lush, almost rhapsodic lament. The violins seem to strain out the notes over a static cello background, all the while sustaining this feeling as they overlap melodic lines to great effect. This is a most melancholy mood. Gradually the violins rise in pitch and intensity as they move into a serious chordal section, which is followed by a brief pause that seems to allow the composer to gather his thoughts. A solo violin moves to the forefront and the ensemble moves in behind it, in a very sparse manner. The violin can often be heard solo here, but the second violin also has plenty to say at other times. A feeling of angst comes over the music with both violins residing in their lowest registers. The cello makes for a mournful sound as the violins

213

slowly edge forward to a prolonged lamenting chord to conclude. This movement has to be worth the price of admission – it's a beautiful piece of writing.

The third movement is a short presto dominated by pizzicato, particularly from the cello and viola. Simple melodies abound in this fantasy of a mood. The music is quite trivial, and it ends unexpectedly.

The final movement starts with a busy solo cello, soon to be joined by a violin, which expresses playfully. At this time, the cello part is as important as the violin. The second violin joins the mood and the music moves forward, all the time increasing in intensity – it is becoming quite manic. A long descending violin line leads to a flourish to end. The cello has been prominent throughout the whole of this movement.

The review CD, titled *Chamber Music*, on the Somm label, and performed by the Bridge Quartet also contains another short, fetching piece, *Souvenir* for string quartet. The rest of the disc is made up of further Ibert chamber works.

This CD is available on Amazon UK and Presto Classical, although they may make you wait for it. Amazon US has it as a download only.

The quartet can be heard on Spotify, YouTube and earsense.

Listenability: A sparkling work, with a deeply felt slow movement.

— oo0oo —

Vincent d'Indy [1851–1931]

Nationality: French
Quartets: Three
Style: Late Romantic

String Quartet No. 1

Interestingly, Vincent d'Indy had an asteroid, (11530 d'Indy), named after him in 1992.

The First Quartet is in four movements and opens with a stark statement played by the ensemble before a solo violin takes over. The statement reappears and the ensemble returns with some elegant, slightly longing chords. There is a strange absence of melody within these chords and, when it does come, it is ever so subtle. The cello sets the piece into a tempo – now it's the violins leading the way. The music bubbles along until a chord change ushers in a tranquil period from which emerges some strong melodies, the first encountered so far. The cello is particularly fine here and leads the quartet into a minor tonality. This is an intense phase and the dynamics change freely several times before settling. A change ensues as the cello leads into a faster tempo, almost racing – the end is in sight. Complex chords and rhythms drive this section which concludes on a chord. The recording engineers were really getting into the reverb on this one. I noticed it in the staccato opening and it is even more obvious at the end, with a long delay on the last chord.

The second movement, marked *lent* (see lento), is the emotional centrepiece of the work. It starts with a sparse minor tonality, the violin gently washing over the ensemble until the viola takes over and a tempo slowly emerges. The violins return with a bright, but calm melody – simply gentle music. A brief crescendo eases into a quiet cello melody and a change back to the major tonality. Overlapping melodies occur here with the viola being salient before the cello takes over for a shared conclusion. It is indeed fascinating, beautiful music.

The next movement begins in a folk-like manner at a slow tempo. Suddenly the viola takes up a dancing rhythm. A change in tonality brings the tempo back – then it is the violin's turn to lead the dance. The skipping tempo is provided by the viola and cello, and the violins are skittish above them. The tempo pauses, and harmonised melodies abound. This is another wonderful movement.

The finale begins with a longing violin, and things happen slowly here. Occasional interjections by the other instruments gradually build into something tangible. It is two minutes before anything like a pulse is felt. Then, breaking into tempo, the mood is dance-like for a time. After a brief pause, the tempo returns, together with a buoyancy as the dynamics rise and fall, all the while retaining the tempo. A new slower passage begins with the cello being especially prominent. As the piece progresses it recalls the first movement and there are lots of sweeping, and swooping of violins as the piece races to its conclusion. What a marvellous work.

I have the three quartets, together with a string sextet, by Quatuor Joachim on Caliope. This version appears to be in a state of uncertainty re availability. Quartets Nos. 1 & 2 are available by the Kodaly Quartet on the Marco Polo label. The first is also paired with Chausson's only quartet by the Chilingirian Quartet on Heliope. Something I hadn't known about the Chausson was that it was incomplete when he died. Vincent d'Indy completed the third movement.

The Kodaly is on Spotify and several d'Indy quartets are on YouTube. All three quartets can be found on earsense.

Listenability: Wonderful French Late Romantic music.

[d'Indy in 1910 – source – Wiki Commons]

— ooOoo —

Andres Isasi [1890–1940]

Nationality: Basque
Quartets: Six
Style: Late Romantic

String Quartet No. 4

Andrés Isasi's string quartets are numbered 0 through 5. A '0' usually indicates that the quartet was discovered later, possibly after his death. Interestingly, he wrote String Quartets 0 & 1 by 1914 and then Nos. 2 through 5 in 1920-1921. No. 3 was never completed. With twenty years still left in him, it's a wonder he didn't get around to it. In any event, it is refreshing to hear the sound of a composer still writing Late Romantic string quartets in the 1920s.

String Quartet No. 4 is a four movement work, written in 1921. The first movement is a sometimes cheerful, sometimes melancholy piece, developed around a strong melodic structure. It is not a music of extremes, seeming to take the middle ground – it's conservative. The movement passes through many different spaces, although it's mostly an optimistic work. It finishes with a light rhythmic passage. I find it amazing to think that at this time, Schoenberg was working on his abstract serial music just a few countries away.

The second movement, marked romanze is just that, romantic. It is a beautifully poignant piece, played at a gentle tempo with superb intertwining melodies. The cello sets the opening tone before the violins give it a pastoral flavour. The cello then moves into pizzicato and picks up the pace, before slowly transforming into a slow phase, which persists until it closes with delicate chords.

The next movement opens with the cello in a folk-dance manner. There is nothing modern about this music – it is anchored in the 19th century. A chord change gives way to a sense of introversion, followed by a recapitulation of the opening cello theme which continues until it concludes in a sprightly fashion.

The last movement begins with a stately theme before moving into a feisty mood that is sustained right through to the conclusion. Along the way, it pauses several times for breath, but it always picks up again – leading to a most enjoyable journey.

Just a brief note on the unfinished String Quartet No. 3 which is also on this CD. Of the three movements, two are attractive slow pieces, while the other is livelier. Another three short pieces for string quartet are on this disc. The first, an Aria in D major, is exceptional – a poignant five-minute piece.

These works illustrate the fact that Late Romantic quartets were still being written in the early 20th century – another case of overlapping periods. They are delightful works, well worth investigating.

The review CD is on Naxos, performed by the Isasi Quartet. String Quartets Nos. 0, 1, 2 and 5 are on two other Naxos CDs. All three discs are on Spotify, and are worth investigating. Several Isasi quartets can be found on YouTube.

Listenability: A delightful piece, not of its time – music to be savoured.

Charles Ives [1874–1954]

Nationality: American
Quartets: Two
Style: Early Modern

The Eccentric Salesman
String Quartet No. 1

Ives sold insurance by day, with great success, enabling him to write music that did not try to be popular. He pretty much succeeded, but the popularity came anyway, although it took some time. Ives won a Pulitzer Prize for his *Third Symphony*. His music can be eccentric, drawing from hymns, marching band music, popular song, and generally for his highly unusual sense of harmony, rhythm, juxtaposition and atonality.

His First Quartet is a student work, composed when studying at Yale University. It is significantly less progressive than the Second and is tonal in conception. The CD liner notes state that Ives quotes melodies from at least seven hymns or popular songs and the work is titled *From the Salvation Army – A Revival Service*. It contains four movements – three of which have multiple tempo markings so I shall only refer to the first mentioned.

The quartet opens at an andante tempo with a fugue of stately style. This is developed for a time until a rise in tempo brings a slightly rhapsodic feeling. Now, echoes of the opening fugue are heard and transformed with various melodic developments. There is a strength about these melodies, likely from some hymn source. A quivering section leads to a faded chordal end.

Next, an allegro movement brings forth a lilting melody, followed by variations on this melody. Some sweet sounds are heard as the composer expresses an appealing, positive feeling – this is joyful music. There are many tempo changes, which give rise to multiple wonderful moments. A slow section of rich chords leads back into the opening melody and the violins again dance with vigour and joy. A totally contrasting passage is quite powerful, but soon gives way to a lyrical feeling to finish.

The third movement, marked adagio, is hymn-like in its purity. Gentle, wistful violin melodies are harmonised to create a most attractive pastoral soundscape. A new section evokes Mozart, but soon returns to the pastoral feeling – there are some rich melodies here. A quivering chordal passage leads into a quicker tempo which is quite powerful before a return to adagio leads to some further stunning melodies. The end comes in a high register.

The final movement begins as an allegro, featuring rhythmically incisive ensemble playing. There is a great sense of forward movement, which eventually is becalmed. Now the violins are more expressive, at a slower tempo, before moving into another pulsating passage where the violins duet with marvellous melodic ideas. The ensemble gathers forces, projecting a feeling of great strength

218

and assertion. The violins rise above the ensemble, and conclude the work on a strong chord.

The review CD, by the Emerson Quartet also contains Ives' String Quartet No. 2, together with the only string quartet of Samuel Barber, Opus 11, written in 1936. This three movement work has a stunning adagio movement that Barber subsequently arranged as *Adagio for Strings*, which is possibly the most popular piece of classical music from the twentieth century. Personally, I don't find the other two movements very engaging so I don't intend to discuss it here.

This CD is available on Amazon US and UK, along with many other pairings of Ives' two string quartets.

There is also a plethora of versions of both quartets on Spotify, YouTube and earsense.

Listenability: Pre-modern Ives at his finest.

String Quartet No. 2

The Second Quartet was written between 1907 and 1913 and is in three named movements.

Discussions opens in Ives' personal atonal style, although there is some harmonic movement. There is even part of a descending major scale. However, dissonance prevails and short energised, frantic even, passages drift in and out of the basic harmonic framework. Ives always features surprises and there are many in this movement. There are incredible contrasts, including a quote from the American song that is something about *Dixie*. Being Australian I didn't notice two other songs but I am reliably informed that he also quotes *Marching through Georgia* and *Columbia, the Gem of the Ocean*. Ives' method is to quote, and then, totally deconstruct and reharmonise melodies. Now follows some heavy chordal interjections, interspersed within this movement, but there are also many charming, slightly dissonant parts. The movement concludes on one such instance.

Arguments is fairly short and commences with highly energised violins featuring a savage tone. This suddenly stops and a gentle violin interlude is introduced. It is constantly interrupted by the sound of the opening. Now an assertive violin statement is presented, which proceeds to practically engulf itself. As arguments go, this one is very heated. The tension is maintained for a considerable time until what is likely to be another popular tune is hinted at and deconstructed. The end is emphatic.

The Call of the Mountains is the longest movement and begins with sustained tones – it is incredibly peaceful – no matter that there is not a melody within earshot. The piece is static for some time until the violins proceed to build atonal melodic lines at a tempo. Things become increasingly busy, but the dynamics are still measured. It is entropic music – it goes nowhere and everywhere at the same time. Finally, the tension breaks, and a brief, intense violin interlude gives way to another, gentler space. There is even some harmonic movement here. As one who thrives on abstraction, I really enjoy these seemingly random moments. An excited section unfolds, with strong cello lines underpinning the violins' atonal statements. Slowly, the intensity decreases and, eventually, the music fades on a long sustained note.

I am a bit ambivalent about Ives. His music can change in an instant from beauty to garbled popular melodies, jerking rhythms, from tonality to atonality, and from simple to staggeringly complex, and many other modes of expression. He is definitely his own man. It's worth noting that jazz composer Ornette Coleman wrote a magnificent orchestral piece, *Skies of America*, which plainly owes a debt to Ives.

My CD review copy, by the Emerson Quartet, and mentioned previously, also contains Ives' First String Quartet and Samuel Barber's famous Opus 11 quartet.

Over two hundred versions of Ives' two quartets can be found on Amazon US, many reasonably priced.

Both of the works can be found on Spotify and YouTube. There are three versions of the work, including the Emerson Quartet on earsense.

Listenability: Ives' music may have been difficult a hundred years ago, but now it just seems a little quirky.

[Charles Ives x 3 – Images – Wiki Commons]

Leos Janacek [1854–1928]

Nationality: Czech
Quartets: Two
Style: Late Romantic

The Kreutzer Sonata
String Quartet No. 1

This title was inspired by Leo Tolstoy's short story, *The Kreutzer Sonata*, which was itself inspired by Beethoven's *Kreutzer Sonata for Violin and Piano*, No. 9, Opus 47. It is of interest to be aware of the short story as I believe that it sheds light on the piece. A man, Pozdnyshev, and a woman, are happily married but after five children the wife, who is a pianist, takes lessons from a music teacher, a violinist. They play the *Kreutzer Sonata* together. Pozdnyshev, in a jealous rage, goes away on a trip. When he returns early he finds his wife and the teacher together, then stabs his wife to death. You can hear feelings expressed in this quartet that relate to various parts of the story, which is obviously more complex than my scant version of events. This story is a terrific read.

The first, fascinating movement, begins with a longing theme, played by the first violin, and answered by the three other players. It then moves into tempo and introduces another delightful theme, filled with passion. There follows a recapitulation of the first theme, this time much quicker and the violin takes over again before it leads into a quiet, busy passage. A recapitulation of the second theme brings the movement to a close. Words can't do justice to this fine music.

The second movement introduction is in a joyful, almost skittish manner. Then follows a period of intensity. Here, Janacek reveals his mastery at restating themes, in different contexts. The conclusion is a wonderful restatement of the first theme, with an awesome cello part.

The next movement again opens with a feeling of longing, almost desperation. The solo violin absolutely yearns with occasional interjections from the ensemble. Then follows a succession of more longing until it gently concludes.

The final movement is a fine denouement. There is a long period of introspection before the music comes to life again. The composer reintroduces the opening theme from the first movement, this time in a chaotic manner. It moves into a gallop and then to a passive conclusion.

String Quartets Nos. 1 and 2 are often paired on a single CD. In terms of availability of the pairing, there must be over 100 versions out there. I have it with the complete Bartok String Quartets by the Tokyo Quartet on RCA Red Seal. There are at least three versions on Spotify and many on YouTube. A fine Hagen Quartet performance of the Kreutzer Sonata can be found on earsense.

Listenability: A marvellous, passionate work – another one of the 50 string quartets you should hear etc.

Intimate Letters
String Quartet No. 2

This work, titled *Intimate Letters* also has an interesting story. It is associated with passion as was the first. This time, the passion was personal. In 1917 Janacek became infatuated with an antique dealer's young wife – she was 32 years his junior. Janacek wrote over 700 letters to her, hence the title. Apparently the young woman was neither interested in the man nor his music. The work was completed during the last year of his life and Janacek threw everything into it. The music oscillates between energetic, emotionally charged statements, to melancholy moments where the composer bares his soul and writes in the language of love. Some pundits have asserted that the dominant viola in the third movement represents the object of his desire. This fascinating piece has been recorded many times and performed even more. Janacek died just after it was completed and never heard it performed.

The quartet opens with a tension which cuts back to being barely audible, before rising again. Another quiet moment ensues before a melody breaks through, which continues for some time. A solo violin statement tempers the music which follows, but it eventually builds into a passionate atmosphere. Things are melodically active and later, move into a slightly less intense space, then back to an intensity. A brief pause brings in a solo violin with a feeling of melancholy. The solo violin passage is repeated, this time with a strong accompaniment, which is quite a contrast and very effective. It ends in a powerful flourish.

The next movement, marked adagio goes straight into a slow violin melody – the ensemble drifts in to provide support. Again, there is a sense of melancholy before a recapitulation of the opening occurs. It is becoming a feature for the first violin as it blossoms into a virtuoso part, with strong accompaniment. Now the music becomes uncomfortable, with the violin seemingly searching for peace. It finds it with a melancholy passage that has a moderate tempo and a reduced intensity, which however, soon increases. There is a short moment of a longing violin, with soft, abstruse interjections before the violin strengthens to conclude.

The third movement commences with a gently harmonised violin melody – it is reflective and the feeling persists for some time. A new melody appears, and the ensemble wraps around its joyless form. An appealing melody is heard briefly, before it is overwhelmed by the ensemble and strong rhythmic thrusts appear, leading to a hectic passage at a brisk tempo. A pause brings more melancholia, featuring mostly solo violin and a short, dynamic flurry brings a conclusion.

The finale is taken at a jaunty tempo which soon dissolves into a quiet space. It is a passionate, ambivalent movement as the intensity rises and falls, frequently and dramatically. A characteristic pause leads to a brief recapitulation of the movement opening. The first violin soldiers on with its melancholy nature, as the ensemble come and go around it. A virtuosic violin passage ensues and eventually we do have a change of ambience with further references to the opening. The work concludes with some striking violin trills and heavy chords.

I believe I can hear Janacek's passion and frustration in this piece – it sounds slightly confused. These are both highly emotionally-charged quartets, and magnificent works. If this was all that Janacek had ever written, it would be enough. With what went on in his life, he would probably say – enough.

As previously mentioned, being two of the most popular quartets in the repertoire, they are freely available on Amazon US and UK. I've enjoyed lately the Panocha Quartet on the Supraphon label.

Both quartets are on Spotify, YouTube, and earsense.

Listenability: Another blazing, passionate quartet from Janacek.

— oo0oo —

Jewish String Quartets – Compilation

Nationality: Jewish
Quartets: Five
Style: Contemporary

Five Jewish String Quartets

This compilation is intriguing. The composers represented are Darius Milhaud, Abraham Wolf Binder, Ruth Schonthal, John Zorn and Sholom Secunda. I have selected the two longest pieces for discussion.

Ruth Schonthal's String Quartet No. 3, *In Memoriam Holocaust* consists of two named movements. The work is performed by the Bingham Quartet.

The first movement is titled *Grave*. It opens in a wonderful chordal manner, with no melodic development but expressive, in a serious way. It pauses and then returns to the opening, allowing the cello to soar as the individual voices start to become clear. Hyperactive violins quiver frantically until the music drops back to a quieter period. The violins reappear to constantly pierce the ambience – cello interjections are also heard. Now we have a plucked cello interlude leading into a cello-driven passage which is intense as the violins reach for the sky, with the ensemble providing striking chordal interjections. The intensity drops back to cello and one violin for a time. A recapitulation follows and the violins grate in their attack. String sound effects abound before a restless violin alternates with ensemble jabs and an intense violin signals the end of the movement.

The second movement, titled *Lament and Prayer* is introduced by a lone cello in a deep register, exploring an ethnic melody at some length. Eventually a violin enters, with the cello persisting. Now a sustained chord sets the violins free to express themselves, again with ethnic-sounding melodies – there is a considerable amount of tension here. The violins become predominant again, working in a peaceful layer of sound before a solo violin begins and the second violin responds – there is also some dialogue with the cello. The cello asserts itself as the violins converse. Its sound is deep and the statement is interspersed with quivering violins. As the end approaches violins speak out over a sustained cello background – the conclusion is solo cello. The writing for the cello is wonderful, bringing forth a powerful texture.

The second work is Sholom Secunda's String Quartet in C minor, which is in four movements. It is long, clocking in at thirty minutes and is performed by the Bochmann String Quartet.

This work opens with a symphonic chord which then forms the backing for a solo violin melody. The second violin enters and a dance feeling ensues as a violin reaches into its highest register for a dramatic effect. The sound now becomes folk-like with simple melodies over simple harmonies. The cello takes over the melody for a time, while still maintaining the simple nature of the passage before the violins move into a style reminiscent of the Baroque era. This is a most appealing section, light and airy. A new melody appears, this time, Romantic in style and featuring a great deal of melodic development. A change to a minor tonality increases the intensity and the violins are front and centre. There are some brief violin flourishes as the movement ends. To my ears, this is very Western-sounding music.

The next movement shows more of its Jewish roots. A tranquil opening has a solo violin leading the ensemble – it rises and falls as it progresses and sometimes cries out in a lamenting manner. The melody is developed with both violins taking part. Now we have a new mood where the violins express in a sparse manner where the use of harmonics concludes this relatively short movement.

The third movement begins with a folk sound – again I hear a Jewish touch here. It is a social space, evoking images of family gatherings. The opening melody is followed by a quick, dance-like tempo with ethnic scales evident. The intensity drops but the feeling remains the same. A false ending introduces another Romantic melody, which eventually leaves the harmony behind and moves into a modal feeling – the harmony returns and the melodies take account of this. It leads to a quicker tempo with what I take to be ethnic rhythms. Lastly, we have another Romantic melody which finishes on a loud chord.

The final movement is the longest and commences in a bright manner. The melody is gentle, and is complemented with interesting harmonies. The cello now leads the melody, which has morphed into a folk tune. The violins return to dominate but the cello occasionally has a significant role. Moving into a minor key, the music becomes gentle in a short passage but the feeling soon returns to a dance-like nature. An extended solo cello statement moves through a modal scale, with sporadic input from the other instruments. A slight ensemble flourish concludes the work. This is light music, optimistic in its melody, harmonies and flavour.

The music from the other three composers is also interesting. I was surprised by the relatively mellow feeling of the John Zorn piece as his string quartets have so far proved to be totally impenetrable to me.

The review CD, *Jewish String Quartets*, on the Naxos label is available on Amazon US and UK.

It can also be heard on Spotify. The Ruth Schonthal and Sholom Secunda quartets can be found on YouTube – I didn't look for the other pieces.

Listenability: Two very satisfying quartets, and something different for the collection.

— ooOoo —

Daniel Jones [1912–1993]

Nationality: Welsh
Quartets: Eight
Style: Contemporary

String Quartet No. 1

Daniel Jones wrote some of my favourite quartets of the twentieth century. It is such a shame that they are so difficult to obtain. The First Quartet was written in 1946 and is in four movements.

The work opens with a sparse feeling and there is a long pause after the first tentative phrases from the violin. The ensemble responds, and another pause follows before the violin continues with the opening melody, which is longing. After another long pause, the whole ensemble is engaged, moving into a serious musical space for a short time. All the while the melody is being developed before a further pause– this time the texture lightens a little and all of the instruments come into play. Now we have forward movement, and a much lighter feeling until the texture thickens again, leading to a most captivating moment. The music starts to become busy – then returns to the opening melody. A long pause and a short theme statement concludes the movement. Such bliss.

The next movement commences in a playful manner, with simple melodies prevailing – one theme is particularly charming. A pause leads to a new phase with pizzicato filling out the sound. Now we are back to the atmosphere of the first movement, out of which emerges a lone violin statement with minimal accompaniment. This new melody is developed and the intensity increases, before dropping back to a sparsity and another serious theme, which is very longing. Suddenly a rhythmic passage begins, developing a strong melody and concluding with a flourish.

225

The third movement is marked adagio and begins with a low cello introducing a melodic mood. There is plenty of space here as the composer takes his time and the introspective nature of the first two movements is again evident. Slowly a tempo develops but then abruptly stops, leading to another pause. The music returns, just so sparse – it is almost stasis, just a murmur now and again. It finishes on one lonely note.

The final movement begins in a pastoral manner as a folk melody is developed and the music is swept up in it. The sound becomes full before the cello introduces a rhythmic phrase as a carpet for the violins – it is delicate music. Another pause follows before a recapitulation of the first movement opening theme. It is developed ever so slowly with the other instruments adding abstract colour to the main violin melody. Another long pause ensues. The theme is stated once, then a few selected notes complete the work. It is a deeply moving piece of music.

If this is Wales, I want to go there – this is a fine set of largely introspective music. There are several modern moments here but it is mostly in a peaceful, introspective place. Somebody had this to say about Jones on YouTube, in a Second String Quartet listing:

It's baffling why Jones' music is still relatively unknown. This is intelligent, intellectual music that exploits the genre brilliantly. Jones does not compromise and write easily approachable music and therein lay the possible reason for his neglect. There is a toughness about this music that reminds me of Bartok. Like Bartok, Jones never gave in to fashion nor abandon tonality completely although tonal goals are often disguised or delayed.

There is a 2-CD set of the complete String Quartets by the Delme Quartet on Chandos. However, availability of the set is uncertain. Sometimes it is on Amazon US or UK, other times the dreaded *currently unavailable* appears. If melancholia appeals to you then I suggest you make an effort to obtain it soon. I recently acquired a used copy, but they are becoming harder to locate. At the time of writing, there were still new copies available on Amazon US, and also from Amazon UK resellers. Someone told me they located one from Japan.

Some of Jones' quartets, including No. 1 are available on YouTube and earsense.

Listenability: This is deeply moving, transcendent music. For those inclined to the melancholy, I can highly recommend it.

John Joubert [born 1927]

Nationality: British
Quartets: Three
Style: Early Modern

The First String Quartet

John Pierre Herman Joubert's String Quartet No. 1 in A-flat major was composed in 1950 as his Opus 1, containing three movements. The work opens with a questioning melodic line, harmonised by all four instruments, in an abstract manner. There is dissonance here but it has a certain warmth, particularly as a dialogue develops within the ensemble. Rhythmic interjections occur for a time, before another questioning passage delivers responses to the first violin's melodies. A powerful tempo is established, with slightly frantic, atonal violin lines sparring with the ensemble – there is an underlying ferocity contained within this music, which continues to an abrupt termination.

The second movement, marked lento, is a wonderful piece of writing. Meandering in and out of atonality it features harmonised melodic lines to produce my favourite feeling, the abstract soundscape. The violin laments, with minimal accompaniment, which gradually increases in intensity – to me, the music sounds very British and slightly intellectual. Further lamenting melodies are presented, contrasted with aching ensemble passages, before a stasis is invoked. With a delicate feeling, the violins edge their way forward, against the background of a faint pulse. A shrill violin is persistent as a second voice expresses loneliness in support – the cello drones in the background for a time before stepping forward and initiating a further measured, dissonant passage. Nearing the end, it is another lament, occasionally interrupted by a throbbing cello. The end is sombre and very precious.

The final movement begins in a light-hearted manner, with the cello playing a strong melodic line against a background of rhythmic violin phrases. The roles are soon reversed and the violins build intensity with a supportive cello. There is a lot of forward momentum here as the violin jabs at the rhythm, which is momentarily muted. A sense of ascending harmonies allows the violins to investigate various melodic motifs, with the cello rumbling to its own tune. Virtuosic lines suddenly leap to the forefront, I think I detect a quote from Beethoven's late quartets here. A pause allows the mood to express a state of peace, with the cello and violin producing an almost pastoral mood of sparse, atonal character. A return to forward movement is intense as the violins and cello again produce virtuosic, contrasting lines before a sharp, dissonant flourish concludes the work.

I must admit that I am drawn to early British modernism, it seems to venture into emotional musical soundscapes that are not necessarily found elsewhere, although there are some parallels with European quartets from the same era. Joubert fits firmly into this mould.

The review CD, *John Joubert: String Quartets 1, 2 & 3*, on Somm Records, and performed brilliantly by the Brodsky Quartet, is available on both Amazon US and UK.

This disc is also on Spotify, and some, but not all movements are on YouTube and earsense.

Listenability: A moving work, steeped in the British tradition. Modern but eminently rewarding.

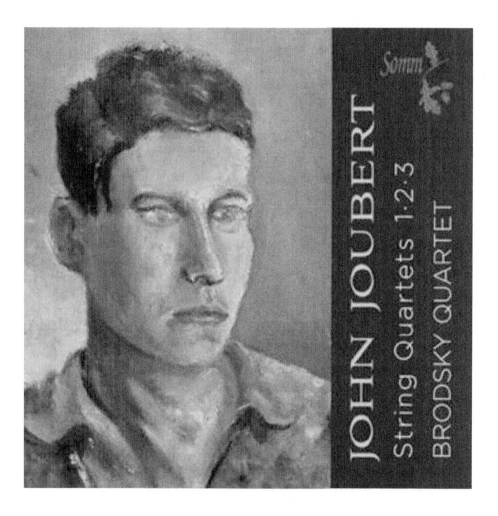

[Image courtesy Somm Records]

Viktor Kalabis [born 1923]

Nationality: Czech
Quartets: Seven
Style: Modern Contemporary

String Quartets Nos. 3 & 4

My review CD contains String Quartets Nos. 3 to 6, all performed by different ensembles. I am going to discuss Quartets Nos. 3 and 4.

The Third Quartet was composed in 1977, is in three movements, and is performed by the Talich Quartet. The first, short movement opens with a spirited violin, soon to be joined by the other players. There is a slight tension, which breaks into a driving passage before the intensity drops and the violins craft atonal melodic duets. There is a hint of microtones at times and the end comes with several more violin duet lines.

The next movement, marked adagio, begins in a sparse, calm manner where the violins could be early morning bird-calls. Into this eerie feeling steps the cello, which leads to a thickening of the texture for a time. A return to the opening leads to more tension. Now the violins scurry with a repeated phrase and then lapse into silence. When they return, it is with an introspective purpose. One violin carries a lamenting melody as the other instruments probe the mood. The cello leads into another pause and there are virtually inaudible sounds to conclude. It is an interesting movement, noticeable for its domination by introspection.

The final movement commences with a tempo, the first that we have heard for a while. Harmonised violin lines alternate with seemingly random violin interjections until powerful chords overtake the violins. Now there is plenty of music happening as the violins express freely. A fabulous descending motif is carried by all four instruments in turn and the violins continue in their excited state until an assertive solo cello statement leads to an exchange with the violins. The tension is now palpable as all instruments engage in rhythmic exchanges. The cello goes solo again, then chaos returns. The music is just so busy, until the tempo dissipates and we are left with a slow, dissonant passage where the violins feature large intervallic leaps. A motif from earlier is repeated and the violins are shimmering. That motif is referred to again, this time it is deconstructed. A solo violin moves into its highest register and slowly the other instruments make an appearance. A new section is filled with activity and violin flourishes. Strong, harmonised melodies abound and the end comes with a flurry of dissonant violins.

I find this to be a well-balanced work, with wonderful highly contrasting second and third movements. To me it is very satisfying, but may be a little confronting for some listeners.

229

String Quartet No. 4 was written in 1984 and is performed by the Doleazal Quartet. It is in one movement and bears the title *Tribute to J S Bach*. We shall see where that takes us.

There is no tempo specified, and the music gently drifts into a sparse space. The violins are conspicuous, but the cello also has an important role to play with the melodies slightly longing, and measured. Slowly some intensity is brought to the atmosphere, as the violins lead into a pulsing rhythm. Their energy is gradually tempered as they dissolve into a sparsity, only to be interrupted by some strong melodic lines. This doesn't last and the longing feeling returns, interspersed with some atonal violin sounds. A slow tempo leads to a passage where the cello supports violins that reach skyward. Another rhythmic episode ensues and the violins express freely, roaming far and wide emotionally. There are some solid interjections, but the violins push on. Now, they are ever so quiet and melancholy – barely audible. Some uncharacteristic harmony is heard and the violins slowly fade in intensity to a conclusion.

I'm not surprised that I didn't hear any connection with Bach, it is a Contemporary work and an interesting one at that. There is not much action, but a lot of musical soundscapes that I found to be particularly attractive. It's worth mentioning that String Quartet No. 5, also on the CD, has a beautiful adagio movement.

There appear to be two CDs containing this music. My review copy is titled *Viktor Kalabis: String Quartets Nos. 3 - 6,* performed by the Zemlinsky Quartet on Koch Records. There is also another 2-CD set – *Viktor Kalabis – Complete String Quartets* on Praga Digitals, this is an SACD disc. Suffice it to say, both of these versions are available on Amazon UK. Only the SACD is on Amazon US.

There is one quartet, No. 4, on Spotify, while earsense has many quartets.

Listenability: I enjoyed the contrasts on this disc but it is definitely Modern.

— oo0oo —

Aaron Jay Kernis [born 1960]

Nationality: American
Quartets: At least three
Style: Contemporary

String Quartet No. 1

Kernis' Second Quartet, titled *Musica Instrumentalis*, won the composer a Pulitzer Prize. I am going to discuss the First Quartet, titled *Musica Celestis*. The work commences with a free flowing ensemble filled with gracefully expressive melodic ideas – some harmonised lines are very effective in their unique sound. A slightly chaotic passage ensues and hints of the opening melody flash in and out. A calm comes to the music and a solo violin expresses soulfully over gentle sparse string sounds before the ensemble eventually comes to life with a slightly confronting passage. A brief pause brings about a change into a charming, melodic phase, which is interrupted by a pulsing viola, however, the melodic nature is maintained. This mood is sustained for some time, with occasional interjections of frenzied activity as the violins reach into the high register with a bird-like sense of flight – another frenzied interruption unfolds. Now hints of the opening melody are heard, soon to be swamped with the energy of the ensemble, although they are still audible. The frantic feeling takes over, but a brief pause leads to a gentler scene, which doesn't last. Nearing the end, a solo cello statement leads the violins into a thoughtful section and again, hints of the opening melody are heard. The conclusion is a very moving piece of writing.

A composer marking, *Musica celestis*, which is the title, is found on the second movement. It opens with sustained chords, in an adagio fashion. This is quite spiritual really, with low and slow, soft melodies to be heard. There is a sense of ascension at times and the melodies are not far removed from those of the first movement opening, albeit at a much slower, gentler tempo. The violins reach out, as if searching for the heavens, and make for a wonderful soundscape. Now strong ensemble chords are heard and the violins respond with more energy. A new section unfolds, with the violins almost frantic in their endeavours as they reach into their high registers. A return to the spiritual feeling with delicate violin harmonies, again reaching into the shrill range makes for a fine moment. A long pause is followed by one violin meditating on a gentle mood – the end is two violins evoking a similar feeling.

The next movement is a short, pizzicato based romp. I must confess that I have never been drawn to the sound of pizzicato and rarely find it musical – oh well. There are almost random violin musings and the dynamics vary continually throughout. Strange interjections occur between violin passages and the pizzicato is mostly present. The end seems to be a random collection of notes.

The finale again, is not long but has a considerable amount of energy. One violin chases another, between frantic moments of pulsing rhythmic statements. Now a rapturous sound ensues, which is quite a surprise and almost incongruous – it doesn't last and we have a return to the previous frantic activity. The cello introduces a brief fugal passage, leading into another section of a seemingly random nature. Finally we have some more peace as a violin laments over a quiet chord until the end comes with a flourish.

I am tempted to call this work *neo-classical* which was a movement in the early twentieth century formed as a reaction against the influence of Schoenberg et al. However, I would have thought that too much time has passed for this to be appropriate for works written in the 1990s. Kernis seems to draw from Classical and Romantic forms but his music still sounds Contemporary due to the way that he manages these forms.

The review CD contains String Quartets Nos. 1 and 2, performed by the Duke Quartet, however it no longer seems to be available. The same music can be found by the Lark Quartet on Arabesque Records and is available on Amazon US and UK.

Both works can be heard on Spotify, YouTube and earsense.

Listenability: A mostly mild Contemporary work

— ooOoo —

Leon Kirchner [1919–2009]

Nationality: American
Quartets: Four
Style: Early Modern

The String Quartets

I am going to concentrate mainly on String Quartets Nos. 1 and 2. The First Quartet, written in 1949, contains four movements. Opening with a slightly entropic feeling – a sort of muted chaos, it reminds me of a large city, like *Metropolis*, a 1927 silent movie. Moving into a period of tranquil solo cello, the violins enter to complete the mood. The tempo returns, with associated string sound effects, which to me, make for the sound of an urban landscape.

The second movement opens with pizzicato and strange, distant sounds coming from the violins. It brings to mind the early hours in a vast city, with things going on in back alleys and mysterious places. It is an introspective, mildly atonal scene. There is no forward impetus, just sketches of a murky soundscape.

The third movement opens with a violin flourish before moving into a tempo, no stasis here. This piece just won't settle – it wants to be somewhere. The violins scuttle here and there and I can feel rats in the environment.

The final movement is an adagio, with dissonant melodies prevailing. This **is** stasis, with no forward movement. It does eventually pick up tempo, and nearing the end, is assertive.

I need to hear it again, but my first impression is that it is an early modern American quartet, which paints a mesmeric, although bleak, scene.

The Second Quartet is in three movements. Written in 1958, it appears to be of the same mid-1950s style as the First. I'm amazed how many American composers go for this type of emotional sound space. The first, short movement opens in a pensive manner, set up by an early melodic statement. Nearing the end, the atmosphere turns peaceful.

The next movement, marked adagio, goes straight into abstraction. I wish I could find another word for this type of feeling. There are synonyms, but they don't seem right for a sound that I have been seeking my whole musical life. It's a rumbling, slightly dissonant world that is definitely of this era. I first experienced this atmosphere way back in 1970, on our national radio broadcaster, the ABC, which played a lot of strange music at that time. It's an inexplicable type of beauty. Such is the mystery of music.

The final movement is agitated and insistent. The instruments clash, both harmonically and rhythmically. This feeling mellows only slightly and it retains an intangible quality throughout its short duration.

Kirchner's Third Quartet is for String Quartet and tape. I find it appalling. It's like Peter Sculthorpe arranging all of his quartets for String Quartet and didgeridoo - totally unfathomable to me.

The Fourth Quartet is in one movement, and of ten minutes duration. It was probably written in the early 2000s, as it does not make my fabulous reference volume, *The Twentieth-Century String Quartet* by Ian Lawrence, which is mostly reliable. This one opens in high drama, before lightening up. The melodies become gentler, and the cello walks for one bar. It is an emotionally static work, but still worth hearing.

Interestingly, the composer doesn't seem to have modified his style in these works, which were written over a period of fifty years.

Kirchner's complete quartets are available in several versions, some of which only contain the first three quartets – watch out. On the Albany label, the Orion String Quartet version on Amazon is complete, with all four.

This performance is also available on Spotify. Many Kirchner quartets can be found on YouTube and there is also a fine performance of the First Quartet by the Orion String Quartet on earsense.

Listenability: Satisfying but has a limited emotional range.

— oo0oo —

Zoltán Kodály [1882–1967]

Nationality: Austrian
Quartets: Two
Style: Early Modern

String Quartets Nos. 1 & 2

Kodály was a lifelong friend of Bela Bartok and introduced him to the techniques of collecting folk songs. He was initially drawn to Modernism but this interest waned as he developed his composing style.

String Quartet No. 1 is long, complex, and in four movements. It is an epic work, clocking in at thirty-eight minutes on my review CD. The work commences in a sombre mood with a solo violin being accompanied by a sensitive backing. The violins begin to spin out long melodic lines before moving into a tempo, with the cello leading over a rhythmic background. Now the first violin takes over, but still leaves room for cello statements. The violin cuts back and moves into a simple folksy statement, which is very becoming, while the cello and violin continue to dominate the music as they converse through various rhythmic musings. There is a certain Gypsy element to this music, as the violin leads the cello into another rhythmic passage. Mostly, the melodies are modal, with little harmonic development. So far, this piece strikes me as being a not very mature work, but feels like a composer working out his personal style. A harmonic change brings a flurry of violins, before they subside and one violin brings a conclusion with a flourish.

The next movement, marked lento, evokes a wonderful ambience. The first violin builds short melodic lines, but there are long answering responses from the ensemble. The cello walks and provides a harmonic underpinning and a connection between sections. Again, this music has a modal feeling, and is lamenting. Two prominent violins take over, but soon the cello begins to walk in a solo fashion to delineate sections. Now a pizzicato violin emerges, as a stasis unfolds before moving into a tempo, where the first violin is intense. A slightly energised episode gives way to a pause, leading into another solo lament before the accompaniment returns, with a sensitive trilling of strings. It is a most poignant moment – the trills are just so subtle. A pause leads to more sparsity which concludes on a sustained violin tone.

The third movement, which is short, has a strong pulse and is filled with simple melodies. These melodies are developed and the music becomes stronger as it progresses. A key change brings a renewed vigour and heralds a new optimistic nature, which sees the movement out.

The finale is rhythmically interesting. It is a potpourri of different rhythms and textures, mostly vigorous. Another folksy statement is heard, with the violin being followed by the cello. A key change continues with lyricism for a time, until it eventually retreats into a mild melancholy. Now a jovial violin introduces another folk texture, with a lightness of rhythm. The tempo quickens considerably, with violins flashing in and out of the passage. A duelling violin phase follows and the mood is brought back to a melancholia. Several melodies are developed before the music breaks into a rapid tempo again. This feeling is carried through to the completion of the work.

String Quartet No. 2 is substantially shorter and contains two movements. An ascending motif played by all instruments opens the work. There is a short section in tempo but it soon dissolves and returns to a placid soundscape. The melodies are cleverly crafted with much overlapping of different instruments. Now the violins produce long motifs contrasted with shorter, rhythmic bursts. A call and response pattern is introduced and the music becomes a conversation, with the violins following each other melodically. There is a degree of dissonance but the violins push on with their dialogue. Now one violin takes precedence, reaching into the high register, leaving the ensemble to finish on a gentle chord.

The second, and final movement, picks up where the first movement left off. A violin reiterates a strong phrase before developing it over a sparse backdrop. A solo violin now moves skyward again and a brief pause has the same violin conversing with the ensemble. A lamenting section brings in the cello. Many pauses can be found in this movement and the next music heard is a brief dancing violin which soon drops back into a longing feeling. I can hear a modern sound trying to break through. Instead we have a tempo with a viola and cello ostinato motif – the violins dance freely over this backdrop. The motif continues, and the sound is prancing, with assertive, busy violin lines. A drone is introduced and the violins spin modal lines over a sensitive accompaniment. The violins have a clarity about them that is wonderful. Energy returns to the piece, but as usual, doesn't last for long. This music is filled with constant variations as simple melodies have their say, and a long solo violin melodic line leads to a slightly frantic conclusion.

Several performances containing Quartets 1 and 2 are on Amazon US and UK. My review CD is by the Dante Quartet on Hyperion. They include two short works as filler. I'm sure that the Kodaly String Quartet have a version somewhere. Both quartets can be found on Spotify and YouTube. Several different recordings of the two works are available on earsense.

Listenability: Mild Early Modern works.

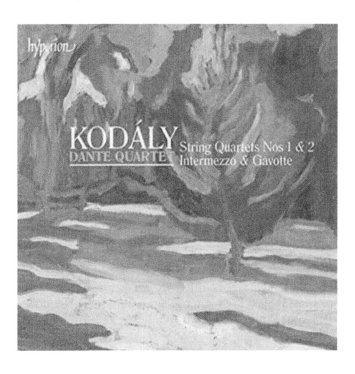

[Image courtesy Hyperion label]

George Kontogiorgos [born 1945]

Nationality: Greek
Quartets: Three
Style: Contemporary

String Quartets Nos. 2 & 3

To my ears, the chronology of these works reveal them to become less modern as they evolve. The First, titled *Unicorn,* is contemporary and interesting. However I am going to discuss the Second and Third Quartets, and will endeavour to illustrate the above concept.

The Second String Quartet, titled *de Profundis,* is in three movements. It features a moderate level of abstraction, which I particularly enjoyed. It starts with some lightly dissonant chords before a hint of a melody begins to emerge. The composer seems to be more concerned with rhythm at this point and some punctuating moments occur. The two violins, after a period of meandering, engage in an atonal conversation. The cello adds to the mix of sounds – it's very busy. The violins continue with their atonal musings until the conclusion.

The second movement is short, about two minutes. It opens with a two-note viola motif, and after each set of four bars, a new instrument appears to build the texture. A pulsating feeling dominates proceedings, which end with the two violins having the final say.

The last movement is based on a moderately dissonant three-note viola motif, which is heard in different guises throughout the movement. A brief, but slightly hectic violin exchange occurs around the motif as they accentuate with forceful phrases. A pause ensues and we hear the opening viola motif again. The violins first harmonise it, then develop it, as one of the violins drops into pizzicato for a time. The viola motif is now distorted rhythmically and it gives way to the two violins, one in the high register, leading to a frantic passage which drifts back into an eerie soundscape. The distorted motif returns and the violins mock it as they swoop and fly. Now we are back to the original motif which is soon subject to fierce examination. Each time the motif is repeated, it is changed by the ensemble, usually frantically. An explosive episode gives way to the motif one last time and a harmonised version concludes the work. This is a fabulous piece of writing, and is very evocative.

The Third String Quartet is titled *Byzantine*, which perhaps explains its nature. In four movements, the opening has a Baroque stateliness about it. The two violins carry poignant melodies while the cello provides a harmonic underpinning. They maintain a partnership for the duration of the movement – it sounds like music from another time. When it finished, I paused it and the atmosphere, almost ancient, seemed to linger for a while.

The next movement again starts with a gentle flowing melody. The violins respect the sparsity of the moment as they tread lightly through the cello harmony. There is some development, but the violins stay close to each other.

236

The music meanders as notes join together to create a most gorgeous canvas of sound. It is delicate music, which is again, not of its time.

The third movement opens ever so softly with an ascending scale using all four instruments. The phrase is continued a number of times until the violins move off into their own space with overlapping melodies. Now the opening phrase is again heard repeatedly, at a quicker tempo. This time it is with variations, and the intensity rises, but not for long, as the violins continue their development to a conclusion.

The brief final movement is much brighter and for the first time in the quartet, we have energy. The violins and cello are expressive, spinning out melodic lines, seemingly from long ago.

I don't know what to make of this music. These two quartets could have been written by different composers in different eras. Make of it what you will – I find it to be magnificent.

The review CD is titled *de Profundis*, performed by The New Hellenic Quartet, but I can't find these works anywhere, except as a download from Presto Classical. Being on Naxos I'm sure it could be located, probably even from Naxos.

It is on Spotify – watch the spelling, and all of the quartets are on YouTube and earsense.

Listenability: A diverse blend of fascinating, sometimes lyrical music.

— ooOoo —

Hans Krása [1899–1944]

Nationality: Czech
Quartets: One
Style: Early Modern

String Quartet No. 1

Hans Krása was murdered during the Holocaust at Auschwitz. His one string quartet was written in 1921. The work, in three movements, opens in a slightly dissonant manner, with furtive atonal phrases, at a slow tempo, but then quickens, leading to a dialogue between the violins, before returning to the opening feeling. The ensemble picks up on a melodic motif and deconstructs it. The cello probes with a call and response pattern together with all instruments involved. That earlier motif returns and is subject to rhythmic interjections. A pause brings another change, this time a morose passage with a conspicuous violin – the mood is abstruse. New motifs are introduced and the ensemble briefly works its way

237

into a frenzy, which doesn't last. Now a beautiful melody appears, although it is still quite sullen. The end comes with a violin note, way up in a high register.

The second movement features a cello and violin ostinato, which appears, disappears and constantly reappears. A lamenting violin now takes precedence, this is a fine moment. The composer moves on, into a propulsive section before a return to a stunning rubato mood, which is very abstract. The cello intervenes, setting up a tempo with another pulsing motif – this causes the violins to break free, before settling back into a cello supported phase. A pause returns to the opening theme and feeling, which is subjected to ensemble interjections. The violin attempts to keep up with the melody, but is overwhelmed. Its last iteration leads to a solo violin end.

The final movement, marked lento, commences with a violin in the low register, before it is gradually joined by the ensemble. This leads to a splendid passage which is very peaceful and longing. The cello rises into its highest register – such a serene sound. A pause continues the very measured mood, there is little movement here. Suddenly, a pizzicato pop is heard, and the music moves into tempo, with the cello providing great support. After a bit of frantic activity, the morose feeling returns and a lone violin plays a lamenting melody. The second violin joins in to harmonise with the first violin and the music is now just two violins. Not for long however, as the cello leads the ensemble into an energised, abstract section. Again, not for long and the status quo is resumed – two violins expressing over a sombre accompaniment, notwithstanding the occasional frantic interjection. The violins are very longing, and the cello purrs with a violin to conclude.

My review copy has the quartet paired with two string quartets by Pavel Haas, including the magnificent *From Monkey Mountains* in the *Entartete* (degenerate) *Music* series, performed by the Hawthorne String Quartet. This has recently been difficult to locate but, at time of writing is on Amazon UK – there also seem to be *New and Used* copies. In any event, there are several versions of the work available, with different pairings, although they seem to be getting scarcer. One fine version is *Czech Degenerate Music: Hans Krasa - String Quartet*, on the Praga Digitals label, performed by the Kocian Quartet, paired with some Haas quartets, which is still available on Amazon US.

The work can be sampled on Spotify, YouTube and earsense, which also has a link to Krása's *Theme and Variations for String Quartet*. This piece is a little more conservative.

Listenability: Fine, serious Early Modern work.

Ernst Krenek [1900–1991]

Nationality: Austrian
Quartets: Eight
Style: Early Modern

String Quartet No. 4

The Fourth Quartet, written over a period in the mid-1920s, was a transitional one in Krenek's output. It was the last quartet composed before he completely changed to a serial-based approach. It contains seven movements and is therefore a longish piece, but some of the movements are short.

The work opens with a catchy solo cello motif that could have been written in the 1980s on a synthesiser – such a wonderful tone and first impression. A spacious melody emerges out of the motif. A slight change briefly reintroduces the cello motif, and then a significantly different melody is presented. Chunks of harmony are powerfully put forward as the cello motif returns for a third, and then a fourth time. A solo violin interrupts the flow and after a time, all players join in with a strong ending. It is a crackerjack movement.

The second movement, which is short, opens quietly with harmonious violins – slightly dissonant but sublime. Eventually the other instruments have their say and build to a slight crescendo ending on a dissonant chord.

The third movement is even shorter, just two minutes. The violins open again, playfully engaging with each other. It is nearly the end by the time the cello can be heard. The melodies become more dramatic and it ends on a quiet solo violin phrase.

The fourth movement is by far the longest and is marked adagio. It opens with a sense of such sweet serenity as the violins share melodic duties with the cello. This occasionally develops into a tempo, interspersed with sombre moments – there is little or no pulse in this music, it must be inferred. Finally a new sense of purpose is felt as the ensemble works as one into a powerful, but still slow, introspective section. The dynamic drops back and we are in a wonderful soundscape. The music briefly pauses and the violins lament, first two, then back to one. A solo violin line concludes the movement. It leaves me with a feeling of 'Where have I been the last ten minutes?' – it is just so moving.

The next movement is again short and takes off at a gallop. The cello pulses and the violins dance. Suddenly the violins are solo again and establish a new structure. The cello returns and we have a motif similar to the opening movement and the violins spar before they are joined by the cello and musical games are played to a conclusion. For two and a half minutes, it is a most enticing mood.

Movement six is shorter still. A solo violin sets the atmosphere with little accompaniment. The viola has a say in the melody but this music is not going anywhere. It is tranquil and drops to a whisper as a violin plays a sustained long tone to finish.

The final movement begins in a rhythmic fashion. There are some allusions to Spain here as a result of Krenek hearing some Spanish records at the time. It is joyful music, replete with strong rhythms and melodies to go with it – not complicated, it just rollicks along. There is a change in the ambience as the violin leads the ensemble into a more gentle space. The Spanish tinge remains but things are sparse as two violins bounce ideas off each other until we are left with one violin to conclude. What a strange ending to a marvellous string quartet.

Krenek's work is starting to become harder to find. I have this piece as part of a complete 4-CD set by the Sonare Quartet on the MDG label. It is still available on Amazon US but only as *New and Used*, and fairly expensive. At time of writing, String Quartet No. 4 is available, paired with No. 6, at Amazon UK. There are also many other of the composer's quartets on Amazon UK.

Three of Krenek's string quartet CDs are on Spotify and many more can be heard on YouTube and earsense.

Listenability: I hadn't heard this in a while and it was a lot more conservative than I expected. Still great music.

String Quartet No. 7

This quartet is purportedly composed in a completely serial style. It was written in 1944 and contains five movements.

The work opens in a freely melodic manner, with abstract statements being made by the whole ensemble. The two violins are especially prominent for a time, until a cello-led interlude thickens the texture. Eventually, the mood abates, only to be resurrected with some striking dissonant violin lines. The cello underpins this moment beautifully and the abstraction continues. The violins take many chances in their endeavours, leading to a most interesting sound. A solo violin brings with it the cello, and finally, the second violin. Nearing the end, the cello expresses deep in its low register and contributes a moving solo statement, with occasional accompaniment from the ensemble. The music then passes straight into the next movement, without a pause.

Now the cello delivers a sombre solo statement, and the violins develop introspective lines around it. There is no tempo here, just slow, deliberate phrases. It is a fabulous, early modern soundscape, which is just so peaceful. The cello engages again as the violins continue with slow, sweeping melodies allowing it to contribute to a powerful atmosphere. The cello then recedes, leaving the violins to lament. Now we are down to one violin, which lets us down slowly.

The third movement opens with a solo cello statement soon to be joined by a pizzicato viola. The violins continue with their previous dialogues and there is much abstraction expressed here. I have always been totally fascinated by these intangible sound spaces. The end is a series of sustained, aggressive violin tones.

The fourth, short movement opens loudly, but soon meanders into a solo violin, with minimal input from the ensemble. There are murmurings from the cello, and the first violin is oh, so sparse. It ends on a faded note, at 1:41.

The final movement has a tempo, albeit a little obscured. Harmonised descending melodic violin lines are jaunty, and spirited, which persist – it's a great passage. Now the two violins engage in a measured frenzy, until the cello rejoins. The longing feeling returns as the violins casually meander through a philosophical mood. Now they launch into an excitable state which concludes the work.

I call this piece modern, because while being serial, it just sounds dissonant to me. Whether it was created using a tone-row is all a bit academic for my purposes. It is not particularly challenging, if you are used to abstract music. I really like it.

The CD under discussion is titled *Krenek – String Quartets Nos. 1 and 7* on the Capriccio label, performed by the Petersen Quartet – it is now a little hard to find. As mentioned earlier, I like the sound of the Sonare Quartet on the MDG label.

The Petersen Quartet disc is on Spotify and there are many Krenek quartets on YouTube and earsense.

Listenability: A marvellous work in a mildly Modernist style.

— oo0oo —

Ezra Laderman [1924–2015]

Nationality: American
Quartets: Twelve
Style: Contemporary Modern

String Quartet No. 8

The Eighth Quartet, in one movement, is a dark, brooding work, unlike most of Laderman's other quartets. It opens with foreboding, gentle string sounds as a violin investigates an atonal melody against this wonderful abstract background. Soon both violins are using glissandos. Now one violin quivers and a crescendo occurs, with sharp interjections in between peaceful moments.

The violins and cello play in a random fashion for a time, which is intriguing. A more powerful texture emerges, although it is not loud. It is reminiscent of some of John Tavener's string quartet writing. There is a lot of dissonance as the music drops back to calm, ambivalent chords before the violins re-enter in an abstract fashion, leading to a virtuosic solo violin and ensemble thrust. The cello is salient here, and plays in a racing tempo. This gives way to a

241

fascinating descending chromatic section with more atonality present, together with changeable dynamics. The cello thrusts, and the violin answers.

A fascinating space follows with the violins jousting, both in a high register. This is quickly followed by a crescendo, which leads to another atonal chordal episode. The texture here is transcendent, complete abstract expressionism. It softens but the atonality persists, with the two violins going at it as if their lives depended on it. Now the cello has a solo part, deep in the low register. A solo violin takes over, until the second violin begins to contribute gentle harmonies. The solo cello returns and formulates a rhythmic phrase which is dominant, even though the violins continue in the background.

A quiet pizzicato ensues, and leads into another atonal pastiche, with the cello again pressing. The violins gradually build the intensity almost to a frenzy as they scurry about with scattered melodies. Then the opening returns, with gentle dissonance while melodies become longer, and the dark background is just magnificent. Now it becomes more conservative and builds into a brief crescendo, followed by some string sound effects.

As we near the end, the violins conjure up a previously unheard sound, with pizzicato underpinning the work of the violins. Now they set a racing tempo with a sense of dissonance again prevailing. This leads into a false ending, followed by a handful of notes, and the piece concludes on a chord.

This is a fascinating work, modern but never grating, with a high level of abstraction, entropy and atonality, together with a great deal of diversity in texture.

Six of Laderman's string quartets are available – they happen to be the later ones. The review CD, titled *Music of Ezra Laderman – Vol. 3* on Albany Records, by the Cassatt Quartet is on Amazon US and UK, while Presto Classical has it as a download.

Only String Quartet No. 2 is on Spotify but many of the later quartets are on YouTube and earsense.

Listenability: Fascinating Modern quartet, featuring many different flavours and textures.

Laszlo Lajtha [1892–1963]

Nationality: Hungarian
Quartets: Ten
Style: Contemporary

String Quartet No. 7

All ten string quartets have been recorded but they are disappearing fast so I thought I'd get in before they are all gone. More on availability later. This quartet is in four movements.

A low bass-like cello statement opens the work before a violin comes in over the top, and then another. The mood is gently inward-looking and the blend within the ensemble is very precious. The cello returns to dominate, establishing a displaced rhythmic pattern that doesn't seem to affect the violins as they sustain their ambience. It is a fine moment. The first violin is the predominant voice but the cello is particularly effective. Now the violin develops a phrase and the cello repeats it – this occurs several times, each time increasing in intensity until they finally overlap and move into a sustained rhythmic section. The cello is brilliant in this slightly chaotic period which eventually dissipates into a slow rubato feeling, leaving just two violins to finish.

The second movement opens in a prancing manner, but there is conflict in the air. The violins converse in a busy manner while the cello has an assertive role to play here, as it joins in the melodies. Suddenly the feeling changes to a much slower, almost plodding tempo. There is no harmonic movement here, it is left to the violins to sustain interest. A new section allows the cello to add some melodies and the tempo changes again. A solo violin snippet is taken up by the cello and they swap melodies. This is positive music. It constantly lowers the intensity only to pick it up again with strong melodies. There is some harmonic movement now and all players respond. The end is a long thrilling violin phrase, which leads to a chordal conclusion. I don't think I've come across a movement like this before with so many tempo changes. It's rather exhilarating.

The next movement is a slow lament with precious, expansive violin melodies. A cello melody comes to the forefront, with minimal backing – it is very strong. The cello digs deep into its lower register and a violin moves in to join it for a sensitive duet. Now we have a hint of a tempo with the cello walking and strings shimmering as the first violin skims across the surface. It finishes quietly.

The final movement begins with solo violin, followed by the second violin as a duet ensues. There is a scattered melody. When the cello enters, it brings impetus and the music moves forward and harmonised violin and cello melodies are heard for a period until the cello returns to its anchor role. The cello won't be silenced however, and it adds lines to the violin melodies and follows them through several phases. The ending has a sound all of its own, with pizzicato, hurried melodies, chordal interjections and a final cello phrase.

This work sometimes sounds Late Romantic but its intensity is definitely Modern. I love the cello, it just has so much to say.

Now on to availability – it's complicated. There were four CDs containing all of the composer's quartets, on the Hungatron label, performed by the Auer Quartet. However, only Volume Two is still obtainable on Amazon. This contains String Quartets Nos. 5, 7 and 9. All four CDs are available as MP3 downloads from Presto Classical.

Volumes 3 & 4 are on Spotify and many Lajtha quartets are on YouTube. Fortunately, most of Lajtha's quartets are on earsense.

Listenability: Hmmm – sort of Late Romantic updated for the 1950s. How does that sound?

[Image courtesy Hungatron Classics via Naxos]

Simon Laks [1901–1983]

Nationality: Russian-Polish
Quartets: Five
Style: Early Modern

String Quartets Nos. 4 & 5

Russian-born Simon (Szymon) Laks took on Polish nationality and was held in Auschwitz for several years, where he became leader of the camp orchestra. I discuss his String Quartet No. 3 in a review of the *Voices of Defiance* compilation later in this book.

The Fourth Quartet, in three, shortish movements, commences with a pizzicato, ostinato feeling. Two violins dominate and, after some initial accompanied melodic development, which is quite rhythmic, the violins continue with harmonised lines over a sparse recapitulation of the introductory motif. Then left to their own devices, the violins spin out atonal melodies. The ostinato briefly returns and the violins reach into their high registers and construct a harmonised dialogue, leading to the end.

The next movement, marked andante, introduces a lamenting mood with a solo violin predominating. A cello line leads into a harmonised chordal passage, which is very beautiful. This feeling is maintained for some time and eventually increases in intensity as the violins give up their harmonies for strong melodic lines. A short section of eerie violin statements over another ostinato doesn't last. We now have a return to the harmonised chords, which is quite an intangible sound. The intensity returns, and, nearing the end only two violins can be heard.

The final movement pulsates from the beginning and strange rhythmic harmonised violin lines push the music. Now a solo violin steps forward, with a hurried rhythmic melody, soon to be joined by the ensemble to create a driving passage. The violins are busy as they surge forward. There are many variations here, but all contain harmonised violin lines – the intensity is high and the conclusion sharp. This is not a long work and, interestingly, it has also been arranged for a string orchestra.

The Fifth Quartet consists of four movements, opening with a solo cello line which is soon taken up by the violins – there is a strong sense of abstraction here. A pulsing cello can be heard and the feeling continues. Powerful, rhythmic chords interject sporadically as the music continues its rather formless structure. The dynamics and intensity rise and fall, the cello scurries about the music and a solo cello moment again encourages the violins to express energised, duelling melodic lines. A short, varied section ends with a strong flourish.

The next, andante movement, starts as a quiet, random soundscape with all instruments contributing to this unusual mood. A change of texture to just two violins initiates a fierce dialogue and, with the intensity rising, the violins negotiate new harmonies with vigour. A sparser, gentle passage ensues, where the music is almost pastoral for a time. A strong flourish leads to another brief atonal moment with faded violins.

The brief third movement begins with a frantic violin, occasionally interrupted by an energised ensemble. The frantic violin returns, this time harmonised and sometimes subject to a throbbing cello. The energised violin persists, solo, and races to an end.

Strong harmonised melodic lines introduce the final movement. This is another formless phase, until some heavy chords are heard. Now the violins begin a frantic section, culminating in a fascinating passage filled with strangely harmonised violin lines, powering the music forward. The energy here is intense with the violins unrelenting. Suddenly a peace comes over the music, and it is only a short time before a firm flourish concludes the work.

I have reviewed these quartets from different CDs but they can both be found on *String Quartets Nos.3, 4 & 5*, performed by the Messages Quartet, on the Dux Recordings label. This disc is available on Amazon US and UK.

Quartets Nos. 3 and 4 can be heard on Spotify and there are various movements on YouTube. All of Nos. 3, 4 and 5 are on earsense.

Listenability: Powerful, rhythmically incisive works.

— ooOoo —

Rued Langgaard [1893–1952]

Nationality: Danish
Quartets: Six
Style: Late-Romantic

String Quartets Nos. 2 & 3

Of Langgaard's six string quartets, No. 1 was abandoned and some of the material composed was used in quartets Nos. 4 and 5. I will be discussing Nos. 2 and 3.

String Quartet No. 2 was written in 1918 and revised in 1931. It consists of four named movements.

Storm Clouds Receding opens in a dashing manner. It is also chaotic until a solo cello makes a statement and is then joined by the ensemble. The chaos resumes briefly before transforming into a stately, peaceful moment which is conversational. The first violin leads but there is plenty of ensemble interaction – it is most satisfying. The tension begins to rise as the violins are like rapiers cutting through the atmosphere. After a brief pause, the music becomes melancholy, and slightly longing, especially the first violin – and just so peaceful.

Now the cello dominates for a time, with violins responding to its call. There is a gentle fade to the end.

Train Passing By is brief, just over two minutes – but its effect is powerful. It opens with a resolute cello ostinato. This is picked up by one violin while the other makes interjections of string sound effects and various melodic phrases. The tonality is constantly changing, which adds to the train-like effect.

Landscape in Twilight begins in a pastoral manner, and is very delicate. Simple folk melodies predominate and the feeling is sparse. A violin now sets up a tempo and the sound intensifies, constantly alternating between melodic and rhythmic sections. A recapitulation of the opening theme occurs – we only have two violins at this stage. The cello and viola eventually make their own statements, before the instrumentation drops back to two violins again leading to a tender moment. A further recapitulation leads to a gentle conclusion.

The Walk commences with a dialogue between two violins in a sparse space until the cello creates a hint of chaos and the ensemble thickens. The music is soft, but the intensity is high, which creates an interesting effect. Shimmering violins take over, making for an abstract mood – there is no tempo, just seemingly random phrases. Eventually a tempo emerges and we are into a dance where the whole ensemble becomes joyful for a time. As the ending approaches there is a certain spacious feeling, and nothing concrete to be heard. A powerful section now takes over and the work is complete.

This is definitely program music and the titles are played out in the piece very effectively.

The Third Quartet, written in 1924, is in three movements. It opens with a series of staccato chords before any melodies occur. When the melodies begin, they are taut, stretched tightly around the chord interjections. After a brief pause, the cello introduces a peaceful space. The violins drift around a sparse melody and the chord rhythm proceeds with the cello predominating until the piece settles into a beguiling pattern, with cello and violins competing to be heard. It becomes a little frantic with string sound effects to the fore. The peace returns as we near the end. After several violin flourishes, the finish comes with three staccato chords. It is an interesting movement.

The second movement is brief, at 88 seconds. Its ethnic melodies meander through the music, ending in a perfunctory manner with the solo cello playing five notes.

The final movement is peaceful, sounding like the introduction to a hymn which then leads to a cello and violin dialogue. The music is anxious and won't settle – a solo cello ostinato occurs for a brief interlude. Now the intensity lifts and the music is more insistent as further dialogue, together with string sound effects, abound. The cello is conspicuous as a sustained chordal section with an implied melody concludes the work. This quartet is not long but I found it fascinating.

Wikipedia refers to the composer as Late-Romantic, which sounds pretty close, although there is an argument for Early Modern. As an aside, of the several Nordic composers that I discuss in this book all seem to have an interesting regional sound to their works.

Various CDs are available on Amazon US and UK. My review copy is a 2-CD set by the Kontra Quartet on Marco Polo. I believe this contains the complete early quartets. There are now three single discs of the complete quartets by the Nightingale Quartet on Da Capo, in SACD format – these also contain incidental works for string quartet that are not numbered. I have been listening to this set on Spotify, they are quite superb.

It appears that everything that is on Amazon is also on Spotify and several full quartets are on YouTube and earsense.

Listenability: Slightly serious at times, but also beautiful.

— ooOoo —

Lars-Erik Larsson [1908–1896]

Nationality: Swedish
Quartets: Three
Style: Early Modern

String Quartet No. 1

Apart from Larsson's three string quartets, he also wrote an early suite for the medium, *Intimate Miniatures* (English translation). He studied under Alban Berg, but his quartets do not appear to reflect this experience. To me, he is a twentieth century composer who appears to look back, rather than forward.

I am going to discuss String Quartet No. 1 and *Intimate Miniatures,* both performed by the Stenhammar Quartet.

The first numbered quartet, in three movements, opens in an optimistic mood with a harmonised cello and violin line. The violin eventually breaks free for a time, but the opening phrase reoccurs at various intervals. A pizzicato interlude leads to variations on the opening melody, and more harmonised cello and violin melodies unfold. The mood changes with the violin leading the way, supported by a very fluid ensemble background. It now becomes more abstuse, before an extended pizzicato section ensues and the violins suddenly leap into a dialogue, with some atonal lines. Harmonisation of the melodies is particularly fine, especially when they include the cello. A pizzicato interlude brings us into a solo violin passage, which is then taken up by the ensemble – however the first violin dominates. The musical texture is now thickened, as it moves to a conclusion with a final, sweeping chord.

A violin duet introduces the second movement, with the second violin paraphrasing the melodies of the first. There is a lot of harmonic movement here, and the viola provides a subtle pizzicato accompaniment. Now the music comes to a standstill, and begins again with a violin and viola section. A pulse is created and the violins move forward, in duet formation once more. The melodies become busier and an animated pizzicato viola enters. The cello adds strong melodic lines, then retreats back into the ensemble. An extended section finally leads to a full sound, before the movement starts to wind down, becoming very sparse, and soon peters out.

The final movement opens in a quick, but slightly stilted manner. There is a lot going on and the instruments seem to have a complex relationship. While the violins lead in a forceful way, the accompaniment seems strangely independent. A very dynamic passage slowly fades to a whisper before leaping into a rhapsodic moment. The stilted style reappears momentarily, before we return to a positively racing section, which leads to the conclusion of the work.

This is a very busy, but charming quartet. It is replete with fine melodies, harmonic changes and strong rhythmic impetus.

I have a slight issue regarding *Intimate Miniatures*. On the Spotify recording, the movements are not played in order – in fact the first movement concludes the piece. I am going to take the movements in their numerical order, and shall treat it as one continuous piece.

The opening is a very slow, enchanting piece of writing. The ensemble all contribute an equal voice and a special mood is created. The music is filled with interplay and features a long fade out before a warm, melodic section follows. The work gathers intensity as the violins begin to assert themselves and a chordal passage is featured between violin statements – this is fine writing. A solo cello passage leads to a return of an earlier melody which is very light and wistful – whimsical, even.

A new mood unfolds with a dichotomy – there are strong positive melodies in the foreground, with a slight minor feeling to the accompaniment. This feeling dissipates and the violins move up a notch in intensity before they positively dominate for a time. The dynamics rise again and then move into a quiet passage, where I recognise a melodic phrase that I have heard before. The positive nature continues at a moderate intensity, slowly increasing, before a brief conclusion.

A stately Haydnesque melody appears and the ensemble sounds very warm in accompaniment. The melodies rise and fall in dynamics, but retain the stately feeling, albeit updated for the twentieth century. A very beautiful passage follows with a violin in its highest register bringing forth wonderful melodic lines over a sparse background. A solo violin section where the violin answers itself is followed by a pastoral mood until a violin interjects with some dynamic statements, but order is soon returned. A plucked cello accompaniment is most pleasing.

A brisk section follows and the violins drive the music forward. There is a violin duet passage, which again builds into a tempo. The violins assert themselves once more and, nearing the end, they revert to attractive harmonised lines, before ending the work in an abrupt manner.

These two pieces are both quite conservative, but have a wonderful optimism about them and mostly, feature a strong pulse.

There are two fine versions available. The first is on Daphne Records, performed by the Stenhammar Quartet, then there is the Helsingborg String Quartet, on the Big Ben Phonograph label.

The Stenhammar Quartet version is on Spotify, YouTube and earsense.

Listenability: Very fine, slightly conservative works.

[Image courtesy Daphne label]

Aleksander Lasoń [born 1951]

Nationality: Polish
Quartets: At least seven
Style: Modern Contemporary

String Quartet No. 1

Lasoń is Modern, but in a delightfully cerebral manner. I am going to discuss his First String Quartet. The work opens with sustained notes, featuring a smattering of microtones before the cello drones and then interjects. The violins express no melodic development, it sounds mildly like police sirens. Sometimes a sustained note soars into the high register. After a brief pause, the feeling returns, this time for me evoking Alfred Hitchcock's *The Birds*, mainly due to the use of glissandos. A rhythmic moment ensues, but it doesn't last and the violins continue with their musings. Suddenly we have a loud episode of block chords, featuring all instruments – they are mostly sustained notes. When they stop, a lone violin delivers up a gentle phrase to finish. What do you say about music that just 'is'? It's a magnificent soundscape, I really enjoyed it.

The second movement sounds more like a string quartet, albeit a little chaotic. All instruments have an equal voice in this random, atonal section. Now a rise in tempo brings about a change, although the level of entropy is still high – violins concoct strange melodies that overlap with each other while the tempo is moderated, but the random feeling persists. Then follows a quiet, almost hymn-like sound – this is a stunning introspective moment. Now some harmonised violin lines are heard, negotiating slow, sometimes ethnic scales as they craft a series of most interesting melodies. A scurrying moment leads us back into the chaos. This is reminiscent of the beginning, sounding like purely random music.

The final movement opens with strong sustained notes and is much more conservative than the first two movements. These are real melodies, with changes in harmony leading to some interesting note selections. It reminds me of the theme statement of Miles Davis' treatment of Joe Zawinul's *In a Silent Way*. They inhabit a similar sound space – there is a longing feeling here, the key feature being the sustained notes, they are very effective. The piece gently winds down for a time, and there are also glissandos featured, making for a very soulful sound. One violin concludes the work. This is a beautiful mood.

The work contains the three elements that make up music: melody, harmony and rhythm. However I am sure some people wouldn't see it that way. I just love the measured, atonal chaos, and the deep feeling of the final movement.

The Third Quartet opens with a sharp note and then moves into a period of stasis, where the two violins play slow, and long sustained melodies. Now an abrupt interjection of notes occurs, before moving into further slow melodies. This passage does not have the intensity of the First Quartet, but features sparser melodies. The interjections occur sporadically, but the music always returns to its predominant feeling, one of a desolate landscape. Now the violins intensify,

251

with a strong attack of their bows, and notes in the high register. Several interjections interrupt proceedings, but the feeling keeps coming back. There is tension now, with the violins exploding into action. A solo violin and a flourish leads to the end.

The second movement begins aggressively, with the violins being particularly so. Now they recede to a position of a duet, quite dramatically and the mood darkens as the violins spin out disparate melodic lines with a rhythmic intensity. After a time, a brief solo cello statement occurs, which leads to a chaotic violin conclusion.

The next movement is 68 seconds long. Opening very slowly, it appears to consist of a series of random notes, ending on a descending glissando. Just a point about the opening of this movement – it was so soft as to be inaudible. I adjusted the levels with a sound file editor so that I could hear what was going on. For the technically minded, I had to increase the level by 12 dB and it was still soft.

The final movement is again short and after a sharp chord, the tempo basically races with a rhythmic motif to support it. It's all about the rhythm here. Violins skim across the top but the ensemble is dominant. There are many harmonic changes until it concludes.

Lasoń is basically very modern and I don't think I've heard anything like his music before. The nearest would be Terry Riley's *Salome Dances for Peace*.

The review CD, *Aleksander Lasoń: String Quartets Nos. 1, 3, and 7,* performed by the Silesian String Quartet on the Pro Bono label is only available as an MP3 download from Amazon US and UK. A second disc of his string quartets suffers from the same fate.

The review CD is on Spotify and YouTube. All of the quartets can be heard on earsense.

Listenability: Very modern and mildly confronting, but I like it.

— ooOoo —

Mario Lavista [born 1943]

Nationality: Mexican
Quartets: Six
Style: Contemporary

String Quartets Nos. 1, 2 & 4

Lavista's six string quartets are so short that they all fit on to a single CD. Three are one movement works – the other three consist of many very short movements. I am going to discuss the former, which run for a combined total time of 33 minutes. Normally, I would regard that length as approaching epic, but this composer has a liking for space. They are all named works, in Mexican, and I had trouble with translating them. Oh well.

String Quartet No. 1 is titled *Diacronia* and is rather short at seven minutes. It opens with an ambient atmosphere and a sustained violin backdrop. A random cello note is heard and eventually, musical statements begin to appear. I wouldn't call them melodies – in any event they are outweighed by the many interjections from all instruments. These take the form of varying textures, sometimes the timbre is quite crude. The interjections can be a phrase, a rhythmic motif, or a string sound effect. The sustained tone has persisted and can still be heard in the background. For me, the interjections, which are the heart of the piece, defy description. I guess I would go with static soundscape. Not your average string quartet.

String Quartet No. 2 is titled *Reflejos de la Noche* which I gather translates to *Reflexes at Night*. It opens with a sound pastiche of assembled instruments, sustaining a mood, while string sound effects emulate wild animals, possibly monkeys. The harmony and the attack of the ensemble does change, but only marginally. The animal noises persist until some melodic fragments rise to the surface, leading to a section that is quite propulsive, with different instruments contributing to the sense of a rhythmic pattern. As the work progresses, there are more, abstract melodic ideas presented. Occasionally, chordal passages are heard. This, like the First Quartet is basically a soundscape, but definitely not of a static nature. Nearing the conclusion I sense some movement in one of the violins as it fades into nothing.

String Quartet No. 4 is titled *Sinfonias*. Sinfonia is an English musical term meaning small orchestra. This work opens with a throbbing cello not unlike the introduction to Miles Davis' *Bitches Brew*. The basic sound resembles the drone of the Indian tamboura, and brings a modal sound to the music. Some melodies occur here, as the violins overlap with lines and phrases. This piece is on the move, albeit slowly. A repeated motif is set up and the ensemble meanders about it, as the cello makes statements, both bowed and pizzicato. A sustained note brings about a change, with the first violin becoming quite assertive. The ensemble responds to this, as it does when the violin mellows. The drone is still present and things become very quiet. The cello makes further statements, sometimes using microtones. The drone changes texture and becomes more like the rhythmic, but static nature of the Second Quartet. The dynamics recede slightly and individual voices are able to be discerned clearly. A sustained note introduces an Indian Classical music flavour, being totally bereft of harmony – modal statements are the mood at this time. A pizzicato ostinato is briefly heard before the pizzicato becomes more melodic in nature. The cello returns, in its lower register, and makes strong statements. Another ostinato passage ensues, and one violin fades to a close.

On the basis of these three quartets, I would class the music as strongly ambient, with little development. I also listened to the remaining three multi-movement works and found the presence of movements allowed for a lot more variety, although some of them were cut from the same cloth as the discussed

253

quartets. Strangely, there are no angry or aggressive passages to be found here – the composer certainly had the opportunity to present some. Lavista definitely has his own unique style – I've not heard music like this before, which is not to say that there isn't any out there.

The review CD is *Mario Lavista – Complete String Quartets*, on the Toccata Classics label, performed by Cuarto Latinoamericano. It is available on Amazon UK and US.

The CD can be found on Spotify and there are several quartets on YouTube. All of the contents of the CD are on earsense.

Listenability: It's not difficult listening, but is clearly in a strange Modern Contemporary style.

— ooOoo —

Benjamin Lees [1924–2010]

Nationality: American
Quartets: Six
Style: Contemporary

String Quartet No. 5

This work opens with a stunning solo cello passage, its rich tones evoking a Bach cello suite. Gradually it works itself into a frenzy and is joined by the ensemble. With all memories of Bach gone, the violin dominates with a rich melody, although the cello still remains prominent. Intense, rhythmic thrusts punctuate the violin's expression, leading into a strong, atonal section with dense, harmonised flourishes producing a feeling of great intensity and drama with a lot of musical activity. Now an ostinato unfolds, made up of several powerful motifs. The cello returns with strong statements as the violin moves into a shrill register that lingers for some time, commencing a section of strong cello and violin dialogue – this is a fascinating soundscape, filled with atonal rhythmic thrusts and frantic violin expressions. The mood moves into a chaos, with all instruments providing dissonant interjections. A change in character emerges as a soft passage unfolds, with a further violin and cello dialogue until the two violins begin to evoke the sound of bees, ever-intensifying in their attack on the strings, and providing a dissonant duet. The end comes with another atonal flourish.

The second, slow movement features the sound of two lamenting, seemingly unrelated violins. A piercing violin, occasionally supported by resonant cello strokes, endures for an extended period until it drops in register and is merely shrill. A conversation develops between two violins and the cello, again in an atonal manner – this extended passage creates a most beguiling emotional feeling. After a pause, the music becomes the sound of just two violins, featuring

254

bird-like string sound effects, eventually leading to a very shrill and beautiful conclusion.

The next movement is quite brief and commences with virtuosic violin and cello statements, including many glissandos and strong rhythmic impetus. Again, the sound of bees is evoked as the violins storm their way to a climactic end.

The finale opens in a dynamic manner, with much quivering of bows and a resultant forward propulsion, featuring sweeping atonal melodic phrases. A short solo cello statement leads the music into an abstract, contemplative space which continues until the first violin soars above the ensemble with a sustained note. The cello and second violin are very active during this passage and a pizzicato viola adds to the texture. Glissandos abound, together with other string sound effects. The bee analogy is also useful here as a distinct rhythmic hum underpins the music. Eventually, another solo cello section emerges and the violins gently blend in with its musings. Nearing the end, the violins drift into a solemn duet – the cello returns and the sound becomes positively dynamic, with a racing tempo to an almost orchestral-like rhythmic conclusion.

Lees' compositions seem to have been guided by his heart, not his musical environment of Modernity. He once said:

There are two kinds of composers. One is the intellectual and the other is visceral. I fall into the latter category. If my stomach doesn't tighten at an idea, then it's not the right idea.

The review CD, titled *Lees, B.: String Quartets Nos. 1, 5 and 6*, performed by the Cypress String Quartet on the Naxos label is available from Amazon US and UK. There is also a wonderful version of his String Quartet No. 2 performed by the Juilliard Quartet, available only as a download although it is included on their recent set *The Complete EPIC Recordings 1956-66*, which is currently on my wishlist.

Both the Naxos and the Juilliard No. 2 are on Spotify and Nos. 2 & 6 are on YouTube.

Listenability: Unique-sounding Modern quartets.

Jón Leifs [1899–1968]

Nationality: Icelandic
Quartets: Three
Style: Contemporary

String Quartet No. 2

My feeling is that Leifs' three string quartets are a trilogy based on the life and works, particularly the religious paintings, of Italian artist El Greco. There is an interesting website on the life and works of the artist here:

https://www.artsy.net/artist/el-greco

More information can be found on Wikipedia. Most of the quartet movements have titles, referring to items such as the birthplace of El Greco and the names of some of his paintings. I have selected the Second Quartet, which is in three named movements, for discussion.

Childhood – The work opens with a selection of quivering strings before a brooding melody begins to develop – there is a sense of ascension here. An ostinato ensues, at quite a low volume. The mood is somewhat reminiscent of Arvo Pärt and it continually builds with the ostinato driving the development. The harmonies have a feeling of Early Music, which sits well with El Greco's life – he died in 1614. Now a lilting passage begins, strutting even. Again, this is developed and it moves into a gentle pizzicato section. I feel as if I am describing music not of this time as the violins continue with a gentle rhythmic motif. A new section has some melodic development and the cello exchanges phrases with the violins. Now the tempo becomes dance-like for a moment before the violins return to their dialogue with the cello, which makes an extended statement. The music never sounds modern, but it is extremely purposeful. It ends on an expansive note.

Youth – A flurry of quivering strings opens this movement. It's only short-lived however, as the violins play long notes over a sustained tone – a tempo emerges. Again it's not of its time, sometimes even the timbre of the violins suggest an early wind instrument. An increase in tempo resumes a strutting feeling, eventually leading to some melodic material being developed. There is a brief flurry of intertwining lines and a return to the introductory quivering. A slow lamenting passage develops, featuring just two violins. The mood lightens a little, but the texture is still very measured. A violin becomes shrill, before returning to its middle register. This atmosphere is sustained for some time until a sparse, but frenzied phase leads to an almost inaudible, shrill violin note to conclude.

Requiem and Eternity – The final movement opens in a modal style which is quite beautiful with a violin wandering in a rubato fashion – there is no tempo here. A slight hint of harmony occurs occasionally and adds interest. Now a new mood is formed with a violin duet, increasing in intensity, coming into play. The viola goes into pizzicato as the piece begins to move forward. A transient phase features the two violins, which are also pizzicato, and then, moves back into a tempo. The violins again develop until the pizzicato viola rapidly increases the tempo and the cello delivers long tones. Nearing the end, sparsity returns and shrill violins perform an inaudible fade, I think produced more by the recording engineer than the musicians.

Several things have come to me while experiencing this quartet which may be worthwhile noting. I have never come across a connected series of works written over such a long period, 26 years in fact. Having also listened to the other two quartets I can tell you that they have a similar emotional content, some sections are even more ambient than this quartet. Finally, the work has vast dynamic ranges throughout, I was constantly reaching for the volume control – some of the music was simply inaudible. I found this more than a little disconcerting.

This CD is available on Amazon US and UK as *Jón Leifs: The Three String Quartets*, on the BIS label, performed by the Yggdrasil Quartet. I could only find a listenable version on Spotify.

Listenability: Strange, sustained gentle music. Seemingly not of this world.

[*Penitent_Magdalene* by El Greco c. 1580-1585]
[Image – Public Domain - courtesy Wiki Commons]

Roland Leistner-Mayer [born 1945]

Nationality: Czech-German
Quartets: At least seven
Style: Modern Contemporary

String Quartet No. 5

Czech-born Leistner-Mayer, after studying in Germany and residing there, is now considered to be a German composer. I intend to discuss his Fifth Quartet.

The first movement is of truly epic proportions, variously in length, emotional scope and dynamic range. It opens with a very full sound – a flurry of quivering violins, evoking bats emerging into the night. This soon moves into a chordal, melodic passage, all the while constantly referring back to the fluttering sound. Now a violin emerges, leading to a more measured ensemble texture. A loud flourish, more powerful than the opening brings forward strong, if somewhat random melodies. Solo cello engages in a dialogue with the violins, eventually leading into another display of power, which slowly dissipates into a conversational section with further strong melodies. A brief pause brings a hint of the opening feeling, in a very controlled manner, with the quivering constantly varying in intensity – this is some powerful music. I should also mention that it is a very long movement.

A return to the dynamic flourish is heard and the violins become insistent in their expression. The cello and violin dialogue again before leading back into the previous dynamic. After an extended period of intensity, the opening mood is resumed and with it, some sense of peace. Sombre violin melodic lines intertwine with solo cello statements for a time but another rise in dynamics follows. A rhythmic pattern is heard, with all instruments contributing – the music often sounds like more than four instruments. A swirling, giddying moment leads to the end.

The second movement begins with a strong ostinato feeling, a little unusual in that various different motifs contribute to the effect. Violin statements seem to be constantly interrupted by these ostinato motifs. A dramatic change features a pizzicato section – out of this emerges a violin melody, and after a brief pause, a solid wall of sound ensues with dramatic violin statements prominent. This turgid passage develops through several mood changes and concludes on a powerful ensemble chord.

The next movement begins on a series of rhythmic chords, before a violin rises out of the ensemble and is joined by the second violin. This leads to a diminution of the intensity with less voices available to carry the chordal rhythm, which is now pushed into the background with the violins dominating. A terse atmosphere unfolds, with a sense of mystery as the violins temper their attack and are absorbed back into the ensemble. Melodic arpeggios prevail for a time, then the ensemble strengthens, only to release the tension, allowing the violins to step forward. A short period of sparsity leads to a dense passage of aggressive

259

violin lines – this slowly moderates and there is a conversation unfolding – the sense of mystery has returned. This feeling is sustained to a gentle end.

The final movement features a solo violin, eventually joined by the other instruments, one at a time. When this mood has fully developed, it is one of abstraction, with the violins being particularly busy. With a drop in dynamics, a pizzicato cello walks, jazz style for a time until the violins overwhelm it with a feeling of chaos. A peaceful section gives way to further dramatic violin lines, with a sense of urgency, slowly moving into a very powerful section. The work concludes on a dynamic rhythmic flourish, followed by a final pizzicato chord.

This is a quartet with moments of great intensity, interspersed with some reflective, albeit atonal passages – I was drawn to its strength.

The review CD *Leistner-Mayer: String Quartets 5-6-7*, on the TYXart label and performed by the Sojka Quartet is available on Amazon US and UK.

This disc can be sampled on Spotify, YouTube and earsense.

Listenability: Very powerful, non-confrontational Modern quartet.

— ooOoo —

Guillaume Lekeu [1870–1894]

Nationality: Belgian
Quartets: One
Style: Late Romantic

String Quartet No. 1

Lekeu wrote just one string quartet in his short life, but it is a masterpiece. The quartet contains six movements, and is a bit of an epic, clocking in at thirty-five minutes.

The work opens with an elegance beyond words, as the ensemble mesh as one. A slightly plaintive melody suddenly adds a bit more life, and the cello writing is wonderful here. A pause brings about a change into a violin-driven section, based around a melodic phrase. Now the rhythm picks up and the cello still provides outstanding accompaniment. The texture drops back to two violins for a time, with negligible ensemble support, before all four instruments come into play, with the violins continuing to lead the way. A cello-dominant passage is impressive and allows the violins to express themselves freely until the tempo suddenly quickens and the texture intensifies, with very fine harmonised violin lines. Another pause brings about a change as the violins temper their approach with gentle phrases. The end comes with a cello and violin duet that slowly moves into one violin, which dissipates.

The second movement, marked adagio *sostenuto* – a little faster than adagio, starts with a melody resembling something that I recognise, I just can't place it. I think it might be a Bach transcription that I've heard. In any event, it is indeed very precious, played by just one violin for an extended period. There is a hint of cello and then a transcendent harmonic background becomes apparent as the ensemble lends gentle support. This too is most precious. Now a tempo takes over with the violins creating a rhythm, and the cello makes a positive melodic statement before moving into a period where the violins soar over the cello, which now creates pizzicato interludes for a time. The texture cuts back to one violin and the cello, such a beautiful sound, with stunning interplay. A tempo returns and the ensemble regathers for a moment. This brings a return of the previously mentioned harmonic background, and a shrill, striking violin line. A fine melody ensues as the violin goes it alone but for an occasional cello statement. This feeling continues to the conclusion of a fabulous movement.

The next, brief movement has a sparse violin melody that sets up a marvellous melodic statement from the cello – it is positive and evokes much harmonic movement. The cello establishes a call and response with itself, by alternating between two registers. Nearing the end, it changes texture and slips into a walking pattern and concludes. This movement is basically a cello solo, and very fine it is too.

Solo cello opens the fourth movement and again it works in two registers. Then a violin continues with the same melody, while the cello uses a pulsing technique. The solo cello makes a statement, and is joined by two violins, which play a long sustained chord that fades. Again the cello returns, in a melodic manner, and continues to alternate between two registers. It almost sounds like two cellos. The violins return, but it is in a support role to the cello, which soon continues its solo musings. The violins are back and a tranquil ending ensues. I can't believe how much the cello has dominated the quartet thus far.

A brief fifth movement begins with a conservative waltz for the two violins. At times they increase the dynamics but soon return to the basic waltz melody before the two violins fade to a conclusion.

The final movement begins with a loud flourish before the cello leads the ensemble into a busy passage. The violins briefly assert themselves – we then have another solo cello statement. The violins eventually take up the challenge and produce some strong chords. The cello again leads and the violins join in. The texture now changes as the cello walks, briskly, and is loud, with the violins in support. This leads to the end of the piece, with a dynamic flourish.

I can't remember the last time I heard such a prominent cello in a quartet. It certainly adds a lot of interest as the writing for the cello is wonderful. Who said Romantic music can't be exciting? And written before he was 24 years old, if you don't mind – what a tragic loss for music. If you only want to own one Late Romantic string quartet, I highly recommend it, it is a simply superb work. There are too many fine features to mention but I was particularly taken by the constant references to earlier melodic phrases, and the way in which Lekeu is able to draw new life out of them, by the sheer brilliance of his craft.

My review copy is on the Timpani label, performed by Quatuor Debussy, titled *Lekeu: Works for String Quartet,* and contains two other, not insignificant, beautifully meditative works for quartet. While doing my final proof-read of this edition, I have been listening extensively to this quartet in my car, along with some of Lekeu's orchestral works. They are all magical.

The quartet is available on Amazon UK, with several different versions. It is always paired with at least one other piece. Amazon US and Presto have my review copy, as does Spotify, but you have to search for Lekeu Quatuor. It's there, you just need to find it. There are also several versions on YouTube. It is on earsense as String Quartet in G Major.

Listenability: Simply wonderful must hear Late Romantic work.

[Image courtesy Timpani label]

Arthur Lourie [1982–1966]

Nationality: Russian
Quartets: Three
Style: Early Modern

String Quartets Nos. 1-3

Lourie's three string quartets are of varying proportions in length and complexity. One is substantial, one is medium and the third, short. I'm going to discuss them all.

Quartet No. 1 runs for thirty minutes and is in two movements, marked lento and grave – both indicating an extremely slow tempo, which sounds interesting. The first movement runs for nineteen minutes and opens with a meandering, intangible theme. It rises in intensity before falling away and a loud rhythmic passage gives way to the opening again. It is repeated for a while – from recondite serenity to loud chordal sections. These strange melodies are enticing – slightly dissonant and sometimes a little agitated. The piece then moves into a dialogue between the cello and the ensemble. This is mysterious music, I love it. A touch of chaos leads into some string sound effects interspersed with melodic chordal moments.

About halfway through this movement, we have a return to solo violin with occasional sparse interjections. It develops into a set of dancing melodies, again mildly dissonant, eventually breaking into a rhythmic pattern and becoming a little darker. It is controlled, modern music. Some string sound effects are heard and the piece now is fully in tempo. Further attractive, slightly ethnic melodies, drift in and it finishes with a measured atonal flourish.

The second movement opens with some slightly dissonant chords in tempo. The violins wander around the accompaniment and there are hints of middle-eastern scales here. A charming melody develops in the first violin against a static harmonic background. This persists for a time, until a chord change has the music turning slightly chaotic with more dissonance. It then settles into a positive rhythm, building in tension until it just stops. It continues with another gentle period with the strings playing as one. Nearing the end, the piece moves into tempo, and features lyrical melodies. These are soon transformed back into dissonance. It has a false ending with three pizzicato ensemble flourishes, a five-second silence and then a seemingly random sequence of notes. There you have it.

I can really appreciate this quartet. It features the kind of musical spaces where I like to spend time.

String Quartet No. 2 runs for only seven minutes. Opening with a slightly dissonant march, it then changes into a more positive flavour. The dissonance returns and is followed by a folk-like section, and a series of chordal interjections. The volume then drops to a whisper before the violin leads the ensemble into a dance section with many different sound spaces and tempo changes. As the piece winds down, some of the opening themes reoccur. Now we have another false ending with a five-second break, and a seemingly random passage to conclude.

This work, being so short, makes me wonder what it was all about. It was written in 1923, so I guess there were different ideas floating around at that time. I'm constantly surprised at how some Modernist composers end their movements. I can recall a number of times writing – it just stops. Oh well.

The Third Quartet has four movements. The first, marked *Prelude*, opens with a sparkling little interlude, and wanders around this for the whole 90 seconds of the movement.

The second movement, marked *Chorale* begins tenderly and slowly edges forward. There is a little dissonance towards the end, but I find it be spiritual in nature. It is also very lyrical.

The third movement, marked *Hymne,* is a little march-like although I could imagine a hymn being sung to it. Featuring a slow, but pronounced tempo, the attractive opening theme is developed in various ways. It is a lot more confident by the time the conclusion arrives.

The last movement, marked *Marche Funebre* (funeral march), opens with a low cello melody, and a small violin diversion before a return to the introductory cello theme. The composer then applies a set of variations to a melodic phrase for some time. The cello is still prominent, offering up dark melodies, as befits the title. As it nears the conclusion, there is a beautiful short statement with whispering violins. Then it just fades away.

These are relatively youthful quartets, all written before 1927. For me, they fit the mould of the composer's time, although the two long slow movements of the First Quartet surprised me. Basically, Lourie's quartets are reflective and, if I may speculate, seem more than a little spiritual.

As to availability, there is a set by the Utrecht String Quartet on the ASV label on Amazon US and UK.

I couldn't find it on Spotify, but some quartets are available for sampling on YouTube and Quartets Nos. 1 and 3 are on earsense.

Listenability: Mostly introspective – I like it.

Albéric Magnard [1865–1914]

Nationality: French
Quartets: One – FOSQC
Style: Late Romantic

The String Quartet

Lucien Denis Gabriel Albéric Magnard's one string quartet is officially titled String Quartet in E minor, Opus 16 and was composed in 1903. This makes him one of the later members of the French One String Quartet Club. Significantly, he would have had a chance to become familiar with the quartets of Debussy and Ravel and I believe I can hear this in the work. It is in four movements.

The opening movement is long, as are most of the movements and the work runs to over forty minutes. The flavour is Romantic but with a touch of introspection, although one could argue Impressionism. After a jaunty start there is a period of sombre violin lines, which meander for a time before the music coheres into a positive mood, with overlapping violin melodies contributing. A sense of urgency is heard, before another gentle, sparse passage. Slowly the dynamics return, this time stronger than before and the music has a sense of drama as violins express powerfully over the ensemble. Another lilting passage ensues with beautiful violin writing, quite alluring really. The cello supports the violins with purposeful lines and the energy rises again. The dynamics continue to rise and fall, with periods of lyricism contrasted with more assertive lines. Eventually, the lyrical nature prevails for an extended phase, which slowly drifts into sparsity, with little movement. The ending is a quiet fade of the violins.

A much shorter movement, marked *serenade*, commences with a passage featuring predominantly a violin duet – this is rather attractive. A hint of pizzicato changes the mood as some fine new melodies are presented, with appropriate variations. A section of shrill violins doesn't last and the previous feeling is resumed. This **is** a serenade, very melodic and it finishes on a brief but charming pizzicato passage.

The third movement is marked *chant funebre* – two translations I found were *lament* and *funeral song*. Funeral it is, with minor key melodies over a sparse accompaniment. The violins are longing, but not dark – there is a hint of optimism here. Slowly the passage unfolds with the melodies becoming progressively more powerful and positive. Now the dynamics recede, however, the melodies remain positive and the violins begin to fly higher again, with a hint of tension to be felt. A strong violin in a low register takes control and is complemented by the second violin, which eventually moves into a rhythmic role. Gradually a chaotic mood unfolds, to be followed by a reprise, which features the two violins back in duet mode. This whole movement has a succession of charming melodies. Nearing the end, the sound is Beethoven-like with lilting violins in the high register – a sustained shrill chord is absolutely perfect.

265

Further assertive violins commence the finale and the mood is filled with violin swoops and overlapping lines. A chordal passage is strong and leads to a cello supporting the dancing violins with intermittent phrases. Now the cello becomes part of the dance and playfully combines with the violins for a busy passage. Another rhythmic chordal section unfolds and the violins emerge from it with more attractive melodies. A return to the strong cello brings on a charming moment where the violins exchange phrases. Except for the cello interludes, the violins dominate this movement. A gentle passage has the cello conspicuous again – this is maintained for some time. Next we have a slightly dramatic moment and a lot of music happens in a short time. The conclusion is a brief racing passage for violins into a final flourish.

The review CD, on Ysaÿe Records and performed beautifully by Quatuor Ysaÿe, is paired with Fauré's only string quartet. There is another version, by the Via Nova Quartet which also contains the only quartets of Roussel and Chausson. Both of these CDs are available on Amazon US and UK. The Via Nova seems to be much cheaper and represents a bargain.

The Ysaÿe version can be heard on Spotify, YouTube, and earsense.

Listenability: Exceptionally fine melodic work.

— ooOoo —

Gian Malipiero [1882–1973]
& Paul Dessau [1894–1979]
Two Contrasting Styles

Italian composer Gian Francesco Malipiero and German Paul Dessau were born twelve years apart and died six years apart. Having said that, their styles are very different, which reinforces the observation that composers don't think in terms of named periods, they just write. Of course they are influenced by their musical environment, but I think the idea of putting composers into categories based on time periods (which I have done in the Appendicies), is only marginally useful, especially in the twentieth century. In light of this I thought that the idea of comparing two composers, basically from the same era, would be an interesting exercise.

Malipiero composed eight string quartets. It wasn't until the seventh that I could hear any modern references. Dessau however, embraces Modernity from his First String Quartet and develops rather quickly into a highly abstract style.

I could have picked Italian Malipiero's String Quartet No. 1, which is Late Romantic, but I have gone for a later work, No. 7, written in 1947, for contrast. This quartet begins with an insistent theme, with all four players given opportunity for expression. It then transforms into a quiet passage building a wonderful melody. This occasionally hints at slightly dissonant sounds but they are usually supported by traditional harmony, which tends to diminish the effect.

Another brief rhythmic moment occurs but this is quickly followed by an alluring bout of introspection. How wonderful. Another strong rhythmic phase follows before it gives way to slow Romanticism again. This cyclic approach continues to the end of the piece – rhythm-slow-rhythm-slow, with occasional forays into mild dissonance. The end is soft and gentle.

Now on to Dessau, who was German. He composed seven string quartets. String Quartet No. 1 was written in 1932, fifteen years before the Malipiero No. 7 and is in three movements. The first starts with a soft, atonal, morose feeling, which is just how I like it. A solo cello statement ensues, and then the other instruments enter with swarming dissonant melodies. It's already more modern than the Malipiero. For variation, Dessau rarely goes into rhythmic episodes, he just increases the intensity of the melodies and accompaniment. It is similar to the cyclic nature found in the Malipiero.

The second movement is short, only three minutes. It consists of a series of atonal musings, mostly soft. It's actually quite playful.

The last movement opens as a solo violin alternating with dissonant chords from the other instruments. There are duet violin passages, sometimes with pizzicato accompaniment – abstract but pleasing ensemble episodes, and almost always without a pulse. The piece concludes with a series of dissonant chords.

Listening to the later quartets, Nos. 6 and 7, reveals a whole new sound world. The dissonance is more prevalent and the attack of the quartet is more aggressive. However I wouldn't call them harsh or confronting.

Both of these composers are worth investigating. Malipiero is obviously more conservative, while Dessau, who is definitely more modern, manages to maintain a deep introspective feeling.

I have listened to two 2-CD sets for this review. The review Malipiero set is no longer available but I am recommending the Orpheus String Quartet on the Brilliant Classics label. I just noticed that it is currently priced at $87.91 on Amazon US, which is about the price of the first violinist's 1709 Stradivarius, although they have it as *New and Used* for under ten dollars. The Dessau is performed by Neues Leipziger Streichquartett on CPO.

Both composer's complete string quartets are on Spotify, YouTube, and earsense.

Listenability: Contrasting contemporaries.

Vincenzo Manfredini [1737–1799]

Nationality: Italian
Quartets: Six
Style: Classical

String Quartets Nos. 1 & 3

Not quite after 1800, but close enough for something different, and interesting. Most of the six quartets are in an early Classical form and predate the influence of Haydn. Each consists of only three movements, with only one movement going above four minutes in length. I am going to discuss String Quartets Nos. 1 and 3.

The First Quartet is basically a *divertimento*, in that the first violin contributes the melodies, while the other three members all play together with the same phrasing, only differing in their note selection, leading to a harmonic accompaniment. There are no individual passages for the second violin, viola or cello. It commences in a Baroque manner, very stately. The violin crafts a fine melodic statement, of course it is quite conservative. There are some interesting rhythmic passages from the ensemble, which feed off the first violin. The end is a solo violin phrase. This is very fine, attractive, almost sweet music.

The next movement, marked largo, is not your traditional largo – it's quite a bit faster. The divertimento concept continues, with the violin playing all of the melodies. Again, this has a stately feeling, probably due to its tempo. The first violin constructs many fine melodies, and the ensemble creates a marvellous harmonic canvas. A change to the minor tonality, leads to a new, more subtle mood, with the first violin creating some splendid lines, given its changed circumstances. A series of decelerating violin phrases leads to a conclusion.

The final, very short movement is energised, and taken at quite a tempo. The ensemble follows the first violin as it negotiates some propulsive melodies. There is a sense of brilliance here. Now a slight pause resumes the process, with the ensemble continuing to chase the violin. The ending is very fine.

The Third Quartet opening, marked allegro, begins as basically a divertimento, and is dominated by the violin. But for the first time, I sometimes notice the appearance of the ensemble without the solo violin. The violin continues through a change to a minor tonality, which doesn't persist. Towards the end, it moves into its high register, and floats freely above the ensemble to a close.

The second movement, marked adagio, is the longest movement of the two quartets. Again, it reminds me of a Baroque feeling, played with a small ensemble, in a minor key. I suppose this is part of the Classical tradition. For the first time, the cello makes a solo melodic statement, and sometimes the ensemble makes further appearances without the violin leading. It always comes back, however. The cello steps forward again and there are many false endings in this movement where the violin slows to a pause. The accompaniment is highly attuned to the melodies of the violin, making for a very satisfying quartet sound. The violin develops some fine rhythmic patterns, as it leads the ensemble to a gentle finish.

The brief final movement again begins in a Baroque manner – it's a little like a pared down version of one of Bach's *Brandenburg Concertos*. This is a very rhythmic section, with a full sound. The violin and ensemble strike a delicate balance and keep to a Bach-like ambience. I think I hear a passage for solo viola in there, before the rhythm returns. The end is a series of strong flourishes, which is a little out of character, and shows indications of the composer moving forward.

By String Quartet No. 6, the style has developed considerably, with a much wider dynamic and emotional range. The andante movement is very precious.

The review CD, *Manfredini: Complete String Quartets*, on the Brilliant Classics label, performed by the Quartetto Delfico is available on both Amazon US and UK, at a very reasonable price.

The CD is on Spotify, YouTube and earsense.

Listenability: Simply delightful, with wonderful slow movements. One for the Classicists.

[Image courtesy Brilliant Classics]

Bohuslav Martinu [1890–1959]

Nationality: Czech
Quartets: Seven
Style: Early Modern

String Quartet No. 1

Martinu wrote a student string quartet work, *Three Horsemen,* when he was twelve. Coincidentally, Mozart also wrote his first string quartet at age twelve, but his is not considered to be a student work – he had already written his first symphony at the age of eight (although this has been subject to debate).

Martinu's first quartet is of epic proportions, running to a length of just under 40 minutes. Essentially a conservative piece, it has four movements and the writing reveals a significant influence of Dvorak. It is fine early 20th century music. It opens tenderly and peacefully with a fugue. The cello is not heard until nearly a minute has elapsed. Some delightful folk melodies can be found here, then the composer slowly works his way into some solid rhythmic melodies and forms. A pause seems to suggest a new movement, which is not the case. The tempo picks up, revealing some stately melodies where again, the cello stays silent for a time. Themes constantly reappear, and the introductory theme is restated softly as the movement ends peacefully.

The second movement also has a false ending. It begins as an andante but then becomes rhythmically driven and features a dance-like quality. The movement finishes with a deep sense of calm.

Movement three starts in a jaunty style and mostly sustains it. Selected themes are constantly reinvoked, giving the work a sense of organisational unity. It is a very melodic movement.

The fourth movement runs for thirteen minutes. It opens in a minor key, the first time that this tonality appears in the work. In contrast to the first three movements, it mostly maintains a brisk tempo feeling for its entirety. Several slower sections occur, but they are not substantial. Some fine melodies are to be found throughout the movement.

In essence the quartet is constantly moving from the refined to the rhythmic. For me, this is music of the mountains and valleys, with a strong Czechoslovakian flavour. There is unbridled joy and the changing moods have so much to offer the listener. I feel that my brief musings don't do justice to this quartet. It seems that, sometimes, critical analysis doesn't work. There are just so many beautiful features here, constantly being stated and re-worked in a myriad of different ways. It is an uplifting piece.

String Quartet No. 1 can be found on various Martinu CDs. The one I have, by the Martinu Quartet on Naxos also contains Quartet No. 2, which is excellent, albeit a bit more serious, and the student work *Three Horseman.* There are several CDs available on Amazon US and UK.

This quartet can be heard on Spotify, YouTube and earsense.

Listenability: A fine first quartet from a composer who obviously had great empathy for his country.

— ooOoo —

Vladimir Martynov [born 1946]

Nationality: Russian
Quartets: At least three
Style: Contemporary

Der Abschied

Vladimir Ivanovich Martynov has written at least three string quartets, or works named as such. I believe his early music was in a modern, confrontational style, but after having spent time in a *Spiritual Academy* to study traditional Russian Orthodox chant, his works seem to have taken on a more spiritual nature. I regard *Der Abschied* (The Farewell) composed in 2006 and in one long movement, as an essentially spiritually inspired work. Apparently it quotes from some of Mahler's lieder, but as I never got much past Mahler's symphonies, I can't comment on that. Reading the CD liner notes may give listeners some insights into the composer's rationale on music – a marvellous essay can be found there.

This quartet opens in an ambient manner, and the sense of space created is continued, in various guises, throughout the whole work. Gentle repeated chords are the first sounds heard. After three or four well-spaced repeats, a slow tempo ensues with similar chords being constantly harmonised. There is no melody but the changes of harmonic structure within the chords create interest. To me, this section, which is sustained for some time, hints at a sparsity that evokes Morton Feldman and forms the basic framework for the whole piece. Eventually a solo cello is heard, in the same rhythmic manner, that is, playing one note with a constant pulse until the ensemble returns to continue the ever changing chords, and maintaining the strict rhythmic structure. Now a violin goes solo, similar to the previous cello interlude, however, it changes register and leads to a lamenting moment. After a brief pause the ensemble again enters, this time with a change in approach. A measured rhapsodic feeling is heard as all instruments contribute a diverse range of sounds – this is a quite beguiling episode. A return to the previously dominant pulsing chord approach settles in, seemingly for the long haul.

Once more, the harmonic changes sustain interest. After a time, and following a brief pause, an ensemble motif is repeated with a long pause between each occurrence. This again leads to another fine rhapsodic passage, which is cut short and the sustained pulsing chords are resumed. These sections are normally prolonged for minutes and this is the case here. Another pause leads to a return of a melodic passage, which is very beautiful with the blend of individual voices rather wonderful. This time the section is extended and a most attractive soundscape ensues. The dynamics increase until the ubiquitous pulsing chords return, again for an extended period. A paring down of the ensemble and another pause brings a hint of a melodic motif, repeated twice before moving back into a more traditional form with sweeping romantic melodies, this time with a gentle ostinato in the background. The violins soar in a most emotionally expressive manner, with ecstatic, long descending phrases being a feature of this extended passage. One particularly passionate violin line is heard many times, to great effect.

Now a new mood is created, with a combination of the basic chordal pulse overlaid with the previously mentioned violin line. This leads to a return of the rhapsodic nature for a brief period, before the pulse resumes, again with the overlaid violin line. A solo violin, in its shrill register, muses for a time until a solo cello takes on the character of the pulsing chord feeling – by way of contrast, it descends into its lowest register and is deeply resonant. Another substantial pause is followed by an almost inaudible shrill violin which leads the ensemble back into a melodic phase, filled with emotional warmth. A period of sustained chords brings with it a total sense of calm – this time without the previous pulsating.

Another melodic violin section, with occasional chordal interjections, proceeds into an extraordinary lilting violin passage with further sustained chords. This gentle feeling is continued over an alternating two-chord harmonic structure until an unusual chord breaks the mood and an extended pause ensues. The two-chord pattern is again heard in a very elegant moment before a pause leads straight back into the preceding section. This occurs several times, with the appearance of the strange chord constantly being the catalyst for change. Nearing the end, there seems to be more pauses than music, and that strange chord followed by another sustained chord is played twice to conclude the piece.

I considered assigning letters to the sections, allowing me to be able to say that it was in an AABACAACB format – I made that up but I hope you get my meaning. The work is a series of constantly recurring sections, although there are subtle differences in the flow between them at times. It is also worth mentioning that the work runs for just under forty minutes, so some of these sections are heard for long periods. It is essentially an introspective soundscape, evoking an almost meditative nature.

There are two other works on the review CD. One is *The Beatitudes*, a six minute work that has a melodic, pastoral feeling in a major tonality, which despite being a fine piece, to me didn't evoke the biblical passage, commonly known as *The Sermon on the Mount* – maybe it wasn't meant to.

The other work is a deconstructed version of the two completed movements of an unfinished string quintet by Schubert. A bonus here is that the quartet is augmented by former Kronos cellist Joan Jeanrenaud, who left the quartet in 1999. Even after reading the composer's CD liner notes, I didn't find this piece very stimulating. The first movement seemed very stilted, only the second movement worked for me. It seemed to be a nod to populism – but that is just an opinion.

Having said that, the Kronos Quartet have also headed down a path that hasn't resonated with me. I am not drawn to their world music collaborations. It was rewarding to come across this 2012 CD, which is classical music. However, their current approach has at least seen them maintain their economic viability and sustained audience support.

The review CD is titled *Music of Vladimir Martynov* performed by Kronos Quartet on the Nonesuch label. It is available on Amazon US and UK.

The album can be heard on Spotify, YouTube and earsense.

Listenability: A very spiritual, calming piece of music.

— ooOoo —

Joseph Marx [1882–1964]

Nationality: Austrian
Quartets: Three
Style: Late Romantic

Quartetto Chromatico
String Quartet No. 1

Joseph Marx' First Quartet, in A major, was written in 1936, and rearranged in 1948, bearing the title *Quartetto Chromatico*. Thus the first quartet also became the last that he published. The other two were written in the intervening years.

The work opens with a lush set of chords which set up a fine atmosphere. Slowly, individual melodies begin to emerge and become quite stately. A drop in the dynamics leads to a slightly winsome phase before moving into a duet for the two violins but soon the full ensemble join in and the cello plays a repeated phrase. The music never remains still for long, and there is plenty of harmonic movement. There is a catchy moment where the violins converse before a solo violin leads into a new, poignant section which is much sparser than that which we have previously heard. It is a terrific piece of Romantic writing, which continues for some time. A change to a minor chord acts as a bridge to an attractive melodic section, which rises and falls with both violins being particularly active. A gentler space emerges and the violins spin out sweet melodies with a minor feeling. One last time, the violins move into a new phase leading to a conclusion on three, measured chords.

The second movement commences in a positive fashion, rhythmic and engaging. The violins surge briefly but are slowed by a pizzicato relief, which is attractive. An open feeling leads to a slightly crowded interlude, transforming into a cello-led section where both violins carry the music forward. There is a depth to this feeling that is sustained until the violins become more animated, in a Modern way. The dynamics rise and the piece ends on a fluttering violin statement with a strong final chord.

The third movement is marked *sehr langsam und ausdrucksvoll* which is German for *'very slowly and expressively'*. Slow and expressive it is, which is my kind of music. The violins are sparse as they investigate enticing melodies over minimal accompaniment. It is classic Romantic writing. The ensemble inserts occasional lamenting phrases – the cello is wonderful here. It is a taut atmosphere, as the violins maintain a feeling of great depth, which leads to some light chaos occurring, together with fine harmonised melodic lines. The two violins point to the conclusion, which is a sustained violin note. This is a wonderful movement, filled with melancholia.

The final movement starts with a hint of folk music, bringing with it a sense of optimism. The tempo is brisk and the two violins project joyous melodic lines until a change comes over the piece and the tempo slows to a walk as the violins continue with their stately phrases. There is a dance-like quality for a time, which moves into a feeling similar to the opening. Shrill violins hesitate, creating a gentle soundscape. Suddenly a short intense rhythmic passage ensues, and the violins end on a chord.

It never ceases to amaze me that so many wonderful quartet styles existed in Europe from 1900-1950. For me it was the zenith of the string quartet genre. Fortunately, there are many great quartets written in all time periods, but the above time frame has always held a special place in my heart.

These three quartets are freely available on Amazon US and UK as *The Complete String Quartets*, on the CPO label, performed by the Thomas Christian Ensemble. The cover art is the distinctive style of Austrian painter Gustav Klimt, who commonly mingled with European Modern musicians of the early twentieth century.

Several versions of *Quartetto Chromatico* can be found on YouTube and all three works are on earsense.

Listenability: Save for the slow movement, bright and breezy.

[Image courtesy CPO Records]

— ooOoo —

John McEwen [1868–1948]

Nationality: Scottish
Quartets: Seventeen
Style: Late Romantic

String Quartet No. 6

There is a definite stylistic progression in McEwen's string quartets, as the composer moves from an early Romantic approach through to a more complex style that embraced Modernism in his later years. This style change is reflected by an increasing tendency to abstraction, which in no way detracts from the

275

inherent beauty of these works. Wikipedia quotes from several sources on their McEwen page. I found two worth mentioning:

McEwen's large output of chamber music reveals a creative mind disposed towards more abstract, polyphonic thought.

McEwen's music synthesizes Scottish (and sometimes French) folk idioms and the Romantic legacy of Berlioz, Liszt, Wagner, and the French and Russian schools; Debussy was particularly influential.

The Sixth Quartet, titled *Biscay*, is apparently inspired by oyster collectors on the French coastline of the Bay of Biscay. Written in 1913, it consists of three named movements.

Le Phare (lighthouse) begins in a delightful mood with a joyous violin wispily drifting over sustained harmonies. A cello passage grounds the music, before it rises again, although not to the heights of the introduction. The cello is again firm and leads into a swirling, dramatic section with a strong violin melodic line that prances over a fascinating harmonic accompaniment, before moving back into the sustained chordal effect. Now a return to a more placid, but mesmeric soundscape ensues. Nearing the end, the violins fashion an attractive, sparse duet, again with sustained chords, moving on to a fade.

Les Dunes (sand or dunes) opens with a delicate, sombre mood, out of which rises a series of plaintive violin lines – the feeling is very precious. Eventually the music becomes more expansive but still retains a serious nature. A lamenting violin moves this movement forward, accompanied by an ensemble drone. A period of light, romantic melodies drift casually as a violin duet unfolds. These very simple melodies tend to be modal, and the passage fades to an end.

La Racleuse (scraper or skimmer) is simply prancing, seemingly in a French manner. A brisk underlying backing supports a violin conversation with an almost burlesque rhythm. Now the mood changes and a further violin duet unfolds, this time with sparse ensemble interjections. A slight increase in intensity initiates a tempo, before a recapitulation of the opening statement is heard. The resultant energised passage has a charm all of its own and concludes with three soft tones.

This simple, beautiful quartet has to be some of the most sublime music I have heard in quite a while. Being from the composer's early-to-mid period, it fits into a Romantic form and yet, gives indication of the development of his style, especially when compared with Quartet No. 13, from 1928, which is also on the review CD and represents a more complex form compared to the Sixth, with two wonderful slow movements.

This CD, *McEwen: String Quartets, Vol. 2*, on the Chandos label, performed by the Chilingirian Quartet is part of a series of three volumes that together contain a significant portion of the composer's quartet output – all three CDs are available from Amazon US and UK.

All three volumes are also on Spotify, but only a handful of individual movements can be found on YouTube. There are two splendid versions of No. 6 on earsense.

Listenability: Magnificent and pleasing writing.

— oo0oo —

Elliott Miles McKinley [born 1969]

Nationality: American
Quartets: At least seven
Style: Contemporary

String Quartet No. 3

I have selected the composer's Third Quartet for discussion as it contains two slow movements, which is where I love to spend my time.

The work, in four movements, commences with a slow tempo, a largo, which is a little unusual. The first sound we hear is a melodic line by the cello which carries on unaccompanied for some time. A pause brings the other instruments into play as they harmonise the cello line – all remain in their low registers, leading to a feeling of great depth. The cello still leads while the violins offer up random melodic phrases in the background. Now we are back to solo cello, until several pizzicato interjections ensue. The cello persists to the end, which features two pizzicato interjections and some seemingly perfunctory violin phrases.

The next movement begins with an energetic solo violin, at tempo, which is soon joined by pizzicato statements from the ensemble. The violin persists in its melodic endeavours, interrupted only by some deep, cello-driven blocks of musical statements. There is also plenty of pizzicato violin here, as it forms a call and response section with the ensemble. Now the pizzicato becomes the melody and the ensemble reverts to answering flourishes before the violin moves into a slightly burlesque mood and the ensemble takes over again. Harmonised violin lines lead into a section of strong, rhythmic thrusts. A return of the pizzicato brings all manner of sound effects and a shimmering violin concludes.

The third movement is based around a simple violin melodic fragment that is sustained throughout the entirety of the movement. There are many responses to it, some of them quite beautiful. The solo motif returns and develops some variations of its own and the ensemble is all around this motif, appearing to be playing as they please. Sometimes, they seem to mock the thematic material, other times presenting alluring responses – one of which leads to a conclusion.

The final movement, the longest in the work, is marked lento. A lone violin searches for a melody and settles on a sustained note which brings in the other players, creating a sustained droning sound. A pause brings a slightly dissonant section into play, but it is still mostly a drone. Dissonant sustained chords prevail, with some string sound effects before a charming solo violin drifts over a rhythmic motif and the ensemble joins in. This section contains no melodic development or forward movement. The solo violin picks up again and, after a time, the ensemble returns with more sustained notes and sound effects. The violin is longing now and quivering strings form a backdrop. There is a hint of melodic tension as the solo violin breaks into sound effects and furtive phrases, over a sustained background which slowly ends the work.

I don't quite know what to make of this music. I like it, but I'm not sure why. There are very few melodies but plenty of ambient sections.

The review CD, titled *Elliot Miles McKinley - String Quartets,* on the MMC label, performed by the Martinu Quartet and the Stamic Quartet also contains Quartets Nos. 4 and 5. I really enjoyed No. 4, not so sure about No. 5. There is another release by the Martinu Quartet on the Navaro label which contains Nos. 4, 5 and 6. I particularly enjoyed No. 6. Both versions are available on Amazon US and UK. It's a pity you can't get Nos. 3, 4 and 6 on one disc – that would be perfect – maybe digital download would be the way to go.

Both of the aforementioned CDs are on Spotify and the Martinu Quartet version is on YouTube, which also features a version of String Quartet No. 7, which I haven't heard yet. There are several late quartets on earsense.

Listenability: Intriguingly satisfying, I also really liked No. 4 and No. 6.

[Image source Navona Records]
[Could not be contacted]

Incidental Images #8

Legendary Beethoven Manuscript

[Image courtesy Wiki Commons]

This image of a scrawled manuscript contains part of Beethoven's original final movement of his *String Quartet No. 13 in B-flat major, Opus 130.* At its first public performance in 1826, the audience were in awe of this fantastic new work. That is, until the finale. People began screaming, hooting and leaving the hall as a response to this titanic movement. Such was the nature of the response of his friends that Beethoven, for the only time in his career, rewrote a new final movement. The original took on a life of its own, later titled the *Grosse Fuge* (Great Fugue). Now most contemporary string quartet ensembles include both movements in their recordings of the piece.

Marc Mellits [born 1966]

Nationality: American
Quartets: At least five
Style: Contemporary

String Quartet No. 4

I believe that Mellits' Quartets Nos. 2 to 5 have been recorded. Wikipedia tells us that *His music is influenced by minimalist and rock music, and has been identified with the postminimalist stylistic trend.* On that note, I'm not sure about the 'post' in minimalist as String Quartet No. 3 is classic minimalism and there is a fair quantity to be found in the work under consideration.

The Fourth Quartet, composed in 2011 and titled *Prometheus*, is in eight movements – many of them are rather brief.

The opening lento has a strangely synthesised sound to it, although it is performed by a physical ensemble. Light cascading phrases lead to a decelerating tempo, eventually finishing on a sustained chord. This happens to be the shortest of the movements, at just 98 seconds in length.

The next movement, marked moderato, also features that unusual string sound, particularly on ensemble chordal passages. The melodies are sparse, and the music very peaceful. Slowly the first violin rises out of the background and some melodic development is heard. The intensity gradually increases with melancholy, overlapping violin lines and perhaps a little too much repetition. Nearing the end, the music takes on a diaphanous texture that you can almost see through. A section of held chords with a hint of quiet pizzicato tones allows for a faded ending.

The third movement opens with a minimalist ostinato that evokes the sound of industrial machinery. Changes to the harmony introduce new motifs as the ostinato persists. The end is sudden with a staccato chord, the tones of which resonate for some seconds.

The next movement features gently pulsating, rhythmic chords with no apparent melody, just changes of harmony. Eventually a lonely violin muses over this background until the music briefly pauses. Now the background is stronger and again features many changes in harmony, but no melody is to be heard. Another pause brings the return of a melodic violin as the ensemble continues with the chords becoming sparser, and a faded closing.

The fifth movement is again underpinned by a rhythmic ostinato as two violins express, and eventually, begin to intertwine, all the while in a very metrical manner. The violins slowly dissipate and we are left with another fadeout.

A rubato movement follows, with a pulsing pizzicato viola tone underpinning a series of violin chords wafting gently. Now melodies are heard and changes in harmony produce a measured passage that slowly moves forward.

An increase in dynamics continues with a sense of repetition that seems a little laboured, to the end.

The final movement evokes the third movement with its ostinato motifs occasionally changing with the harmony – sometimes the music is quite forceful. The conclusion is a sharp stop.

My impression of this work is that it lacks definition and sometimes, music. Several times the harmonies seemed to be based on simple chord changes that could be found in popular music. I've already mentioned some sense of repetition. A visit to the composer's website also indicates that often compositions are arranged for many different combinations of instruments, including Bluegrass String Band and Saxophone Quartet. The Third Quartet, titled *Tapas*, has also been published as *Concerto for String Quartet & String Orchestra*.

The review CD, titled *Mellits: String Quartets Nos. 3, 4 & 5*, on the Evidence Records label and performed by Quatuor Debussy is available from Amazon US and UK.

This disc is on Spotify and Quartet No. 4 can be found on YouTube. There are several full quartets on earsense.

Listenability: Possibly one for the minimalists or New Agers.

— oo0oo —

Melomania – Compilation

Nationality: N/A
Quartets: Seven
Style: N/A

Women String Quartet Composers

This compilation contains string quartets by the following female composers: Fanny Mendelssohn, Ethel Smyth, Germaine Tailleferre, Elizabeth Lutyens, Grażyna Bacewicz, Violeta Denescu and Gloria Coates. The music spans 150 years of string quartet composition and is quite diverse. I have picked out several pieces to review.

I am very fond of Tailleferre's solo piano music – I would call it profound in its simplicity. She was also a member of *Les Six*, a group of French composers who eschewed the works of Wagner, and the influence of Impressionists, Debussy and Ravel. There is a fine article about this group on Wikipedia. Tailleferre's short String Quartet from 1930 is a charming piece of writing. It opens in an expansive manner, with gentle melodies, all occurring at once. A change in tonality brings about a violin and cello dialogue. This music sounds contemporary, and the short first movement concludes with some fine melodies and a trill to end. The second movement is more rhythmic, and produces many attractive pastoral melodies. Gentle harmonies are of their time and continue to the conclusion, which is two plucked pizzicato notes. The third movement is more intense with a pulsating melody accompanied by chordal interjections. Now it turns positively dark – all the while, the propulsion continues. The music ebbs and flows here, at one time the violin soars into the high register, leaving the darkness behind. A violin phrase builds in intensity, and there is great emotional depth. The violins create a fabulous feeling which moves into a long, powerful passage. The harmonies mellow and the peace goes quiet, trailing out on a cello note.

The only string quartet of British composer Ethel Smyth was written from 1902-1912 and begins in a sentimental manner before taking on a rhythmic nature, which soon dissipates. A serious mood comes over the piece and the rhythm returns. Then some classic, warm folksy melodies move into a serious episode of tense violin. Dramatic violin flurries lead into a powerful chordal phase, where the first violin dominates. Now the rhythm falls away for a time, which is reflective, only to return to a tempo as a galloping feeling briefly appears and the violins spin out strong melodies. A joyous period ensues and the violins express freely over a warm background. Nearing the end, a slight darkness appears again and the violins become animated, finishing with a double flourish.

Violeta Denescu is Romanian and was born in 1953. Her named quartet, *Lin Terra Lonhdana* – I wasn't able to find a translation – is a torrid affair. A dramatic, aggressive opening, featuring mostly a dissonant violin with a crude tone, dominates proceedings. There is little accompaniment but copious amounts of space in this introduction. As the piece progresses it features several string sound effects, including many glissandos. The arrival of the cello thickens the texture. It is very atonal music and a solo cello is taunted by the violins which quickly return to take charge. I'm hesitant to say that the sound effects overshadow the music, but at times it appears to be true. The use of microtones occurs as the piece progresses and the level of dissonance also increases. I'm now lost in sound as the first violin transcends music in its endeavours. More aggression follows, with agitated string sound effects. The ending is hostile.

Of course, many contrasts exist on this CD, due to the long time period over which these pieces were composed. There is some fine music to be heard here.

This CD, titled *Melomania*, on the Troubadisc label and performed by the Fanny Mendelssohn Quartet, is available on Amazon US and UK.

It can be heard on Spotify and YouTube and two versions of the Tailleferre are on earsense.

Listenability: A mixed bag, mostly accessible, some reservations.

Felix Mendelssohn [1809–1847]

Nationality: German
Quartets: Six
Style: Romantic

String Quartet No. 2

Jakob Ludwig Felix Mendelssohn Bartholdy was a chamber music child prodigy. At the age of sixteen he wrote his *Octet for Strings*, generally considered to be one of the most brilliant chamber music works of all time. It is a magnificent piece, the opening movement being exceptional, with a forward propulsion that has probably never been matched. He also wrote five symphonies which are still popular today.

Two years after the octet, he commenced his String Quartet No. 2 in A minor, Opus 13. He was born just at the right time, enabling him to study the Beethoven late quartets, hot off the presses. Apparently his mother kept him in good supply and he was able to spend much time with them. This study certainly bore fruit as the musical references to Beethoven, especially *String Quartet No. 15, Opus 132*, also in A minor, are manifold throughout this piece.

The first movement is marked adagio - allegro vivace and within the first 30 seconds, two obvious references to Beethoven are stated. There is a slight pause at the end of each phrase, and, in that instant, I can hear in my head the music that followed Beethoven's from Opus 132. Then Mendelssohn comes in with some of his own material. I find it strangely disorienting when this happens. In any event, the influence of Beethoven is profound and throughout, and I shall not mention it again.

The adagio progresses into some shimmering and then some folk material. Overall, the movement slips in and out of a forward thrust and energy, contrasted with slower parts, which are captivating, with some appealing, playful melodies. There is a lot more allegro vivace than adagio but, when the contrasts arrive, they are extremely effective.

The second movement opens with sombre chords. It then moves into a quiet adagio fugue, ever slowly building in intensity, until the composer relieves the tension and sets the quartet free. They move into double time and develop the momentum again, and, when things become positively raucous, the piece is stripped back to a solo violin. It then slowly returns to the grave mood of the opening before a tranquil conclusion unfolds.

The third movement opens with a stately melody, gently taken up by all four players as it progresses. After some minutes, the meter moves into double time for a playful joust. Inevitably, it returns to the stately melodies of the introduction. The texture of a solo violin accompanied by the pizzicato cello makes for a wonderful atmosphere, which eventually takes the movement out.

The final movement starts dynamically and the first violin appears to struggle with the rest of the ensemble. It finally wins out for a brief period before the intensity rises again. This dichotomy continues until we have a moment of solo violin which is mesmeric. It then looks back to a previous movement, and some sombre chords which just drift into silence.

Mendelssohn was truly a marvellous melodist. All four movements show evidence of this. His enthralling melodies shape the piece into something of great beauty and substance. Considering he was eighteen at the time makes it all the more noteworthy.

There are many Mendelssohn CDs on Amazon US and UK. My review CD was *Mendelssohn – The Complete String Quartets* on the Cedille Records label by the Pacifica Quartet. I also liked the 3-CD Cherubini Quartet at a nice price on Warner. There would be many other versions, including single-CD formats. But then you don't get to hear the rest of his fabulous melodies, do you?

The Pacifica set is on Spotify, along with others. Some versions of the Second Quartet are on YouTube and there are many fine performances of the work on earsense, especially the Escher String Quartet.

Listenability: Youthful and enchanting, a magnificent quartet.

— oo0oo —

Krzysztof Meyer [born 1943]

Nationality: Polish
Quartets: At least fourteen
Style: Contemporary

String Quartet No. 12

Meyer's Quartets Nos. 1 to 13 have all been recorded. A feature of these quartets is that they tend towards more introspection in the later works – some of the earlier quartets are quite confronting. The Twelfth Quartet contains nine movements, which I will sometimes to refer to as sections.

Lento –The work opens with a gentle atonal landscape which slowly builds in tension. Expressive violin melodic lines are insistent, but never confronting, with sporadic cello and viola mutterings in the background

Con ira –A stark introduction opens this brief movement. A sense of dissonance is heard, together with pizzicato, creating a measured assertive passage. A mild chaos slowly develops, with the violins prominent, which ends on a flourish.

Vivo – Strong, dissonant harmonised violins are accompanied by a walking pizzicato cello, making for a marvellous mood – somewhat reminiscent of jazz composer Ornette Coleman's writing for strings. Rhythmic thrusts give way to strong, dissonant violin lines – the walking cello is particularly effective throughout and the mood is completed with a sense of evanescence.

Dolente – This, the longest section of the work opens with a wonderful feeling of lamenting as a solo violin is occasionally complemented by a sensitive arco cello. Gradually, other instruments join in but the feeling is very subtle. Quivering bows evoke a spiritual feeling, one that allows the violin to craft a most expressive passage. Now the violin soars and the ensemble strengthen and sometimes harmonise with the violin – this is deeply poignant Contemporary writing. Nearing the end, the violin laments freely, leading to another quiet conclusion. For me, this section is the highlight of the work.

Furioso – A challenging opening soon disperses into a series of violin glissandos, creating an atonal, abstract mood. The introduction of pizzicato brings a sense of chaos, where dissonant melodic lines abound. Now a solo violin softens the feeling briefly, before two violins express a powerful ending.

Largo – This moves straight into another atonal soundscape with the cello prominent. The violins complement each other wonderfully as the shortest section of the work concludes.

Adagio – There is no pause before this section and it again features a sombre feeling with a deep cello expressing long lines, occasionally interrupted by string sound effects, which eventually become the music. A return of the cello leads to an increasing atonal intensity, which then gives way to a lamenting cello and various string sound effects from the ensemble. The cello persists, reaching into its highest register before fading on a sustained, shrill tone.

Prestissimo – A powerful harmonised violin duet expresses over a sombre background and a forward momentum is established – quite unusual for this work. A pause leads to a passage of glissandos before the violins then surge in a dramatic manner to an abrupt end.

Appassionato – Strong chords set the mood for this final section. Out of this develops an alluring passage with a violin expressing sparse phrases against a carpet of quivering bows, which are very distant. A pause leads into a lone violin which simply disappears.

I find this work to be fascinating and most appealing. Its Modern tendencies are always very measured and it contains moments of profound beauty.

The review CD, *Meyer: String Quartets Nos. 9, 10, 11 & 12* is performed by the Wieniawski String Quartet, who I believe have recorded the first thirteen quartets on four discs for the Naxos label. All four CDs are available on Amazon US and UK.

Spotify features the four CDs but YouTube only has the earlier works.

Listenability: Wonderful, brooding, Contemporary quartet.

Darius Milhaud [1892–1974]

Nationality: French
Quartets: Eighteen
Style: Early Modern

String Quartet No. 1

Milhaud was a prolific composer, as seen by his being responsible for 18 string quartets. A bit of trivia – String Quartets Nos. 14 & 15 were written to be played individually or together as an octet, and this has occurred in performance a number of times.

String Quartet No. 1 was composed when Milhaud was 20 – such a tender age. Dedicated to painter Paul Cezanne, it's one of the loveliest first quartets that I have heard. The work consists of the traditional four movements.

The quartet opens with a sound of a sweeping chordal phrase – it is a joyous moment, and is followed by a pristine melody. Gentle harmonies support a variation on the original melodic line, which returns verbatim. The violins rephrase the melody and then move into a shimmering state, before rephrasing the melody again. A calm ensues, where the cello is featured and the music then leaps into life with a long solo violin descending line. The ensemble provides background, and the cello makes a melodic statement before a soft rhythmic phrase introduces a new passage where the first violin follows the harmonies of the accompaniment. After a brief pause, the ensemble is set free and cello converses with violin in an engaging manner. A precious moment follows where the first violin projects winsome statements over a minimal background of strings, leading to a faded conclusion.

There is a wonderful start to the next movement. A solo violin expresses a transcendent melody that ends on a strange note. This is a cue for the ensemble to provide a lush background as the violin expresses freely in a low register. The fine mood continues for some time and, eventually, the other instruments blossom and increase in intensity. A tempo is established, only to return to the lone violin with minimal backing. It is a wonderful place to be. The two violins converse, with a viola pizzicato accompaniment. The opening melody is revisited and rephrased – we are now down to one violin, which finishes on a gentle, sustained note.

The third movement has a longing opening that builds ever so slowly in intensity. One violin follows another, as the dynamics increase. The cello carries the melody here, with subtle violin phrases – the cello and violin converse again. Now we have some rhythmic movement and a strong ensemble phrase carries the first violin into its upper register, until the feeling subsides back into its melancholia. A sparse fragment of violin and cello lead to a faded end. What an incredible piece of writing.

The final movement returns to the joyous feeling of the first. An energetic first violin dances over various ensemble rhythms and the melodies are strong for a time. Now we are back into the territory of the previous movement, so gentle, and pure melancholy. A new melody starts to build and a viola phrase leads back to the opening. The first violin is strong and is constantly probing for new melodic lines. The pace quickens and we have a sustained chord, with a flourish, to conclude the work.

The outer movements (1 & 4) are rhythmically up tempo and charming, with the introduction being exceedingly joyful. The inner movements (2 & 3) are slow, with wonderful long melodies to be found here. In fact I would describe each movement as lyrical. For a youthful first quartet, it is a delightfully rewarding experience. Interestingly, some people have noted a hint of Debussy in the work. Later in his life, Milhaud edited the work and discarded the third movement. What a pity – I really enjoy it.

I am aware of two worthwhile performances. The Quator Parisii have recorded all 18 quartets on the Naive label, on five CDs, but they omit the third movement on this one. I recommend the Arriaga String Quartet on the budget Discover label. This excellent performance of the original four movements comes paired with String Quartet No. 2. Please disregard the negative reviews on Amazon about this disc. It is a wonderful rendition at a great price.

The Complete Quator Parisii set of the 18 quartets is available on Spotify and various versions of the work are on YouTube. A number of the quartets, including the first, can be found on earsense.

Listenability: A wonderful first string quartet.

— ooOoo —

Ted Moore [born 1987]

Nationality: American
Quartets: Hmmm
Style: Contemporary

Gilgamesh and Enkidu

To my knowledge, Moore has not written any works for a standard string quartet. He has however, composed several for string quartet augmented with other instruments. The work under discussion is designated as *for string quartet and laptop computer*. Normally I would shy away from such a concept but I believe that this piece, titled *Gilgamesh & Enkidu* contains some worthwhile chamber music. The work has six named movements and appears to be inspired by a pre-Christian Babylonian mythical tale. You can read a comprehensive article from Encyclopaedia Britannica via Wikipedia. Suffice it to say, it is an epic work of early literature and this quartet plus one is an epic piece of mostly music, running to just under an hour. Not exactly Feldmanesque proportions but one of the longest quartets that I have heard. Let's get into it.

The Fall of Enkidu – The work commences with a drone that sounds like an Australian native didgeridoo, before a violin gradually appears, its probing phrases being answered by the cello. The drone persists and I now believe it to be electronic. Violin glissandos give way to a brief pizzicato interlude, followed by further glissandos. At this point, it is more about sound than music. Having said that, a passage emerges with a violin offering up a rich, harmonised violin lament, together with a wonderfully reverberant cello part. Moving forward, a fascinating passage unfolds, with poignant violin melodies. The end is a long sustained drone.

The Dark – Some electronic, distant storm-like sounds introduce this movement – they continue as violins firstly express a feeling of pathos before moving into the full ensemble in a slightly agitated passage. The music is stretched tight, with powerful, intertwining ensemble lines. A period of string sound effects leads into a solo violin part, which soon gives way to a concluding section of sound effects. This is by far the shortest movement in the work.

Lament – A brief section of cloudy electronica introduces a mournful solo violin melody, which is then harmonised by the ensemble to create a fascinating atmosphere. The dynamics ebb and flow, eventually settling back into the previous quiet mood – this is terrific writing, and the violin is magnificent. Stunning harmonies unfold and a sense of drama is revealed. A further gentle passage for two harmonised violins is occasionally interrupted by ensemble thrusts, leading into a fine solo cello passage. A dramatic section follows, with all instruments displaying a high level of intensity. Out of this a descending melodic phrase emerges before dissolving into an impalpable feeling with glissandos as the music mocks itself. A sense of sparsity prevails as the melody is deconstructed with abandon. Solo cello now comes to the forefront, with only a hint of the ensemble present for the duration of the movement. This could be music from Bach's *Cello Suites*, it is very Baroque in style.

The Silence Was Deeper Than Before – More electronics introduce a sparse solo cello, which varies in intensity. It is sometimes difficult to discern the difference between the cello and the electronica at this time until the solo cello predominates, projecting a powerful sound, arco alternating with pizzicato. For me, it evokes the bass solos of Jimmy Garrison from jazz saxophonist John Coltrane's last quartet, especially the extended performances from 1966 in Japan. The cello is variously: rhythmic; probing; subtle; and sometimes orchestral. Running the full gamut of sounds available from the instrument, it is a virtuosic workout. Sometimes there can be heard a distant rumbling in the background, I take this to be electronics. The cello persists in its journey, rising high into its upper register, before descending to craft a sparse lament, as the strange background also continues intermittently. Finally it is just the cello that moves into the last notes of the movement, which has been a 13-minute fantasy for cello with only sporadic sounds for company. The style is just so different from the Bach-like nature of the cello role in the previous movement.

The River, the Flood – Gentle sounds of water bubbling and further electronica are heard for some time – no music here. There is variation as the volume and intensity continually increase, leading to the sound of a raging torrent. Explosions appear, silencing the river. A quiet, sustained period introduces string sounds, but they are synthesised. A brief return to the torrent transforms into a sustained chord, which fades to the end. There is no ensemble playing in this movement.

Epilogue - Names and Monuments – The longest movement in the work starts as a solo cello over a mournful string background. The cello ceases and the strings continue with a sparse selection of sustained sounds. A burst of activity leads to a return of the cello as it exchanges phrases with the ensemble. Now the background is synthesised with interjections from the acoustic instruments, again, it can be difficult to discern the source of some of these sounds. The mood is quite evocative however, as gentle washes of sound create a delicate ambience. A sustained electronic background allows the violins to express long melodies in a most appealing manner before the electronic sounds completely take over. Slowly the quartet instruments re-enter with their distinctive acoustic tonalities being music to my ears. A repeated descending melodic motif builds in intensity as the acoustic melds with the electronic. This motif continues for a considerable time before finally allowing the cello to express over the quiet sustained background, leading to a moment of bliss. A series of ensemble chordal interjections signal the beginning of the end as the didgeridoo sounds heard at the opening of the work resolve it to a peaceful conclusion.

Discounting for a moment the use of a laptop computer to provide electronic sounds, this work is highly stylised, program music. The composer seems to specialise in compositions involving electronica, and has come up with a comfortable blend of sounds that sustained my interest for its entirety.

The review CD, *Ted Moore: Gilgamesh & Enkidu*, on the Ravello label, performed by the aptly named Enkidu String Quartet is available on Amazon US and possibly Amazon UK.

It can be heard in full on Spotify and YouTube.

Listenability: One of a kind Contemporary work – well worth a listen.

Eddie Mora [Born 1965]

Nationality: Costa Rican
Quartets: At least three
Style: Contemporary Modern

String Quartets Nos. 1 and 3

I found information on this composer to be very difficult to obtain, but his works deserve to be heard.

The First Quartet, titled *Retrato V*, is quite brief and consists of just two movements. The work opens with a solo violin repeating a melodic phrase, soon to be joined by an ensemble background of a rather abstruse nature. The violin melodic motif persists until a section of powerful glissandos ensues, before a violin line with a rich tone, and great beauty, appears. A previously heard violin section is recreated and an obtuse passage follows, before a return to the opening violin motif, which ends with a series of solo violin harmonics.

The second movement begins as a low cello drone and the violin enters with a line not dissimilar to the previous movement. A thundering violin in the low register makes occasional interjections. Now an almost Romantic feeling is heard as the instruments engage in a conversational manner with the violins delightful and the cello being very expressive. A slowing of the tempo leads to a further uplifting passage, gradually developing into a more modern texture with pulsating phrases that end on a flourish.

Considering the very modern music which follows on the CD, this quartet doesn't feel of its time.

The Third quartet, titled *JRM*, is significantly different from the First. It is in one long movement and is filled with contrasts in emotional quality and style. The first notes heard are an almost inaudible bowing of a violin in a high register. This is overlaid with a fascinating violin part that projects a morose beauty. The ensemble inject sporadic statements that contrast with the sustained bowing. On occasions, a violin simply cries out against a taut background. A new section commences with some strong, abstract chordal passages and serious glissandos. A repeated violin motif gathers strength and the sustained bowing effect evokes Vivaldi's *Four Seasons*, 250 years on – however this music is far removed from Vivaldi in terms of its emotional character.

Surging violins propel the music forward, sometimes with an ethnic flavour, possibly Middle-Eastern – a return to peace also evokes the ethnic feeling. This is music of great diversity, with the composer constantly changing the instrumental texture. A solo violin expresses in the highest register, only to encounter a response that is very sparse. As the piece progresses, there is much beauty to be heard as a funereal passage features a lamenting violin over a throbbing ensemble. String sound effects and pizzicato punctuate the throbbing texture – the shrill violin continues its contemplations and constantly moves into the high register, creating a wonderful contrast with a bass-heavy ensemble.

The throbbing becomes more insistent as the solo violin meanders through this abstract soundscape, now in a lower register. The ethnic feeling is again presented, sounding sometimes like the Middle Eastern stringed instrument, the oud. The work concludes on a series of shrill, solo violin lines that are positively haunting.

I must admit that, on my first listening to this music, I found it to be a bit confronting, but as I hear it again, that feeling is no longer there. String Quartet No. 2, again in one movement, is also on the CD. This piece in some ways acts as a bridge between the two discussed quartets, although it is more emotionally tied to the Third Quartet. I would personally rate this composer as very Modern, but never confronting.

The review CD, *Eddie Mora: String Quartets Nos. 1, 2 & 3*, on Ravello Records also contains a measured piece for symphony orchestra, *Sula'*, and a three movement, *Bocetos a Yolanda*, performed by University Contemporary Ensemble which is wonderfully abstruse. These two works run for just over 20 minutes – the quartets take up 43 minutes.

This music is on Amazon US and UK as a download only, but it is currently available on Presto Classical and likely elsewhere.

The works on this CD can be found on Spotify, YouTube and earsense.

Listenability: Brilliant, unique and fascinating Modern works.

[Image courtesy Ravello Records]

291

Nikolai Myaskovsky [1881–1950]

Nationality: Russian
Quartets: Thirteen
Style: Early Modern

String Quartet No. 1

Myaskovsky's First String Quartet was written in 1911 and revised in 1935. Just as an introductory remark, I was surprised by the significant level of abstraction in this early work. Also, he doesn't have that heavy sound often associated with Russian composers. The quartet is in four movements.

The first movement is marked poco rubato, which I take to mean – a little freely. It opens with a solo violin phrase before the second violin and cello add support. The violin melodies are taken up by the other players until a peace emerges. A pastoral melody takes over, the intensity rises and abstraction makes an appearance. Shimmering violins support a cello melody and the piece moves into an ostinato for a time. A violin dialogue ensues, which is slightly tonally ambivalent. Now we have a peace, still abstract, but quietly so – it is most attractive. Soon the music is on the move again but quickly settles back into a pastoral feeling. As the ending approaches there is some gorgeous cello work, together with a response from the violins. The violins lament and the cello anchors this feeling which fades to a conclusion.

A brief fanfare begins the second movement, which is short. The viola is salient and it provides the background for the melodic development – it actually sounds a bit like a bassoon. Things are intense for a time and there is a lot of rhythmic impetus – insistent moments come and go, and the melodies do the same. Violin statements are quoted by the cello, and then passed around the ensemble. A surprisingly stately section comes out of nowhere but is soon overwhelmed by determined violin chords. There is a scurrying feeling for a time, which becomes rowdy before the cello repeats the opening theme and the violins join in. A subdued section ends the movement.

The next movement starts with a funereal motif and the violin meanders around it, until we have a solo violin statement. The violin remains prominent as the motif keeps returning. The cello now steps out to take over and it hovers over the music – there is wonderful writing for the cello here. A long solo violin leads into an abstract moment where the violins mimic each other. The cello keeps up with a melody that creates a gentle chaos within the violins as dynamics vary appreciably within the movement. Sometimes it's like a whisper to a scream. A remarkably poignant moment ensues where the cello supports a solo violin. This is another beautiful piece of writing – the violin is just terrific. An ostinato is established by the cello and another opening motif returns, leading to the ending which is delicate and ephemeral.

The final movement opens in a disjointed manner and nothing seems to settle for a while. Eventually the cello and violins combine for a wonderful melodic passage. Soon a degree of chaos occurs with some violent interjections. This is cut back to almost nothing until the violin leads the ensemble into a slightly atonal episode which is quite evocative, if a little out of place. A measure of calm reappears – now it becomes folksy again, albeit slightly atonal. A scurrying cello rushes toward the end which comes with a flourish.

This quartet is filled with contrasts: ostinatos; introspection; chaos; many melodies and great variations. I would like to have heard the 1911 version – it's just so beguiling at times.

There are five individual CDs containing the complete quartets by the Taneyev Quartet on the Northern Flowers label. *Volume 1* contains String Quartets Nos. 1, 2 and 3. They can all be found on Amazon US and UK. String Quartet No. 1 is available on Spotify and there are many quartets on earsense. A handful of various quartet movements are on YouTube. I love the photo of Stalin accompanying the clips. Not sure how Stalin would have reacted to this music. Apparently he didn't think much of Shostakovich.

Listenability: Quite enjoyable Early Modern quartet.

String Quartet No. 11

Unusually, there is no great divergence of style between this and the previous work, although they were written many years apart – I suppose you could call that conservative. This work is in three movements.

The quartet opens with a charming melody, which is developed for a time. Then follows murmurings from the ensemble as the violin leads it into a slight piece of abstraction. There is a wonderful duet violin line in here, which leads to a sound space similar to that of the beginning. A four-note theme is put through its paces and out of this comes that amazing duet harmony again. Then the violin alludes to the opening melody and a graceful period ensues before the texture becomes one of call and response with the violin and ensemble. The four-note motif returns, giving the movement impetus until the end beckons, and the violin fades out.

The next movement, marked andante, commences with the violin working one note until it breaks out into some variations. The cello rises above the ensemble for a moment and a chordal episode follows, with the violins picking up on a stilted melodic line, which progresses into a graceful state. Now the intensity rises with slight chaos being the order of the day. The music briefly jumps into life until the violin returns with a longing melody which is sustained for a few minutes with the mood slightly dark, before distinctive chords interject. A brief crescendo introduces a quiet space and the end is a sustained chord.

The final movement begins in a brief, but thoughtful manner which transforms into some rhythmic playing. The violin performs a virtuosic, but gentle line before it returns to the opening theme. This is continued for a time until a shimmering of violins makes for a fine soundspace. The ensemble sounds full here and contains some admirable melodies. A tempo is established which evokes the beginning again – the composer certainly feeds on this melody. The conclusion comes slowly.

As to availability, *Volume 4* of the previously mentioned set contains String Quartets Nos. 9, 10 and 11. They can all be found on Amazon US and UK. String Quartet No. 11 is on Spotify and a handful of various quartet movements are on YouTube. Many of the quartets are on earsense.

Listenability: Conservative but ultimately lush, lovely quartet.

— ooOoo —

Per Norgard [born 1932]

Nationality: Danish
Quartets: Ten
Style: Contemporary

Early Works
String Quartets Nos. 1 & 2

Norgard's First String Quartet, marked *quartetto breve*, which means short quartet, runs for just under seven minutes. It is in one movement, of course. It opens with a lilting rhythmic phrase before the violin enters with a superb melody. This melody is then developed over about three minutes of beauty and is followed by some striking cello interjections, as things become a little torrid. The peace returns with a recapitulation of the opening theme. This is a splendid lament, which is again interrupted by the cello, bringing with it a period of chaos. The melody breaks into a tempo and the chaos continues with a dialogue between the violin and cello. The cello is conspicuous, leading the work to its conclusion. This quartet is an outstanding piece of miniaturism – there is just so much beauty compacted into the seven minutes. A remarkable example of musical concision.

The Second Quartet is again in one movement, this time running for 20 minutes. It is marked *brioso*, which means spirited – and so it is. It definitely has a spirited opening, skittish, with unrelated melodic lines competing for the space. The high register dominates, especially for the first violin. There is a period of dialogue between the violin and cello before the music eventually settles into a passage led by the cello – however the violins soon have their way. After a time, the mood settles down a little, even allowing for a brief pause. The violin and cello re-enter slowly – long melodies develop here. You could reach out and touch this music, it's like standing behind a waterfall. It slowly develops into an intense period where the cello and violin again converse. Now the cello is the soloist as the violins shimmer in the background.

At around the halfway mark, a brief pause occurs, and we are in for a change as the music returns with a strong chordal section. There is no tempo, things just

294

happen. Melodic lines drift over a sparse harmonic background and the viola has a lead role to play here. The volume drops back to almost nothing and we only hear the barest of whispers – this is pure evanescence. The mood gently lifts, still quiet but increasing in volume. Now the violins are back to full intensity, the loudest so far in the work. It suddenly cuts back to string sound effects, with no development here, just mild chaos. The volume and intensity return as the end is in sight and the cello leads the way with the intensity gone. The violin takes over and the music recedes. It is a wonderful quartet.

No problem with availability here. Amazon US and UK both have *String Quartets 1-6* by the Kontra Quartet on the Kontrapunkt label and also *String Quartets 7-10* by the Kroger Quartet.

Many versions of Norgard's quartets are on YouTube and earsense.

Listenability: Early works from a Modern composer.

Late Works
String Quartets Nos. 7 & 10

String Quartet No. 7, marked andante, opens ever so gently with a cello and some intermittent violin pizzicato. The cello continues to lead the way, and the violins drift in. A change ensues, with probing violin interjections, and a serious nature. There is a measured chaos here, as the violins make startling statements. This feeling softens for a moment but then continues with slightly chaotic violins and a brief pause brings about another random section. The cello contributes positive statements as the violins opt for string sound effects. The violins continue with a hint of pizzicato, then fade out.

The next movement, marked lento, builds from a whisper with sustained tones. It is a tranquil opening, and totally without tempo, just pure rubato. The sustained notes continue, interrupted by string sound effects before a violin slowly appears out of the ensemble for a brief interlude, with the sustained notes soon resumed. Brief pauses abound, and there is little to be heard here. A violin repeats a phrase over the ensemble's murmurings, and then hints at a melody. It rises in register and intensity and a cello note completes the movement.

The final movement has a strong cello introduction, as the violins wrap string sound effects around it. Again, this music is played rubato. The violins move into glissando and microtonal statements. Then follows an ascending melodic trend, as the viola makes pizzicato interjections, with the violins now playing purely string effects. A cello statement spurs the violins on into an atonality, and the work concludes on a seemingly random violin statement.

String Quartet No. 10, titled *Harvest Timeless,* is in one movement. Violins create a gentle opening, with soft cello statements – it is very pensive. A change brings about a sense of optimism, and the violins dance lightly over the ensemble. There is a hint of a concrete melody, but this soon dissipates and we have an extended period of quivering violins. Normality returns and the violins continue in a dialogue, which becomes subdued. The music edges forward until we have one violin in the high register, followed by a pause which leads into another, brisk period, where the violins again exhibit a pensive manner.

Now a slow tempo is heard, and the viola introduces a melody, with the violins busy in the background. Eventually they prevail and continue with a sparse duet. More string sound effects lead into a brisk tempo, with a slight aggression in the violins. They reach into their high registers and become agitated. This continues for some time, until it moderates into a sparse passage, bordering on silence. The violins become more prominent and their glissandos dominate, until a brief repeated phrase brings the work to an end.

Two points about this quartet. Firstly, it spends a lot of time investigating the regions between music and sound. Secondly, it seems much longer than it actually is. I'm not sure how the composer has achieved this, but it is fascinating.

I consider both of these works to be what I would term Modern Contemporary, and they are significantly more technically and emotionally advanced than the previously discussed Quartets Nos. 1 and 2.

Amazon US and UK both have *String Quartets 7-10* by the Kroger Quartet, on the DaCapo label. This *7-10* disc is on Spotify, and many versions of Norgard's quartets on can be found on YouTube and earsense.

Listenability: Fine late works from a Modern composer.

— ooOoo —

Norwegian String Quartets – Compilation

Nationality: Norwegian
Quartets: Four
Style: N/A

Four 20th Century
Norwegian Composers

This compilation contains string quartets by the following composers: Klaus Egge [1906-1979] – Fartein Valen [1887-1952] – Johan Kvandal [1919-1999] – and Alfred Janson [born 1937]. I shall be discussing Egge and Kvandal.

Klaus Egge wrote his one and only String Quartet in 1933 and it contains four movements. Commencing with a largo, it gently eases its way into a pastoral manner. The cello is beautiful as it wraps itself around the violin melodies. A stately section ensues, then the music returns to two violins. The melodies are very fine, it sounds a little like a tone poem. Soulful violins move the piece forward slowly, with the occasional ensemble chordal interjection. The violins conclude on a sustained tone.

The next movement opens in a brisk, dashing manner and a strong melody is developed, and redeveloped, as it moves forward. Variations abound, with pizzicato added to the mix. The first violin is especially strong, and suddenly becomes tense, leading into a brief, slightly harsh cello section. Now we have a flurry of action – all instruments sound excitable until a pizzicato cello statement takes the movement out.

The third movement, marked andante, is again of a pastoral nature, and somewhat melancholy. The melodies are quite something as the two violins seem to spiral about each other, with a viola pizzicato accompaniment in the background. The cello makes a brief, strong, solo statement before it is joined by the violins. The melody has a lot of forward momentum, and grows in intensity until it develops into a swirling passage, before dropping back to a state of sparsity. It is a tremendous musical space, with great contrasts in feeling, reminiscent of the opening. The end is a false one – as it leads straight into the next movement, it begins to take flight.

Out of this feeling comes the final movement, which commences in a busy, excited style. This energy gives way to a punchy, multi-instrument sound. Rhythmic interjections litter the movement and eventually lead to a drop in intensity. A melancholia ensues and the violins resume their seats as they produce slow, sustained lines with a viola pizzicato adding to the texture and taking us to the end of the quartet.

Johan Kvandal wrote his String Quartet No.3 in 1983 and it also contains four movements. The opening, marked andante, is very orchestral, in a melancholy manner. The four instruments are as one in the opening passage before a violin asks probing questions of the ensemble, which answer in kind. A brief solo violin lament has an intensity, with the violin being aggressive. A solo cello line drops the intensity and a folk sound is presented. This does not last, and the feeling intensifies again with the first violin showing the way. Now we have a pastoral mood as the violins explore new melodies. Eventually this gives way to some drama, which then leads to a brief, quiet section before the movement finishes with a flourish.

The next movement, marked adagio, is gentle with a lone violin lamenting over a sombre ensemble. Slowly, the cello adds support, through soft, plucked notes – some forward movement can be felt. Slightly spirited melodies begin to form, only to recede back into melancholy. This whole movement is a feature for the first violin as it leads the music through many lamenting moments. As the end approaches, the violin descends into a low register and is absorbed back into the ensemble, where it stays until the conclusion. It is a fine movement.

The third, brief movement, opens in a frisky manner and investigates some wonderful harmonised melodic lines that are slightly folksy. A short pizzicato fragment leads to a final violin phrase to finish.

The last movement opens in a serious, sparse mood. However, after a time, the violins take flight, in a similar manner to the previous movement. There is a lot of solo violin, combined with periods of ensemble accompaniment, which seem to chase the violin. A dynamic texture leads to a strong conclusion.

These are two fine quartets, as are the other pieces on the CD. The Valen No. 2 is similar to the previously mentioned works, while Janson's only string quartet, in one movement, investigates several different moods.

The review CD, *Norwegian 20th Century String Quartets*, on Naxos, and performed by the Oslo Quartet is available at Amazon US and UK. It is also on Spotify and YouTube – earsense features works for all composers individually, so you will have to search for them.

Listenability: Charming, melodic works with great slow movements.

— ooOoo —

Viteslav Novak [1870–1949]

Nationality: Czech
Quartets: Three
Style: Romantic

String Quartet No. 2

Novak's three string quartets are a little hard to find but they are out there. I shall be discussing String Quartet No. 2, which is in two long movements, and was composed in 1906.

This work begins with a fine solo introduction by the cello. The ensemble gently eases in and begins to fashion a peaceful scene. Violins wander freely, but there isn't much melodic development – it seems ambient for its time. All the while the piece is gaining substance as more interplay occurs. Although it's not strictly a fugue, the feeling is, with a constant interweaving of voices. A slight change brings an optimism, but the effect is subtle. Suddenly, the intensity lifts and we have drama, which is sustained for several minutes before the mood changes again with a solo cello leading into a tempo – this features particularly attractive melodies. I'm now finding it again to be static. Some drama returns, but it's only transient – we are soon back into the ambient feeling. The ending is most pleasurable as the violins go high and gently fade.

The question to ask is – where did the last 14 minutes go? Wherever it went, it was a beautiful sound...

The second, longer movement moves straight into a tempo. The violins are busy and their energy drives the music forward. It's a little folk-like in melodies which push hard. A pause allows the viola to express itself, with a measured

298

ensemble backing. There is still a tempo, but nothing like the beginning. Now a new melody ensues, with just two violins and the viola joins in the stabbing chords that accompany this jaunty feeling. The tempo and feeling are set now and the violins constantly surge forward with new melodic phrases, bringing a sense of tension to the music.

There is a slight moderation here and more simple melodies come to the fore. Then some rhythmic punctuation takes place, leading to a period of shimmering violins. A solo cello emerges out of this and the violins return, at a moderate pace. There seems to be more folk melodies in this movement than there were in the previous. Finally a longing is felt as the violins look inward while an undercurrent of viola and cello keep up the tempo, which has decreased considerably. The violins move way up into a high register momentarily, and then drift back into simple melodies which are sustained to a peaceful conclusion, the last notes being played in the highest register of a violin.

These two movements are quite contrasting – the first static, the second, freewheeling.

My review CD is by the Kubin Quartet on the Centaur label, and is paired with a piano quintet, a genre that I don't normally enjoy. However, this one is fabulous, there is a lot of string quartet in there. Several other versions of String Quartet No. 2 can be found on Amazon US and UK. I like the sound of one by the legendary Janacek Quartet, which is coupled with the two quartets of Janacek, at a very nice price. There is a bit of confusion when searching because there exists an ensemble, the Novak String Quartet, who have recorded quite a few CDs.

The review CD is on Spotify and the work can be found on YouTube and earsense.

Listenability: Contrasting, but ultimately interesting Romantic work.

— ooOoo —

Buxton Orr [1924–1997]

Nationality: Scottish
Quartets: Two
Style: Contemporary

The Painter
String Quartets Nos. 1 & 2

A few thoughts about Orr. He writes music that has a peaceful, often atonal background, with constantly occurring melodies. I like to think of him as an expressionist painter. He sets up an abstract background and then applies paint, a dash here, a couple of brush strokes there, and moves on. Furthermore, he seems to have been influenced in some ways by the works of Bela Bartok and Dmitri Shostakovich.

I am going to discuss his First String Quartet, titled *Refrains IV*. It's unusual in that it consists of nine movements. Five of them are under two minutes and as most of the movements run together I shall not name every movement, just occasionally.

The work begins with a fractured theme, which is repeated with some variations – the piece is already atonal. A further theme is played which becomes a bit more energised. All instruments contribute to a slightly agitated space which turns into chaos, followed by a rare moment of tempo. The instruments produce excited sounds until a violin invokes a peaceful section. This doesn't last as an abstract conversation proceeds to the end of this section.

The third movement is sparse with a lamenting viola behind the violins. The melody is static and there is little melodic development. However, the mood is wonderful – just so intangible. Now the cello takes a prominent role, leading into some beautiful harmonies. The intensity increases, or is it chaos? It is quickly subdued in any event. A solo violin enters for a time and it is joined by a calm ensemble. Those harmonies return and sparsity predominates.

The next movement opens with a solo cello theme, which is repeated to the accompaniment of the violins. A brief pizzicato phase gives way to another violin lament. The pizzicato breaks out again into a theme, before an ensemble interjection occurs. Now it is time to put on some paint and the composer introduces another abstract section, as the cello scurries around the violins. Again we have a conspicuous cello theme. The violins move into the middle register with a hint of pizzicato. They are just so wonderfully expressive.

The seventh movement is a short violin interlude over a smattering of string sound effects. A hint of a crescendo ensues and the cello scurries again, before taking the lead with interjections from the violins. There is forward movement, with the violins leading the charge. This leads to further abstraction and an atonal dialogue. A delicate texture ensues and is only broken briefly by a flourish. There is a brief change of tonality to conclude.

The final movement has an interesting tonal background and the piece quickly becomes quiet. Occasional notes are heard but the quartet is essentially over.

The Second Quartet consists of four movements and probably is encapsulated even more by the painter analogy. I commend this music to those who like mild, interesting abstraction – no noises here.

Both of these works, together with some other assorted string chamber works can be found on a single CD, *Chamber Music for Strings* on the Toccata Classics label and performed by the augmented Beethoven String Trio of London, on Amazon US and UK.

This album is on Spotify and both works can be found on YouTube together with several versions on earsense.

Listenability: Beautiful, sparse, thought-provoking music.

Andrzej & Roxanna Panufnik [1914–1991]

Nationality: Polish
Quartets: Three
Style: Contemporary

String Quartets Nos. 2 & 3

Roxanna Panufnik [born 1968] is the composer's daughter. She contributes two quartet movements, and an arrangement of a string sextet written by her father, to the review CD. They are performed by one of my favourite ensembles, the Brodsky Quartet. I intend to discuss two of Panufnik's String Quartets, Nos. 2 and 3, and also a work for string quartet by his daughter.

String Quartet No. 2 was originally a one movement work, titled *Messages*. The Brodskys perform it as a seven movement piece, not sure why. I have another CD containing it as one movement, and, as the movements are all short, for convenience I shall consider it as one movement.

The quartet opens in a lamenting atonality, with the other instruments following the lead of the violin. It's a terrific, abstruse soundscape. Now the violin again leads, but with slightly dissonant interjections. The sound is then transformed into a gentle melodic episode where the two violins express freely, eventually becoming rhapsodic. The mood ends with a sweeping chord and, after a brief pause, the first violin engages the cello in a gentle dialogue. The cello dissipates and the violin goes it alone – this is a very moving moment. Eventually a sense of agitation arises with the violins becoming aggressive.

A solo cello now takes over, using mostly pizzicato, and is rhythmically incisive. The ensemble returns in an agitated way and the music becomes chaotic, almost frenzied. We then have a march-like section, which starts conservatively but quickly moves into another agitated state. The solo cello returns with a rich texture as it negotiates all of its registers with ease. The violins again take control, but the cello is still strong, until a softening leads to another intriguing, introspective soundscape. A dialogue between the first violin and the ensemble is jerky, and seems to lack direction.

The two violins now take precedence and again the music is sporadic. They move into another atonal duet and the cello returns, leading to another wonderful feeling – the gentle atonality is enthralling. The first violin now goes solo, and is so soft, as it fades to a conclusion.

String Quartet No. 3 is in five movements and is titled *Wycinanki*, which translates as *Cutouts*. It opens with a sustained violin note, with minimal support – notes are hinted at initially, then build slightly. All the while, the violin keeps up its sustained tone, it's mostly all you can hear and it remains to the end. I should mention that these are all relatively short movements.

The next movement begins in a wonderful, slightly intangible, joyous manner before the violins concoct strange atonal melodies. For a short period they become agitated, but soon return to sparsity and gently fade out. This movement runs for just over two minutes.

Now we have a pizzicato opening to the third movement, which is even shorter. Nearing the end, the cello makes for a scurrying passage, and the violins finish it off.

The fourth movement begins with a frenzied atmosphere. A solo violin assumes a strident manner, and there are no holds barred. It is a virtuosic interlude which ends abruptly at 1:27.

The final movement is the longest at little over three minutes. It is a fascinating adagio, with sustained violins, and a hint of microtones that bring a powerful character to the piece. It is static, with a minimum of development. The end comes with a fade of the sustained violins.

These are two fine quartets. There is some agitation, but much admirable music to be found here. The last adagio is particularly magical.

As previously mentioned, Roxanna Panufnik contributes two movements for string quartet. They are titled *Memories of my Father – I and II*. I intend to discuss the first work, as it is a beautiful piece of writing, and very moving.

It opens with a lamenting cello, complemented by a violin. Longing atonal melodies are expressed and, for me, it inhabits a sound world similar to that of Arvo Pärt. The music ebbs and flows, but all the while the underlying tone is melancholy. It gently fades after having sustained the mood for over six minutes. This is a transcendent, sublime and, dare I say, spiritual work.

The review CD, titled *Messages: Chamber Music for Strings,* on the Chandos label also contains String Quartet No. 1 and two string sextets – *Song to the Virgin Mary* is simply wonderful. The same can be said for the playing of the Brodsky Quartet.

This CD is freely available at Amazon US and UK.

It can be heard on Spotify and YouTube and there are several recordings of works from both father and daughter on earsense.

Listenability: Modern with some sublime spaces.

[Image courtesy Chandos label]

— ooOoo —

Jean Papineau-Couture [1916–2000]

Nationality: Canadian
Quartets: Four
Style: Contemporary

String Quartets Nos. 1 & 2

The First Quartet, which is in two short movements, opens with a fascinating atonal mood. Marked grave, a lamenting solo violin is soon joined by the ensemble in a slow, but pulsing manner that sits firmly on the beat as it moves forward. The violin expresses long tones and, after a time, there is some harmony and the dynamics rise momentarily, before dropping back slightly. Now there are

303

strong harmonised interjections, followed by a return to the pulsing feeling. Powerful violin statements are augmented by the second violin – the end comes as a short, peaceful lamenting sound. This music reminds me of Charles Ives' magical hanging chords and also some of jazz composer Ornette Coleman's stunning orchestral work *Skies of America*, which was plainly influenced by Ives.

The second movement, marked presto, features an excited violin leading the music into a wonderful soundspace, at tempo. The melodies are very interesting – slightly atonal, but ultimately fascinating. As the music unfolds, the tempo abates slightly and the violin leads the ensemble into a different feeling, somewhat tense, before it expresses a short virtuosic solo violin passage. The rhythm returns immediately and the mood is propulsive as it moves through several chord changes. The violin repeatedly works on a distinctive melody, which is echoed by the ensemble. A strong chordal passage brings about a dynamic ending.

The Second Quartet is in four movements and is longer than the First. The music again commences with a dissonant flourish, complemented by ensemble mutterings. A dark chord ensues and the sound becomes rhythmic – there is again, a sense of tension here as the rhythm is discarded. A solo cello passage is thoughtful, before a sombre violin returns to muse above the cello, with fine, sparse, dissonant melodies. A pause leads to an energised atonal passage which diminishes into another quiet, introspective mood. The ending is a long, quivering solo violin line.

The next movement opens in a thundering, chordal manner, interrupted only by a short, atonal cello statement. Now the chordal rhythm is played at a lower intensity and soon moves into a quiet passage of violin expression. The opening strength returns – it is somewhat reminiscent of the final moments of Grieg's *In the Hall of the Mountain King*, played by a string quartet. The finish is a lone violin melody, followed by a long pause and then a most confronting flourish.

The third movement is marked andante, and is similar to the opening movement of the First Quartet. It is a burbling, atonal soundscape with the violin conveying strong, long melodic lines over a desolate ensemble sound. A solo violin flourish leads into a harmonised section, which brings to mind some of the early symphonic writing of Hans Werner Henze. A pause leads to a change into a sparse mood, with intermittent pizzicato strokes accompanying a distant violin. Now the violin lifts in intensity and the ensemble follows with sustained, harmonised chords. A brief period of chaos ensues but is soon dampened, and the violin leads into an engrossing faded ensemble conclusion.

The finale is very short and commences with a powerful solo cello statement which is eventually joined by the violins as they investigate the dynamics. This is quite a stark feeling, but also rewarding. A loud, aggressive passage rushes to the end.

I really like these works, especially the brief First Quartet, and especially appreciate the composer's tendency towards powerful, orchestral style writing. The review CD, performed by the Molinari Quartet is a superb set – it also

304

contains String Quartets Nos. 3 and 4, both one movement works, together with a string trio, which just happens to be the longest piece on the disc.

The CD, titled *Papineau-Couture: Quatuors à cordes Nos. 1-3 & Trio Slanò* on the Atmar Classique label, is available on Amazon UK and Presto Classical, and as a download on Amazon US.

The works can be heard on Spotify, YouTube and earsense.

Listenability: Fine, absorbing, Modern music.

— ooOoo —

Louis Pelosi [born 1947]

Nationality: American
Quartets: Three
Style: Contemporary

String Quartet No. 2

Pelosi's Second Quartet, dedicated to his late wife, is titled *Rosemary Koczy – in Memoriam*. It is in one eighteen-minute movement.

The work opens with the cello leading the way, and abundant harmonies being introduced. Once the violins have appeared, the mood settles into a gentle, drifting passage. This leads into a hint of anxiety – I detect a portion of a motif from Shostakovich – before moving into a brief section in tempo. It soon dissipates and meanders along with several pauses interrupting the mood. The tempo returns and the violins express charming melodies. The cello is conspicuous here, but not for long as a solo violin emerges for a brief moment. It is soon joined by the ensemble and leads to a slightly stilted feeling.

Now some powerful rhythmic chordal thrusts ensue, but they are only transient. The gentle melodies return and the cello is again prominent. There goes that Shostakovich motif again. A solo violin takes over and eventually the ensemble enter at various times. The violin is still the driving force although some slightly dissonant interjections add to the mood. The chordal thrusts make a reappearance, before things become very quiet. Some dissonant touches are quite pervasive.

The prominent violin pushes ahead with a second violin in evidence, together with pizzicato viola. Another familiar phrase occurs, it may be from a Bach *Brandenburg Concerto*. The intensity increases – the phrasing is again Bach-like. A pause introduces a solo cello statement, which is joined by the violins and later, a strong rhythmic passage occurs.

This gives way to a gentle mood with cello pizzicato complementing the violin duet. The Bach-like phrasing returns for a time – it definitely has a Baroque feeling. Now some strong chords raise the intensity, and cello interjections seem to quieten the violins as they become very sparse. The cello interjections return and a repeated violin phrase leads to the conclusion.

This work seems to contain both old and new elements, especially as it progresses – a mixture of Bach and Shostakovich is an interesting concept.

The review CD is titled *Music by Louis Pelosi: A Triptych Memorial to My Rosemarie, Part I*, on KASP Records, performed by an unspecified string quartet. It also contains String Quartet No. 1 and is available on Amazon US and UK.

I could only find a listenable version on Spotify, together with a CD featuring the Third Quartet.

Listenability: Aesthetically pleasing, without being overly sentimental.

— ooOoo —

George Perle [1915–2009]

Nationality: American
Quartets: Eight
Style: Contemporary

String Quartet No. 8

Perle was a prominent music theorist with a particular interest in the *Second Viennese School* – Schoenberg, Berg and Webern – conducting numerous analyses of their works and adapting their serial techniques to his own personal style. These issues are covered in a fine article on Wikipedia. The Eighth Quartet, titled *Windows of Order,* is in one movement and is a far-ranging work. It was written in 1988.

The quartet opens in a laconic fashion, both harmonically and rhythmically. The energy soon rises however, and notes and phrases are flung about with gay abandon. A smoother passage calms the piece temporarily, and then we return to the entropy. After a time, a calm period containing a lot of space appears in the music. Perle's use of his personal techniques is characterised by scurrying violins followed by laments. It is modern music, sometimes evoking Elliott Carter, as he descends into calm atonalities quite often.

A stasis comes over the work, and the ensemble probe gently, with deep, abstract feeling. This is a wonderful soundscape, filled with harmonic twists and turns. Slowly, the music moves forward, without any hint of a tempo. The sparsity really works for me, it's almost meditative. All of the instruments add their presence to this state of tonal ambiguity. It seems to have become even more static, with little development of any kind.

Now we have a flurry of violins, and the original scurrying feeling returns, together with a rhythmic density. The cello is wonderful here, as it navigates its way through the tension while the violins are positively racing, but the ensemble does not engage with them. A peace returns, but is driven back by some spiking interjections from the violins, with brief fragments alternating frequently, this music won't be tied down. Expansive violin phrases occur and the work finishes on the highest note in the piece. Finito.

This review seems short to me, but each of the sections described in a few words or sentences, in fact last for some minutes. The work is more like a painting, it is that abstract.

Two other string quartets are on the review CD, Nos. 2 and 5, in which you can hear the progression of the composer's style. No. 2 has a wonderful adagio movement. There is also a stand-alone twelve-minute masterpiece simply titled *Molto Adagio*, a magnificent piece that sustains a melancholia for its duration. Violin lines drift in and out, but there is never any sense of a tempo.

As to availability, the CD, *Perle: The String Quartets [Molto Adagio]* on Bridge Records label, performed by Daedalus Quartet can be obtained from Amazon US and UK. This CD is also on Spotify and the complete *Windows of Order* is on YouTube, and earsense.

Listenability: A fine example of Contemporary progression.

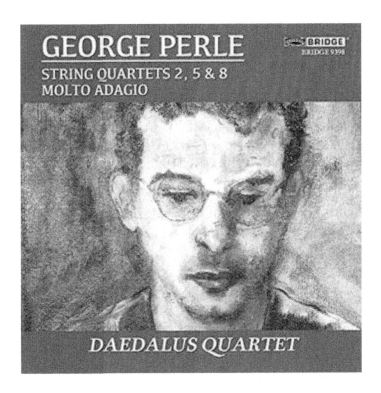

[Image courtesy Bridge Records]

Vincent Persichetti [1915–1987]

Nationality: American
Quartets: Four
Style: Contemporary

String Quartet No. 3

The Third Quartet, which is in one movement, opens with a shrill solo violin, which may be using harmonics for effect. The second violin joins the sombre atmosphere and assorted cello sounds are heard. There are also some pizzicato viola strokes and the shrill violin persists, while the other instruments subside. There is absolutely no tempo until the feeling changes to one of mild rhythmic chaos where all instruments are now present, in an ambient mood. Now we have a return to the previous rhythmic interchanges, which slowly revert back into a section for the two violins. They lower the intensity and produce a slightly dissonant passage, which is quite becoming, and turns out to be an extended phase, with just the two violins meandering. The violins suddenly intensify, and the ensemble gather for support. The violins continue with their random musings and the feeling is quite strong. Now there is a chaotic scene where the violins fire out rapid phrases, and engage with the cello, which becomes the dominant voice for a time. This insistence dissipates and a solo violin is heard, with interjections from the ensemble.

An abstract passage follows with a walking cello, jazz-style, and viola pizzicato gestures. The violin duo return, in a subdued section, and the ensemble makes short stabbing statements. The walking cello resumes and the violins continue with their mildly dissonant exchanges. Soon they are on their own with a seemingly random discourse as the cello picks up on an implied tempo and makes its own random sounds. It then moves into positive statements which reduce the intensity back to a drone with sparse violin sound effects. A pause brings about another change as the violins are once again energised – the mood is almost combative. The violins combine in a fascinating section as they intertwine with mildly intangible phrases before a return of the intensity leads to a melodious passage, which is complemented by a recondite background. Dynamic violin phrases occur until the cello goes solo. The violins are very sparse here, producing a tender moment. The end is a sustained chord with intermittent cello notes.

This is a mildly modernist work, with the mood constantly changing, but the basic emotional nature covers only a handful of different soundscapes.

There is a definite progression in the composer's string quartet output. Nos. 1 and 2, written in 1939 and 1944 respectively, are in a relatively approachable style. The Third, from 1959, shows a significant progression into modernism, while the Fourth, from 1972 is slightly confronting and quite abstract. It is also a named work, the tenth in a series of disparate compositions titled *Parable X*. The other *Parable* compositions are for various ensembles – for instance, *Parable II* is for brass quintet.

The review CD titled *Persichetti: Four Quartets*, on Centaur Records and performed by the Lydian String Quartet is available on Amazon UK and Presto Classical. It can also be heard on Spotify, earsense and YouTube.

Listenability: The music features a profound progression from the early works to the later, fairly modern style.

— ooOoo —

Astor Piazzolla [1921–1992]

Nationality: Argentinian
Quartets: Possibly three
Style: Contemporary

Five Tango Sensations
Bandoneon and String Quartet

Piazzolla has been a significant part of a revival of the tango on the world's musical stages. This work, *Five Tango Sensations*, has the composer on bandoneon – an accordion-like instrument, supported by the Kronos Quartet. It is one of the many CDs on which Kronos have joined forces with other musicians. Since encountering the bandoneon on this album, I have formed an attraction to it. I particularly enjoy the work of Dino Saluzzi, who has many fine albums on the ECM label. If you like sparsity, check out his solo album *Alina* on ECM.

Five Tango Sensations consists of five named movements, as follows:

Asleep – A fabulous opening with slow solo bandoneon, which becomes haunting when the strings enter. Then a key change enhances the texture. The violin eventually takes up the main melody until the bandoneon re-enters – such an alluring passage. It then cuts back to a solo, before the cello comes to the forefront until the tranquil conclusion.

Loving – Features another lonely, slow, solo bandoneon opening. It is an arresting movement as the bandoneon meanders over the string background, while never straying too far from the melancholia. The strings switch to pizzicato for a time, but the melancholy returns as they take it out with a repeat of the melody.

Anxiety – This is more insistent. A repeated phrase accompanies the bandoneon until the cello takes over, to wonderful effect. There is some stunning interplay and the piece concludes as it started, while fading out.

Despartar – A simple melody and a deeply moving, restrained piece.

Fear – This starts at a medium tempo, with solo bandoneon, until it is joined by the viola for a dancing duet. Then the rest of the ensemble enter. Virtually the whole piece is based on a single rhythmic pattern, occasionally broken up by pizzicato moments.

These are fabulous, beautifully layered pieces of music. The textures are wonderful. The thing that strikes me the most is the wistful sound of the bandoneon – it's just so expressive.

The CD, on the Elektra label only runs to 26 minutes and, when I purchased it, was at a commensurate price. It's still available on Amazon and reasonably priced. I have also seen other versions of the piece, but not heard them.

It is on Spotify and many versions of individual movements are on YouTube. The complete work is on earsense, together with recordings of three other short works for string quartet, which are most interesting. I particularly enjoyed the four-minute *Oblivion for String Quartet*.

Listenability: A miniature magnificent, sustained state of wonder – a must have.

— oo0oo —

Willem Pijper [1894–1947]

Nationality: Dutch
Quartets: Five
Style: Early Modern

The Last Two Quartets

Willem Frederik Johannes Pijper wrote five string quartets, with the last remaining uncompleted. I am going to discuss String Quartets Nos. 4 and 5.

The Fourth Quartet, written in 1928, contains four movements. It opens in a hesitant mood with a gentle, intangible, almost formless structure. Atonal violin lines drift along until eventually, a tempo is established. There is also a sense of scurrying violins, together with a rather oblique cello. This creates a fascinating, early twentieth century soundscape, with minimal melodic development – I should also mention that the sound is very quiet throughout, until it finally drifts into oblivion.

The next, very brief movement, is marked allegro and starts in an energetic manner. Again, there is no real sense of structure as the instruments thrust and parry with each other. The end comes quickly with a feeling of susurrus as the music quietly dissipates.

Lamenting violins, a little more conservative this time, introduce the third movement. The sound is one of tonal violins over atonal cello and viola, which paints a marvellous picture. The texture gradually thickens, led by the cello, but this is only temporary, as a return to the opening feeling is this time almost completely atonal. A pizzicato cello and violin provide a rhythmic structure and the intensity is quite strong (for Pijper). The ending, again, just falls away to nothing.

The final movement features a pizzicato viola and walking cello. String sound effects combine with sporadic sombre melodies, which are transformed into a positive mood and then into a more atonal feeling, at tempo. Now the violins express wonderful, transcendent dissonant melodies as the music moves back into rubato, casting aside all semblance of rhythm. This is very delicate music, wistful in spite of its atonality. A period of longing cello and violin lines concludes the work.

The unfinished Fifth Quartet contains only two movements, apparently both written in 1946. The first, marked allegretto, begins with a similar feeling to the previous work, which I find unusual as they are eighteen years apart. There is however, possibly a maturity in evidence as the music is slightly more coherent, even exhibiting some melodic development and conversational sections. The violins are assertive at times but the effect is still that of an introspective soundscape, interspersed with some lyrical melodies, which are attractive. This lyricism persists, leading to a wonderful, extended melodic section. The end comes with a feeling of great tranquility.

The second movement is slow and sombre, with the cello particularly prominent in supporting the violins as they gradually develop an intensity, which does not last. A moving solo cello statement is joined by soft, lamenting violins – this is definitely music of the heart. A period of intensity is brief and the status quo is resumed. Plucked cello accompanies two quiet violins to a conclusion.

I can only speculate as to what this music would have sounded like if completed. I can say that the composer has a strong continuity of style which permeates the last two quartets, at least. Listening to the first three, composed between 1914 and 1923, reveals them to be more conservative, with a gradual tendency to introspection as they progress.

The complete quartets can be had on *Five String Quartets*, on the Olympia Label and performed by the Schoenberg Quartet, which is available on Amazon US and UK, mostly *New and Used* and through Amazon resellers. The Schoenbergs are also on a box set of Dutch string quartets, a 5-CD set titled *The Dutch Legacy*, from Amazon UK and Presto Classical, which looks rather promising. There is a further version of String Quartets Nos. 4 & 5 on a separate release, paired with a symphony – useful if you only want the two mature quartets. This is available as a download, and sometimes from Amazon resellers.

Both of the single CDs mentioned are on Spotify and the five quartets by the Schoenbergs are on YouTube and earsense.

Listenability: Fine, non-confronting Early Modern works.

311

[Image – Olympia label – could not be contacted]

— oo0oo —

Walter Piston [1894–1976]

Nationality: American
Quartets: Five
Style: Early Modern

Two Early Quartets

Walter Hamor Piston Jr was an academic who taught a plethora of Contemporary composers, including Leonard Bernstein. I believe him to be a major influence on the burgeoning American 1950s string quartet revival. Influenced by Schoenberg, his music is often atonal or serial, and for me, somewhat intellectual. This does not hinder his emotional expression however, examples of which can be found in the three slow movements on the review CD. I am going to discuss String Quartets Nos. 1 and 3.

The First Quartet, written in 1937, and in three movements is mainly tonal in character, with some exceptions. The work opens with an allegro tempo and a strong sense of rhythm, a feature that permeates throughout the composer's quartets. A wistful atonal melody emerges, to thoughtful accompaniment before a dance-like section unfolds, leading to a more tonal passage – however the music is still dissonant and at times, frantic. Slowly the dissonance subsides and a harmonically rich section is established, and an intriguing tonal duet between the two violins is especially fine. A return to a rhythmic pulse leads to a strong ending.

The next, adagio movement features a lamenting cello introduction, accompanied by a gentle ensemble layer of sound, which gradually rises to the surface, producing a magnificent abstract soundscape. Mutterings continue in the background and the cello begins an ostinato while the violins lead for a time, only to have the cello return – its resonant statement is most beguiling. Now the violins construct a jagged passage and melodic themes are repeated by various solo instruments. Again a solo cello is superb for a time, with intermittent violin lines adding a poignant touch. A hushed chordal passage leads to a quiet termination.

A brief finale is energised from the start as the violins create stabbing melodic patterns, before moving into a passage of string sound effects as the violins persist with their stark interjections. Approaching the end, the violins combine with rhythmic thrusts to bring about a firm conclusion.

The Third Quartet was written in 1947 and has the same structure as the First – a slow movement bookended by two allegro movements. In fact, the Fifth also has this structure.

The first movement is more assertive than anything in the First Quartet, and more atonal, possibly even serial at times. The mood changes to one of introversion with the violins contributing various random statements. This is followed by a return to the opening feeling which does not last but moves quickly into a marvellous violin duet. Again, the opening theme returns but is soon transformed into another thoughtful passage. The cello is strong here, constantly urging the violins forward and a building sense of chaos leads to an abrupt end.

The slow movement is marked lento and again features a deeply resonant cello part that combines with the violins to create a beautiful sound. The music meanders through a very sensitive emotional soundscape, with atonal melodic lines dominating. An increase in intensity is strong but soon subsides back into a peaceful section. After a pause, a solo cello sets about slowly rebuilding an earlier mood, before long sustained chords take out the movement.

The finale is assertive, featuring prominent violins with ensemble string sound effects. Strangely, the mood turns pastoral for a time before returning to a busy, multi-instrument dialogue. The first violin steps in briefly but is overwhelmed by the rhythmic energy of the ensemble. A change brings about a measured passage until a sweeping of violins concludes the work.

The review CD also contains String Quartet No. 5, which has another fine slow movement. This CD, titled *Walter Piston: String Quartets 1, 3 and 5* by the Harlem Quartet is on the Naxos label and is available on Amazon US and UK.

The CD is on Spotify, and the three quartets can be found performed by various ensembles on YouTube and earsense.

Listenability: Fascinating, slightly intellectual works with brilliant slow movements.

— ooOoo —

Ildebrando Pizzetti [1880–1958]

Nationality: Italian
Quartets: Two
Style: Late Romantic

An Italian Romantic
String Quartets Nos. 1 & 2

Pizzetti was a member of the *Generation of 1880* along with Gian Francesco Malipiero and Ottorino Respighi. They were among the first Italian composers in some time whose primary contributions were not in opera – thanks, Wiki.

These are Romantic works and I regard them as sumptuous due to their texture and orchestral approach. Each contains four movements.

String Quartet No. 1 is in A major and was written in 1906. The opening is breathtakingly beautiful. It sustains this attractive mood and the composer's orchestral style really shines through – it is such a full sound. The violins continue with the opening melodies while the cello and viola slip into variations. After a time, there is a hint of a minor tonality but the beauty is untouched. There are also orchestral-like crescendos that soon return to the natural dynamic level of the quartet. Minor crescendos continue to surface but the piece sustains its natural state for nine minutes. It is a miniature masterpiece.

Movement two is an adagio in a major key, which is a little unusual. The writing is again orchestral-like and the effect is similar to the first movement. It has a long attractive melody that is sustained for two minutes, before it drops into a subtle minor tonality. There is little variation, but it really doesn't need it. It is a place for just being in.

The third movement is again slow and reflective before it jumps into tempo. The melodies are busier here and there is forward movement for the first time in the work. This doesn't last for long and it returns to a slow tempo with the two violins engaging in conversation – sometimes it is strangely reminiscent of

Vaughan Williams' *The Lark Ascending*. Now the tempo picks up again, and many new melodies emerge, before ending with a peaceful conclusion.

The final movement is totally out of character, in a pleasant manner, as it skips along in a moderate tempo. I love the way Pizzetti subtly shifts from major to minor for a short time, before embracing the major again. The tempo then drops a little, allowing for longer melodies to be presented. The tempo returns, as does the joy. There goes that minor again, but not for long. The violins begin to ask questions, then provide their own answers. Nearing the end, the cello has a voice before the piece goes out with a flourish.

String Quartet No. 2 is in D major and was written in 1933. That is quite a gap but it's not uncommon for string quartet composers to leave a considerable time between quartets. I'm not sure what to read into that. Many composers leave a ten year gap between quartets. Others write in consecutive years.

The opening of the first movement signals a completely different approach to No. 1. It is a melancholy piece, stately and rewarding. What Pizzetti can achieve in a major key is stunning, as he is seemingly able to express a wide emotional range. The tempo and strength increase for about three minutes until there is a drop in the dynamics. Gentle melodies follow – we are in a respite. The composer works his way into more intensity, which is in no way chaotic, even though the melodies are flying past at a great rate, before a dignified melancholia returns. The harmonies are so close it sounds like Early Music. Nearing the conclusion, a pleasing melody returns to finish.

The next movement is an adagio, a tempo at which Pizzetti excels. More shades of *The Lark Ascending* – it's beautiful. There is a certain element of stasis here as the violin wanders through various textures and yet the ensemble is soft. It is an attractive passage. Five minutes have elapsed but it still sounds reminiscent of the opening, and definitely a feature for the solo violin. Finally some tension emerges but it soon reverts to peace. I detect a hint of Beethoven here.

The third movement is relatively short, opening with a pair of violins playing a harmonised line. It then moves into a solid ensemble sound at a tempo and there is also a quote from Beethoven. A chord change signals a new melody and a swell in intensity. Now we enter a totally new rhythmic space and a melodic fragment takes it to the conclusion.

The final movement is substantial – eleven minutes, I'm looking forward to it. It opens with a forceful flourish and a slightly aggressive melody. This is already the darkest music on the CD. Settling into a more moderate mood, the violin melody is a lot more conservative, with sweeping lines. It then becomes serious again, this time with swirling violin melodies. That brief minor to major and back again reappears and seems to bring the piece under control. The ensemble bubbles along as the violins intensify again. This becomes pastoral, and is very idyllic. After a time, a moderately tense moment is heard but it fades to a solo violin melody that is searching for something, and it finds it with the help of the ensemble. It is poignant and becomes even more longing as the section progresses. We are nearing the end now and it concludes with a flourish.

Considering the 27-year gap between the two quartets I would expect a little modernism and that's what I heard in this movement, a **little** modernism. This music was an unexpected pleasure, given that I had not heard of Pizzetti before yesterday.

These works can be found on Amazon US and UK, performed by the Lajtha Quartet. Both are on Naxos and Marco Polo, which is a Naxos subsidiary.

They can both be found on Spotify and the Second Quartet is on YouTube and earsense.

Listenability: Somewhat conservative music. Deep, not intellectually, but emotionally.

— ooOoo —

David Post [born 1950]

Nationality: American
Quartets: At least four
Style: Contemporary

String Quartets Nos. 3 & 4

The Third String Quartet is in one movement and opens with an optimistic melody and chordal punctuations. These eventually disappear and we are left with a burbling melody. It then softens a little and a solo violin pursues a different emotional feeling. There is a lot of forward propulsion in this work and occasionally the punctuations return. Now the melody is more melancholy and the accompaniment sparse, quite lyrical really. It is wonderful, and the opening seems like it was a long time ago. Having said that, to me this music evokes a contemporary landscape, possibly a city.

A pause is followed by a pastoral melody. The cello provides a subtle tempo whilst the violin develops a wonderful new atmosphere. It descends to the bottom of its register and for a moment, there are some more interjections. The lyrical feeling reappears however, and the melody persists. Now the cello sets up a brisk tempo and the violins scurry about, with some agitation. A new tempo finds the ensemble providing slightly dissonant thrusts – but not too powerful. There is some marvellous harmony here – again it evokes the feeling of the present age. A violin repeats one note rapidly and the other instruments insert various seemingly random notes to achieve a slightly ambivalent feeling.

Another pause introduces a somewhat quieter nature, totally lacking in tempo. Sparse violins bring about a most precious soundscape, reminiscent of

316

Charles Ives' quieter moments. The music begins to darken as the violins investigate new melodic possibilities, but it doesn't last. There is another pause and the two violins return to draw out long melodies, with the cello to be heard occasionally in the background. The violins continue the dreamy, abstract, Ives-like atmosphere and slowly fade out to conclude.

This quartet is really in three parts – the intensity decreases as each one arrives. The third part is a fine piece of writing, evoking a feeling of serenity and sparsity. It's a terrific work.

String Quartet No. 4 is titled *Three Photographs of Abelardo Morell* and consists of three named movements.

Camera Obscura Image of Brookline View in Brady's Room – The quartet begins with the cello, then the violin plays an interesting phrase that seems to ask a question. This continues as the phrase is again featured with the other violin in support – it is also developed at some length. A flourish leads into the next passage which is pulsating and the violins sustain a moderate tension. Now appears some intermittent, startling chordal interjections. The cello is salient for a time but finally, it is just two violins that lead the movement to a conclusion.

Book: Pieta -The second movement again opens with a conspicuous cello while a violin meanders freely. The second violin enters and adds to the ambience, which takes me to a special place where the cello is strong and the violins are beautiful. Then it is just the violins for a time, until the cello eventually returns, bringing with it a full sound while a change in harmony leads to a propulsive rhythmic episode. The music then cuts back to a lamenting solo violin. After a time the cello emerges, in a very subtle manner. The movement ends on a shimmering violin phrase which is quite enchanting.

Map in Sink – In the final movement, the viola plays a repeated phrase and a pizzicato violin cuts across the rhythm. Another harmonic change brings more intensity and the violins produce some stabbing chords. The violin begins to ask questions and the ensemble responds with vigour. A slight chaos ensues and it's all over. This has been a short movement.

These are fine quartets. The review CD, *Post: String Quartets 2-4,* performed by The Hawthorne Quartet, also contains a short piece, *Fantasia on a Virtual Chorale* – much music to listen to. It is available on Naxos at Amazon US and UK.

This CD is on Spotify and String Quartet No. 3 is on earsense and YouTube.

Listenability: Not as modern as I would have thought, but impressive nonetheless.

Sergei Prokofiev [1891–1953]

Nationality: Russian
Quartets: Two
Style: Late Romantic

The Two String Quartets

Prokoviev's two string quartets both contain three movements. A prancing, melodious violin passage opens the First Quartet before a touch of melancholy arrives, but the violin pushes through it with wide intervallic leaps before settling again. The feeling increases in intensity, and with rhythmic thrusts from the violins, it becomes a little chaotic. Now the opening atmosphere returns, with the second violin providing wonderful supporting melodies. This is an extended section, which eventually leads into a brief period of uncertainty, before the opening is revisited. The final moments are contrasting, and rhythmically incisive – the end comes with a solid chord.

The next movement, marked andante and vivace, starts in a melancholy mood, mostly created by the violins. After a time, the violins surge into action and the viola and cello pick up on the motion. The andante is left far behind as the music is stretched tight, and the violins are positively dynamic. There is a great feeling of forward movement in this passage. It continues to grow more intensely rhythmic, with many chordal punctuations. Now a solo cello statement brings a warmth to proceedings and continues as the violins return – this is magnificent. Eventually, and it is for quite a while, the violins parry with the cello to the end. This is a most satisfying experience.

The final movement, again marked andante, begins in a minor key with violins repeating phrases as the cello quivers in the background. The violin melodies are particularly attractive, and distinctly Russian, with the feeling of musical strength that many Russian composers seem to possess. Powerful chords now predominate for a short time, before the andante tempo returns. There is gradual melodic development and the cello is superb in the accompaniment. Suddenly, the texture becomes heavy, with chords projecting in a minor key. A cello-based theme develops, but it is only for a short while as the music returns to the opening. The rhythm resumes and leads into a strong solo cello melody. This is followed by gentle violin melodies that lead to a wistful violin and cello conclusion.

This is a passionate work, in a conservative style – no modernity here. It was written in 1930 and can be contrasted with the feeling of the later work.

The Second Quartet, titled *On Kardinian Themes*, features a stately disposition. Violin melodies assert themselves over a static background, which occasionally dissipates, leaving the violins to go it alone. A pause brings about a new phase which settles into a measured march-like tempo, while one violin crafts various pleasing melodies. Suddenly, the work is hectic with dissonant chords being superimposed over the violins. The chords continue but the dissonance gives way to a rhythmic motif, while the violin investigates various melodic possibilities to the end, which is strong.

The second movement starts with lamenting violins and a gentle melody, which is slowly developed. It is an alluring, atmospheric feeling. The mood becomes slightly more insistent but the basic melodies persist, as the passage moves into a tempo. It definitely has a Russian feeling – the rhythms are quite stiff. This section is vaguely reminiscent of Ravel's *Bolero*, with the rhythm pronounced. Now we have a change – there is no tempo and things become quiet. A brief pause introduces an achingly beautiful, solo cello statement, which stirs the violins as they flutter above with sympathetic melodies. The cello persists, again solo, and concludes the movement. Oh, what a feeling.

The final movement has an underlying intensity with the ensemble creating another of those military march-like tempos. A rhythmic motif is created, allowing the violins to strut above the tension as a violin quivers feverishly, and various types of sounds are produced at different places in the piece. The tension is eventually released, and a brief pizzicato interlude introduces another taut period. The cello goes it alone in a stunning solo statement until the violins take up the challenge and we have further tension. More dissonant chords occur, together with a powerful cello, as the violins take a back seat. They eventually emerge in an abstract manner and investigate pizzicato possibilities. As we near the end, the military tempo returns and is maintained by the violins until the quartet finishes on a chord.

I would have to say that the Second Quartet is even more passionate than the First. It was composed in 1941, which would have been military times in Russia, and it shows. Again there is nothing modern about this quartet. I would speculate that Prokofiev's work was influenced by the political climate of his times, similar to Shostakovich's difficult political experiences. For those interested in such things, I found an interesting internet article on Stalin and Prokofiev, here:

www.rferl.org/a/prokofiev-stalin-deaths/24920002.html.

These two works are brilliantly performed by the Pavel Haas Quartet on the Supraphon label. The CD also contains a third work, *Sonata for Two Violins*.

At least a dozen pairings of both quartets are available on Amazon US and UK. Most have another piece to fill out the CD. The Pavel Haas Quartet is on Spotify and many versions are on YouTube. There are ten recordings of the Second Quartet, including a fine performance by the St. Petersburg String Quartet, at earsense.

Listenability: Emotionally charged works, not really of their time

[Image courtesy Supraphon label]

— ooOoo —

Joachim Raff [1822–1882]

Nationality: Swiss-German
Quartets: Eight
Style: Romantic

String Quartet No. 4

Swiss-born Joseph Joachim Raff is considered to be a German composer as he spent most of his life there. I am going to discuss his Fourth String Quartet.

The work opens with a gentle, pulsing mood. A high violin melody is very elegant as the ensemble muses beneath it – I could listen to this violin forever.

Next follows a solo cello statement, while the ensemble continues with the pulse. The first violin soon returns and there are some harmonised violin lines along with conversational forays. The opening violin melody is still heard, occasionally broken up by ensemble interjections. Now the cello again comes to the fore, with a lyrical melodic line. At this point, the violin melody changes and is more expansive, even expressing some rhythmic passages which are harmonised by the ensemble. The violin then rises above to construct a beguiling section, constantly moving forward. The intensity increases and the violin again soars above the propulsive ensemble, bringing great beauty to the music. A mellowing of the feeling has the cello again expressing lyrical melodies as the violin takes a backward step. Now the violin starts its journey towards the end. The dynamics drop and the cello again speaks out, leading into a strong rhythmic section, led by the violin until the music comes to an abrupt stop.

The second movement, which is the shortest in the work, is closely related to the first movement but slightly faster. The first violin again gives a stunning performance, while being more expansive. Many instances of harmonised lines occur, together with call and response. There is a drama in this music, as the violin again leads us to another abrupt finish.

The next movement, marked andante, begins with a stately feeling, in a minor tonality. The manner in which the two violins interact brings a very satisfying contrast to what has come before. They reach out together, to fashion an alluring mood. Now the music begins to develop and some intense playing produces several powerful rhythmic passages which lead the music into a tempo. The violins are strong and very active as they direct the ensemble through this fascinating section. The intensity slowly subsides and we are left with the violins expressing gentle, sparse melodies, sometimes in harmony. Even though the melodies are soft, there is a certain rhapsodic feeling to be heard at times. Slowly, a pizzicato sound enters and the violins waft over it – this is another marvellous mood. Nearing the end, the violins lift in intensity before drifting to a conclusion with a sense of evanescence.

The finale, marked presto, commences with a short solo violin section, before it is joined by the second violin. Now the presto is felt, and the music moves into a tempo with swirling violin sounds as a rhythmic motif initiates a new, positive section. The violins begin an extended duet and they are eventually joined by a conspicuous cello. A three-way conversation makes for another beguiling passage before the violins reassert their position and drive briskly towards a final flourish, which completes the work.

The review CD, performed by the Mannheimer String Quartet, on the CPO label also contains String Quartets Nos. 2, 3 and 8. It is available on Amazon US and UK.

The full CD can be heard, along with other Raff quartets on Spotify, YouTube and earsense.

Listenability: A wonderful, charming Romantic quartet.

John Ramsay [born 1931]

Nationality: British
Quartets: Four
Style: Contemporary

Two Named Works
String Quartets Nos. 2 & 4

The Second Quartet is titled *Shackleton*. It refers not to Ernest Shackleton but to Robert Milner Shackleton, a personal friend of the composer, and a distant relative of the Antarctic explorer. The work is in four movements.

This short quartet opens with a lamenting passage. Long notes contribute to this feeling, which happens to be sustained throughout the work. There is a flowing melodic line, with the dynamics varying to good effect. It is slightly intangible, always seeming just out of reach, and finishes as it starts, with a great depth of feeling.

The second movement is slower than the first and begins with a somber background overlaid with a violin in a high register. The melody is yearning and again, long notes are featured in the accompaniment. A brief pause brings forth a solo cello which makes for a stately melody, which ebbs and flows until we are left with two violins. Eventually, the viola plays a rhythmic figure in the background and the movement moves to its conclusion.

The next movement, which is short, features a strummed cello. The violins again work with a melancholy melody, changing as the cello varies its harmony. The end comes with a slow transition into nothingness.

The finale is positively racing, compared to the previous movements. The melodies are strong and eventually they drift back into the default nature of the piece. Another pause introduces a tempo which is carried by the whole ensemble. Melodies move through different textures until a further pause leads to a slow cello figure with sparse violin melodies in abundance. This has a certain inevitability and a final lament concludes the work.

It's been a while since I have heard such a sustained melancholy in a string quartet. There is not much joy in its sixteen minutes duration. It is definitely a poignant piece of music.

String Quartet No. 4 is titled *Charles Darwin,* and is in one long movement of twenty-two minutes duration. It opens softly, so much so that it takes a little while to work out what is going on. Eventually a violin melody meanders over a sustained chord backing, before a second violin comes into play. The music gradually intensifies and the violin becomes a little frantic. A drop in intensity and a long descending violin line introduce a new passage which is not unlike John Tavener or Arvo Pärt.

Powerful chords take over – the dynamics change frequently and there is much movement in the textures. A strong melodic phrase comes into play, repeated at a diminishing volume. Now there is a peace, with the cello ruminating over a quietly sustained chord. A change in harmony brings a new folk element to the melody in the violins which is picked up and repeated by the cello. The melody is retained, and variations on it are expressed. The cello then repeats the melody at a quicker pace. Strangely, we then have a direct quote from *All Creatures Great and Small*. This is definitely English eccentricity.

The melody now assumes an ethnic character with more emotional intensity than has been heard thus far in the work. There are some dissonant chords and it's a busy section that lasts for a time. Previous phrases are repeated and they bring on a crescendo which wanes ever so slowly before leading into a dramatic texture which gradually brings peace. The first violin states a lonely melody and the work appears to be looking to the conclusion. Two violins feature in a touching moment which begins to build, but soon fades into the distance.

These quartets, together with String Quartets Nos. 1 and 3 can be found on a 2-CD set *String Quartets 1-4*, on the Metier label, performed by the Fitzwilliam Quartet, famous for their complete Shostakovich cycle. Bouquets to the Fitzwilliam for their incisive and elegant playing throughout.

The set is available on Amazon US and UK and can be found on Spotify, and many individual movements are on YouTube. Both works are on earsense.

Listenability: For me, these are slightly eccentric works, very much in the British tradition and quite interesting.

— ooOoo —

Karol Rathaus [1895–1954]

Nationality: German-Austrian
Quartets: Eight
Style: Contemporary

String Quartets Nos. 3-5

Only Rathaus' Quartets Nos. 3, 4 and 5 are currently available. He is probably the gentlest Contemporary composer I have heard, although I guess you could argue Morton Feldman. They are both very different.

The Third Quartet contains five movements. The first begins with a plaintive, introspective melody, and a wonderful feeling – I love the way the composer probes at the music with the melody. Nearing the conclusion, the music deepens a little. The second movement, marked sarabande, continues in the same emotional space, perhaps a little more peaceful than the previous movement. An up tempo movement follows, again with a gentle sense of agitation as a solo cello leads into a stately, appealing moment before the tempo quickens to conclude the movement. The short, slow fourth movement again occupies the emotional space that I crave. It is understated, with an eerie sound. The final movement, while ultimately abstract, is never particularly challenging. The first violin is busy and constantly plays games with the ensemble.

The Fourth Quartet is in three movements. It opens with a flourish but continues in the same vein as the previous piece. This movement is rhythmic, but there is no violence or anger here. Towards the end it breaks into a solo cello with sparse accompaniment. It's soothing really – belying its marking of allegro energico which I take to mean energised. The next movement is slow, perhaps a little harsher than the preceding movements. I like the soundscape it evokes – a sense of the desolate. The last movement is a bustling affair, almost sprightly. Again, atonal, but with only a minimum effect of dissonance.

The Fifth Quartet also contains three movements. The first continues with some of the previous textures. It has a measured sense of Modernism about it. However, it is a little confronting. The same could be said of the second movement, it just has a bit more of an edge to it. The final short movement is busy, and again, a little confronting.

These works confuse me slightly. They are definitely atonal with a degree of Modernism. However, the modernist traits of anger, chaos, agitation and aggression are not to be found here, except in a measured manner. There are some exquisite slow moments that I find introspective and particularly attractive.

The review CD, Complete String Quartets, by the Amar Corde Quartet on the Acte Prealable label is freely available on Amazon US and UK. It contains the subtitle *11th September 2001 Victims in Memoriam* on the CD cover.

Unfortunately, Rathaus's quartets are available neither on Spotify nor YouTube.

Listenability: Let's call it tempered Modernism – fabulous just for the quiet movements.

— oo0oo —

Maurice Ravel [1875–1937]

Nationality: French
Quartets: One – FOSQC
Style: Early Modern

String Quartet No. 1

The two classic quartets from French Impressionists Claude Debussy in G minor and Maurice Ravel in F major are strangely the only pieces they composed in this genre. Interestingly, both eschewed the term Impressionism but history seems to have labelled them as such.

The Ravel Quartet, in four movements, opens with a lilting melody which is soon restated, slightly modified. A moment of dissonance appears before the intensity is lifted with a recapitulation of the theme. Peace returns with a beautifully harmonised version of the opening melody. The harmony changes and affects the melody in many different ways. There is dissonance in abundance now, but the melody keeps reappearing. It reaches several crescendos before dropping back to a moderate level. The opening melody eventually sustains the whole movement and the ending is a cello arpeggio and one last violin note. It is a brilliant, rapturous piece of music.

The next movement starts with a short pizzicato statement, then a melodic phrase, before the pizzicato is repeated. Shimmering violin chords over this backdrop are especially effective. A new section ensues with two violins and a melancholy melody, before the cello and viola join in to produce a slow lament that eventually moves into a tempo. A lot of dynamic changes occur and still the opening melody is heard, as pizzicato. The recapitulation races towards the end, with assorted pizzicato phrases and chords.

The third movement commences with a cello conversation, which is continued by the violin. Over a string backdrop, a new graceful melody unfolds, which gathers strength from a deep cello and rapidly rises to a crescendo which concludes with more spacious violin phrases. The cello returns to push toward the end, together with the ensemble. It ends on a hanging note.

The final movement introduction is aggressive in nature and eventually settles into a melodic pattern before a passing reference to the introduction leads to some agitation, which is sustained for a good while. Now the melodies return – they are everywhere, from all instruments. The chaos returns briefly before a charming passage takes shape. There is one more chaotic crescendo which ends the quartet. That was something, Mr Ravel.

There are many fine versions available, Amazon US has at least 1500 listings for this quartet. I have the Borodin Quartet on Chandos and the Quartetto Italiano on Eloquence – both paired with Debussy's string quartet. I suggest a set with the Debussy, the two works are often paired together on a CD and they fit perfectly. This music has a universal appeal – it is akin to jazz trumpeter Miles Davis' *Kind of Blue* – everybody owns or should own this timeless jazz classic. It has an impressionistic flavour too.

Many versions of the Ravel Quartet exist on Spotify and it also can be sampled on YouTube. The Alban Berg Quartet is featured in a stunning performance on earsense.

Listenability: Impressionism with a slightly harder edge than its frequent companion, the Debussy.

[Image courtesy Philips via Universal Music]

— ooOoo —

Alan Rawsthorne [1905–1971]

Nationality: British
Quartets: Three
Style: Contemporary

String Quartets Nos. 1 & 2

Rawsthorne wrote three published string quartets and an unpublished work, which has fortunately found its way into the repertoire. The composer has a mysterious style, which is quite forward looking for its time.

The First Quartet, composed in 1939, is in one movement. Titled *Theme and Variations*, it is brief and commences with a typically British Modern sound from that period, featuring a gently, mildly dissonant passage – this creates an eerie feeling. It progresses rather quickly with rapid violin phrases, while the two violins lead the way into an animated conversation. Now the tempo is replaced by a tranquil sparsity, which then returns to the previous character. The music is wispy, filled with short pauses. Suddenly things become lively and the violins lead the piece into some busy abstraction. There are chordal and rhythmic punctuations which support the two violins for a time.

Abruptly, the intensity drops and a funereal moment ensues. The violins express minimal phrases at first, and then they gradually become more expansive. Even this slight increase in intensity does not last, but dissolves, almost into a stasis. Eventually we have movement, and melody. Both violins converse while the cello supplies an appropriate harmonic underpinning. It is about as animated as this piece has become, with violins spinning out discrete, atonal phrases. Finally, nearing the end, there is a flurry of atonal activity featuring the two violins. They briefly pick up on a motif with the cello and continue until an extremely loud flourish finishes the quartet. This is an introspective work, filled with thought provoking, atonal soundscapes.

The Second Quartet was written in 1954, and is in four movements. The opening features a dissonant fanfare, which quickly leads into an intense melodic section. Again, this is the Modernity of its time. There is some eventually some melodic development from the violins, which I don't believe is a significant feature of this composer's style. A brief, calm fragment, with a lamenting first violin, leads straight into a melodically chaotic episode. The cello makes some significant statements which propel the violins forward. The end is a lone violin which peters out.

The second movement is more of the same – atonal melodies carried by the ensemble. Having said that, it moves on to an introspective, peaceful soundscape. A brief, measured atonal frolic gives way to another satisfying piece of introspection before the cello draws out long lines that complement the sparsity of the violins, which slowly fade to the end.

The third movement has a viola playing a rhythmic motif as the violins express quiet, dissonant melodies. The motif persists and now it is only one violin, together with sporadic cello statements. A pastoral feeling comes over the work, but, although tainted by the dissonant nature of the violins, is still very peaceful. A pause leads us back to the opening motif and the violins are just so sparse. A lonely violin carries the music to a conclusion.

The opening of the final movement fits with the preceding sounds – soft violins with the occasional cello presence. Again, atonality prevails, but it is measured. A violin motif suggests a tempo, which, after a time, is taken up by the ensemble. It is a most enchanting passage, as the violins dance over and around the viola and cello. It slowly retreats to a lone violin, way up in the high register, which is joined by the second violin. The cello repeats a familiar phrase a number of times and it's all over.

To me, this is very melancholic music. I happen to like the European style from 1900-1950, and these quartets fit squarely into that genre. They may not suit everyone's taste.

The review CD, titled *Rawsthorne: Four String Quartets*, on the ASV label and performed by The Flesch Quartet, includes the unpublished work. There is also a Naxos CD, which contains the first three quartets. Both versions are available on Amazon US and UK.

The CD is on Spotify and several quartets are on YouTube. The First Quartet is on earsense.

Listenability: Melancholy and mildly atonal. You would have to be in the mood for this one, but definitely worth a listen.

— ooOoo —

Max Reger [1873–1916]

Nationality: German
Quartets: Five
Style: Early Modern

String Quartet No. 3

I heard someone recently offer an opinion that German composer Max Reger had written a string quartet which pointed the way from Late Romanticism to Contemporary Modernism. This particular work, String Quartet No. 3 in D minor, Opus 74, was completed in 1904. Just to put things into perspective, Schoenberg's revolutionary String Quartet No. 1, was completed in 1905, a year later. With my interest piqued, I was prepared to give it a solid listen as I had never heard any of Reger's Quartets before. This work is in four movements. The first and third are long, and the core of the work. The second and fourth are relatively brief.

The first movement is wonderful – it surprised me. It is rich with melodies, some that look back to Beethoven and Brahms. However there are many passages that look forward to the new sounds of the twentieth century. It has a melancholy and ambience that is not of its time, leaving Brahms and Beethoven to look on. The movement opens with a moment of dissonance, then breaks into several gentle melodic phrases, before moving through many changes of mood. These contain some of the sweetest of melodies you could find, bound together with rich chordal harmonies. Nearing the end, it touches on the opening dissonance, then finishes with a Romantic flourish.

The short second movement has a jaunty, dance quality. It moves along for about two minutes before it segues into a slow, melancholy passage. This is followed by a quick recapitulation and it's all over.

I found the long third movement a little disappointing at first. Now having listened to it several times, I'm beginning to warm to it. It starts with a pastoral feeling but soon becomes dramatic. It evokes Brahms to me and shows no evidence of any modern characteristics. Many melodic themes are presented and developed, at various tempos. It is most satisfying.

The last movement is another jaunty outing as it moves briskly through some chords. A brief slow melody follows, but not for long as it soon resumes its journey with contrasting periods of slow and moderate tempos. Albeit conservative, this is positive, enjoyable music.

So where does that leave me in considering the direction and style of this work? I'd have to say that I'm slightly ambivalent. The first movement is absolutely enthralling, full of twists and turns and some charming melodies. It has some modern sounds that are beautiful – I love it. The two short movements are attractive although conservative. The long third movement holds its own. Is it at all modern? Yes, the first movement definitely has elements that are not of the nineteenth century. Having said that, the other movements are conservative – I must try Reger's other quartets.

This work is available on a single CD, and on a 3-CD Complete Quartets set on CPO, performed by the Berner String Quartet, at Amazon US and UK. It is worth noting that it is mainly referred to as Opus 74.

Only string quartet Opus 109 is on my Spotify. Some of the quartets – but not No. 3, are available on YouTube. There are two recordings of No. 3, together with some others, on earsense.

Listenability: Slightly enigmatic, but ultimately a successful work.

[Image courtesy CPO label]

— ooOoo —

Terry Riley [born 1953]

Nationality: American
Quartets: At least twelve
Style: Contemporary

Salome Dances for Peace

Terry Riley first made an impression on the music scene with his famous and influential early <u>minimalist</u> work, *In C*, recorded in 1964. He met Kronos Quartet member David Harrington at Mills College in the early 1970s and has since composed over a dozen works for that quartet.

Salome Dances for Peace was written in 1989, specifically for Kronos. Conceptually it appears to be based on a new age mythical theme. I can't find any references to the biblical account of Salome dancing, either spiritually or aurally in the work, or the movement titles.

The quartet consists of five named suites: *Anthem of the Great Spirit, Conquest of the War Demons, The Gift, The Ecstasy* and *Good Medicine.* These suites each consist of a number of named movements.

I am going to discuss the first suite, *Anthem of the Great Spirit,* which runs for about 40 minutes.

The Summons – The movement opens with a sparse, solemn, almost rubato statement, using an ethnic scale. The theme is a series of long notes which are played by all four instruments in unison, to a striking effect. Even the timbre of the sound is strange, similar to a snake-charmer's pungi, which is an Indian wind instrument. After a time, it moves into tempo and the quartet take up their traditional roles of solo violin with cello in support. You find yourself walking through a Moroccan market and can almost smell the hashish...

Peace Dance – Surprisingly, given that it is based on the title of the work, it begins peacefully, muted, offhand even. The first five minutes of this movement is a restrained mood of quiet, abstract motifs – there is no rhythm here. Then the cello makes its move with a long, ascending melody that is breathtaking. After this brief interlude, the volume drops and the music takes us to a marketplace again, albeit in a different place to *The Summons*. To conclude, we have a return to the opening – muted and restrained. This is the longest movement in the suite, at eleven minutes.

Fanfare in the Minimal Kingdom – Underpinned by a rhythmic motif, this begins as a tour de force for the cello. As the passage continues, the movement briefly pauses, before breaking into agitation. This contrasting pattern continues throughout until it moves into a pizzicato section to conclude.

Ceremonial Night Race – The introduction is quiet and the composer uses micro-tones, which are the notes between the notes. They work particularly well on non-fretted stringed instruments such as the violin, viola and cello, giving the music a slightly out of tune ethnic quality. Then follows a brief period of chaos before a return to the opening. As the melodies unfold, the micro-tones are just superb. The end comes as a short period of chaos. What a fabulous movement.

At the Ancient Aztec Corn Races Salome Meets Wild Talker – Features another quiet micro-tone introduction which is maintained to the conclusion. It is a beguiling movement, not morose, but not far off.

More Ceremonial Races – This unbelievably short 50-second movement is aggressive, particularly for the violinists. It is worth noting that the CD tracks run together so that the timid ending of the previous movement thrusts you straight into this one, leading to an incredible contrast.

Old Times at the Races – Beginning with a repeated motif and a wonderful cello part – it sometimes sounds like a double bass, as it goes so low. Midway through the piece the tempo is quickened and it descends into chaos. It slowly drifts back to the opening motif and closes with a fade, the first one that I've noticed. It gives one second of silence before launching into the next movement.

Half Wolf Dances Mad in Moonlight – Fortunately, we have that one second break as this movement also has a frenzied opening. It is sustained for a time until it moves into a conversational mode – again the cello is magnificent. Storm clouds gather as it nears the finish and slowly fades out to completion.

And that's just the first suite. I find this to be a pretty amazing piece, sometimes challenging, mostly just interesting. I wouldn't want to hear it every day, but I would call it a great piece of music.

This album was originally issued on vinyl and runs for just under two hours. It's extremely rare to find an LP with a thirty minute side. They were really pushing the technical boundaries of records when they pressed this one.

Just a small point. Cellist Joan Jeanrenaud left the Kronos Quartet nearly twenty years ago. She will be, and has been, sadly missed. Her playing was just so integral to their sound.

I don't think that anyone else has recorded this work but the Kronos Quartet version on the Elektra/Nonesuch label is still freely available on Amazon US and UK. You can even have the vinyl edition for a king's ransom.

It can be found on Spotify and you can hear some of *Salome Dances* on YouTube.

Listenability: Rewarding, and probably not as difficult as I may have made it sound.

— oo0oo —

Guy Ropartz [1864–1955]

Nationality: Breton
Quartets: Six
Style: Early Modern

String Quartets Nos. 4 & 5

Ropartz's six string quartets were composed from 1893 to 1949, yet, for me they show no evidence of stylistic development, or for that matter, any stylistic influences. Here is a man with a personal style, which is to be admired. I shall discuss quartets Nos. 4 and 5.

The Fourth Quartet starts with a flourish but soon moves into a period of strong melodic statements. These are particularly attractive – with the music conservative, but elegant. The violins negotiate several harmonic changes as they constantly put forward positive melodies. It does, in some ways, feel like the kind of music that one would write when raised in a small locale, as Ropartz was. Towards the end, the melodies have a poignancy not previously noticed.

332

A pizzicato line introduces the second movement, which allows the violins to fashion rustic melodies. There is an intensity here that is not in the first movement. A pause reintroduces some marvellous melodies, leading to a double-time rhythm, which is exhilarating. Again, as we approach the end, it has a feeling all of its own, with the cello leading to a slight, but effective arpeggio. After a brief melodic phrase, the movement ends on a flourish.

The third movement is slow, and commences with a probing cello, coupled with a searching violin line. The cello continues as the violins tease out beautiful overlapping melodies, with minimal accompaniment. The interplay between the violins and cello is terrific. Now the cello feeds out short phrases, allowing the violins to meander – the cello is wonderful here. Slowly the intensity drops, leading to a conclusion.

The final, short movement is energised, and the cello follows the lead of the violins, with discrete phrases. The violins continue with brisk melodies that abound with joy, and there is a constant dialogue with the cello. The end approaches with haste and again ends on a flourish.

The Fifth Quartet opens with a brief sense of dissonance, but this is dissolved in an instant. The violins construct a rhythmic passage which eventually settles into a rubato feeling. A playful period follows and the composer's characteristic melodies come into their own. A prolonged section of busy melodies, made up of short notes, gives way to a stasis. Here the melodies are refined, and they drop in intensity altogether, as they move towards a peaceful conclusion.

A brief second movement, marked adagio, is a relief from the previous activity. It is quite precious, as the violins interact with the cello. It ceases on a chord at 1:47, which also happens to be the length of the fourth movement.

The third movement opens in a positive manner, which is now becoming a familiar pattern. The violins are expressive here before they are interrupted by a slowing of the tempo, featuring one violin lamenting, as the ensemble responds in kind. Suddenly, the bright feeling returns and the violins become loud as they stretch out in an emphatic manner. A cello interlude closes the movement.

The next movement, as previously stated, is brief and also at an adagio tempo. This is most tender, and the cello contributes beguiling phrases, as the violins craft long melodies. It is so short, it seems to be over before it started, while leaving you wanting more.

The final movement is again positive, and violins float over an intermittent pizzicato backing. The melodies are more stately than I had noticed before, and they have much to offer. The composer's unique style is definitely on show here. A more measured mood is established but does not last. Again, melodic movement prevails and the end is a joyous one, with a flourish from the violins.

The Ropartz string quartets are on a series of three CDs by the Stanislas Quartet on the Timpani label. The review copy is titled *Ropartz String Quartets*

Volume 2, and all three discs are available on Presto Classical and Amazon US, but not UK, which tells me that these discs are not long for this world.

All of the quartets are on Spotify and earsense while many quartet movements are on YouTube.

Listenability: Uniquely personal and mostly joyful, with a touch of melancholy.

— oo0oo —

John Rose [born 1928]

Nationality: British
Quartets: Two
Style: Contemporary

String Quartets Nos. 1 & 2

John Rose's two string quartets are both one movement works, each lasting over twenty minutes.

String Quartet No. 1 opens softly with two violins. A dissonant chord doesn't do anything to change the status quo – the two violins remain focussed on their melodic development. Eventually the ensemble gathers forces but keeps the same slightly dissonant atmosphere – it is gentle music. A pause brings about a more dominant violin and a stronger melody. This is carried along with some fine work from the cello as it moves to the centre of the sound. At around four minutes, the piece becomes energised and transforms into a dance feeling which is constantly subjected to variations. It is ever so mildly chaotic, with overlapping melodies to the fore. This is sustained for around six minutes and probably overstays its welcome.

The two violins introduce a more propulsive nature for a time and then drift back into a dance again. With pizzicato accompaniment, the texture is light. A new passage ensues with a call and response between the instruments before a new motif takes over – it's constantly changing and the violins continue to paint their images. Now the tempo stops and there is a rubato dialogue. A solo violin makes a statement, soon to be joined by the second violin as the cello sweeps in to provide a harmonic backdrop. The tempo returns and a few shaky chords are heard as the violins return to their dialogue. The music is propelled forward as we near the end – the violins gradually lift in intensity and with a flourish, we have a conclusion.

Most of Rose's compositions were completed late in his life – the above quartet being composed in 1997. I find this work to be conservative in the light of that date.

The Second Quartet was composed in 1999 and begins with a lamenting violin melody, together with a sustained cello and a wandering second violin. Now the full ensemble enters at a measured pace as contrasting cello lines provide interest, complementing the meandering violins. The cello briefly moves into a rhythmic motif, then has a moment of development before returning to the motif. The music moves effortlessly between these two cello patterns until it settles on a fast motif, with the violins just keeping up. More dialogue occurs and the mood starts to become a little feisty – there is plenty of forward movement here, together with several harmonic changes. The cello exchanges rhythmic phrases with the violins until the violins conclude.

A new phase of slight abstraction appears as cello and violins engage again in their dialogue. Now we have another solo violin statement breaking the mood which, as in the previous quartet, probably goes on for a bit long with minimal interest. Joined by the second violin, the sound becomes thoughtful – then the cello enters. It is a beguiling piece of writing, with a lot of music going on. Suddenly everything stops. A creeping feeling develops as the ensemble examines a new soundscape. The music is laced with tension as it struggles to sustain this atmosphere, which is maintained to the end.

Again, I find this quartet to be quite conservative – I believe the composer is just writing in the style that he developed through his long life.

There are also three solo piano pieces on this disc, two *Preludes and Fugues* and *An Essay on DSCH*, which was Dimitri Shostakovich's musical moniker. In German it represents the notes D, E-flat, C and B. More information can be found on Wikipedia. Presumably the piece used that phrase at some point. To be honest I didn't listen to the piano pieces so I have no opinion.

Back to the string quartets. The review CD is on the Divine Art Records label titled *Rose: String Quartets 1 & 2*, performed by The Edinburgh Quartet. It is freely available on Amazon US and UK.

These two quartets can be found on Spotify, earsense and YouTube.

Listenability: These works sound older than they are and quite conservative – with a hint of Shostakovich.

Hilding Rosenberg [1892–1985]

Nationality: Swedish
Quartets: Fifteen
Style: Early Modern

String Quartet No. 1

Rosenberg's First String Quartet, written in 1920, was premiered in 1923. The composer was definitely looking to express himself in an Early Modern fashion as, at the time, he had fallen under the spell of Schoenberg. The reaction to the performance was extraordinarily negative. The local press had a field day, one paper apparently stating that the music '*sounded like a chaotic and horrifying vision, a vision, indeed, of a mentally deranged person!*' As a result, the composer withdrew it and did not return to it again for over 30 years, when he revised it in 1955. It was then performed in 1956 for Swedish National Radio.

This piece has one of the most uplifting openings I have heard. The opening movement, which lasts for seven minutes, begins in a light, joyful manner, offering nothing that would point to the style of its later movements. It then moves into a lament. The chords hang like a waterfall, in a manner similar to some of Charles Ives' works. It's as if you could reach out and touch them, they are so close and shimmering. Then the tempo quickens and slightly dissonant melodies begin to reappear. They come in cascades, and in a flash, it's all over.

The second movement, marked andante, starts with a slow fugue. It is nearly one minute before all four instruments have made their entry, and is a wonderfully melancholic section. Slowly the tempo picks up and the cello dominates for a while, before returning to the first violin. Following are more of those hanging chords, though their texture makes them a little farther away this time. They eventually fade into nothing.

The third and fourth movements are played without a pause. They begin in a lively manner, the cello being particularly conspicuous. As it builds, I believe I hear a quote from Grieg's *Peer Gynt Suite*. Now the tempo drops for a short time, folk melodies abound, with more rhythm, then less, then more again. The fugue theme from the previous movement comes again, played in double-time. Vigorous statements continue until, like the first movement, it just stops.

This is a lovely first quartet, full of wonderful melodies and sparkling rhythms. It makes me wonder what all the fuss was about in 1923.

The recording I have is on the Caprice label, and also includes Quartets Nos. 6 & 12 which are a lot more modern, with some wonderful slow periods, together with some slightly dissonant passages. Each quartet is played by a different ensemble.

Caprice issued Rosenberg's Complete Quartets as a 6-CD pack, with the last disc containing bonus material. I once saw it in Tower Records in Singapore and should have picked it up then. The five individual discs are still available separately but I don't think they will be around for much longer. When stocks run out...

I just had a quick look at Spotify and they have three of the CDs, but not this one. There are many Rosenberg quartets on earsense and the first quartet is available on YouTube.

Listenability: A wonderful first quartet.

String Quartet No. 4

Rosenberg is one of my favourite string quartet composers. He has a unique style, sounding nothing like his Scandinavian contemporaries. His style transcends Modernism and he goes about his own way, mostly eschewing the Modernist trappings of anger and vast dynamic ranges. He has a distinctive method of harmonising duet violin lines which leads to some interesting sounds. The later quartets exhibit dissonance and a high level of abstraction.

I am going to discuss String Quartet No. 4, a brilliant composition, which is much more introspective than No. 1, and rather moving. It is in four movements, with the second being the emotional centrepiece of the work.

The quartet opens with a short solo violin statement, before it moves into a tempo. As this happens, the violin establishes an attractive melody. There is a brief conversational section with the cello and violin in dialogue. A succession of flourishes follow until the previous melody returns. Now a lively passage has the violins taking the lead and a wonderful harmonised violin line brings a conclusion.

The second movement opens with an incredibly plaintive melody which forms the basis of that which follows. A slight variation on the melody brings the other instruments into play. There is another solo violin statement before the other instruments start to fall into line, producing a much stronger tempo. Suddenly a hectic violin-led march tempo is introduced, then repeated. Now we are back to the introduction as the viola and violin work the same opening melody. This is subtle, as the violins drift in and out. The opening melody is continued with the full ensemble, and there is a wonderful passage as the cello converses with the violin. The introspection here is profound, and beautiful – it is writing of the highest order. Previous themes begin to re-emerge and we even have the cello stating the opening theme. The violins skip lightly across the surface. The end comes with a solo cello playing the theme.

The next movement has a march-like sound. The violin plays a strangely static melody but it eventually develops into something more varied before a cello phrase changes the tempo and the music starts to race before returning to the opening. This time however, it is a lot more intense. The march-like tempo continues and still references the opening melody. There is a slight flourish which leads to the completion.

The finale begins in a strong manner and yet it is only two violins. Eventually the ensemble merges and strengthens the tempo before we have a return to the feeling of the two violins. It is energised for a time – then the intensity drops and the violins meander over a cello phrase. As the end approaches, the energy returns with the violins being particularly prominent. This doesn't last and the two violins lead to a propulsive conclusion.

This is wonderful music. The second movement in particular has some fine moments. If you want a Rosenberg CD, I suggest now is the time as stocks are running out.

My review CD also includes Quartet No. 7, together with a set of miniatures *Six Moments Musicaux*. Both quartets and the *Six Moments* are played by different ensembles. This disc is available on Amazon US but not on UK, although they do have other discs of his complete quartets.

It is also on Spotify and all four movements are available on YouTube. As previously mentioned, there are many Rosenberg quartets on earsense.

Listenability: Scandinavian heaven.

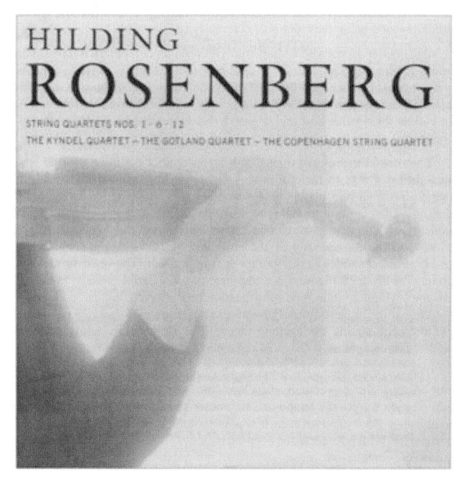

[Image Caprice label - could not be contacted]

Arnold Rosner [born 1945]

Nationality: American
Quartets: Six
Style: Contemporary

String Quartets Nos. 2 & 5

Apparently many of Rosner's compositions were influenced by his original Jewish beliefs, but also later, by Catholicism – thanks, Wiki. I shall allude to that concept later. Both String Quartets Nos. 2 and 5 are one movement works.

The Second Quartet was written in 1963, and revised in 1993.It opens with a resonant, reflective cello line. As the other instruments enter, a melancholy fugal texture evolves. A chordal background allows the cello to answer and there is harmonic change. A series of rhythmic chords follows, and quivering violins allow the cello to make a substantial melodic statement. After a time the music drops back into a pastoral feeling which is fetching. A solo violin gently investigates a melody, over a peaceful harmonic background.

Now the harmonies disappear, leading to a modal atmosphere. All instruments come together to create open melodic lines with a mood that is again peaceful. There is also movement, as the violins create a dance-like flavour at a moderate tempo before an interjection of four chords is followed by a return to the dance. The melodies are more serious now, and also more rhythmically incisive. This feeling doesn't last for long however, and it leads into an extended, reflective episode. Eventually, a tempo is established and the music almost becomes folk-like, but for the intensity that inevitably takes over.

A pause brings a period of slightly dissonant chords, leading to several solo cello statements with the music becoming ever so quiet, and a violin rises high into the sky with minimal accompaniment – what a beautiful sound. Slowly, the intensity rises, before dissolving back into another pastoral phase. A light sense of dissonance colours the music, and a slightly orchestral passage brings forth lamenting melodies. A cello leads the violins to a faded conclusion.

String Quartet No. 5 was written in 1977, so, in a sense, it is earlier than the revised Second Quartet. It begins in a modal form, with one chord introducing a solo violin, soon to be joined by a second. This is an incredibly profound passage as the cello makes a pensive melodic statement and there is no tempo to be found, just pure atmosphere. It does have a sense of the spiritual, with the two violins expressing gently via the modal scale. Another solo cello statement occurs – this too, stays within the mode. An ascending and descending theme seems to be building, before being interrupted by a solo violin.

Suddenly there is rhythm and harmonic movement as the first violin moves with the harmonies, and fashions a recurring phrase that cries out, again, this is wonderfully introspective. The modal feeling returns and the violin expresses a melody while the cello inserts random notes. Now we have rhythm once more, and the violin sounds modal as the harmonic changes are rare.

Another rhythmic tempo ensues, with rapier-like ensemble interjections and a period of strong chords drops back into a section of a searching violin over a pizzicato viola. The modal feeling persists, and gentle violin statements carry the work forward. A more complex moment arises, and the tension between the violins is palpable. A phrase develops and the violins play with strength, with the ensemble pushing out chords in a serious manner. At this point, the intensity drops, but the tempo remains – we are back to harmonic movement, and the first violin swirls above a striking accompaniment. The violin picks up on a melodic phrase and repeats it to a faded close.

These are basically peaceful works. Emotionally, they are governed by the persistent use of a modal approach. Even when changes in harmony occur, the melodies do not necessarily embrace the changes, as one might expect. For me, the pieces are contemplative, but apart from the moments mentioned specifically, I didn't feel that they were overtly spiritual. Of course, they may have been spiritually inspired.

Along with String Quartet No. 3 and a *Duet for Violas*, this music is on a CD titled *Chamber Music of Arnold Rosner, Vol. 2*, performed by the Ad Hoc String Quartet on Albany Records. It is available on Amazon US and UK.

The complete CD is on earsense and YouTube.

Listenability: Basically introspective, with an occasional rhythmic edge. Conservative for its time.

— ooOoo —

Miklós Rózsa [1907–1995]

Nationality: Hungarian
Quartets: Three
Style: Early Modern

String Quartets Nos. 1 & 2

Rózsa's first quartet was not approved for publication, and although a manuscript exists, he never included it in his list of works. Thus we are left with two string quartets, both in four movements.

The First Quartet opens with a solo cello moving into a fugue. It features a light and breezy subject, in a very attractive section. This becomes quite busy, led by the violins before moving into a lamenting passage with both violins prominent. The cello interjects and a violin picks up on the phrase to establish a tempo with the viola pressing the music forward while the cello and violins take up the challenge. After a short rhythmic phase, the calm returns with a salient cello. Moving towards the end, the sound is most graceful.

The next movement starts in an agitated manner, with propulsive violins. A trill from the cello leads to a tempo taking over as the music becomes a little chaotic. This emphatic mood moves into a cello motif, then the violins are set free to duet briefly, before a passage in half-tempo ensues. The duet returns, with a call and response between the violins and a single pizzicato note leads into an attractive fade.

The third movement, marked lento, is in a longing mood as one of the violins plays in a low register, while the other is much higher. There is an ethnic sounding modal moment – this is very beautiful. A mournful phrase becomes prominent and is picked up by all of the instruments before a tempo commences and there is gentle chaos which lingers for a while. The violins collect themselves, and we have a striking fragment which fades to nothing. A solo violin is gradually joined by another and the cello offers support in a most appealing way. There is no rhythm here, just two sparse violins. It all ends on a cello beat – what a fascinating movement.

The final movement starts in an aggressive fashion, with strong rhythms to support it. The violins again engage in a conversation – this seems to be a characteristic of Rózsa and many instances are to be found in these works. Now the cello joins in and we have a slightly anguished but enjoyable atmosphere. The opening rhythmic pattern returns and now the conversation includes the cello. There is a lot going on here with the violins creating some strong rhythmic statements. The work ends with an ascending motif leading to a flourish, which is a sparkling conclusion to a fine piece.

The Second Quartet opens on a sharp chord and soon moves into atonality. The ensemble pauses, leading to a return of the violins and gradually the ensemble re-enters. This is taut music, pushing the extremes of tonality. There is a slight easing of texture for a time until the tension returns. Another slightly chaotic mood ensues, but it is not without its attractions. Abruptly, a solo cello plucks a few notes and it ends on a chord.

The next movement starts with a slow, sparse, intangible flavour, seemingly both happy and sad at the same time. The mood is broken by a pulsating rhythm and the violins interlock into a motif. The cello leads the piece back into sparse territory and each member takes turns in solo melodic statements. The violin is in the high register and the music becomes dissonant as it fades.

The third movement begins with a recurring cello motif which gives impetus to the violin lines. Things are slightly hectic in this short movement as the solo cello glides over pizzicato violins and the music becomes almost rhapsodic. However, it won't settle and concludes with a series of atonal notes.

The finale sounds modern with a lot going on until it segues into a cello motif, which anchors a violin conversation. For a brief time, the cello is silent and the violins continue their duet. The music then turns to into a lilting, introspective phase. A key change heightens the effect and a sense of chaos ensues before the cello finds its voice and we reach a sustained climax. A long, ascending, frenetic phrase leads us to the final chord.

341

These are fine works, with some beautiful writing. I was particularly taken by the many violin duets – they really give character to the music.

The quartets are available in at least two versions, both available on Amazon US and UK. My review CD is titled *The Two String Quartets* by the Flesch Quartet on the ASV label, which also contains a *Sonata for Two Violins*. There is another version, on Naxos titled *String Quartets 1 & 2 – String Trio* by the Tippett Quartet.

These works are available on Spotify, YouTube and earsense.

Listenability: Wonderfully performed mid-twentieth century quartet.

[Image courtesy ASV Digital Records via Universal Music]

Albert Roussel [1869–1937]

Nationality: French
Quartets: One – FOSQC
Style: Late Romantic

The String Quartet

Roussel's single string quartet is in four movements and is fairly lively, with three movements featuring an allegro tempo.

This work opens with an ever so slightly dissonant mood, quite rhythmic, which is soon transformed into a charming, free-flowing section. The violin is very lyrical while the ensemble provides all manner of musical colour in accompaniment. A recapitulation of an earlier theme ensues, but the intensity soon drops, allowing the violin to craft a serious melody for a time, followed by cello and ensemble interjections. Now the violin returns to lyrical and is a little serious as it reconsiders an earlier melody. The accompaniment becomes quite hectic with strong rhythmic statements from the ensemble. It ends on one of these statements.

The next movement, an adagio, develops a classic Romantic feeling from the start. A poignant violin melody leads into an even more poignant ensemble, bringing about a slightly pastoral feeling, which is very European. The first violin expresses a soft melody while the ensemble can scarcely be heard, it's merely a harmonic drone. Now the cello steps forward to contribute its own variation on the mood. The music is just so sparse, until the violins lift in intensity for the first time in this movement. They soon return to the default subdued feeling, and the violins fade to a close.

The third movement begins in a jaunty, loping manner as the violins happily exchange melodic ideas. A section of pizzicato provides interest until a change comes over the piece. A serious moment leads to a return of the opening moments to conclude. This is a very short movement.

The finale opens with a solo violin, soon to be joined by a second – then the ensemble enters. This is a strange mood, moderately intense, but there doesn't appear to be a tempo. A brief pause leads to a solo violin conveying a lamenting melody over a measured, but scurrying ensemble. There is a lot of pleasant chaos going on, and the cello institutes a passage of chordal interjections. This movement features many changes of emphasis and texture, as it leads the listener through various moods. A very brisk moment has the violins conversing, and a pizzicato cello has a brief role to play before it ends on a sharp chord.

It seems that this work is not particularly popular but it is featured 27 times on Amazon UK. The obvious version to recommend is by the Via Nova Quartet on the Warner Classics APEX label, which also contains the string quartets of Chausson and Magnard who are also members of the French One String Quartet Club, which I believe I have almost exhausted by now. I previously discussed both Chausson and Magnard.

This disc is on Spotify, and versions can also be found on earsense and YouTube.

Listenability: Quite a conservative work for its time. Very pleasant.

— ooOoo —

Edmund Rubbra [1901–1986]

Nationality: British
Quartets: Four
Style: Contemporary Modern

A Master of Abstraction
String Quartets Nos. 1-4

Sir Edmund Rubbra's four string quartets were usually written about 15 years apart, so he had a lot of time to think about the next one. He is a master of intangible feelings that take you somewhere you've not been before. This permeates throughout the quartets. I intend to briefly discuss all four quartets.

String Quartet No. 1 is a very strong first quartet. Rubbra is capable of creating long melodies and the opening has many fine examples. These melodies are evident from the start, leading into the murky waters of his developed themes. The second movement, which is long, opens with a lament, featuring solo violin accompanied only by the cello. Then a repeated motif really drives the movement forward. The volume and the theme intensify before drifting into a beautiful tranquil place – this is wonderfully evocative. The composer is able to sustain this for many minutes. Now all four instruments come together in a serious manner before drifting to an appealing conclusion. The third and final movement starts optimistically at a vivace tempo which is sustained, with constant dense interplay, continuing to the end.

String Quartet No. 2 is in four movements. The mysterious opening gives way to a powerful section. There is a recurring motif that drives this movement forward. After a time, the writing becomes dense and orchestral, before returning to pure melodies, which drift until the end.

String Quartet No. 3 is in three movements and opens with a haunting, lyrical melody – it has already taken me somewhere as I write these words. The first movement becomes almost orchestral as all of the instruments soar to the top of their range, making for a shimmering sound. It's another one of those – you can reach out and touch it moments. It continues this before descending into a dissonance to conclude. The second movement is an adagio with emotional links to the Beethoven Late Quartets. Brilliant harmonies support the first violin, and the cello is also salient as a source of melody. The third and last movement is up-tempo and brief – it represents Rubbra at his most pastoral.

String Quartet No. 4 is dedicated to the memory of a friend who had recently died. Containing only two movements, it commences in an appealing manner as the melodies, in my mind, evoke a walk through a forest. There are many gentle stops upon the way and manifold little skips and it is surprisingly uplifting. It ends on one of these positive moments. The second movement is a singularly beautiful tribute to the lost friend. The mood is consistent throughout, with long heartfelt melodies. It is somewhat reminiscent of the sound of Arvo Pärt, although it was written many years before Pärt became prominent.

For me, Quartets Nos. 1 and 2 are simpler and slightly more approachable than Nos. 3 and 4 but ultimately, they are all magnificent. I find it amazing that Rubbra can conjure up so many fascinating soundscapes. No wonder he was knighted.

Regarding availability, I have these four works on a 2-CD set by the Sterling String Quartet on Conifer Classics and can recommend them. Naxos have a set of Nos. 1, 3 and 4, performed by the Maggini Quartet. Both versions are available on Amazon US and UK.

The Naxos is on Spotify and some of Rubbra's quartets on earsense and YouTube.

Listenability: A wonderful set of quartets in a British Modernist style.

[Image Conifer Classics – Could not be contacted]

Elena Ruehr [born 1963]

Nationality: American
Quartets: At least six
Style: Contemporary

String Quartet No. 4

Ruehr's total musical output is quite varied in style, especially the string quartets. I have chosen a middle-term work for discussion.

The Fourth Quartet opening movement, titled *Sonata*, begins in a mysterious manner – sporadic violin lines are played with a strong tremolo attack on the notes, making it sound a little electronic. The music soon settles into a pizzicato rhythmic motif which, when joined by the cello, becomes a full-blown ostinato with various violin melodies expressed. A dramatic moment ensues with percussive, rhythmic chordal interjections. The ostinato continues and a solo cello phrase evokes the opening tremolo effect, this time applied to a chordal passage. Gradually the music develops into a lamenting mood, with stark violin lines, before moving back into the ostinato. Again there is drama with strong melodies in abundance as dissonance prevails. The end comes with a slowly pulsing pizzicato cello.

There is no pause leading into the next movement, *Aria*, which features a violin using various micro-tones and glissandos to express a deep sense of sadness over a droning accompaniment. Melodically, the lines are modal, taking their cues from the drone – this is a wonderfully melancholic passage, sounding slightly ethnic. Eventually the cello enters, with more ostinato, but the violins now combine to emphasise the ethnic nature of the music. A rising intensity further develops a Middle-Eastern mood. Unusually, the music just stops with a few cursory pizzicato cello notes.

The third movement, *Minuet*, opens gently rhythmical, in a strange time signature. Soon the rhythms become powerful and loud, until they return to the mellow feeling. As the music unfolds, it continually oscillates between the mellow and the powerful, while the harmony also moves regularly, leading to a subsequent change in the melodic material – the modality is long gone. As the music rises and falls, the rhythmic flavour persists through the various sections and continues until an abrupt ending.

Finale features an opening flourish, before settling into a dynamic ostinato which serves as a grounding for the violins to craft long melodies. Again the rhythmic intensity comes and goes, sometimes there are quite dramatic thrusts – at other times, pensive melodies are heard. As the music progresses the strong motifs seem to predominate. Occasionally, moments of morose, harmonised violin lines are heard, but the almost inevitable thrusts return. Nearing the end, an extended melodic passage unfolds, again hinting at an ethnic feeling. The conclusion is a flurry of quivering, sustained violin tones.

This piece seems slightly unusual. The first two movements are very melodic, while the last two have rhythm at their core. The First Quartet is a bit similar – it features three rhapsodic movements while the finale is very assertive and powerful. The Third Quartet almost sounds medieval to these ears and, mostly very light and positive.

The above three works are all contained on the review CD, *How She Danced: String Quartets of Elena Ruehr* on the Cypress Performing Arts Association label by the Cypress String Quartet. There is also a 2-CD set, *Elena Ruehr: Six String Quartets* on Avie Records, by the Borromeo Quartet & Cypress Quartet, which I presume has the same versions as the review disc, combined with new recordings. These can both be found on Amazon US and UK.

All of the music can be heard on Spotify, YouTube and earsense.

Listenability: A varied mixture of Contemporary styles.

— ooOoo —

Russian String Quartets – Compilation

Nationality: Russian
Quartets: Five
Style: Various 20th Century

This CD contains music by a disparate selection of five Russian composers. I have selected the two longest works to discuss.

Elena Firsova [born 1950] has written at least twelve string quartets, most of which have never been recorded. Her fourth, titled *Amoroso* (Loving) from 1989, is in one movement.

A quiet, sustained chord opens the work and several other softly, sustained slightly atonal chords follow. The first violin begins to express a melody containing long tones and the second violin complements it. With the ensemble in full voice the melodies become slightly confronting, but only for a time. A return to the opening feeling is wonderful, leading to a passage for the two violins which has an intangible beauty all of its own. The cello entrance initiates a tension with the violins moving into a brief agitated moment. Pizzicato notes follow, over a sustained cello tone leading to a return to another ambient atmosphere as the violins drift peacefully, this time in a tonal manner – what a fascinating soundscape. An increase in tension and a tonal ambiguity develop, as the violins bring forth torrid melodic lines. Atonal violin thrusts are quite aggressive, with many glissandos before a brief pizzicato section is followed by a pause. Now the opening mood is recreated with soft, shrill violins combining with strange harmonies and the viola and cello offer up atonal mutterings as the tension begins to rise again. With the end approaching, the tension recedes and

347

leads to an almost inaudible fluttering violin to conclude. This is a fascinating, other-worldly piece.

Dmitri Nikolaevich Smirnov [born 1948] has written at least eight quartets, but again, most of them have not been recorded. I am going to discuss String Quartet No. 2, from 1985, which is in two movements.

A dominant violin leads the ensemble into this work, in a rather vague manner. Some agitation follows and there is a scurrying of violins. This has a very modern feeling as string sound effects are superimposed onto the violin's dissonant lines and there are several conversations going on simultaneously. A pause brings about a peace, based on a cello drone as the violin makes bird sound assertions. The second violin adds to the harmonic background with slow, interesting melodies. Another pause doesn't change the sound, except perhaps making it a little quieter. The end is a wispy solo violin statement.

The second movement commences very sparsely with a violin expressing long tones over an occasional pizzicato cello. Another violin and a viola join in the accompaniment, with the mood still being retained. Slowly the first violin edges into its high register, supported by the second violin. The mood is delicate and a harmonised melody begins to develop – this brings a feeling of great depth and emotion. The mood now becomes more rhythmic, but the sound is still very measured. A return to the sparsity is quite precious as a long solo violin section unfolds before the ensemble enter again, all the while retaining the sensitive feeling. Nearing the end, there is a slight fluttering of a violin but it concludes with a handful of solo violin tones.

The review CD, *Russian String Quartets*, on the RCA Catalyst label and performed by the Chilingirian Quartet also contains brief works by Igor Stravinsky and Alfred Schnittke, together with a fascinating rhythmic piece by Nikolai Roslavets, a composer I intend to discuss in a future edition. The music has been on two separate releases, one of which is still available on Amazon UK. It is download only at Amazon US and Presto Classical. There are also several *New and Used* copies at Amazon resellers.

This disc is on Spotify and both of the discussed quartets are on YouTube and earsense.

Listenability: Russian string quartet music in a broad range of styles.

Incidental Images #9

A String Player's Survival Kit

[Image courtesy Sophie Curtis – Sartory String Quartet]

Camille Saint-Saëns [1835–1921]

Nationality: French
Quartets: Two
Style: Romantic

String Quartet No. 1

Firstly, let me quote a little trivia from Wikipedia – '*Saint-Saëns had been composing since the age of three – his mother preserved his early works, and in adult life he was surprised to find them technically competent though of no great musical interest. The earliest surviving piece, dated March 1839, is in the collection of the Paris Conservatoire.*'

I am going to discuss the First Quartet, in E minor, written in 1899, consisting of four movements. The work opens with a stunning solo violin statement, which is soon joined by the ensemble in a gentle manner. The solo violin continues to dominate until, suddenly, we have a rise in intensity and dynamics. This is followed by a virtuosic melodic line, with the ensemble hanging on every note. As the mood is tempered, the cello becomes prominent and engages, first with the violin and then the ensemble, which returns to dominate, until the energy dissipates for a time. Strong harmonised violin lines return and propel the music forward before the cello returns with an alluring statement and dialogues with the violins for a most attractive passage. The violins eventually prevail and a pause ensues. Now a solo violin again leads the ensemble, this time, in a charming folksy manner. The violin here is superb and the cello steps out to complement it – this is ravishing writing. The energy starts to increase and the ensemble finishes with a strong flurry of notes.

A considered melodic violin line commences the next movement, which is marked allegro. The violins parry with each other and the accompaniment is very strong as many sweeping violin lines are to be heard over a positively propulsive ensemble. The dynamics vary many times, from one violin and a cello to pizzicato based sounds. All the while, strong violins dominate, as they constantly return to very rhythmic phrases. Nearing the end, the violins return to this world and gently conclude.

An adagio movement provides welcome relief from the previous energised sections as a solo violin muses over a gentle layer of sound. Now a rhythm ensues and the two violins spar before a solo violin crafts a marvellous mood, which is eventually joined by a restrained ensemble. The music is sparse and stately, as a minimal backing allows the violin to move into a tempo. The backing is still measured, although the violin soars. This section continues for some time and the violin is most appealing in this ambient texture. The cello has a role to play as it changes the feeling, allowing the solo violin to bring about a resolution.

The final movement begins in a more modern, intriguing manner. It soon moves into a violin directing proceedings over a harmonic atmosphere before the violin then leads the ensemble through a jaunty section, where it expresses freely

350

– now we are back into Romantic territory. After a long period of melodic development, the mood becomes subdued and the cello features prominently in reining in the tempo. There is a false ending, then the whole ensemble come together in a brisk tempo to terminate the work.

I must confess to having a weakness for French string quartets, and this one is very elegant. The review CD by the Fine Arts Quartet also contains the Second Quartet. It is on the Naxos label and is available on Amazon US and UK. There are three versions on Spotify, including the Fine Arts, and several versions on YouTube. There are also many fine performances of both quartets on earsense.

Listenability: Another marvellous Romantic French work.

— ooOoo —

Aulis Sallinen [born 1935]
Nationality: Finnish
Quartets: Five
Style: Contemporary Modern

Pushing the Boundaries
String Quartets Nos. 3-5

Sallinen wrote his five string quartets from 1958 to 1983. The CD that I am going to discuss contains all five, but I will be concentrating on Nos. 3, 4 & 5. Nos. 1 & 2 can be difficult at times, although they are still worthwhile pieces. It is significant they were written in his mid-twenties. I think that it is just a case of a young composer trying to be modern and changing his philosophy with the passing of time. It's great if this is so, for many composers have continued on the modern path, some losing their way and crossing the barrier between sound and noise.

Except for String Quartet No. 1, which has three movements, all of the others are named, single movement works.

String Quartet No. 3, titled *Some Aspects of Peltoniemi Hintrikin's Funeral March*, was written in 1969. It opens as a gentle, slightly ethnic sounding march which is attractive and made me look forward to what was coming. This persists with some minor harmonic changes for two minutes and then the pulse becomes more insistent and dissonance starts to appear. It doesn't last, but moves into a pizzicato mode. The opening theme returns and the music wanders as the march disappears revealing gently dissonant violin sounds, which make for an enthralling section as they play variations on the opening theme. Now the tempo quickens and the music becomes conversational. First fast, then slow, now fast again and so on – a dialogue between two different tempos. It then reverts to the opening march theme for a moment until a solo violin takes over, with the cello

351

responding to the violin. The insistent tempo returns for an instant before dissolving into a folk-like melody, again slightly dissonant. Solo cello takes over now, and is then joined by the violins. This is as dissonant as it gets but it doesn't last – it is taken out by a quiet solo cello statement.

String Quartet No. 4, titled *Quiet Songs* – is exactly that. Written in 1971, the opening sounds like a church organ with sparse playing from the quartet. The melody is simple but haunting. It continues in this manner for some three minutes until the cello tries to introduce a pulse, which doesn't persist, but is replaced by an achingly mournful dissonance. A tempo establishes itself, still haunting, a little like a slow Gypsy dance as the cello touches on ethnic folk scales. There is a brief pause and the cello and violin then converse before the violins take the lead, over a soft and slow tempo. Previous segments of music constantly reappear. Suddenly, the piece becomes energised as a violin propels it forward and then, after a time, there is almost a stasis, manifested as a drone with little variation. A slight burst of movement is heard before the piece ends. This is quite a funereal work.

String Quartet No. 5 is titled *Pieces of Mosaic.* Written in 1983, it runs for twenty-four minutes, nearly double the length of all the other works on the CD. The movement opens with violin interjections which transform into a fluttering, abstract, but beguiling soundscape. Soon some rhythmic impetus is felt, with scales not unlike those found in Terry Riley's *Salome Dances for Peace.* European string quartet composers have often gone to folk music for inspiration and so it is here. The tempo quickens and rhythms appear until the music becomes stately, with an occasional hint of chaos. Emphatic passages come to the fore in an extended section until around the 12-minute mark when it all dissolves back into nothing.

Now we have some subtle playing from the violins as they cry out. The loneliness is palpable – it is a desolate soundscape. The ethnic scales continue in this muted moment and, finally a rhythm emerges, albeit a little disjointed, but it does give form to the music. The violin interjections reappear. I keep hearing its similarity to *Salome* but in other ways they are worlds apart. As the piece moves towards a conclusion, the anger of the interjections give way to a morose feeling. It finishes with some quiet violin flourishes.

I feel like I have been through the wringer discussing this piece – there is no joy to be found here. But I believe the music does tell a story – we just don't know what it is. All we have are our imaginations to make sense of such abstraction.

The CD is titled *String Quartets 1-5* and is admirably performed by the Jean Sibelius Quartet on the Ondine label. It is available at Amazon US and UK – I leave it for you to ponder.

It is on Spotify and you can hear many versions of Sallinen pushing the boundaries on YouTube. There are also multiple recordings of all Sallinen's quartets on earsense.

Listenability: This is not easy music, but sometimes I like that.

[Image courtesy Ondine label]

— ooOoo —

Vadim Salmanov [1912–1978]

Nationality: Russian
Quartets: Six
Style: Contemporary Modern

String Quartets Nos. 1 & 2

Salmanov wrote his six quartets from 1945 to 1971. Each is more modern than its predecessor, leading the textures from gentle and sparse to a quite modern No. 6. I am going to discuss his first two efforts.

The First Quartet contains four movements and opens in a minor key with a strong emphasis on chords. When this concludes, two violins enter, then the cello, with the music sparse until a minor key fanfare reintroduces the feeling of

353

the opening – stately with long tones, becoming a bit chaotic with the use of atonal melodies. This continues to the conclusion. It is extremely powerful music.

The second movement is marked allegro and is rhythmic. After a time, it becomes even more so for a brief period before all goes quiet, until the impetus returns. The violins maintain the pace – they are busy. A series of staccato chords leads into a slight chaos as the violins conduct a dialogue. The movement then fades out.

The next movement begins with string sound effects which linger in the air, creating a sparse scene as a lone violin plays over a quiet cello for a time. Finally all of the voices are heard and we have an attractive, sparse, conversational passage. A hint of pizzicato leads into a crescendo and the music remains loud as chords punctuate the air – it is all rather serious. The tension slowly drains away and a lone violin backed with pizzicato produces a wonderful melody. The tempo slows here and the ending is particularly calm. Quite a beguiling movement really.

The final movement, marked allegro, has the violins soaring with string sound effects in abundance. The tempo is brisk and all instruments seem to have an equally important role. The intensity is maintained and leads to the sound of shimmering violins, while the cello is full in tone and plays a significant role. Finally, nearing the end, the music becomes peaceful and a tranquility finishes the work.

There is something mysteriously intangible about this piece for which I cannot seem to find the right words. Oh well.

The Second Quartet is, on the whole, peaceful, and contains many attractive sounds. Beginning with gentle violins, it often moves into the high register. A tempo is introduced and the violins sustain a wonderful atmosphere. After a pause and a brief violin flourish, we have more peace as solo cello converses with the violins, before setting them free again. Suddenly, an intense chordal passage is injected, however it only has a brief part to play, then it is back to the soft cello and the longing violins. Another crescendo comes out of nowhere and there is much activity but, it doesn't last and we are taken back to the violins and quiet cello. As the end nears, the violin lightens and, together with the second violin, leads the movement to a gentle conclusion.

The second movement begins with a pizzicato accompaniment and the violin is agitated. Settling into a rhythm, the two violins propel the music forward. Now it is just two violins for a time which makes it quite melancholy until we are back into tempo, with almost manic violins leading the way. Filled with chordal punctuations, a change in tonality leads to a crescendo and the violins strut over the pulse. Now all is peaceful again as a solo violin laments and the second violin comes in to conclude. This movement is a little ambivalent, containing music of great beauty, together with episodes of aggression.

The final movement starts with a solo cello in the low register. Slowly, some string sound effects appear, leading to a sombre atmosphere. The violin makes its entry, conversing with the cello – it is a most enthralling moment. The intensity slowly increases and the violin rises above the ensemble. Now we have a change in tonality, however the violin still dominates before the cello enters with great force, leading to a crescendo with the violin eventually prevailing. The intensity drops back to nothing and the cello burbles in the background while the violins feature with beguiling melodies. There is a touch of atonality in this relative calm, which ultimately leads into a solo violin statement. The sparse feeling lifts for a time, only to return to two violins gently wafting over the cello to conclude the piece. This is fabulous music.

These works are available on Amazon UK and US as *The Complete String Quartets Volumes 1 & 2* on the Northern Flowers label, by the Taneyev String Quartet. Vol. 1 contains Quartets 1-3. The whole six quartets are available on Spotify and earsense, with several single movements on YouTube.

Listenability: Fine, mysterious works.

— ooOoo —

Ahmed Saygun [1907–1991]

Nationality: Turkish
Quartets: Four
Style: Early Modern

Middle-Eastern Influences
String Quartet No. 3

Saygun's music is steeped in the Western Classical Music tradition but he does draw on Turkish folk music influences. These are manifested in exotic scales leading to interesting melodies and abstruse soundscapes. There is also a strong rhythmic focus at times. I would like to stress however, that these are bona fide string quartets in the classical style and are not, in any way, examples of world music.

The first two quartets are wonderful, and very interesting. I love the ambience and the sense of space, together with the ethnic melodies. However, I am going to discuss the Third Quartet, which is slightly more intense and I like it. It is in three movements and, as with the first two quartets, contains many instances of the previously mentioned Turkish leanings.

The first movement, marked grave, is magnificent. It runs for fifteen minutes and covers plenty of emotional territory. Beginning ever so softly, but with a restless feeling, two violins probe thoughtfully and a dialogue occurs. Now a violin scurries about and the other instruments enter with the same approach.

The music intensifies and becomes propulsive and a sense of moderate chaos is sustained for a time before the violins scurry again. There are string sound effects and the chaos returns. A pause brings in the cello and a violin answers in a whisper – it is a wonderful moment, one to be savoured. More chaos returns before a longing violin statement introduces another fine mood where there is plenty of movement. String sound effects abound as the music becomes more intense but the feeling seems to be ever-changing, sometimes delicate, other times chaotic. Several ascending and descending folk sounding melodies appear, and as we move toward the end things become gentle.

This movement is a tour de force. It is modern and contains many instances of mild dissonance, atmospheric spaces and rhythmic intensity.

The next movement is marked lento and again starts gently. A solo violin is joined by a second, this seems almost like a canon. There is little from the ensemble until the cello begins to offer up supporting statements and a mild chaos briefly develops, only to descend back into a variable dynamic where the volume oscillates through differing melodic fragments. The violin tone is just so pure, as instances of strong, but soft melodies lead us to the end where chordal interjections gradually dissipate into nothing.

The final movement opens with a strong rhythmic figure leading to an interesting chord. The music breaks into tempo with an excitement factor and a strongly harmonised melodic phrase leads to an ostinato figure constructed from an ethnic scale. The violins are intense and there is a lot of energy. A solo violin statement is interrupted by a pizzicato cello which leads the music into abstraction, with the violin reaching into the high register. Gradually it descends and is joined by the ensemble. Now follows a short held violin note, very powerful, which develops into one of those intangible soundscapes. The end comes with a strong violin figure which fades out and it's all over.

This is a fascinating work. On reflection, it is not as ethnic as I first thought, but it is more modern. Apparently, *The Times* newspaper referred to Saygun as:

The grand old man of Turkish music, who was to his country what Jean Sibelius is to Finland, what Manuel de Falla is to Spain, and what Béla Bartók is to Hungary.

This interesting music is contained on a 2-CD set, *Complete String Quartets*, on CPO, performed by the Quatuor Danel. It can be found on Amazon US and UK. There are also several quartets on individual CDs.

Unfortunately, I was not able to find a version of No. 3 that you could sample. String Quartet No. 1 is available on Spotify and a handful of various quartet movements are on YouTube. There are two complete quartets on earsense, but not No. 3.

Listenability: Modern and eminently profound quartets.

356

[Image courtesy CPO label]

— ooOoo —

R Murray Schafer [born 1933]

Nationality: Canadian
Quartets: At least twelve
Style: Modern Contemporary

String Quartet No. 4

Schafer's string quartets span a time period of more than 30 years, and the composer covers a vast musical territory within these works. They have been unavailable for a while, but I just noticed them on Amazon again. I am going to discuss String Quartet No. 4, written in 1986, which is in one movement, as are the majority of his quartets.

The Fourth Quartet commences with a sustained dissonant chord, until a violin expresses a melodic line. The music soon settles into a drone and a violin in the high register makes for a remarkable mood. The drone subsides and the ensemble dialogues underneath the first violin. The violin goes solo again and after some very shrill melodies expresses a remarkable descending phrase that seems to cover the whole range of the instrument. This is a cue for a brief period of dissonance to return. The violin goes solo again, with occasional cello throbs in the background.

The music is all about the violin until the ensemble fashions a hectic chaos, while the violin returns to the lower register. It soon resumes its former shrill level and the ensemble responds with aggressive, rhythmic phrases with the violin constantly varying its register. A pizzicato passage leads to a moderation of the mood, but it doesn't last. Dissonant thrusts are now the focus, and a rhythmic passage allows the violin to dominate again. A chord change intensifies the feeling, but it soon drops away – reverting to the former thrusts. A hint of pizzicato softens the proceedings.

Thus far, the piece has been all about contrasts. It seems a case of so much music, so little time. A dissonant glissando section leads to the first peaceful moment in the work. Quiet, pensive chords sustain this thoughtful mood, which is other-worldly. More glissandos lead back to a prominent violin in the highest register before a solo cello phrase is heard and we almost have a stasis. Now the energy returns, with dissonance and excited violin melodies. The solo violin returns and ascends again into its highest register.

At this moment a soprano voice enters – it is truly wonderful and also very shrill. The wordless vocal and the violin combine for a magnificent soundscape – after a time, the violin is left on its own, and leads to a conclusion at the top of its range.

The soprano voice is that of Marie-Danielle Parent – she also appears on one other work on the review CD. Speaking of which, all of the 12 string quartets are available as two 2-CD sets, on the ATMA Classique label, performed by a Canadian Ensemble, Quatuor Molinari. This one is titled *String Quartets 1-7* and can be found on Amazon UK and US.

These sets are both on Spotify, together with a performance of the early works by the Orford Quartet, which appears to be no longer available. There are many quartets by both ensembles, including No. 4 on earsense and YouTube.

Just a point about the Orford, some of the music is so soft as to be inaudible – the levels are quite drastic on the Molinari as well. It certainly makes for difficult listening.

Listenability: Some dissonance, but ultimately very rewarding.

[Image courtesy ATMA Classique label]

— ooOoo —

Artur Schnabel [1882–1951]

Nationality: Austrian
Quartets: Five
Style: Early Modern

String Quartet No. 5

People may be surprised to find that Austrian piano legend Artur Schnabel was also a serious composer. Schnabel was the first pianist to record the complete cycle of Beethoven's 32-two piano sonatas, the Mount Everest of the piano world. As a composer, he wrote three symphonies and five string quartets.

I am going to discuss his Fifth Quartet which was composed in 1940. It is a four movement work which opens in a slightly agitated, densely textured, modern manner. This gives way to a solo cello part which is quite moving and the cello remains salient as the ensemble returns. There is a recapitulation of the opening – this makes it busy but not quite chaotic. Now follows another, restrained, solo cello statement as the movement finally fades to a whisper and concludes.

The second movement is again busy, this time with a pulse. The flavour is abstract as the violins bubble along, creating a brooding soundscape. Towards the end of this short movement, a new sense of melody appears, then it just stops.

The next movement is marked adagio and is pure introspection and, pure magic. All four members combine as one to paint a picture of intense loneliness. After a brief time in a tempo, we have a return to the contemplative mood. As it progresses, it becomes even more sparse and introspective. Nearing the end there is a brief flourish before it settles into another period of longing. The end comes with a violin soaring over some dark chords before it fades to a conclusion. This is very moving writing.

The final movement is marked presto and at last there is some joy to be found here. A brief pizzicato leads back to the slightly chaotic feeling of the earlier movements, and we have a conclusion.

I would also like to mention String Quartet No. 1 as it is a fine work. Running for a little under 50 minutes, it is almost symphonic in nature.

String Quartet No. 5 is available on Amazon by the Pellegrini Quartet on the CPO label. String Quartet No. 1 is also available on Amazon US and UK.

Some of Schnabel's quartets can be heard on Spotify, earsense and YouTube.

Listenability: Slightly strange but appealing works.

— ooOoo —

Arnold Schoenberg [1874–1951]

Nationality: Austrian
Quartets: Four
Style: Early Modern

String Quartet No. 1

Arnold Schoenberg's four mature string quartets were composed over a period of 32 years, and you can hear the change in musical approach as he moved from a basic Romantic style, through to an atonal and finally, serial nature. Quartets Nos. 3 and 4 have no key signatures assigned.

The First Quartet is one of my favourite string quartets. For me, it defines an era. Schoenberg stipulated that there were to be no breaks between its four movements. The opening theme has an urgency that propels the music forward – I just love it. The intensity is maintained with a recapitulation, culminating in a brilliant descending violin phrase. Another recapitulation brings a deconstruction of the theme before a brief pause allows for a melodic and pleasing, gentle section, which continues for some time. Eventually the music is enlivened and we hear a hint of a previous phrase before the mood becomes almost pastoral, as the violins spin out Romantic melodies, which can be quite pleading at times. A gentle first violin is most precious, with supportive statements from the second violin. Now a quivering violin leads into a period of abstraction, followed by a slightly burlesque sound, before we return to a previous theme. The violins again become precious, and the music is sensitive. Nearing the end, an earlier phrase is repeated, and the violins complete the movement.

The next movement comes in immediately, and is light in texture. The piece proceeds at a gentle pace and violin melodic lines dominate as a hint of dissonance leads into some harmonised melodies – a gentle pizzicato ensues, leading to a delicate texture. Appealing melodic lines are captivating, very Brahms-like, until a slow tempo appears, with violin murmurings over a salient cello. The energy returns in a jaunty manner, and a measured chaos unfolds. Now a lamenting violin, reminiscent of the first movement, takes the lead role and the opening theme is quoted verbatim. This theme is varied after a time and a solo cello interlude leads to a conclusion.

The third movement, marked langsam, opens with a sparse, searching, lone violin. There is no tempo here, as a second violin and eventually, the ensemble, can be heard. Sporadic periods of solo violin, and minimal accompaniment, can be found here. A previously heard melody is repeated, but the texture remains melancholy throughout, with the feeling one of sparse atonality, which is most beguiling. The violin slowly gathers momentum and the ensemble goes with it. For me, there is a sense of romantic longing in this passage as it develops. A sustained tone leads into a period of quivering violin, no notes can be distinguished. Now the longing continues, this time with more prominent harmonised lines, as another theme is revisited. The ending is abrupt – in fact, you don't notice it as it moves straight into the next movement.

Measured gentle melodies introduce the final movement. A busy passage ensues and the melodies become more complex, and almost obtuse as many new melodies are introduced with no obvious development. A shimmering violin interlude is pure sound and it eventually transforms into another melancholic statement – I still hear a longing present. Now the violins combine to produce a thoughtful soundspace with warm melodic lines, leading to sustained tones to conclude the work.

This work drifts between occurrences of blatant Romanticism and charming melodies, contrasted with dark, dissonant angular periods of deep abstraction – a pointer to the composer's later works. There are several thematic sections that are reintroduced in different movements, sometimes with a modified harmonic background. For me, the overall mood of the piece is a journey, constantly moving between light and dark places. For some listeners, this may be a slightly difficult piece. But hey, you'll never know if you don't give it a try.

Recommending performances is a little difficult. I have three versions, all of which are in box sets. The LaSalle String Quartet 4-CD box on Deutsche Grammophon is probably my first choice. This also contains the string quartet works of Berg and Webern, Schoenberg's students. If you can find the version with the 200-page booklet, all the better – it's a fascinating insight into the era – I have read it several times. The Schoenberg Quartet have a 6-CD set containing all of Schoenberg's chamber music. Their version is a little lighter than the La Salle's. As I enjoy historical performances I find that the Juilliard String Quartet *Early Works 1948-52* 5-CD set is also a worthwhile candidate. They take the piece at a faster tempo than the others and this makes for an interesting, contrasting performance. I used this version for the review.

Many other versions are available on Amazon US and UK. A version on Naxos, performed by the Fred Sherry String Quartet, also contains the composer's wonderful string sextet *Verklärte Nacht* (Transfigured Night). It sounds like a great introduction to Schoenberg.

The Naxos disc is on Spotify and several versions of the work are on YouTube, with eight recordings to be found on earsense.

Listenability: Dissonant at times but many fine moments.

Transfigured Night

The work under discussion was written in 1899 as a one movement string sextet – in this instance, a string quartet ensemble augmented with an extra viola and cello. It was based on Richard Dehmel's poem *Verklärte Nacht* and is normally played in five movements, corresponding to the five stanza structure of the poem. It was later arranged for orchestra by the composer – both versions are stunning. Details relating to the programmatic nature of the composition, the personal circumstances surrounding it, and the poem itself, can be found on Wikipedia. I believe that this would be Schoenberg's most popular composition, and yet it doesn't really sound like him.

The work commences with low, sustained murmurings from the ensemble. Out of this formless soundscape a melody slowly emerges, gradually moving from long tones to a lamenting passage which drifts into the violins' high registers. A brief intense moment ensues, before the violins again bring further peace. Now the music becomes very dramatic as it crosses the line into the second movement.

This is most animated, but soon moves into a sparse section, only to be interrupted by a questioning violin with an answering ensemble. The melodies here have a lyrical purity about them as a slight crescendo is heard before a return to sparsity. A melodic phrase is repeated by the ensemble and is further developed – all the while, a tremendous sense of lamenting is present. Suddenly, the music erupts briefly and brings forth a strongly melodic passage, and then a reduction in the dynamic level. Wonderful, flowing melodies are very engaging, until another brief crescendo again changes the mood with a passage of introspection, replete with assertive melodic statements and string sound effects. A further intense passage is orchestral-like and very foreboding. Nearing the end, the texture reverts to a single violin expressing a feeling of loneliness with the occasional ensemble interjection. The violin is totally solo as the movement concludes.

A brief third movement follows without pause and is of a solid, somewhat tempestuous nature, with several iterations of the opening movement theme heard. A short solo violin passage is followed by a series of slow, rich chords, in which the cello is prominent.

Again the next movement begins without pause. A strong, hymn-like melody which for me, evokes Charles Ives, is presented and then, harmonised in a wistful manner, with the first violin leading the ensemble. The introduction of an ascending melodic line brings to the music a sense of charm, with occasional pizzicato and string sound effects adding to the development. A Romantic style is featured as two violins drift in a perfunctory manner across a rich harmonic tapestry – this mood is sustained for some considerable time, before returning to the dramatic nature of some of the earlier sections. Now some fabulous slightly dissonant melodies are heard, and the intensity again builds to near chaos, before settling back into the predominantly peaceful nature of the work. Another soothing violin melodic section, featuring the sparsest of accompaniments, prevails to a transcendent end.

The final movement comes straight in with another handsome melody, slowly moving forward. The texture gently thickens and the violin lines are splendid. A new section is introduced with stunningly effective pizzicato and the piece softly concludes.

It has been a while since I have heard this work and I had forgotten how beautiful it is. To think that, soon after, Schoenberg composed his radical First Quartet, also a stunning composition, but one that illustrates his rapid stylistic development.

My review source is a 5-CD set containing the composer's complete chamber music, performed by the Schoenberg Quartet, on the Chandos label. There are however, approximately fifteen single CD versions available on Amazon UK and US. I quite fancy two pairings, Richard Strauss' *Metamorphosen for Strings*, arranged for string septet, performed by Les Dissonances, or Korngold's *String Sextet* by the Raphael Ensemble, but there are many other issues to be found, including the Naxos mentioned in the previous review.

There are several versions on Spotify and many of the sextet and orchestral arrangements on YouTube. A further eleven sextet recordings are on earsense.

Listenability: Brilliantly evocative work from a youthful Modernist master.

[Image courtesy Chandos label]

— ooOoo —

Franz Schubert [1797–1828]

Nationality: Austrian
Quartets: Fifteen
Style: Romantic

Death and the Maiden
String Quartet No. 14

Schubert died before his 32nd birthday. He wrote over 20 string quartets but only 15 were ever published. His most famous quartet is undoubtedly No. 14, known as *Death and the Maiden*. Written in 1824 and containing four movements, it is generally recognised to be one of the chamber music masterpieces of the Romantic era.

This work opens with a spirited, minor key chordal phrase and then moves into a gentler, melodic statement, before slowly increasing the intensity until it redevelops the opening melody at some length. Now we have a charming moment, where virtuosic violins display their wares. A key change takes place, and the melodies keep coming. I'm now starting to realise how influential Schubert was, as I hear hints of later composers' works. The melodies remain sprightly, but eventually become more agitated. The intensity drops to introduce a serious passage and then wonderful melodic variations on the opening phrase are heard. A brief pause leads into a dynamic section, and again, further variations are examined. As the movement winds down, a fade out occurs.

The next movement, an andante, begins in a funereal manner, with quiet violins almost droning. A sombre melody evolves, and the harmonic nature here is beguiling. A tempo now emerges, with a skipping melody and a pronounced cello part, leading to the music becoming slightly rhapsodic, in a gentle manner. The minor tonality again becomes evident here, with measured violin melodic lines. A slight rise in intensity follows and a longing feeling is established, with a hint of a sound from the first movement. Now the violins generate a more rhythmic feeling, which is strengthened as the music moves forward. A new theme is introduced, which is convivial – no minor key here. After a time, it darkens slightly, then a delicate fragment gives way to a more dynamic feeling. Nearing the end, the music retreats into itself and the sound is sparse. A quiet interlude concludes this movement.

The third movement commences with a joyous melody, filled with life. Variations occur but the mood is maintained – it is a beautiful sound. Now a delicate melody, with gentle harmonies, moves forward. A recapitulation of the opening melody is heard, and this short movement reaches an end.

The final movement is of a galloping nature, featuring some harmonies that were introduced earlier in the work. The music is suddenly busy, both melodically and rhythmically. A Beethoven-like phrase is heard and strong chords introduce a new passage, while the rhythm is still strong. The galloping feeling returns, this time with the rhythm broken up at times, allowing the violins to express freely and return to previous melodies. A dramatic moment ensues, as a minor tonality alters the sound of the melodies. An earlier part is repeated, and reharmonised. The rhythm remains insistent, and several false endings only add to this wonderful feeling. Another recapitulation follows, and strong violins move to a conclusion with a flourish.

As this work is so popular, it is no surprise to find more than 1600 recordings on Amazon UK. It seems that every string quartet in the world has recorded it. It is also featured heavily on Spotify and YouTube with ten versions to be found on earsense.

Listenability: An iconic, marvellous Romantic quartet.

The Last Quartet
String Quartet No.15

Schubert's String Quartet No. 15 in G major has a posthumous opus number, but was written in 1826. It is in four movements.

The work opens with a series of flourishes before settling into the merest hint of a melody and ever so slowly the full melody is brought to the fore. The opening flourish returns, this time with a reworked repeat of the exposition, and not for the last time. Then follows several changes where the opening melody is presented in various ways, ranging from the serene to the hectic – some of the writing is almost orchestral. The whole movement appears to be a set of harmonised versions of the exposition, at different levels of intensity, together with brief interludes between the variations. Each time the melody comes back in a new and exciting way. There is a secondary theme that is a variation of the exposition which is also reworked several times. A loud variation concludes the movement. This is magnificent music making with the movement running for fifteen minutes, but more on that later.

A most genteel melody introduces the second, andante movement. After a time, a variation is introduced, then it is back to the exposition. Now follows a loud dynamic, which soon develops into the sound of quivering violins. The volume returns, followed by a period of calm where the theme reappears at a leisurely pace. Constant changes of key appear during these many variations and some of the writing is again of an orchestral nature. Now the music breaks into a tempo and an extended delightful melodic theme ensues, before a fade delivers an ending.

The third movement begins at a sparkling tempo, with all of the instruments busy, but the violins lead the way. This is more rhythmic than melodic. A new mood appears without the rhythm, it is conversational and charming. The texture thickens and leads into a most attractive passage as another key change extends the possibilities. Then we are back to the opening theme, with plenty of energy which races to an ending.

The final movement begins at an allegro tempo, which continues in a rhythmic fashion for most of the piece. A simple, rapid melody dominates proceedings – the accompaniment is strong here. Alternating phrases at half tempo where the melodies change their pace and intensity for lighter colours, contrast with the stronger rhythms all around them. The piece fades, then ends with two huge chords.

Just something about the first movement. I reviewed the Melos Quartet version which runs for 15 minutes. I also have the Quartetto Italiano version which runs for 22 minutes. The reason for this discrepancy is that the Italiano observe the exposition repeats, which are instructions by the composer to repeat basic themes. It is relatively common for string quartets to not always perform all of these.

It has been an intense experience discussing this work – its orchestral scope is just so powerful. For me the heart of the quartet is in the first two movements. It's a marvel how Schubert can present and re-present the melodic material in so many beautiful ways. They are both stunning movements. Words cannot do justice to the music and I feel that I have merely skimmed over the surface of this magnificent piece.

Amazon UK has over 400 versions of this quartet. I can recommend the Quartetto Italiano on a 2-CD recording, *The Last Four Quartets*, on the Philips Classics label, which includes *Death and the Maiden* and a famous single movement work, *Quartettsatz*, all for a nice price.

Quartet No. 15 is also available on Spotify, YouTube and earsense, which has many versions, including the Melos Quartet.

Listenability: Magnificent early Romantic composition.

[Image courtesy Philips via Universal Music]

Erwin Schulhoff [1894–1942]

Nationality: Czech
Quartets: Two
Style: Early Modern

String Quartet No. 1

Schulhoff's two string quartets are augmented by a Quartet '0'. This usually means that the composer rejected the work or it was discovered after his death. According to Wikipedia '*He was one of the figures in the generation of European musicians whose successful careers were prematurely terminated by the rise of the Nazi regime in Germany...*', and '*who died in a concentration camp, probably of tuberculosis.*'

The First Quartet, in four movements, has a torrid opening with a strong forward propulsion, the violins being exceptionally powerful. Most times, melody gives way to rhythm. A slight drop in intensity allows the first violin to moderate the tempo and the opening melody is then repeated, almost mocking itself as it plays it much faster than previously, and the composer inserts atonal phrases freely into the music. This brief movement ends on a chord.

Gentle, swirling melodies introduce the next movement. There are pizzicato chords within the accompaniment and the first violin begins to strut, before breaking into a solo section. A brief pause is followed by a soft scurrying mood where the violin soars above the ensemble. The backing is very soft and the violin works a melody that eventually descends in range and stops. Now another soft, but hectic ensemble phase is heard before a further pause brings about a mostly violin-led passage. The strange backing reappears, again softly, and the violin skims over it. The violin pauses but the accompaniment continues until near the end – it also stops. The movement concludes with the violin playing a short solo section with trills, and a brief final flourish.

The next movement is sprightly and the melodies are engaging, although, rhythm predominates over melody. The introduction complete, the cello sets up an ostinato, and the violins a melody similar to Ravel's *Bolero*. A sudden pause initiates a banjo-like, percussive rhythm as the violin takes up with a new melody and the tempo accelerates – all the while the violin plays at a breakneck tempo. Interjections occur and the first violin is virtuosic. A very busy cello now returns to the ostinato. The tempo is brisk and the violins duel their way to a sharp ending.

The fourth movement, which is by far the longest, commences with a gently, pulsing background while the two violins drift across the surface. The backing becomes as soft as to be virtually inaudible, but it draws the violins into an abstract, measured duel. One of the violins is like a soprano voice, so pure is the tone. Now a solo violin expresses a serious melody, while the ensemble offer up a drone which fades to a silence. A violin takes over, even it is very soft, with occasional sounds emanating from the ensemble. The violin eventually increases the volume and the cello and viola provide sharp interjections, followed by a feeling similar to the opening, which is extended for some time. The violin meanders with no melodic development, now it is just the pulsing backing. It fades quietly to a conclusion.

This is a mystifying work. It was written in 1924 and apparently was well received in a 1928 performance. However, I find it to be a very abstract piece. Not that of a Schoenberg, but in more of an Impressionistic manner. There are few discernible melodies and the dynamics can be very soft at various places in the work. Its rhythmic passages are also consistently soft.

The review CD, performed by the Aviv Quartet, on the Naxos label also contains String Quartet No. 2 and *Five Short Pieces* and is freely available. It does not contain Quartet '0', which was formerly on a CD by the Kocian Quartet that seems to have disappeared.

The Aviv Quartet is on Spotify and there are several quartets on YouTube. Quartet '0' is available at earsense as Opus 25, along with Quartets Nos. 1 and 2. There is also an earlier divertimento there.

Listenability: Fascinating early 1920s work.

— ooOoo —

William Schuman [1910–1992]

Nationality: American
Quartets: Five
Style: Contemporary

String Quartet No. 5

William Howard Schuman wrote five string quartets but withdrew the first from publication in 1935, so we are left with four extant works. I am going to discuss the Fifth String Quartet which was composed in 1987. The work is in two, long, named movements – both are very slow, and mostly lacking in tempo.

Introduction opens with a barely audible violin, which is joined by a second, and then the cello. The music is mostly sustained notes, with little melody to be heard until a violin leads the ensemble into an interesting place, which is quite animated. A very high violin appears, together with harmony from the second violin – this is a most satisfying moment, as the violins reach out over a pulsing cello, which descends into its low register against a slightly dissonant ensemble. A brief pause leads into more solo violin and the ensemble seems intent on providing subtle harmony until a hint of a melody appears and the minimal accompaniment makes for a quietly introspective moment. Now two violins are heard, both sustained, as the cello and viola play gently in the background. The cello provides as much, if not more action than the violins.

369

The cello returns to silence, leaving the two violins to go it alone, again with sustained tones. Now sounds emerge from the ensemble, with the viola featuring a flute-like texture, and is quite energised. A cello and violin phase has one violin, again joined by another and the cello throbs a harmonic web behind them. There is no melody, just a sense of longing. A pause leads to a cello statement of long, sustained tones and the violins respond with a mildly dissonant texture. This builds into the loudest music heard so far, leading into another pause, then a solo, slightly melodic violin that increases in intensity to close the movement. This is a false ending as, after a pause, we hear a series of held chords, quite like the opening of *Beethoven's String Quartet No. 12,* but on the other hand, they are sound-worlds apart.

Variations – Epilogue again begins with a solo violin, this time expressing a gentle major key melody in its high register. It's not long before an answering violin is heard. They duet for a time, and a solo cello makes the same positive melodic statement, which is then harmonised by a violin and the full ensemble creates a fugal sounding mood. A pause leads to some playful violin mutterings, before the second violin enters and they chase each other through the passage, deconstructing the previously heard melody. Eventually, the viola comes in as pizzicato, completely taking control. The cello enters, creating a compelling section as the viola carries on. Now ensues a passage for violin and pizzicato viola, which soon drops out.

After a pause the previous texture is reintroduced – this time the cello has a part to play and the pizzicato disappears. Jaunty violins begin to duet and there are references to the opening melody. The entry of the cello makes for a busy passage and there is a rhythmic melodic phase where the opening melody is again deconstructed. The playful violin returns but a serious tone brings with it morose melodies, sometimes slightly dissonant.

Now we are back to sustained violin tones that eventually begin to hint at a very subtle melody. This creates a wonderful, sparse soundscape as instruments drift in and out. Slowly, dissonance builds while the intensity decreases. Violins express over a plucked cello and the mood is again morose, and deeply moving. There are several solo sections for the various instruments. A solo violin assumes control one last time before it is joined by a second violin, making for a very introspective section. A cello drones long tones and a violin stays until the conclusion.

I feel that I may have overlooked some of the passages in this magnificent piece. It's just so long, with many moods to savour. It would be one of the longest reviews that I have produced.

The review CD, *William Schuman – Three String Quartets* is performed by the Lydian String Quartet on the Harmonia Mundi label and is available on Amazon US and UK. It also contains String Quartets Nos. 2 and 3. These are both likeable, early works. No. 2 is quite energised and No. 3, a little folksy and sometimes serious. Interestingly No. 4, composed in 1950, is very avante-garde, which seems to me to fit the tenor of the American String Quartet at that time. It was thirty-seven years later that Schuman composed his final, Fifth Quartet. Maybe that's why it seems so considered.

Only No. 3 is on Spotify but there are several quartets on YouTube. There are also several quartets on earsense, some featuring the marvellous Juilliard Quartet.

Listenability: I found it to be pensive, but deep emotionally.

— ooOoo —

Robert Schumann [1810–1856]

Nationality: German
Quartets: Three
Style: Romantic

String Quartet No. 1

Schumann's three string quartets all form part of a set, Opus 41. Before he started on these works, the composer spent time seriously studying the Mozart, Haydn and Late Beethoven quartets. This was time well spent as there are hints of all of them scattered throughout his Opus 41.

The First Quartet is my favourite of the three. It consists of four movements, which was normal for the time. Only Beethoven seemed to bend the rules in this regard.

The first movement, the longest of the work, begins with a most poignant introduction as a solo violin melody is joined by a second violin in a fugue-like fashion. This wonderful harmonised melody is most alluring – it could have been written by Beethoven. An increase in dynamics with a few powerful, chordal strokes leads to a brief pause and a recapitulation is heard, gently fading, followed by another pause which leads into a brief, but powerful passage. After a period of melodic development a charged rhythmic interlude is heard. Ensemble thrusts are answered by the first violin, and an earlier melody is developed at some length, again leading to further poignant sounds. Now we have a strutting, rhythmic section but it seems that each variation doesn't last long before returning to the basic character. This duality is in force for some time and significant melodic development is heard. Nearing the end, the intensity lifts for one last time, followed by a fading shrill violin and two pizzicato cello notes to finish.

The next movement, by contrast, is the shortest of the work, and also the most energised. Firstly, a vibrant motif is developed at a brisk tempo then interspersed with occasional thrusting sections, which are quite conversational, and a strong sense of forward propulsion is achieved. Now a return to the opening feeling is started, then developed. This is followed by a very gentle passage with a most alluring, extended melodic section before another recapitulation brings the movement to life once more. Interestingly, while it is very dynamic rhythmically, the playing is often quite soft. The end comes with a surprising flourish.

The third, adagio movement is introduced by a plaintive cello melody which leads to the violins crafting melancholic melodies that are very beautiful – again they reveal some historical influence. This almost aching feeling is sustained for some time until a change in emphasis, but not in tempo ensues, and a series of overlapping, ascending melodic lines portrays great feeling. Changes in harmony add to the melodic interest, and slowly the music builds, as all the while the violins spin out wonderful melodies. The cello now comes to the fore and the violins respond to its contribution. The final stages are very subtle, sublime even – the music lets you down very gently.

A forceful opening to the final movement is characterised by a wonderful melody that threads its way through and around the strongly rhythmic ensemble. At times, the music resembles a footrace, although the earlier melodies are still heard frequently, in various harmonic guises. Shrill violins are at the core of this development, with the playing at times seemingly virtuosic. Suddenly a sweet soft section emerges with long tones, but this is soon overtaken by the earlier histrionics and builds into a final flourish to conclude.

This piece seems to modulate between the Classical and Romantic styles. All things considered, I find it to be a very attractive work.

The version I reviewed is by an historical ensemble, the American Flonzaley String Quartet, which was formed in 1903 – you can hear the surface noise from the acetate pressings. I am very fond of historical quartets, which are freely available on several internet sites, due to the fact that these early performances are out of copyright, even in the US. Feel free to contact me if you have any interest in downloading some of these quartets from earlier times.

Amazon US brings up 1,000 results for a "Schumann String Quartets" search. They are often paired with other composers on 2 or 3-CD sets. I'm going to recommend a version that I have myself – the Fine Arts Quartet on the Naxos label. All three quartets fit onto one disc and the playing is superb.

There are many complete versions of Opus 41 to be found on Spotify, YouTube and earsense.

Listenability: Another brilliant first quartet from a Romantic master.

String Quartet No. 3
Arranged for String Orchestra

I have long thought that many string quartets would be suitable for arrangements to be played by a string orchestra. My search has mainly been in vain. For instance, I purchased such an arrangement of the complete Beethoven Late Quartets and found it terrible. The orchestra overwhelmed the string quartet intimacy with a feeling that could be aptly described as – Andre Rieu in a china-shop.

Having said that I think I have finally found what I was seeking. The CD that I am about to discuss contains String Quartets Nos. 1 and 3 arranged for string orchestra. I have selected No. 3 which is probably Schumann's most popular quartet. The orchestration definitely works on this performance. Obviously the string orchestra takes away some of the original's intimacy, but I find that it tends to come across as a warm orchestral glow around the quartet, particularly in the slow movements. The quicker passages are somewhat more brash.

I feel I should make mention of the melodic theme of the first movement. Schumann is a supreme melodist and I find this theme to be one of the most beautiful in the repertoire.

String Quartet No. 3 is in four movements. It begins in an andante tempo with a lush introduction which is very precious. A slightly quicker tempo contains a hint of what is to come. Then we hear **that** melody in all its splendour. Next we have a development of what I would call a sub-theme, one that is closely related. The orchestration sounds a little like an early Mozart symphony, quite sparse. Now we have a development of the theme until it is stated in its original form again. The sub-theme reappears, to great effect, and a more restrained recapitulation of the main theme follows. A change from major to minor brings in a stronger orchestral presence and a totally new variation is presented as the cello comes to the forefront. Variations abound and the orchestra maintains a subtle backdrop to the violin theme. The violins create another new melody before resuming the variations, then take us through to a calm finish. This movement is a most appealing piece of writing.

The next movement opens in a lightly symphonic nature with a simple phrase. Suddenly the texture thickens, the tempo quickens and short, incisive phrases are featured. Now the orchestra is in full flight in a tempestuous mood. A pause leads into a simple melody with the orchestra in the background – this melody is developed and the violins reach into a high register as a new melody is presented which is longing, but attractive. The next passage has plenty of impetus and is a variation on the theme from the first movement. A further new melody is crafted, carried subtly by a sedate ensemble to a conclusion. This movement has more of an orchestral nature than the first.

The third movement, marked adagio begins in a stately manner as a salient first violin provides the melody. The orchestral writing here is splendid and a tranquility ensues, followed by a rise in the dynamics. This eventually drops back in intensity, the orchestra can barely be heard until they return with a hint of the harmonies of the first movement theme. A crescendo is presented and the orchestra is prominent here. Now the cello walks and the mood becomes sparse. As the end approaches, the music is pared back to just a few instruments and a sustained chord leads to a sublime finish.

373

The final movement, marked allegro, starts in a dynamic manner before moving into a period of busy violins before they prance, with little accompaniment. This mood is sustained for a time until the violins return to their busyness. Eventually the intensity decreases and the violins continue with melodic development and we are on the move again as the music becomes energised once more, leading to an end with some rhythmic violin melodies and a final flourish.

It is worth noting that the string orchestra version of Quartet No.1, which happens to be my personal favourite, is also extremely fine.

This recording, titled *Schumann: String Quartets Nos. 1 and 3: Transcribed for String Orchestra* is on Naxos. It comes and goes on Amazon US and UK. I just Googled it and it came up on Amazon US. Being Naxos it will always be available.

You can listen on the Naxos website but you have to be a member or sign up. It is on Spotify, but I had to search Google to find it there.

Good luck with it, it is out there.

Listenability: I would have to say it is the best orchestrated string quartet CD that I have come across.

[Robert Schumann – Image courtesy Wiki Commons]

Peter Sculthorpe [1929–2014]

Nationality: Australian
Quartets: Seventeen
Style: Contemporary

Island Dreaming
String Quartets Nos. 8, 11 & 13

Of Sculthorpe's seventeen string quartets, the first five are considered lost.

String Quartet No. 11, titled *Jaribu Dreaming* contains two movements. The first opens with an aggressive cello riff, more reminiscent of rock music than a string quartet. A solo violin floats beautifully across this riff and the other musicians enter at differing times as Sculthorpe invokes his trademark use of seabird sounds from the violins. The music then enters a short violent phrase, which fades into a dialogue between the two violins, with viola accompaniment. A strong, rhythmic passage follows, before going out on birdsong. A solo violin starts the second movement and, following a brief chaos, returns to the ensemble, with further seabird sounds in evidence. The violin soars above an insistent cello phrase for a time as the texture becomes dense and then recedes. The violin soars again, birdsong reappears and the dense nature resumes as the violin, inspired by the birds, reaches great heights. Suddenly, the piece ends in a cacophony of seabird sounds and fades away.

Quartet No. 13, featuring vocalist Anne Sophie von Otter, is in one movement, and for me, the highlight of the CD. It opens with solo vocal before the ensemble enters variously in solo, and supporting roles. This is divine music, as the wordless vocals blend perfectly with the quartet, ultimately creating a soundscape with solo vocal and the other instruments phasing in and out. The accent then shifts to a new rhythm, but a similar feeling, with the still wordless vocals, leading to a wonderful moment. The ending begins with a gentle vocal and an ensemble phrase, which gives the music substance. The final notes are a long vocal phrase to end this magnificent piece, which is beautifully realised.

Quartet No. 8 is in five movements. It was written in 1969 and is of its time. A peaceful, introspective opening gives way to more birdsong. A solo cello concludes the movement. The next opens with pizzicato, to my mind, not particularly successfully. It is soon over and a plaintive violin laments over a sparse accompaniment. Suddenly, the opening pizzicato reappears with a few non-musical sounds. It finishes on a single, loud pizzicato cello note.

The third movement begins with a solo cello statement before it is joined by a violin for a time. The ensemble enters, and brings such an emotional depth. The rest of the piece is basically for solo cello – the other strings enter for one chord to bring it to a conclusion. The fourth, pizzicato movement sounds extremely dated, very 1960s Modernism. The final movement is a bit the same with abstract interjections. The only real music comes from the cello.

I once had a chat with Peter Sculthorpe. It was at a concert in Perth with gifted local cellist Sophie Curtis playing his *Requiem for Solo Cello*. He was happy to talk about his string quartets however, that theme ended rather rapidly when he told me he was going to arrange all of his quartets with a part for didgeridoo. That was just too much for me to take. I have noticed that subsequently, some of these arrangements have been released. Hmmm, I don't believe that I'll be going there.

This CD, *Island Dreaming*, on the Challenge Classics label is played by the Brodsky Quartet with guest vocalist Anne Sophie von Otter. I think the concept works well. The disc is freely available on Amazon UK and US.

This CD, along with several other Sculthorpe quartets, is on Spotify, YouTube and earsense.

Listenability: Apart from a little 1960s Modernism, a great pleasure.

— ooOoo —

Leif Segerstam [born 1944]

Nationality: Finnish
Quartets: At least thirty
Style: Contemporary

String Quartet No. 6

Of the many string quartets of Segerstam, there are only three currently available on CD, Nos. 2, 6 and 7. The two latter works are both orchestral in conception and epic in character, which is probably something to do with the fact that he has also composed over 300 symphonies. I am going to discuss the Sixth Quartet as it seems to be more readily available than the others.

The work opens in a slightly mysterious manner, with orchestral overtones. A brief introduction gives way to a solo violin supported by strong string sounds which become quivering before the cello invokes a change of mood. Now rapidly descending violin lines are accompanied by rhythmic thrusts and a pause again introduces mystery – this is a very sparse passage. A violin reaches out and cello glissandos are heard in the background, then more quivering. For the first time we have a tempo, and the sound is atonal. Another pause brings about a solo cello statement over further quivering violins. Pauses seem to abound in this movement and another brings on a delicate, abstruse mood. This formless phase again has the violins reaching out, to a stodgy cello feeling. There is a sense of chaos here, definitely without a tempo as atonal violins make thrusting sounds, and the level of intensity is high. A brief shrill solo violin passage with little accompaniment is soothing to the soul. Now the ensemble combines again bringing more mystery, as the violins are sensitive and lead into a sparsity which ends the movement.

Lilting, atonal violins introduce the next movement and they gently drift along against the background of a recurring viola motif. Gradually the violins increase in intensity and projection – the viola repeats a different motif. A powerful cello statement adds to an emerging chaos as strong violins now dominate with much quivering of bows, while they investigate various changes in harmony. Finally a pause brings about a sparsity, with the violins gently expressing various strange melodies. Again the intensity rises as the violins work themselves into a frenzy, accompanied by a rhythmic cello. A further mood change ensues as the violins trill gently and a long pause leads into a solo violin statement. Nearing the end, there are brief periods of silence as the music just dissolves.

The third movement begins with a frantic flurry of activity – this is sound, not music. Slowly a structure begins to form but it is soon overpowered by ponderous rhythmic flourishes. The feeling is now one of frenzy, seemingly relentless. Minutes pass and there is no relief from the intensity. Finally a solo violin interlude featuring many glissandos brings a peace. The second violin begins to develop a further brief frenzy but soon leads to another substantial pause. There is more silence than sound now and the music simply disappears. I have to say, this is quite a disturbing movement, totally out of character with that which has come before.

Vague, rumbling sounds introduce the final movement. The frenzy has disappeared and the mystery has returned. Sparse melodies overlap to create a measured, atonal mood with the accompaniment solid, but quite mournful. Both violins develop lamenting lines, intertwining with a rubato feeling generated by the viola and cello. The mood slowly intensifies and one of the violins goes into pyrotechnics as it traverses its complete range, in a solo passage. More silence initiates a new, placid but still philosophical feeling with mostly sparse violins interrupted by an occasional cello stroke. The music assumes a sense of transcendence for a time, with minimal activity. This beguiling passage slowly intensifies and what sounds like a piano introduces several loud notes. The conclusion is similar to the previous movements, leaving us with a feeling of evanescence.

I'm not sure what to make of this music, but I feel it may have a New Age sensibility, something that I am not drawn to. Certainly the composer deals in extremes in his music, particularly in the volume of his output. I think I shall leave it at that.

The review CD is titled *Segerstam: String Quartet No. 6 / Rituals in La*, on the BIS label. The string quartet is performed by the Segerstam Quartet. There is also a Segerstam piece for wind quintet, and *Rituals in La*, composed by Lasse Werner. This disc is available on Amazon US and UK. String Quartet No. 7 is also available, but a little harder to find. I believe that String Quartet No. 2 can be found on a disc paired with music of Rautavaara, another Finnish composer.

Quartets Nos. 6 & 7 are on Spotify and YouTube, which also has Quartet No. 28 and Symphony No. 288! No. 6 can be found on earsense.

Listenability: Not sure that this long work has a lot to say – possibly one for the New Agers.

— ooOoo —

Vissarion Shebalin [1902–1963]

Nationality: Russian
Quartets: Nine
Style: Early Modern

A Sense of Wonder
String Quartets Nos. 1-3

Shebalin was a close friend of Dmitri Shostakovich, who dedicated his Second Quartet to Shebalin. There is something intangible about these works – they are not profound, but some of the movements are deep, if that makes any sense. They were written from 1923 to 1938. A disc containing String Quartets Nos. 1 to 3 is still semi-available so I am going to examine them all in moderate detail. As a general statement, I would say that Shebalin's music does not often venture far from its opening moods.

The First Quartet consists of three movements. Opening with a charming flavour at a modest tempo, I am struggling to find the words here – it is just so pleasant and personable. Plenty of major scales make this a charming passage with only occasional changes in tempo or emotional feeling. It also comes across as a little orchestral with the individual voices not always being obvious. It's more about the effect of the harmonies than the melodies, although attractive melodies are to be found here. The second movement is similarly enticing but constant, never straying far from the basic theme. The third movement breaks the mould as it is taken at a much livelier tempo. The brightness still prevails, however. This movement is a little less orchestral, being more focussed on the individual voices.

The Second Quartet opens in a minor key, which is a nice change. There is a brief fanfare before it settles into the piece proper. The cello then leads the ensemble into another orchestral section before the solo violin has a part. The ensemble resumes and things darken a little but retain a lilting quality as slowly a lament appears, with the texture dropping back to nearly nothing, just a violin with occasional interjections from the quartet until it finishes. The second movement opens at a slow walking pace with the violin featured. The tempo quickens and a jaunty mood emerges before there is a recapitulation of the opening theme. The third movement begins with a strangely captivating melancholia as the tension builds and then peters out for the finale. The final movement begins strongly, for Shebalin, but never overwhelms. A plaintive solo violin leads into a restrained rhythm, which brings a conclusion.

Now on to the Third Quartet. The first movement features a cheery opening with some of the previously mentioned orchestral sounds. It continues this to the conclusion. The second, short movement, again features a brisk tempo – this is a delightful romp. The third movement is soulful, and builds in intensity before it drops back to a delightful passage to take it out. Finally we have reached the end. The fourth movement is the most dynamic on the disc, but nary an angry note. It just sweeps you away.

I'm quite fond of this disc. I can't put a label on it as it sounds like nothing I've heard before. It's not of its time. Sometimes it is joyous and melancholy at the same time.

The CD, on the Olympia label, by the Krasni Quartet is still available but the signs are not good. Amazon is featuring those ridiculous *New and Used* prices and that usually means that it's about to disappear.

Several Shebalin quartets are on YouTube and String Quartet No. 5 is on Spotify. There are also many quartets on earsense.

Listenability: Simple, endearing, magical music.

— ooOoo —

Dmitri Shostakovich [1906–1975]

Nationality: Russian
Quartets: Fifteen
Style: Early Modern

String Quartet No. 1

Along with Shostakovich's fifteen string quartets, the composer also wrote fifteen magnificent symphonies – quite an achievement really. Together with Bela Bartok, they would have to be the most performed and best-selling string quartet composers from the 20th Century.

By way of background, Shostakovich had constant problems with the Russian government and battled his way through several political regimes, where he was alternately praised and disparaged, especially for his symphonies. He had a particularly tenuous and troubled relationship with Joseph Stalin. I have just finished a book, *The Noise of Time* by Julian Barnes, which appears to be based on the social and political life of Shostakovich. I recommend it.

To listen to all of the quartets is to enter the composer's world of innovative, magnificent and daring music. I intend to discuss his First Quartet, which is a fine early effort. I am particularly fond of first string quartets – they always seem so innocent but point to the future developments in a composer's later output. Shostakovich's First Quartet is a charming work, almost in a Romantic style. It contains strong melodies, and no slow movements, according to the composer markings. It doesn't quite work out this way. A bit of trivia – the composer referred to it as a *'spring time mood.'* And so it is.

The work, which is in four movements, commences in a Romantic manner with a gentle melody at a slow tempo, which is repeated. A change introduces an ostinato and a new melody, which only lasts for a short while as a pause reintroduces the ostinato, allowing the first violin to slowly soar over this new mood, for a stunning musical moment. The violin fashions a simple melody and a key change allows it to express a wonderful descending phrase. Now the cello enters in a similar manner, fading from nothing into a powerful statement. A return to the ostinato is brief and the first violin is again splendid. This leads to a passage of overlapping, ascending violin melodies, before the ostinato returns and the descending violin melody is again heard leading into a wonderful section, which recalls the movement opening. Variations are heard as the dynamics drop, leaving just a solo violin to close. There is nothing modern about this movement, it's just beautiful.

The next movement commences with a serious solo violin melody until the cello slips in behind it for a folksy section. A change brings about a more dense texture and eventually the power of the ensemble is heard. A sense of optimism ensues with a jaunty violin section, which becomes quite forceful. After a solo cello walk, a pizzicato complements a gentle, lilting passage which ends on a chord.

The brief third movement is in complete contrast to the earlier movements. It sets up a simple melody and applies variations to it. Changes in harmony add interest but it seems to be over before it started.

The finale is brisk and positive, and again brief. A strong cello leads the ensemble through an exciting section before the dynamics are cut back and statements are freely exchanged by the ensemble. The previous busyness returns, then drops back to a solo violin which suddenly transforms into a very strong passage to conclude.

This is fine music, especially the first two movements, which for me, form the emotional heart of the work. The last two movements seem a little perfunctory after the earlier, powerful emotional expression.

The First Quartet can be found on individual CDs, there are around 100 listings on Amazon US and UK, but I suggest you opt for a complete set if you can manage it – the price is right.

There are many versions of the complete quartets. I can recommend two, both containing six CDs and at a budget price (at least on Amazon UK). The Fitzwilliam Quartet, on the Decca label was the first complete version I ever owned and it was wonderful. I then came across the Brodsky Quartet on Teldec which has a more contemporary, energised approach. Lately, I have been re-examining the Fitzwilliams, and still finding them very enjoyable. If you buy the Brodskys, try to seek out the one on Teldec with a photo of the four players on the cover as there are two versions. The one without the border is a quarter of the price of the bordered version. Basically you can't go wrong with either the Brodskys or the Fitzwilliams.

The complete Brodsky set is on Spotify and many of the composer's quartets are available on YouTube. There are also eight versions, including the recent Pacifica Quartet live set, on earsense.

Listenability: A very satisfying first quartet.

String Quartets Nos. 9 & 10

String Quartet No. 9 is in five movements. It is long, with no pauses between movements. Opening with a violin melody over a sustained chord, the accompaniment grows a little more complex as the music unfolds. The texture becomes dense, in a measured manner, as the violin persists with the melody, while the other instruments form a rhythmic background. The first violin duets with the second, but the melody remains until it is interrupted by an ensemble flourish which reverts back to a static background as the opening melody returns to conclude.

The next movement, an adagio, commences with a strong chordal melody. The first violin breaks out into a solo part while the atmosphere is sparse. It is a moving moment which is sustained until seemingly random chords are heard. The music then settles back into the introductory mood, this time a little more pensive. The conclusion is a motif, played twice by the solo violin.

This motif is developed at the beginning of the next movement, there being no pause. Now the motif is rhythmic, which introduces a tempo. The violin creates a slightly chaotic interlude which brings in the ensemble to set up a musically dense situation, followed by a brief melodic passage where the ensemble moves into a tempo again. The opening motif returns briefly and the violin plays with an earlier melody before ending on another motif.

Again, this motif is developed into the new, fourth movement. The violin plays some seemingly random pizzicato and then, after a brief violin melody, the pizzicato returns before a moment of solo violin in the high register. Near the end, some chordal accompaniment appears, leading to the seemingly obligatory motif.

The final movement, marked allegro, begins in an extremely agitated, spirited manner and dense melodies predominate. After a time a repeated motif emerges and the violin struts for a while until a new rhythmic pattern develops – the violin is still salient. The pattern continues at a lower volume and there is some interplay which is chaotic, gradually becoming louder and more intense. The chaos stops and we are left with the solo violin until the cello interjects with some aggressive playing, which eventually becomes soothing and melodic. The cello instigates a new motif and all is quiet for a time. Soon however, we have another chaotic intervention as the violin pushes on, over some aggressive cello playing. Further chaos follows and it ends with a powerful flourish.

This is a fine work, replete with strong melodies, barren soundscapes and rhythmic and melodic variety. It is a complex piece.

Quartet No. 10 begins with a simple, playful violin part. The other instruments pick up on the mood and build into a repeated motif. Now the cello takes over – all the while the violin is scurrying about in the background. The repeated motif reappears, with the cello providing an attractive melody. It is interrupted by a slightly abstract solo violin statement before the motif resumes and the violin concludes the movement.

The second movement opens powerfully with the cello offering forceful thrusts. Suddenly great agitation occurs as melodies compete with rhythmic forces and it is confronting. The agitation continues with many atonal forays. Then it just stops dead. Finito.

The third movement has a chordal introduction with a solo violin melody. The violin sounds almost disinterested as the ensemble moves into a slow, quiet space. The violin is now eerily peaceful, expectant even. The chordal melody returns, and as the piece is about to conclude it drops back to two violins, ever so quietly setting up the next movement as there is no pause.

The final movement begins with a solo viola. The other instruments enter over a period of time until finally there is a tempo. The violin introduces a folk-like, slightly dissonant melody, punctuated by a pizzicato ensemble and then a repeated motif – this is long, with only small deviations throughout. The tempo remains strong and the intensity begins to rise, with interjections occurring more often and the music becoming louder. It is bordering on the chaotic but the motif pushes on. Eventually the composer has had enough and offers up a brief solo violin interlude. A new chordal sound arises out of a pause and the violins extemporise on the melody before a gentle ensemble passage concludes.

These two quartets are freely available and sometimes can even be found as a pairing on Amazon US and UK. Also of interest is a 2-CD set on the Cedille Records label that contains Quartets Nos. 9-12 performed by the Pacifica Quartet.

Both quartets are on Spotify as different albums. Many versions exist on YouTube and there is a fine performance of No. 9 by the Pacifica Quartet on earsense, which also has many other versions of both Nos. 9 and 10.

Listenability: What I have come to expect from Shostakovich – excellent Modern quartets.

String Quartet No. 15 – The Last Quartet

Shostakovich's final string quartet, No. 15 is a fitting monument to his output. Characterised almost completely by adagio tempos, it features a depth of feeling that has rarely been equalled.

The work opens with its longest movement, the beginning of an epic journey. A solo violin plays long tones, hinting at a very simple motif before the second violin enters to create a stunning mood. This is heightened by a particularly resonant cello and a sympathetic viola line – the melodies remain simple, folk-like even. Now the violin goes solo again for a moment and its simplicity dominates the music, as the ensemble supply a drone until a cello line begins to develop and the violins express with a rich tone in their lower register. The beginning of a new melodic phrase is again folksy with slow, emotionally deep feeling. The opening melody is revisited by the first violin, now solo, then with superb cello accompaniment. This slowly leads the movement to a conclusion. There is a vivid sense of despondency in this music, which is rather wonderful.

There is no pause before the next movement, as a sustained violin note is carried over. This is a strange passage as the attack on each violin note has an unusual edge to it. Some rhythmic chordal thrusts introduce a solo cello until the violin returns with its strange sounding musings. Another solo cello section leads into an ensemble passage where intermittent rhythmic interjections are heard, initially supporting the first violin, then the cello. Occasional chordal thrusts are revisited before the end comes with a short, solo cello statement.

The third movement, which runs for only 89 seconds, again begins without a pause. A searing virtuoso solo violin is positively startling in its impact while a dissonant chordal section leads into a solo cello statement. A much more conservative violin now presents a simple melody, which is joined by the cello in a faded final statement.

The following movement represents a different character from that which has come before. The ensemble engages in a harmonious passage which is very controlled – stately even. Eventually a solo violin prevails for a time but the ensemble regather to add to the atmosphere, which is particularly becoming – we are deep in Shostakovich's soundworld here. A solo cello expresses a gentle conclusion.

The fifth movement begins strongly with rich chords. This only serves as an introduction to a solo violin statement, but they return again, this time yielding to a solo cello passage. The cello reaches high and its powerful tone resonates with great emotional depth. A quiet ensemble section again sets the first violin free and it also reaches into its upper register before it is joined by the second violin in a profound duet. Now the cello walks tall, pizzicato fashion, occasionally with an ebbing accompaniment. The ending is just the pure sound of the cello.

The final movement again begins strongly with a chordal introduction leading into another virtuoso solo violin statement. A graceful ensemble passage ensues, as the first violin expresses melodies hinted at in the accompaniment. A wild, passionate cello takes over the music until it recedes into a violin duet where long, slow melodies are developed in a sparse manner, evolving into another solo violin statement. Now a flourish of frantic violin tones leads to another solo cello assertion, with occasional ensemble passages heard. These passages move into a solo cello note, which concludes the work.

This quartet is dominated by its persistent adagio tempos and is a work of great emotional depth.

My review CD is from the Fitzwilliam Quartet complete box set, which I tend to recommend, together with the Brodsky Quartet, who also have a stunning complete set. Of course, the work is available on many single CDs but the complete sets are very reasonably priced. You won't be disappointed.

The work can be found on Spotify, YouTube and earsense.

Listenability: A titanic twentieth century string quartet.

[Image – Teldec label – could not be contacted]

Jean Sibelius [1865–1957]

Nationality: Finnish
Quartets: Four
Style: Late Romantic

Intimate Voices
String Quartet Opus 56

Johan Julius Christian Sibelius' magnificent String Quartet in D minor, Opus 56, is titled *Intimate Voices*. Sibelius was infamous as some critics and composers denigrated many of his works but this quartet has maintained its popularity and there are at least a hundred recordings available.

The quartet is in five movements, and is long. The work opens with a lone violin exploring a poignant melody before the ensemble joins in to create a lush texture and soon the cello comes forward to make a strong statement with the violins accompanying. It then moves into a tempo and a positive manner. A solo violin is answered by the ensemble and then blends with it – the tempo now quickens and the violins become extremely busy. A brief pause introduces a peace, at a slow tempo, where the violin is supreme. Soon, chords are to be heard, taking the music to completion.

The second movement is ever so short, just over two minutes, with quivering violins at tempo dominating. The music becomes almost irreverent for a time as scattered phrases are heard. The intensity returns and the violins resume their brisk tempo. Nearing the end, they just play melodic fragments and fade away.

The next movement, marked adagio, is the emotional heart of the work and begins with a graceful nature. I believe this is where we start to hear the *Intimate Voices*. Measured violins produce a longing melody which lingers in the air – ascending melodies come forth and the intensity rises for the first time. We do however, still have the adagio tempo, and the graceful sound returns. It is terrific writing for strings, and advances ever so slowly until a fugal passage ensues, evoking a sense of wonder. The violins sustain the peaceful nature with varied melodies and harmonised lines. The cello introduces a new statement, with its rich sonorities providing a perfect foil for the violins. The cello now leads the piece and provides a longing, enchanting texture which leads to the conclusion. This movement has a beauty beyond words. It has to be one of the loveliest adagios I have experienced.

The fourth movement opens in a serious manner, before briefly leading into a transcendent section. Now a violin enters at a rapid tempo, overlaying the serious background. Gentle folk-like melodies are slowly brought into being and there is some interplay between the violins. The racing violin returns as the ensemble continue at their moderate tempo and a fine ascending melody brings more intensity to the ensemble with the playing now strong. A pause leads to some fluttering violins which turn serious and the movement ends on a lone, but forceful cello note. This is a movement of great contrast, and is immensely rewarding.

The final movement is again at a fast tempo, and some splendid violin interplay is developed. The ensemble brings texture, and the cello creates a dramatic undercurrent. A brief pause leads to a solo violin absolutely racing, then it is just two violins which drop the tempo and scurry about in all possible registers. The dynamics are loud, and a feeling of measured chaos prevails. It is a strong ending to the work.

This piece deserves its place as one of the classics of the repertoire. A great deal of it is very intimate and the adagio is worth the price of admission.

As to availability, it has been recorded by most of the major string quartets. Several 2-CD sets containing all of the composer's four string quartets can be found but, for me, Opus 56 would be enough. Of the many versions available on Amazon US and UK, I can recommend a single CD on the BIS label, performed by the Tempera Quartet, which contains a stunning version of *Intimate Voices*.

There are eight versions on Spotify and many on YouTube. There are ten recordings of this sumptuous work to be sampled on earsense, including the fabulous Tempera.

Listenability: Fully deserving of its reputation as a Late Romantic classic.

— ooOoo —

Valentin Silvestrov [born 1937]

Nationality: Ukrainian
Quartets: At least three
Style: Contemporary

String Quartets Nos. 1 & 2

Valentin Silvestrov is sometimes known as Valentyn Vasylyovych Sylvestrov. The composer's Facebook page uses the first naming convention so I shall run with that. He began composing in a modern fashion in the 1960s but has evolved through at least two different styles since. His first two quartets, written in 1974 and 1988 respectively, illustrate one of those styles. I have not been able to find a recording of the Third Quartet, which was written in 2011.

The First Quartet is in one movement. It opens in an ambient, almost spiritual manner, with an organ-like sound, and a drone accompaniment. Vague melodies are explored, and the depth of feeling is immense – it could be Arvo Pärt. The first violin dominates the section, while the ensemble produces a graceful backdrop. There is harmony here, and the violin responds to its changes. Gradually, the second violin comes into play, with a persistent, questioning motif while at other times it responds to the first violin's utterances. Repeated melodic phrases give form to the music, while still retaining a gentle feeling although, occasionally, the first violin takes on a rough, hewn tone. On one such occasion, the mood changes and the drone is terminated, as individual instruments express more freely.

This melodic freedom is interspersed with peaceful passages – the cello and viola offer up slightly abstract, insistent lines. Gradually the impetus dissipates and the first violin plays sparse, haunting melodies over gentle, rhythmic thrusts from the ensemble. Now the thrusts increase and the first violin makes angular statements that draw you into the music. The sound diminishes in dynamics and intensity, leaving the two violins and the cello to each make random, intermittent incursions. The first violin responds to a change back to the opening mood, and expresses gentle melodies – this section is like a prayer and is most alluring. Long cello tones resonate into the distance, only to randomly return – we are left with one violin for a period and a sustained eerie chordal section concludes the piece.

The Second Quartet is also in one movement and is considerably longer than the First. A powerful opening features a strong cello and an almost savage violin. When this has concluded, it moves into a similar emotional space to the previous quartet. A quivering cello, slowly increasing in intensity interrupts the mood momentarily but the strength soon resumes. The music then becomes modal, as both violins express wonderful, sparse melodies, which slowly become more expansive, with less spaces, and the cello occasionally returns with its gentle rumblings. This sometimes draws the violins into a more dynamic, agitated feeling, which usually lasts for some time, all the while decreasing in intensity. A single, hurried burst of cello does nothing to change the mood.

Now we are back to extreme sparsity. The First Quartet droning sound presents again and the violins rise above it with thoughtful melodic statements. For a time, the music becomes inaudible until the cello introduces some abstruse utterances as it rumbles beneath the persistent violins. The mood is again, eerie, but to my ears very beautiful in its unfamiliarity. The violins continue with their musings – this is a very different, sparse, although beautiful sound-world. The longer it goes the more I am drawn into this piece. It has more of an intangible sound than the previous quartet and I find it fascinating.

A long section of two violins with occasional quiet cello murmurings continues with the violins investigating gentle melodies. A pause introduces another mildly agitated conversation which represents a definite change in mood. There is a hint of pizzicato from the viola – the level of abstraction has lifted. Slowly the music edges forward with intermittent string sound effects, which cause the violins to be even sparser. Finally the work gives up its spirit and finishes on a quiet chord.

These two quartets inhabit a very similar soundspace and differ mainly in the expression of the minimal pieces of music that constantly recur to make up the works. They are far removed from the emotionally charged, sometimes confronting pieces of the 1960s. Having heard Silvestrov's later piano music, I am aware of a further change. For those interested in these works I refer you to two ECM discs. One, *Bagatellen und Serenaden*, has the composer playing simple piano, while the other, *Nostalghia*, played by pianist Jenny Lin, takes simplicity to an extreme level, with almost constant use of the sustain pedal and long pauses in the music and between tracks. This music contains an intimacy that beggars belief.

I found a quote from Silvestrov that may shed some light on his current musical approach:

Music should be so transparent that one can see the bottom and that poetry shimmers through this transparency.

The review CD, titled *Music for String Quartet*, on the Etcetera label and performed by the Lysenko String Quartet is available at Amazon US as *New and Used*. String Quartet No. 1 is also available on ECM Records as *Leggiero, Pesante*, together with other works for various combinations of strings, and piano.

The ECM disc is on Spotify and Quartets Nos. 1 and 2 can be found on both YouTube and earsense.

Listenability: Extremely captivating, sensitive, ambient music. I found it to be spiritually uplifting.

— ooOoo —

Bedřich Smetana [1824–1884]

Nationality: Czech
Quartets: Two
Style: Romantic

From My Life
String Quartet No. 1

Smetana's most famous quartet, and a staple of the repertoire, is String Quartet No. 1 in E minor, titled *From My Life*. This work is in four movements.

The First Quartet opens on a firm chord and the ensemble immediately slips into a subtle rhythmic motif to accompany a strong Gypsy sounding violin melody. This leads into a change in the tonality of the accompaniment, bringing about a passionate moment. Now the rhythmic motif subsides and the ensemble joins the violin with melodies of their own before the solo violin leads the section into a tempo, which is not sustained. This is virtuosic playing from the violin as it negotiates several harmonic changes, before the violin mellows, whilst still retaining the position of dominant instrument. Now the passion rises to the surface again, although it's nothing like the opening. A very subtle violin leads us to the end of the movement with three cello notes being the last heard.

The next movement marked *allegro moderato a la polka has* a folksy Czech sound. Various melodies are introduced, including one by the viola, and the polka feeling is evident in its simple, dance rhythms. Now the music transforms into a waltz tempo, with simple harmonies. There is not really a melody, just rhythmic phrases from the violins. The music moves into an up-tempo section – this time the violins do play melodies. The tempo moderates then accelerates again, before dropping back to a very brief rubato interlude. A return to the energy for a brief period takes the movement out.

The third, and longest movement is in a largo tempo. A solo violin introduces a longing melody and the ensemble moves in behind it with some most attractive harmonies. The solo violin has disappeared into the background. It gradually returns with changing harmonies allowing it to develop an ever so subtle melody. Now the violin introduces an intensity and the ensemble respond in kind – it's quite tempestuous really. This turns out to be a short section and a more subdued mood is established with the violin expressing over a cello pizzicato. A brief solo violin interlude leads into a slow, aching passage where the violin expresses a gentle, longing melody. The pizzicato cello resumes and it's all very peaceful. The violin continues with minimal accompaniment and concludes with several sustained tones.

The finale opens in an energised fashion, as befitting its vivace tempo marking. The violins are both dynamic, and combine with further simple melodies. This is a feature for the two violins as they negotiate various dance-like moods – however the dance feeling is a little negated by the very brisk tempo. Now we a have a section of quivering bows, together with the solo violin lamenting, as in the third movement. This moves into a lilting passage with the violins expressing gentle melodies. A pause and an extremely quiet violin moment lead to a conclusion.

Being such a popular work, there are many versions available on Amazon US and UK. My review CD, also contains Smetana's Second Quartet, together with Sibelius' *Intimate Voices* performed by the Dante Quartet on Hyperion – that is quite a lineup. Also I like the look of the work paired with Cesar Franck's only quartet, performed by the Juilliard String Quartet on Sony Classical, or perhaps String Quartet No. 1 with the two Janacek quartets, performed by the Jerusalem Quartet on Harmonia Mundi.

Again, there are several versions on Spotify and both of Smetana's quartets are on YouTube. You can also find some video and further audio performances on earsense.

Listenability: A classic Romantic work.

[Image courtesy Hyperion label]

— oo0oo —

Vladimir Sommer [1921–1977]

Nationality: Czech
Quartets: Three
Style: Early Modern

String Quartets Nos. 1 & 2

Sommer wrote three string quartets but I believe only two have been recorded.

The First Quartet is in three movements. The work begins with a slightly pastoral theme, played rubato and featuring delicate violin melodies with wonderful cello contributions. Suddenly the mood changes, still featuring the

390

same melodies, but played with intensity and more attack on the strings. The opening feeling returns, now with different melodies. The cello states a new theme and the violins pick up on it, segueing into a lively tempo with the violins scattering notes freely. Now we are back to one violin over a cello and viola until a second violin subsequently joins in and a mild chaos ensues, with some wonderful harmonised melodic cello lines and a persistent rhythm in the background. The music is quiet for a few measures, before we have a recapitulation of the opening melody – this time, it features the cello prominently. Eventually moving into tempo and out again, the theme is subject to variations of melodic line and volume. It finishes on a solo theme statement.

The second movement is even slower than the first. Languid melodies are the order of the day as the violin is haunting and the second violin responds for a time. The melodic intensity slowly, then quickly, increases before moving back into the sparse opening, this time with a cello and a rapidly bowed, quivering violin. The cello is plucked for a while and then we have one violin, and now two as the tonality changes from major to minor. A solo cello statement is measured and the quivering returns, with barely audible violin lines combining to deliver a fine sense of sparsity. There is some terrific violin here as it reaches out of its loneliness. Now a solo violin goes gently into its highest register and we have a conclusion. It is a very fine movement and another one for my list of favourite adagios.

The final movement is assertive, with a pizzicato interlude thrown in, before it picks up the tempo again. A key change brings about forceful violin thrusts which soon return to a gentler nature. The tempo increases and a violin bows forcefully as another inserts powerful statements. The composer expresses many variations on this texture, but each time, it reverts to a pulsating feeling – at times it is positively frantic. A sustained violin trill allows the other violin to elaborate on a majestic melody which gradually diminishes until there is nothing left. This, again, is a fine movement to finish a fine quartet.

String Quartet No. 2 is in four movements. From the first few notes you can tell it is going to be more modern than the previous work. It breaks into a faltering rhythm, interspersed with atonal thrusts, eventually finding some peace as the cello comes to the fore and the music dissipates around it. We now have an atonality with intermittent violin themes but no melodic development. The intensity rises and falls and a gentle interlude leads to another frantic atmosphere where the violins are simply outrageous. The end comes with a repeated flourish and two strong chords.

The next movement begins with a longing solo violin, soon to be joined by a second. There is no tempo, just a soundscape, and the cello adds to this beautifully abstract texture. It is almost stasis with atonal melodic lines meandering across a harmonic canvas. This is reminiscent of a string quartet by jazz composer Ornette Coleman that I have heard. The violins move into their highest register for a while before dropping an octave, but still persisting with their slow, atonal murmurings. The violins then just fade away to conclude.

An atonal flourish introduces the third movement and it moves into a syncopated rhythmic ramble as the music explores previously unknown territory. A sparsity features string sound effects and microtones. The violins join forces, spinning out magical melodic lines, and a brief ensemble atonal flourish completes the movement, which is a fine piece of writing.

The final movement features a low cello introduction, with violins weaving more atonal magic, over and under the cello. There is a pleading quality to this music – it cries out. Now it progresses, and becomes tender in an abstract way, the violins slowly lift the intensity and reach into the high register for a time. As this unfolds, I realise that I have never been here before – it is a very spacious feeling, with a sense of an unknown landscape. It eventually leaps into life, only to repeat a sparse three-note phrase from another piece I have reviewed recently – I think it was Schumann's *String Quartet No. 3*. Now the cello speaks as the violins shimmer and the work ends on a sustained cello note. That was some heady stuff.

The most obvious thing to mention is the contrast between the two pieces – they sound like different composers from differing eras. While the first quartet is gently introspective, the second takes it to a whole new level. It's absolutely wonderful. I love the way the music flows from one through to the next.

This CD titled, not unexpectedly, *William Sommer – String Quartets Nos. 1 & 2* on the Panton-Protokol-XX label is performed by the Panocha Quartet – and hats off to them – what a performance. I could only find it on Amazon US as *New and Used* and as an MP3 download. What a shame this is happening to the string quartet repertoire.

The CD is on Spotify and the First Quartet can be found on earsense and YouTube.

Listenability: Beautiful mildly Modern abstraction. Highly recommended for those inclined to such qualities.

— ooOoo —

Charles Stanford [1852–1924]

Nationality: Irish
Quartets: Eight
Style: Late Romantic

String Quartet No. 2

My review CD contains String Quartets Nos. 1 & 2. I don't have the dates of composition but the two are in very contrasting styles. The First is in a Classical style while the Second is definitely of a Romantic nature. I intend to discuss the Second Quartet.

This work opens in a slow fugal manner as the first violin introduces a lamenting melody and the second violin soon comes in behind it. Some strong chords present a stately mood – the cello has a say in this before a change in feeling and tempo follows. The tempo, marked moderato, is now in full swing and the violins produce optimistic melodies, with sometimes pizzicato being present. The melodies move into a descending duet for the two violins, making for a more rhythmic phase with the cello harmonising the violins. A slight folk sounding section ensues, somewhat Gypsy-like, as the violins roam freely in their melodic statements. A solo violin passage slowly brings in the second violin and the ensemble follows. I know the composer is Irish but the music reminds me texturally, of early American string quartets. The solo violin keeps returning and eventually leads the ensemble into an endearing passage. The first violin is persistent and, together with the second, they move into a period of reflection before a sparse moment concludes.

The second movement is short, and races from the beginning. The violins are extremely busy with cascading flourishes of notes. The mood becomes slightly tempered and the violins again produce some charming melodies. Now the previous feeling returns, and the distinctive melodic flourish is heard again. The end is three sharp notes and a final chord.

The next movement, marked andante, again takes me to America. Perhaps there was a little Irish in early American quartets. This is pastoral music, for me, evoking hills and valleys. A change brings a degree of tension as the violins become very animated, agitated even. Some loud chords are heard, and then the opening feeling is revisited. The pastoral feeling returns but this time, with more of an edge to it, leading to a most alluring passage. Now some mild tension is heard, with spiking violins – this doesn't last and a winsome feeling unfolds as the violins spin out complementary melodic lines. The end lets you down easy, with a fade on some gentle chords.

The finale, an allegro, has some jaunty violins with a gentle meter and a basic folk rhythm. It slowly gains impetus and a flurry of melodic activity is very sprightly. The violins express with long phrases and a brief change to a minor tonality gives the music a different sound. The major key soon returns and strong violin lines proceed for some time. Another characteristic descending flourish occurs and the violins settle into an accelerated passage – there is intensity here as the violins move into a strongly rhythmic section. Nearing the end, a feeling of measured melancholia comes over the piece. This is soon dispensed with and a frantic passage concludes the work.

The review CD, on the Helios label, performed by the Vanbrugh Quartet, is available on Amazon US and UK. It also contains a *Fantasy for Horn and String Quartet*, which is very emotional – there is some fine string quartet writing here.

To my great surprise neither of these two string quartets are on Spotify nor YouTube. A CD on the Somm label by the Dante Quartet containing Quartets Nos. 5 and 8 is available on Spotify, YouTube and earsense. I have chosen the image from the Dante Quartet disc for its intrinsic artistic beauty – it's a stunner.

Listenability: An entertaining Romantic work.

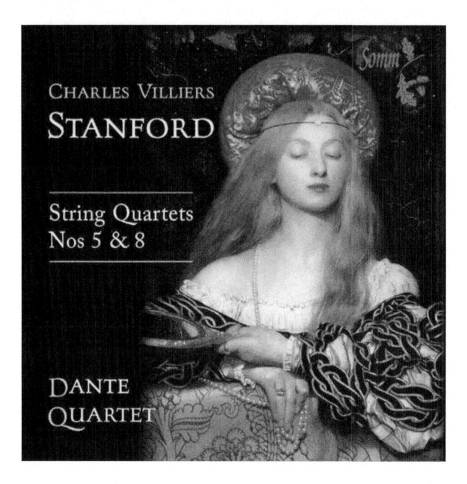

[Image courtesy Somm Recordings]

— ooOoo —

Wilhelm Stenhammar [1871–1927]

Nationality: Swedish
Quartets: Seven
Style: Late Romantic

String Quartet No. 6

Stenhammar's seven string quartets are all Late Romantic works, and are very
lyrical.

The Sixth Quartet opens in a typical Swedish manner, with a touch of melancholy. Soon the violins grow in dynamics for a time, before dropping back to almost nothing. A slow ascending phrase brings about a return to melancholia, and the violins lead us through a gentle phase. The first violin breaks into song and the movement assumes a tempo with overlapping violin phrases – it is splendid writing. Descending violin lines now dominate, and become busy, as the cello rumbles and the violins reach a zenith with strong melodies. The descending lines return and bring about a tranquility. The violins are especially lyrical here, and there is a great depth of feeling before the violins gently waft over the music and end on a chord.

The next movement, marked allegro, is quiet, but insistent in its brief 2:50 appearance. It is a marvellous piece of musical concision.

The third movement, an adagio, begins as a peaceful wander through various, measured melodies. The violins reach out as the melodies become stronger, and the sound is often chordal, eschewing individual melodic lines. The ensemble moves into a period of gentle, pulsating chords and the violins flow effortlessly over this tapestry of sound. As the movement progresses, the violins rise in dynamics but retain the gentle feeling throughout. A solo violin is especially attractive, and continues intermittently until the end of the movement which comes with a solo violin, sometimes gently harmonised, that concludes on a sustained note.

The final movement opens with a dramatic flourish, and is then repeated before the music moves into a chaotic tempo where strong rhythmic, but slightly orchestral melodies, are fashioned as the violins move forward. Some of the playing is frenetic, evoking some unknown memory. A touch of minor harmony brings a slightly serious tone as the violins continue their intensity. It is eventually transformed into a hectic violin passage and is very rhythmic. Some lone ensemble chords change the nature completely and a chord brings about a conclusion.

Several CDs containing String Quartet No. 6 are available on Amazon US and UK. The review version on CPO, by the Oslo Quartet contains Quartets Nos. 4-6.

There are several discs of Stenhammar quartets on Spotify and the work can be found on YouTube. All six quartets, sometimes with multiple versions, are on earsense.

Listenability: Conservative but charming. Music of its time.

Bernard Stevens [1916–1983]

Nationality: British
Quartets: Two
Style: Contemporary

String Quartet No. 2

Bernard Stevens' First Quartet in one movement is titled *Theme and Variations*. It is a fairly significant piece clocking in at over eighteen minutes and is characterised by some poignant sounds, contrasted with a dash of British pastoralism. However, I am going to discuss his Second String Quartet.

The work opens with a lament that lingers for a while. For me, it's not of this world. The violins spread their wings over a tapestry of much beauty until the flow is interrupted by some pizzicato and a tempo ensues. The violins dialogue wonderfully well together as the tempo transitions into another lament. The accompaniment is truly wonderful with such a beautiful background. After a time the tempo lifts again and the violins build into a stately theme before a long descending melody brings us back to the lament. Again, the accompaniment is marvellous as it evokes the introduction. The end comes with the two violins playing enticing, sustained tones.

The second movement, marked presto, begins with some light abstraction until it proceeds into some bright flourishes. The cello is salient, but the violins spur the movement forward. Now the tempo drops and a calm period briefly ensues until the tempo rises again. This time it is forceful and shimmering violins present a most attractive passage which goes out with a flourish.

The next movement opens in a similar manner to that of the first – it's transcendent. Violins harmonise over a delicate accompaniment and there is no forward movement here, it's just pure atmosphere. The cello plays its role in this sustained passage as the volume slowly builds. There is slightly more intensity before dropping back to another lament with the violins particularly expressive. A flurry develops and we now have forward movement as a long, sturdy cello line leads the violins to the conclusion of the movement.

There is no pause before the final movement and it begins at an allegro tempo. This is combative, as the violins and cello compete. The volume drops slightly but the duelling continues, with some chordal interjections. The music then cuts back to nothing, again evoking the opening movement. It is a most mesmeric moment, with subtle playing. Now the tempo is restored, albeit quietly until the violins engage to the point of crescendo. Many flourishes occur as the piece moves towards an orchestral sounding conclusion.

This is a fine, thoughtful work and well worth hearing. Coupled with the *Theme and Variations* there is also a *Lyric Suite for String Trio* on the CD. These pieces are both cut from the same cloth as the Second Quartet and are introspective. The disc, by the Delme Quartet on the Unicorn-Kanchana label is titled *Chamber Music for Strings*.

It is available on Amazon US and UK and the Second String Quartet can be heard on YouTube and earsense.

Listenability: Takes me to a new and wonderful sound world.

— ooOoo —

Alexandre Tansman [1897–1986]

Nationality: Polish
Quartets: Eight
Style: Early Modern

String Quartets Nos. 2 & 8

Of Tansman's eight string quartets, I am going to discuss two of them, an early and a late work.

Firstly, String Quartet No. 2, which was composed in 1925 and is in four movements. This work opens with a light, slightly atonal melody carried by the two violins, creating an atmosphere of a swirling nature as the viola and cello weave in and out. A rise in the intensity has some rhythmic motifs being developed, with a wonderful measured feeling. There is a slight pause and a recapitulation of the first melody. Then the cello and violin set up an ostinato before things becomes focussed and lead to a conclusion.

The second movement, marked lento, is a slow fugue which develops with some sparsity. Again it is mildly dissonant, and somewhat haunting, creating a most interesting soundscape. There is a slight rise in intensity before it moves into a tempo which gives way to the two violins which just fade away.

The third, short movement starts with a singing melody over a pizzicato backing. The violins are energised and propel the music forward. After a few brief rhythmic flourishes, it's all over.

The last movement is strong with cello and viola providing a dynamic opening. A melody is developed with some vigour while the violins constantly repeat a note as the cello pushes hard. The melodies return and the violins repeat a motif which would not be out of place in the 1970s minimalism of Phillip Glass. A strange, stark tone concludes the work.

String Quartet No. 8, written in 1956, is also in four movements. It commences with a torrid mood, the cello being salient. There are many rhythmic flourishes, a certain amount of chaos, and, a sense of ferocious intensity. The violins are like rapiers as they slice through each other's melodies. A propulsive figure ensues before the violins revive their duel. This goes on for some time and is occasionally punctuated by some cello and viola interjections. The movement ends as it began, in a vigorous manner.

The next movement opens slowly, eerily even. It is also slightly Romantic but with a serious tone and the melody is just oh, so sparse. There is a hint of atonality as the two violins move forward on their own before the passage opens up with all players involved. Sometimes the violins sound like film music, not that there is anything wrong with that. They finally fade to a conclusion.

The third movement is centred on a cello figure that dominates the music until the violins take flight. It's all very noisy as the piece develops several crescendos. The violins screech at each other and chaos emerges. The music cuts back to the cello to take it out.

The final movement is marked adagio and is sparse in the extreme. It's hard to imagine the same composer wrote the previous movement. After a time the violins become a little agitated but soon return to the somber feeling. There is some melodic development but the music is barely moving, just extremely understated. A fugue is introduced, which is fascinating at this slow tempo. A sudden violin entrance brings with it another fugue, this time at a fairly moderate tempo, just fast enough to make it chaotic. The music positively dashes to the end.

It's a long time from 1925 to 1956. The Second is a light work while the Eighth, quite intense. This development is common among some twentieth century composers. You can generally experience their progression through their quartets.

These works come on a 2-CD set, *Complete Music for String Quartet* on the Etcetera label, played by the Silesian Quartet. It is available at Amazon US on CD and at Amazon UK as an MP3 download only.

This CD is on Spotify and both quartets, together with some of Tansman's others, can be heard on earsense and YouTube.

Listenability: A most interesting journey.

— ooOoo —

John Tavener [1944–2013]
& Arvo Pärt [born 1935]
Works for String Quartet

This CD contains two one movement, named string quartets by British composer John Tavener, and two works by Estonian composer Arvo Pärt, both arranged for string quartet. These two composers seem to have risen to prominence simultaneously and, in my opinion, sometimes tread similar paths musically. Their works are characterised by a sense of spirituality and an ambience that I haven't experienced very often, particularly with regard to string quartets.

The two Tavener quartets are long with the Pärt arrangements a lot shorter. Due to the emotional, ambient nature of these works, I shall discuss the music rather broadly. The CD is actually under the name of Tavener but the Pärt pieces are important and interesting works in the genre. I will also follow the order of the pieces on the CD.

Tavener – *The Last Sleep of the Virgin*

This work runs for 24 minutes. It begins with sustained chords and moves into an expansive nonspecific melody. This is a common trait for both of the composers. A brief pause brings forth some more ambient sounds as it drifts in and out of various nebulous atmospheres. A lone dissonant note brings about a slight change and another pause introduces a bank of sustained chords which develop into a slightly choral sounding moment. Now we have an ethnic sound and some intensity in melody. Be aware that all of these different sections can last for 3-4 minutes. More sustained chords abound as the music incrementally moves through various changes. Towards the end of the piece, some hand-bell sounds are heard, together with melodic development by the cello. A moment of further dissonance occurs but is soon washed away by another set of sustained chords. It concludes with no obvious ending.

There is an inherent spiritual introspection in this work. Also, while there may be different emotions, the music doesn't seem to go anywhere – it just is. I find it tremendously satisfying.

Pärt – *Summa, for String Quartet*

Repeated motifs define this short piece and the simple interplay of the instrumental voices is soothing. This doesn't go anywhere either, in fact, it seems to constantly grow back into itself like a Mobius strip. A sustained note leads to a peaceful end. It is a mini masterpiece.

Pärt – *Fratres, for String Quartet*

I have heard several versions of this work, all with different instrumentation. It is again based on motifs, in this instance however, they are developed melodically. Sporadic soft percussive sounds colour the background – I suspect that these sounds are made by hands on wooden instruments. Variations of the first motif are slowly introduced into this sparse musical space. There are various pauses and each time they occur, the melodic development is more obvious as the sound becomes fuller. Nearing the end there is a sense of winding down, the music being pared back to the opening texture. It fades out with percussive effects featured. What a fascinating, introspective piece.

Tavener – *The Hidden Treasure, for String Quartet*

There is a sense of ascension in the opening measures as a sparse violin melody wanders above a sustained chord. Occasionally, the second violin contributes a phrase. A pause restarts the process, with the second violin becoming more prominent. Now we have a crescendo – loud ethnic scales spike into the music until it reverts back to a solo violin. Occasionally a tempo is established but it never develops, always returning to the opening mood. At one point the crescendo returns with its strange melodies, continuing for many minutes before subsiding. Now a solo cello keeps the ethnic nature going over a hint of a sustained violin note – the feeling of ascension can again be found here. The cello is positively dynamic but it too succumbs to the underlying sparse texture and a quiet ensues, then we have another crescendo. The conclusion is a long fade of a violin phrase. The work runs for 31 minutes and, while there is more happening than the first piece, I just didn't feel comfortable with it at that epic length.

I hope I have shed some light on this unusual CD. For me they are ambient pieces that may not work for everyone. It is strongly introspective music with clear spiritual overtones. It has probably been claimed by the New Agers but this is a flawed argument. It's real music, not repetitive dross. I would refer to it as meditative, save for the dynamics in *The Hidden Treasure*.

Regarding availability, this CD is performed by the Chilingirian Quartet and goes by the name of *The Last Sleep of the Virgin* on Virgin Records. It is freely available on Amazon US and UK. Some of the works are on Spotify but not this particular CD. Several versions of the Tavener quartets are on YouTube. The Pärt works are too – you will just have to search for them. You can also find them on earsense.

As a postscript, you should make every effort to hear Steven Isserlis play Tavener's magnificent work *The Protecting Veil* for solo cello and string orchestra, also on Virgin Records. It can be sampled on Spotify and YouTube.

Listenability: Mostly extremely introverted, uplifting, spiritual music.

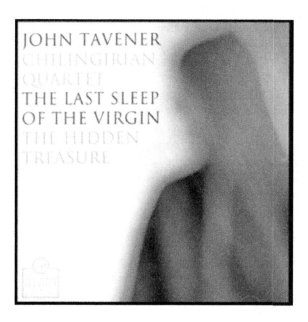

[Image courtesy Virgin Classics via Universal Music]

Incidental Images #10

The Juilliard String Quartet

[Image courtesy Wiki Commons]

The Juilliard String Quartet were one of the most highly regarded ensembles in the middle of the twentieth century. They premiered many composers' new works. This image – date unknown – has the JSQ rehearsing Bartok's First Quartet.

Pyotr Tchaikovsky [1840–1893]

Nationality: Russian
Quartets: Three
Style: Romantic

String Quartet No. 1

Pyotr Ilyich Tchaikovsky was renowned for the use of folk melodies in his works of all styles. He studied the styles and even wrote and published books of folk songs. I am going to discuss his First String Quartet, in D major, Opus 11, which is in four movements. The first two are moderately slow and beautiful, and the last two, brisk and energised.

The first movement opens with a folk sounding melody on one violin. It is repeated and the other instruments gradually enter, leading to a majestic sound. The harmony changes to minor and there is a soft moment where the opening melody prevails again. The music builds and launches into a fast fragment which doesn't last and the precious mood is restored. There is a hint of a terrific melody here – I hope it comes back. Then follows a long pattern of melody and variations before it briefly moves into a tempo and the violin soars above the ensemble, constantly asking questions. The ensemble replies and the piece moves into a most appealing section before taking off again. Now it is racing, the call and response remains, and the first violin brings the ensemble back to a sense of peace. Rumblings arise from the cello and old melodies become new again. The end is at a moderate tempo and goes out with a series of descending motifs. Assessing this movement the phrase *'peaceful heart, gentle spirit'* comes to mind – thanks, Chico Freeman. It is quite beautiful.

The next movement opens with a strong folk-sounding melody based on the ancient Russian folk tune, *The Volga Boatmen Song*. This phrase is worked and reworked for this extended peaceful phase. The music then takes up another simple melody and moves into tempo. A harmonic change allows for further development of the basic melody, before the 'Volga' melody returns with further simple melodic themes in abundance. The conclusion is a solo violin with a handful of cello notes until it fades out with two chords which resolve perfectly.

The short third movement moves into folk territory instantly with an upright, strutting rhythmic structure. The rhythm dominates this movement, with constant slight fragments of straight melody, always coming back into strong rhythmic flourishes. It ends on a solo cello playing a smattering of notes.

The final movement opens at a moderate tempo, again with a simple melody. If it wasn't so brisk it would be dance-like. This movement follows the third in its extensive use of diverse rhythmic patterns, some complicated, with plenty of melodic interspersions. Even the cello has a statement to make as it weaves its way through the rhythmic patterns. Sometimes these patterns are so powerful as to be orchestral sounding, the composer was also a fine symphonist. A salient motif drives the whole last half of this movement, now in a different key which allows for new, varied melodic ideas. There are some marvellous quiet, slow melodic passages between the rhythmic offensives. Following a period of tranquility, the music suddenly leaps into action and positively races to the finish line.

There is just so much contrast in these movements and this work reveals Tchaikovsky to be a fine melodist who is equally comfortable with rhythmic complexity.

These would be some of the most popular quartets in the repertoire, and the composer's quartets are readily available on Amazon US and UK, returning over 1,000 results on both sites. I have them as a 2-CD set on the Apex/Erato label by the Keller Quartet, together with a wonderful string sextet, *Souvenir de Florence*. It is reasonably priced on Amazon UK. As would be expected, they are on Spotify and also on YouTube. Several performances, including the Quatuor Ebène are on earsense.

Listenability: A beautiful Romantic work and a staple of the repertoire.

— ooOoo —

Ludwig Thuille [1861–1907]
Nationality: Italian-Austrian
Quartets: Two
Style: Romantic

String Quartet No. 2
& Quartette-Satz

Italian-born Ludwig Wilhelm Andreas Maria Thuille moved to Austria at age eleven, following the death of both of his parents, where he was raised by an uncle, and is generally considered to be an Austrian composer. Both quartets were written before he was twenty however, there is also a recently discovered one movement work for string quartet, *Quartette-Satz*, which I intend to discuss, along with String Quartet No. 2.

The Second Quartet, in three movements, opens in an allegro tempo, with a strong, pleasing sound, slightly reminiscent of Felix Mendelssohn. A delicate chordal feeling gives way to a sumptuous harmonised melodic phase. Now a rhythm is introduced and the composer crafts melodies that look forward, with a sparse accompaniment. More rhythmic movement unfolds and the first violin contributes some moving lines. The tempo becomes more forceful and further harmonised melodic lines make an appearance, together with some rhythmic punctuation, which leads into another strong melodic passage. This is wonderfully joyous music, and definitely of its time. Accompanied by a sensitive ensemble, fine, gentle violin melodies are expressed and beautifully harmonised.

The cello is prominent for a time, but soon returns to a supporting role, although its influence can readily be heard. The violins continue to dominate, albeit at a low intensity, then there is a slight increase in volume, followed by a soft passage which leads straight into a dynamic flourish to end.

The next movement features a phrase from one of Beethoven's late quartets before continuing the emotional mood of the previous movement. A solo violin section leads to a repeat of the opening passage, which is the subject for a set of melodic variations. A beautiful moment unfolds, with the violins engaging in a harmonised duet – further variations on the opening motif are heard and developed for some time. Rhythmic variation adds to the interest, before there is another flourish to conclude.

The final movement, marked andante, is introduced by slow chordal passages, which gradually drift into a minor tonality. Lush melodic phrases create a great feeling of calm, as the violins meander expressively through an ever changing harmonic landscape. Continually seeking out new melodies, this is a most attractive passage. A pause leads to a slight diminishing of the already slow tempo, which seems to bring a new charm to the music. The violins are splendid here, with gentle but highly expressive melodies in a wonderful section, as the violins bring you back to earth with a subdued ending.

The one movement *Quartette-Satz* again, for me, evokes Mendelssohn, specifically, the opening of his *Octet for Strings*, although, without the extreme propulsion that is a feature of that chamber music classic. All of this is soon left far behind, as many changes in tempo introduce new melodies. Now we have a return to variations on the opening, with its characteristic forward thrust. This feeling is carried forward into the next passage, before a drop in intensity introduces some marvellous melodies and the return of a tempo unleashes wonderful swooping violin lines, in a fascinating violin duet. Once again the tempo rises and the mood becomes almost rhapsodic with the violins very strong, amid several changes in harmony. A recapitulation of the opening has a strength that is palpable. Now the composer has the violins gently unwinding for a period, only to gather in strength for a powerful, orchestral-like conclusion.

The review CD, *Ludwig Thuille: The String Quartets*, on Champs Hill Records and performed by the Allegri Quartet, is available on Amazon US and as a download from Amazon UK. There is also an impressive version by the Signum Quartet, however this does not contain the one movement *Quartette-Satz* and therefore is considerably shorter.

Both performances are available on Spotify and YouTube – the Allegri version is on earsense.

Listenability: Fine, uplifting Romantic quartet works.

Michael Tippett [1905–1998]

Nationality: British
Quartets: Five
Style: Contemporary

String Quartet No. 3

Of Sir Michael Kemp Tippett's five string quartets, I have selected the Third Quartet for discussion as it contains two very expressive slow movements. It was written during 1945-46.

The work opens with an extended chord, leading into a short violin statement, followed by a pause, and a restatement of the opening chord and violin melody. The music is now energised for a time, before gradually becoming more measured. Again there is a pause and the next music heard is the sound of two busy violins in a duet, until the cello and viola move in behind them. The violins begin to make assertive statements and the intensity drops, at least in volume. Another long section of two violins ensues, before the return of the cello and viola as the assertive violins dissipate for a moment, further reducing in volume and intensity. A violin duet carries the movement to the end, which is a sustained chord.

The next movement is an andante and the music commences as a lone cello played pizzicato, jazz style. A violin begins with a lamenting melody as the cello is strummed, sounding somewhat like a lute. A short section of two violins expressing lyrically is most alluring – the combination of the two violins has a quiet, spiritual effect. The cello returns, arco this time, before reverting back to first, pizzicato, and then the strummed sound. Heavenly violins reach out to create a stunning soundscape, with the cello providing occasional support. I could listen to this movement on repeat, it is so satisfying. Nearing the end, the cello becomes more conspicuous, moving from long tones to pizzicato and further strumming, with all instruments concluding on a faded chord.

The third movement is the shortest in the work, and the most rhythmically propulsive. Skipping violins criss-cross at tempo as the cello bounces behind them. The violins are most excited as they carry the music forward. A short, harmonised interlude for cello and a violin is very effective, even dropping in intensity for a moment before the violins return with a race to a final flourish.

The fourth movement, marked lento, is the emotional heart of the work, with an almost inaudible shrill violin being the first sound heard. The second violin, then the cello join the music and the dynamics rise rapidly. A pause brings about a powerful solo cello section, which is quite long and is occasionally interrupted by the two violins. Now the opening feeling is revisited, the shrill violin set against the long, resonant tones of the cello. The violins return to the lower register and rapidly, we have a recapitulation of the previous dynamic passage with the cello repeating its earlier statements. A pause brings about a new mood as the cello drones, and a violin expresses long notes – this is music of great emotional depth. A gradual return to the dynamics results in a chaotic passage which closes the movement.

Without a pause the finale commences with a sense of the mysterious, again slightly chaotic. This soon abates but the violins are still a little hectic and the cello adds to the feeling in intermittent bursts of energy. The violins are insistent and make for a fascinating section exploring a mild atonal mood which eventually concludes the work on a strong, held chord.

The CD liner notes describe this movement as a *'gentle, relaxed fugue'*. I didn't find it relaxed and I doubt whether the audience at its 1946 premiere would have either. But what a pleasure it was coming across a quartet with two slow movements – I find the piece to be beautifully balanced in its construction.

My review CD, which is fairly old, and titled *The String Quartets*, on the Brilliant Classics label, is performed by the Britten Quartet and contains Nos. 1-4. This version can still be found on Amazon UK. The composer subsequently wrote a Fifth Quartet and there is a version by the Heath Quartet on the Wigmore Hall Live label, which contains all five works in a 2-CD live set. This too, is available on Amazon US and UK. There are also two single Naxos discs featuring various quartets.

The Heath Quartet is on Spotify and there are several quartets on YouTube. The Britten Quartet is one of two versions on earsense.

Listenability: Mid twentieth-century modernism. Very listenable with some stunning moments.

— oo0oo —

Boris Tishchenko [1939–2010]

Nationality: Russian
Quartets: Six
Style: Contemporary

String Quartets Nos. 1 & 3

Interestingly, Tishchenko's quartets cover a time span of over fifty years. I am going to discuss the First and the Third Quartets.

The First Quartet, written in 1957 is relatively short, and contains three movements, commencing with an extended solo violin section. The mood is morose and the playing folk-like as the violin fashions a conservative melody. The violin is then joined by a harmonic backdrop of sustained chords – quite beautiful really. A solo cello statement appears and the ensemble soon overwhelms it, creating very tense music before some gentle harmonised cello lines predominate over the sound of strings, which eventually assume control. A return to the opening is this time accompanied by the ensemble. The cello again steps forward and moves to an ending.

The second, brief movement commences with a throbbing rhythm, which is occasionally interrupted by violins. However, the feeling eventually returns for a short time. Now we have a passage of controlled chaos until the throbbing is resumed. A virtuosic cello line leads to a conclusion.

The finale, marked lento, features a longing violin over sustained string tones, making for a most alluring passage. A solo violin introduces a little optimism, which leads to a violin reaching skywards. Upon returning to the ground, it is rejoined by the ensemble and some powerful cello lines are heard. The cello cycles through several changes of tonality, before the opening peace is again heard. The music has now become quiet and it just fades away.

The Third Quartet was written in 1970 and is in four movements. It is a strange piece, as I shall attempt to explain. It again opens with a solo violin, to be joined by some ensemble interjections. This creates a very gentle, expressive mood which persists for some time. There is no pulse to be found here, and the violins restrict themselves to a limited emotional range. The arrival of the cello adds tension, especially when it makes striking melodic statements. The music now becomes agitated, with no instrument seemingly concerned about its environment. This is the first strange section in the work. Having completely destroyed the opening mood, the whole ensemble powers to an abrupt ending.

The next movement leads straight into abstraction with dissonant, rhythmically charged violin flourishes and the cello adding to the sound. A pause leads into a sparse, but disjointed section which is high on entropy and low on structure, consisting mostly of string sound effects. A solo violin makes for a dissonant melodic line as it races to the end. I believe that the movements in this work are to be played without pauses in between, as the music seems to suggest this.

The third movement starts with a robust solo cello, and is soon joined by the ensemble. Again, there is a high degree of entropy. A violin and cello duet proceeds in a most disjointed manner before all instruments become involved and a chaos is achieved. Some rhythmic punctuation is briefly felt, and the violin negotiates this with strange melodies. This is followed by a set of chaotic passages broken up by small breaks whereupon the cello goes solo in a most unstructured fashion. The violins resume their chaotic musings, and proceed to an ending with some powerful flourishes. Strange music indeed.

This time, there is a pause between movements and the finale opens with a most poignant mood, so distant from the third. Two violins reflect with overlapping plaintive melodies, gradually increasing in intensity. A touch of dissonance can occasionally be heard as the mood progresses through an extended period. Now a loud phrase is heard, then repeated and developed, but the ambience of the violins persists. That hurdle crossed, the violins proceed with a gentle cello accompanying. When the cello drops out, the violins lead to an almost inaudible conclusion.

I call this music strange because of its vast contrasts, beginning within the first movement and continuing through the second and third. The last movement is from a different musical world.

Tishchenko's quartets are available, but not many are on single CDs. There is a 3-CD set, *Complete String Quartets*, on the Northern Flowers label, performed by two different quartet ensembles. It has become hard to find but is still available at Presto Classical.

This set can be heard on Spotify. All six quartets are on earsense and Quartets Nos. 1 and 3 can be found on YouTube.

Listenability: Some fine slow passages littered with chaotic moments.

[Image – Northern Flowers label – Not able to be contacted]

Ernst Toch [1887–1964]

Nationality: German
Quartets: Thirteen
Style: Early Modern

String Quartets Nos. 6 & 12

Toch's first seven quartets remained unpublished in his lifetime, and he certainly began early, as No. 6 was composed when he was seventeen. The progression from the Sixth to the Twelfth is pronounced. The Sixth is a conservative work, while the Twelfth is fully mature.

The Sixth Quartet is in four movements, and opens with a magnificent melody and an orchestral approach. The sound levels out into a charming passage where melodies flow effortlessly. A change to the minor key brings a different feeling, very refined while some more orchestral sounding writing unfolds before reverting back to an earlier theme. The minor key brings forth another alluring melody which turns out to be the heart of the movement. This moves through many different textures, from solo violin to the Berlin Philharmonic. Well almost anyway. A cello steps out to craft a new melody, which is significant and is sustained for some time before being subsumed back into the ensemble. As we near the end, forceful chords abound, before it finishes with a flourish.

The next movement, marked andante, begins with a folksy sound as swirling violin melodies evoke ethnic sounds. Eventually, a solo violin takes centre stage before handing back to the full ensemble as they investigate the melody. There are subtle rhythmic changes before the ensemble suddenly jumps into life with a rhythmic intensity, as the music positively races with frantic violin phrases being presented at speed. A slight relief appears, and multiple variations ensue. Now we have a new melody, which is beautifully written, before an earlier phrase returns for a final time. The violins contribute a gentle ascending melodic line to conclude.

The third movement, another andante, is ever so peaceful, until the violins reach into a high register. It leads to a romantic sound and a change into a delightful waltz tempo allows the violins to portray a lyrical feeling. The cello joins in the melody and brings about a dramatic change – this is totally out of character for the movement. The composer builds a wall of sound and intensity, which gradually subsides into another waltz. The violins are delicate and it could be Schumann, or even Mozart. Another dramatic flurry ensues with quivering bows being the order of the day. Now the music settles and fades out ever so slowly.

The final movement opens with a strong chord which leads into a rhythmic ensemble. A violin furnishes the propulsion with some fine playing and busy melodies until the intensity drops slightly, although the tempo remains the same. Now the intensity rises again with harmonic changes leading to development of melodies. The full rhythmic feeling returns for a short while but again, moves back to a more peaceful place. It is actually the shortest movement in the work, but it has a feeling of epic proportions. It finally succumbs and ends on a flourish.

While the Sixth Quartet was Toch's first extant composition in the genre, the Twelfth was the first major work undertaken after WW II. String Quartet No. 12 is 40 years and a world away from the Sixth – there is a striking difference both in conception and realisation. It contains four movements.

The first, marked *calmly*, opens with two violins locked into an intertwining soundscape, with the mood quietly passive despite its insistence. After several minutes of stasis the movement bursts into life with a loud passage featuring dissonant melodic lines. They gradually diminish in intensity, all the way back to a solo violin. The opening is again heard, with the cello now playing a more prominent role. The end comes with a melodic violin and murmurs from the ensemble. This movement is a terrific piece of atonal abstraction.

The next movement opens with loud atonal musings which soon dissipate into another world as the cello leads the violins into another stunning intangible mood. The intensity rises and falls, such that all that is heard are two violins in a duet, filled with intimacy. The duet takes a more melodic turn and the cello joins in, creating a moment that spirals upward, revealing some use of microtones. Now it briefly drops back to a violin duet – such a longing feeling. A minimal violin phrase fades to a conclusion. It is another tour de force.

The third movement starts in a more conservative, rolling manner, which evokes a gentle feeling. The melodies are lyrical, but it is the intertwining nature that captures my attention – it continues throughout the whole movement. A change brings with it a rhythmic emphasis and the violins are stronger, but the lyricism remains. A touch of pizzicato allows for a brief relief, while the cello walks, jazz-like. It is a relatively static movement, but still delightful in its innocence. A few gentle chords lead to an end on a violin phrase.

The finale features a loud, gaudy opening, with the violins crowding each other. Now the intensity drops and the cello plays a repeated note. We have a brief snippet of the opening again, before returning to a mild dynamic. A pause reintroduces the opening, played loudly and the violins compete, seemingly on different stages until the intensity drops again and one violin carries a motif while the other soars. Some string sound effects introduce a strong passage that leads to a return of the motif. There is nothing intimate about this music, but it is wonderful in its strength. A key change adds to the chaos as the violins continue to spar. A heavy chord brings about some violin musings which produce a closing phrase.

This quartet is a marvellous piece of sustained, busy, abstract beauty. I think I shall leave it at that.

Most of Toch's string quartets have been released as a series, but I fear some have been deleted. This disc, titled *Ernst Toch: String Quartets 6 & 12*, on the CPO label, performed by the Verdi Quartet, with a striking red cover, is still available on Amazon US and UK, albeit as *New and Used*.

This CD is also on Spotify, along with two others of the series. There are many of Toch's quartets on earsense and several on YouTube.

Listenability: A wonderful CD, showing two sides of the composer's development.

— ooOoo —

Manfred Trojahn [born 1949]

Nationality: German
Quartets: At least six
Style: Modern Contemporary

String Quartet No. 4

The music of Manfred Trojahn is in a fairly modern style and of the two string quartets on this CD, Nos. 3 and 4, I have chosen No. 4 to discuss – it is a little milder than No. 3.

This four movement work opens with a dissonant four-note arpeggio, with each instrument playing a different note. After a pause, a similar, descending arpeggio is heard. There are a lot of silences within the music, leading to many gaps. The ensemble now moves into tempo with a harmonic backdrop that allows the violin to craft a sparse melody – another pause ensues. Some gentler arpeggios are heard and the violin searches to find a melody of substance, while the cello and second violin evoke an alluring soundscape. It is followed by a brief dissonant intrusion and another pause, which turns out to be the movement conclusion.

The short second movement is busy, but not too intense. The instruments scuttle about, sometimes softly, at other times, moderately loudly. A series of dissonant chords interrupt the proceedings briefly before the busy feeling returns. The dissonance is repeated until a most harmonious chord gives way to some rhythmic phrases which end the movement.

The next movement, marked lento, begins ever so gently, with sustained tones. Melodies slowly emerge as the cello keeps the sustain going until a solo violin statement commences and the cello adds a few notes to the feeling. Now all of the instruments involve themselves in a most attractive section. Long melodies appear, bringing with them a deep feeling. A pause occurs and a layer of string sound effects allows for the development of a sombre violin melody. The cello plays a persistent phrase as the violin, way up in the high register, fades out.

The final movement is rather spirited, and all four instruments converse in a slightly chaotic dialogue. There is a theme to be found in here, I know it. Now a succession of flourishes give way to a charming melody – it could be an English

411

country garden. The violin exchanges phrases with ensemble interjections but it is still pleasant, with a light feeling. A brief chaos breaks the mood and the cello takes over with string harmonics sounding in the background. This leads to more chaos until the violins make light, abstract sounds before finishing with a full chord.

I can't pin this piece down. It's definitely different. There is an absence of cliches, or any recognisable influences here, as far as I can tell. I couldn't find any of Trojahn's other quartets anywhere.

I should also mention two further works on the review CD. Firstly, there is a six-piece suite, *Fragmente für Antigone* which is an assortment of modern sketches. There is also an interesting, dramatic 10-minute piece titled *Lettera amorosa- No. 6. Chant d'insomnie III* – (Song to Insomnia III) which is, and I quote, *'the penultimate movement of the seven movement score Lettera amorosa* (Love letter), *for 2 sopranos, 2 violins and string quartet'*. No sopranos were heard in the piece – I believe it to be a string quartet transcription.

This CD, titled *String Quartets,* on the Neos label and performed by the Henschel Quartett, is available on Amazon UK and Presto Classical. It is on Spotify and both Quartets Nos. 3 and 4 can be heard on YouTube and earsense.

Listenability: Mildly Modern, slightly eccentric and most listenable.

[Henschel Quartett – image source HQ website]

412

George Tsontakis [born 1951]

Nationality: American
Quartets: At least four
Style: Contemporary

String Quartet No. 4

Tsontakis' Fourth String Quartet, titled *Beneath Thy Tenderness of Heart* is in three named movements.

Introduction – Chorale and Meditations is the longest movement of the work. Opening with a hymn-like quality, a peaceful mood is established, which features simple <u>harmonised</u> melodic lines. This proceeds into a <u>fugal</u> sounding passage, with the instruments mimicking each other. A sense of tension then ensues, followed by some severe violin interspersions – the violins are very emotionally deep here. Soon the sound of the music evokes waves, as lines propel it forward, before moving into an introspective section, and then a return to the opening simplicity. A tempestuous passage, with powerful overlapping instrumental utterances is heard before a peace again settles with a violin in the upper register lamenting romantically. This certainly doesn't sound like the prevailing musical climate of string quartets from this era.

An intense cello-driven mood gives way to another powerful passage and a sustained solo violin tone ends with a brief pause. Earlier passages are revisited before some strong chordal melodies are heard. The music seems to move between the powerful and the introspective at will, always filled with interesting textures. A gentler moment evokes late Beethoven, giving way to a chaos which still contains great beauty. Spiralling violins dominate, becoming circular in motion, as they drive towards a frantic finish.

Part Two: Scherzo is comparatively brief and begins with positive, rhythmically satisfying harmonised cello lines. There is an abundance of forward movement here as the two violins converse, within the confines of a strong cello accompaniment. Now the piece is bursting with energy until it fades into a wispy atmosphere, albeit briefly, before the tempo is resumed. Frantic violins navigate ascending <u>harmonic</u> movement, which eventually gives way to a piercing solo violin to terminate.

Part Three: Postlude, the Madonna Weeps starts frantically but soon fades into a dissonant, but alluring section for two violins – there is a great sense of mystery here. A pause leads to another loud flourish but this too returns to a sustained violin duet. The dissonance has gone but the feeling of mystery continues. A pattern seems to develop as another strong flourish leaves us alone with two violins – occasionally the viola and cello offer harmonised motifs in the background. Again a similar passage unfolds which is loud and leads to some considered violin melodies in an abstract duet, with a gentle, pulsing accompaniment. The violins are magical here. The cycle is repeated, although now the boisterous nature lasts for a considerable time. Eventually we are back

413

to a previous soundspace, this time with a shrill, solo violin featured. A sparse harmonic undercurrent sustains the shrill tone of the violin as it slowly fades to a conclusion. This is a tremendous movement, filled with deep emotional moments.

The review CD, by the American String Quartet, also contains a wonderful Quartet No. 3, another three movement work, titled *Coraggio*. The first movement, marked lento isn't even slow, but rhythmic and dramatic while the second, marked *misterioso*, is a stunning piece of writing.

This disc, *George Tsontakis – String Quartets Nos. 3 & 4*, on New World Records is sometimes available on Amazon US and UK and is currently obtainable from Presto Classical.

The CD can be sampled on Spotify.

Listenability: Innovative, emotionally charged Contemporary work.

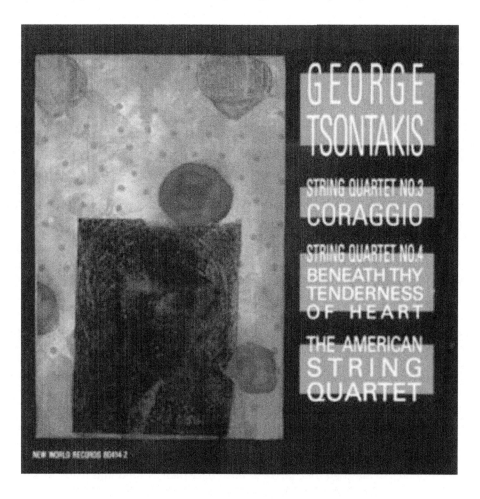

[Image - New World Records – could not be contacted]

414

Joaquín Turina [1882–1949]

Nationality: Spanish
Quartets: One
Style: Early Modern

The String Quartet

Joaquín Turina Pérez' only string quartet is titled *De La Guitarra* and is in five movements. The opening, marked *andantino*, which apparently can be slightly slower or quicker than <u>andante</u>, starts with a brief chordal fanfare, answered by a solo <u>pizzicato</u> cello phrase. The cello then leads the ensemble through an appealing melodic section before the violins eventually take the lead and a deep, distinctive Spanish sound is evoked. Now the violins break free and bring a sense of romance to the music. Superb <u>harmonised</u> melodies slowly rise in intensity but soon return to a calm before a brief <u>recapitulation</u> of the opening moments is heard, followed by a solo violin passage which concludes.

The next movement is optimistic in nature and features warm melodic motifs, again revealing Spanish characteristics, with a charming violin melody again being somewhat romantic in nature. A chordal fanfare, similar to the opening of the work is heard and the music moves into a strong tempo, replete with wonderful melodic sections. The cello is very expressive here as it intertwines with the violins. A pause leads into another warm, romantic mood as the composer again revisits his Spanish roots. A passage of theme and variations is most attractive as the violins investigate new melodies. The end comes with three sustained solo violin tones.

The third movement begins in an introspective style with the cello slowly leading the ensemble into emotionally lighter territory. After a time the music comes to life in a distinctively Spanish manner, leading to a more measured section, which is very precious, before the violins bring the music to life with striking, rhythmic playing. The mood soon settles however, and an emotional depth is restored. A scintillating chordal flourish finishes the movement.

A lone violin opens the next movement, which is quite slow. The violins create soft, drawn-out melodic statements and there is a great sense of peace here. Now the mood is lightened as the violins express positive melodies for a time before they begin to turn rhapsodic, albeit in a stately manner. A solo cello interlude introduces a joyous melodic section which again evokes a feeling of romance. The end is unexpected, but beautiful.

Floating melodies introduce the final movement, which soon develops into a sprightly tempo. The violins soar freely, with much impetus, eventually returning to the ground and a gentler feeling – there is great <u>lyricism</u> here, as the melodies continue to develop through several <u>harmonic</u> changes. A brief pause introduces a new section and frantic violins give their all as they explore the Spanish touches. The music becomes more powerful before receding again, with the conclusion being another flourish, then a sharp chord.

This is a fabulous quartet, filled with joy, sometimes contrasted with feelings of romance. There are two other significant quartet works on the review CD – *Serenata* and *La Oración Del Torero* and also a sublime piano quintet, *Quinteto En Sol Menor* – good value for money here.

The review CD is titled *Joaquín Turina: Música De Cámara*, on the Documentos Sonoros label, performed by the Greenwich String Quartet with Brenno Ambrosini on piano. It is freely available on Amazon US and UK, along with many string quartet compilations containing the work.

The CD is on Spotify and several quartet movements are on YouTube. The full version can be heard on earsense.

Listenability: Wonderful Spanish chamber music.

— ooOoo —

Louis Vierne [1870–1937]

Nationality: French
Quartets: One – FOSQC
Style: Late Romantic

String Quartet No. 1

Louis Vierne's only String Quartet, Opus 12, was written in 1894 and this youthful work is in four movements. The piece opens with a solo cello, before the violins enter. The pace quickly picks up with a series of folk melodies in abundance, this continues for some time. The violins dominate and we have several key changes before it then develops at a more moderate pace, all the while with the violins leading the way. This continues to an ending, featuring a series of chords.

The next movement begins with a skittish violin over a cello and a charming melody develops. A recapitulation allows for some melodic development – it sounds a little like *The Teddy Bears' Picnic*. It pauses briefly, then moves to a tranquil conclusion. This movement is only three minutes long.

The third movement is an andante and offers up a satisfying texture. There are hints of a melody from Wagner's symphonic poem *Siegfried Idyll*. The intensity increases for a time before a solo violin leads the passage into some stronger melodies – the violin goes way up into its highest register and the ensemble begins to support it. There is a recapitulation of an earlier melody and there goes *Siegfried Idyll* again. Now the music just bubbles along until it finds its resting place.

The final movement produces a dance-like feeling as it moves into a brisk tempo until the rhythm ceases and a rubato moment ensues. The violin quickly

416

returns to tempo and, melodically, it is still very simple. After a short pause, a brief fugal interlude is heard as the music struts and is a little orchestral. Nearing the end, the piece is going at a breakneck tempo and the work finally finishes on several repeated chords.

Vierne was also a virtuoso organist who wrote several major organ symphonies, and many works for solo organ, some of which are of a transcendent nature. He died while performing the end of a piece, at the organ. As he fell, his left foot landed on the lowest bass pedal and the note reverberated through the cathedral in which he was giving the performance – thanks, Wiki.

The review CD, by the Spiegel String Quartet on the MDG label also contains a piano quintet. This work is readily available on Amazon US and UK. It is also on a number of Vierne chamber music compilations, it's just a case of finding an appropriate pairing.

There is a 2-CD set, *Chamber Music* on Spotify which contains the quartet and there are several versions on YouTube. The performance from Spotify is also on earsense.

Listenability: A fine piece of French writing.

— oo0oo —

Heitor Villa-Lobos [1887–1959]

Nationality: Brazilian
Quartets: Seventeen
Style: Early Modern/Contemporary

String Quartet No. 15

The work starts with a gorgeous melodic flavour until things start getting a little more serious. The violin constantly spins out melodies over the ensemble as it moves through different moods, with the sound from the ensemble being full at all times. A brief pause leads to a drop in intensity and a slightly lilting section with a fabulous ascending violin line, moving into a serious moment. This music is rhapsodic and also very busy with folk sounding statements from the violin as it takes flight. Rhythmic assertions are prominent but we are left with a brief interlude for two violins until the cello thunders in to conclude the movement on a full chord.

The next movement, marked moderato, is actually played slowly. A shimmering violin and string sound effects are heard during the introduction which leads into a mournful melody backed by a cello phrase. The violin starts in the low register before rising to lighten the atmosphere. A superb chordal accompaniment allows the violins to explore the melody at length. A new, swirling melody develops and the violin moves into its high register before the cello signals the return of a mournful scene and the violin picks up on the cello melody. The cello is salient for a time until the violins return. A brief pause ensues and we are back at the beginning. The introduction of a sustained cello note allows the violins to drift to the conclusion.

For me, this is the emotional centrepiece of the work as the melodies are magnificent in their conception and execution.

The third movement is short at two minutes and comprises mostly a joyful dance flavour, with all instruments playing their role. Not being overly familiar with Brazilian music, I think of it as having a Spanish flavour. The ending is particularly inspired, with a lot happening in a brief time.

Solo cello introduces the final movement before the feeling becomes rhapsodic as the cello interweaves with the violins. There is a warmth to this music that is probably part of the native style. There is much interplay, together with harmonic changes. Suddenly the feeling is intensified and many ascending and descending lines can be heard. The cello recalls the beginning, this time in a truncated form while the violins dance over a warm cello phrase. The cello now dominates for a time and, when the violins return, the phrasing reminds me of the string writing of Charles Ives. A low rumbling passage is heard and the ensemble gathers itself for a slightly dissonant final flourish.

This work is available on several single CD releases, including the Danubius Quartet on Marco Polo, who have recorded the complete quartets. There is also a complete 6-CD set by the Cuarteto Latinoamericano on Brilliant Classics. All of these items are on Amazon US and UK, although some seem to be not long for this world.

The Danubius Quartet version is on Spotify coupled with Quartets Nos. 3 and 10. Several versions are on YouTube and there are many quartets to be found on earsense.

Listenability: A striking, rhythmically incisive work, with a great slow movement.

— ooOoo —

Carl Vine [born 1954]

Nationality: Australian
Quartets: At least six
Style: Contemporary

String Quartet No. 5

Vine's first five quartets, from 1979 to 2007 are all contained on the review CD. Four of these works are in one movement with the First being the exception. A

Sixth Quartet, titled *Child's Play* was composed in 2017. There are probably more coming.

Muffled, organ-like, sparse solo violin sounds introduce the Fifth Quartet. As further instruments enter, some with harmonised lines, the organ effect is even more pronounced. The music now breaks into a period of measured chaos with flurries of violin lines underpinned by striking cello phrases and pizzicato viola. The intensity increases rather quickly, almost to the point of anguish, before a sequence of strong, descending chords is heard, rather like a heavy metal version of a section of Vivaldi's *Four Seasons*, before a return to the more measured feeling. This time the fluttering violin lines are accompanied by an arco cello, using double-stops to create chords until it reverts to murmuring melodic lines. Now a tempo is established and again the strong descending chord section is repeated – I hope Vivaldi is getting royalties from this frantic passage. A solid chord leads to a pause in proceedings and a solo violin muses in a slightly dissonant manner. In a complete contrast the ensemble now embarks on a sumptuous section with alluring harmonised melodies which would not be out of place in a Romantic work, save for a hint of dissonance. Vine then deconstructs this passage, adding more conflict through dissonance – I hesitate to call it self-mocking as it soon returns to the Romantic nature.

The music has become lamenting, with the violins expressing sparse, long melodic lines in a rubato manner. The emergence of the cello brings about a call and response nature. A further change has a sprightly pizzicato backing, with the violin introducing further Romantic melodies until a strange rhythmic pattern leads to a virtuosic violin line, negotiating simple harmonic changes – this is not music of its time. The rhythm is now doubled, but the solo violin persists and puts the virtuosity aside, leading to a wonderful set of unfolding melodies.

A pause leads to a new pizzicato-backed section. A wonderful cello line in a high register creates another alluring passage which doesn't last as the music unexpectedly turns frantic. Dissonant violin lines surge forward and move through a variety of textures from the ensemble. A persistent cello rhythm sets the tone, and eventually makes its own melodic contribution, leading to a hectic series of harmonised cello and violin lines. A brief intense section gives way to a complete contrast as the violin again expresses long lines against a sympathetic accompaniment. This time, the violin soars into its highest register with some stunning playing – this is a simply beautiful, sustained passage. Now the second violin works a motif to underpin the first violin, allowing the music to reach great heights, reminiscent of Vaughan Williams' *The Lark Ascending*. This violin becomes ever so shrill before the ensemble create a jaunty rhythmic pattern which is then harmonised by the first violin. It begins to have fun by responding to the rhythmic motif, and adding variations. The dynamics increase and the violin leads the ensemble through some rhythmic histrionics before an abrupt conclusion.

You will have noticed a sense of duality in this work – in essence, the historical with the present, side by side. After sampling the other quartets, I feel that they tend to be more in a modern style, but, as I only scanned them, I can't be precise about that.

The review CD, *Carl Vine: String Quartets* is performed by the Goldner String Quartet on the ABC Classics label, distributed worldwide by Universal Music. It is only on MP3 download at Amazon US and UK, but is available at Presto Classical, and probably elsewhere.

The CD is on Spotify and most of the works are on YouTube and earsense.

Listenability: Surprisingly contrasting work, with many wonderful moments.

— ooOoo —

Voices of Defiance – Compilation

Nationality: N/A
Quartets: Three
Style: Early Modern

This music, performed by the Dover String Quartet, contains pieces by three composers with all of the works having a link to World War II. The three composers are Dmitri Shostakovich – Russian, Szymon Laks – Polish, and Viktor Ullmann – Czech. I am going to discuss the Laks and Ullmann works.

Ullmann's String Quartet No. 3, in two movements, was written in the Theresienstadt concentration camp in 1943. Given the circumstances, it is interesting in that it opens with a lush mood – romantic melodies abound, this could be popular music. Slowly the music drifts into abstraction, while still maintaining a melodic approach, but changing to a more dissonant note selection. It eventually starts to fall apart and becomes somewhat introspective. There is a small period of rhythmic intensity but it soon returns to its former melodic nature. A period of unrest ensues, but again, not for long as a violin and a cello exchange phrases for a moment. Now a virtuosic violin phrase leads into a tempo, with many rhythmic interjections – this is somewhat reminiscent of Shostakovich's early quartets. The tempo now dissipates, leaving a lone violin to initiate another lush passage which slowly ebbs and flows until a pause brings about another longing solo violin moment. The second violin gently moves into the music and there is a stasis as the two violins muse with an occasional cello phrase in support. The end comes very quietly.

The short second movement commences powerfully with strong, rhythmic, harmonised, dissonant phrases. The violin leads a slightly hectic passage, which then restates the opening. A solid chordal phase leads into another full, rich, dissonant run of chords that conclude the piece.

Szymon Laks' Third Quartet, in four movements, was written in 1945 following his liberation from Auschwitz at the end of the war. It begins with a

420

jaunty passage, followed by an insistent ostinato moment, before returning to the opening mood. This feeling is expanded into an extended passage with a great depth of feeling, which is finally moderated by another jaunty mood. The violins intersperse rhythmic thrusts with optimistic, melodic sections – these thrusts are most effective, evoking a military flavour. This movement already displays great variation, and many fine melodic phrases. A slight tension builds, but it quickly dissipates into a harmonised section, again with a military sound, before it finishes on some strong chords.

The second movement opening suggests a Beethoven influence with slightly dissonant sustained chords producing a delicate melody. A violin plays beautiful, lilting phrases and a slow viola pizzicato leads to another wonderful harmonically rich fabric. The violins are almost searing in their intensity, producing a powerful sound. Now we return to the lilting melodies which drift casually across a viola ostinato. An almost orchestral sounding passage ensues, with rich harmonies underpinning the melodies. Eventually it moves to a faded ending.

The next movement has a pizzicato introduction with all instruments involved. This proceeds for an extended period, with occasional melodic interludes. These melodies are very simple and not of their time, they are most romantic. It's fair to say that this movement is dominated by pizzicato, even with the melodic phases. The end is a long, racing pizzicato melodic line.

The finale begins with a succession of rolling chordal phrases. This quickly changes to a folk sounding solo violin melodic passage, followed by another ensemble section with the same mood. The ethnic rhythms continue, and build in intensity to drive the music forward. A short fiddle-like violin interlude leads back into the previous intensity, but this time it is for an extended period of strong chords which increase in volume. A virtuosic violin passage brings with it a new mood which slows down the chords and concludes the work.

I am not going to discuss the Shostakovich Second Quartet, written in 1944 but I can tell you it is an ominous, foreboding work. Performed magnificently here by the Dover Quartet, it runs for over thirty minutes. A further discussion on Laks can be found in this book.

Being a relatively new release, this CD on Cedille Records is available on both Amazon US and UK. You can also listen to it on Spotify and YouTube. Both Laks and Ullmann quartets are on earsense.

Listenability: A superb, themed album containing some fine music.

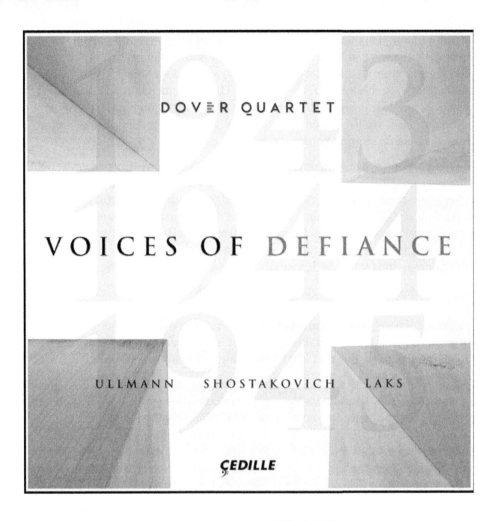

[Image courtesy Cedille label]

— ooOoo —

Kevin Volans [born 1949]

Nationality: South African
Quartets: At least ten
Style: Contemporary

String Quartet No. 4

Not all of Volans' quartets have been recorded and of those that have, some are no longer available. He first came to prominence when the Kronos Quartet recorded his *White Man Sleeps*, in two versions. The second, complete version is still available on the *Pieces of Africa* CD. This work, along with his other early quartets, contain strong influences of African music and minimalism. He befriended Morton Feldman and was obviously influenced by him, as evidenced in the second movement of the Fourth Quartet. This work is titled *The Ramanujan Notebooks*, after the great early twentieth century Indian mathematician Srinivasa Ramanujan. It was written in 1990, and revised in 1994. Consisting of only two movements, it is still quite long.

The Fourth Quartet commences with some brief pizzicato rhythmic string sound effects, slightly African, interspersed with some simple violin phrases. There are also interjections of one iteration of a minimalist ostinato motif. This pattern continues for a time, with the number of iterations of the motif regularly increasing and hinting at what is to come. Eventually an extended ostinato prevails and a new phase emerges, with random violin phrases, together with some rhythmic punctuation. A lone violin now expresses some long tones, leading into an ensemble dialogue. This is quite an abstruse passage, with all instruments having a say. A change to solo violin leads into another dialogue, this time with the second violin and there is also a return of the opening percussive string sound effects. A random section unfolds and we then have a brief pause.

Some further rhythmic dialogues occur, interspersed with seemingly random violin exchanges. The extended ostinato that I was anticipating hasn't eventuated and the feeling is introspective with occasional iterations of a new motif. Solid, rhythmic chordal phrases are interjected sporadically and the first violin negotiates a path around them. The feeling is sustained for some considerable time – it's quite entropic now – before concluding on a sustained violin tone. This music is of a measured, modernist nature and while abstract, is totally inoffensive.

As previously mentioned, the second movement is in a completely different style, opening with a slow, simple, quiet melodic phrase, which is repeated. It could have come from Feldman's *String Quartet II*. A new ensemble phrase is introduced, and then another. There are subtle variations in each group of phrases, a feature not found in the above Feldman work. Now a section consisting of a cello plucked note with a violin response unfolds – the cello is more obvious in the various phrases now. A longer phrase is introduced but this doesn't change the mood, which is basically stasis. A rhythmic strike from a violin leads to some abstract sounding violins; the strikes return and the movement is over.

The review CD also contains String Quartet No. 6, titled *Dancers on a Plane*, which is a long, one movement work which also displays evidence of the composer's African and minimalist interests.

This CD, titled *Volans: Dancers on a Plane / The Ramanujan Notebooks / Movement for String Quartet*, on the Collins Classics label, and performed by the Duke Quartet, is available on Amazon UK and Presto Classical.

There are many Volans quartets, including Nos. 4 and 6 on Spotify, earsense and YouTube.

— ooOoo —

Anton Webern [1883–1945]

Nationality: Austrian
Quartets: Several
Style: Early Modern

Early Works for
String Quartet

There is a little confusion regarding the number of string quartets of Webern because he composed two one movement works and a rondo without opus numbers, which makes them dubious to some scribes. Wikipedia refers to them as *juvenalia,* what a cheek. I intend to examine the two without opus numbers, as they are wonderful, and shall be discussing the Quartetto Italiano recording of the works.

Slow Movement for String Quartet was composed in 1905, and is in a Late Romantic style. It opens with a lush melodic theme, open sounding with the writing very fertile. The quality of the playing of the Italiano is also a feature. The violins develop the melody over a rich texture of cello and viola. The music ebbs and flows, but is always attractive. At times the violin soars, only to drop back into the ensemble. A refashioned statement of the melody is created, and the violin completely dominates until the opening variation is reintroduced, with are blissful melodies. A brief pause brings a recapitulation of the opening theme and a lyrical passage ensues, followed by a splendid section which only hints at the theme. The music becomes lighter until a descending violin phrase leads into an extended variation. Another brief pause and a delicate recapitulation fades to a lone concluding cello note.

I guess you have worked out by now that I like this piece. It was one of the first string quartet CDs I ever owned and I have always been taken by its deeply expressive nature.

String Quartet in One movement was also composed in 1905 and at roughly 16 minutes, it is the longest piece for string quartet that Webern wrote. This work is definitely more vigorous than its predecessor. A solo violin introduces a longing descending melody, and several sparse chords are injected into the solo violin part. Now a bank of chords is created which builds into a melody, and then a melancholia. Suddenly there is dynamic melodic movement. Pizzicato prevails for a time and then the piece becomes forceful – strangely the melodies are melancholic, but they are loud. This is dramatic and lasts for some time. The dynamics eventually recede and we are left with a violin melody that we have

424

heard before, which is slowly joined by the other instruments. The feeling remains precious for a time until a change occurs with a little abstraction in the music – there is also a hint of darkness here.

The mood changes again, becoming slightly chaotic, with the violin dominating. This is a long passage, with some tempestuous writing – the tension is stretched tight. A break introduces a sparsity, which invokes a number of different variations on the main theme. Now we have a sparkling start to a new, warmer texture as more variations occur and the feeling is again sparse. A solo violin returns and the ensemble gently reintroduces the theme in a subdued manner. A series of quiet chords close the piece.

Webern was first a student, then associate of Arnold Schoenberg. Together with Alban Berg, they became known as the *Second Viennese School* and were a tremendous influence on 20th century music. These works are really Part One of the Anton Webern story. His lessons from Schoenberg led to a rapid development in atonal and later, serial compositions.

Webern's works for string quartet are readily available by several ensembles on one CD from Amazon US and UK. Some of them are enhanced with bonus tracks. For instance, the Artis Quartet include a String Trio, and the Rondo for String Quartet. Other good candidates include the Leipziger, Emerson and Arditti Quartets. Be aware that some other releases may not contain these two early one movement works.

Spotify has several CDs, and the *Slow Movement* at least, can be found on YouTube with seven versions on earsense. Bouquets to the Quartetto Italiano on the Philips label – they really get to the heart of Webern.

Listenability: A great mixture of Late Romanticism, beautiful melodies, drama and slight dissonance.

[Image courtesy Philips label via Universal Music]

Mieczyslaw Weinberg [1919–1996]

Nationality: Polish
Quartets: Seventeen
Style: Early Modern

String Quartet No. 6

Mieczyslaw Weinberg aka Moishei Vainberg, was a friend of Dmitri Shostakovich. In 1939 he moved to Russia, leaving his family behind. All were killed in the Holocaust but for his father, who was shot under the direct orders of Stalin in 1948. Weinberg's 17 quartets to go well with his 26 symphonies – that is quite an achievement as very few composers of the last 200 years have contributed so many works to the genre. I am going to discuss the Sixth Quartet.

This work, which was written in 1945, has six movements. It starts with a simple folk melody and accompaniment. The melody sounds familiar to me, which suggests it may have been a folk tune that has turned up in other quartets. It is followed by a prolonged passage of violin and viola. The mood changes as the cello is introduced, becoming more incisive – there is some wonderful writing for the first violin here. The piece becomes more modern as it progresses, leading into some agitation, although this is still musical and listenable. It then segues into a sparse, delightful section which features the cello prominently before ending in a gentle fashion.

The second movement, which is short, begins in an insistent manner. The composer gnaws at the music like a dog with a bone, establishing a slightly frantic mood and carrying it to the end. The third movement, which is even shorter at 1:52, is bleak and daunting. Enough said.

The next movement, which is marked adagio, returns to this world with a solemn lone violin introduction. The other players enter slowly, bringing with them a touch of optimism. After a time, the piece progresses into a bewitching feeling at low volume which takes you out of this world again and into the abstract. This leads to a simply stunning conclusion.

Movement five is captivating. The violin sets up a phrase and regularly refers to it as the other instruments change the dynamics as they please. There are many wonderful musical spaces here.

The sixth, and final movement, begins with tension in the air. The harmonic environment is a sense of descending chords while the first violin prevails. It soon moves into a tempo and the cello seems determined to dominate for a while in an enticing slow statement. The tension returns for an extended period and it ends in the way that it began, with a slightly frantic feeling.

I shall refer briefly to the other pieces on the CD.

String Quartet No. 8 is a one movement work. The opening features a brooding texture with the violin and cello in play. The piece moves through several interesting changes of style and tempo. Very enjoyable.

String Quartet No. 15 has nine movements, with many of them quite short. Mostly it is contemplative, but it does have several movements which make you hang on to your seat.

Sixteen of Weinberg's string quartets were issued on six CDs on the CPO label, performed by Quator Danel. The review CD is titled *The Complete String Quartets: Volume 3*. Most of the six discs are still available from Amazon US and UK, sometimes as *New and Used*. Occasionally a single quartet work turns up on a compilation.

Three discs of this series are on Spotify and many Weinberg quartets can be found on both earsense and YouTube.

Listenability: Mildly Modernist with some wonderful lyricism.

— oo0oo —

Karl-Erik Welin [1934–1992]

Nationality: Swedish
Quartets: Nine
Style: Contemporary

A New World of Sound
String Quartets Nos. 1, 6, 7 & 9

Welin wrote his nine string quartets between 1967 and 1990. The four quartets on the CD under discussion are all one movement works, each running from 17 to 20 minutes. Having listened to them intensely over the last couple of weeks, I must admit I am having trouble pinning them down stylistically. I keep hearing new ideas each time. I first heard them as seemingly four basically similar pieces but I think I could now sum it up by saying the disc is a contrasting series of slow, moody music, punctuated by brief periods of positivity.

String Quartet No. 1 is of a pastoral nature. It has a slightly European sound, with some wonderful melodies. It is a stunning first quartet, and a harbinger of things to come.

String Quartet No. 6 has an opening sound reminiscent of Samuel Barber's famous *Adagio* in that it is expressed totally as long static blocks of chords, with each instrument holding the same note for the duration of the chord. It is one of the composer's distinctive stylistic features, reappearing often in the later quartets. No melodic development appears until seven minutes into the piece. This new melodic passage then continues until a brief interjection leads into a gentle abstraction. After another brief crescendo, the melodies return with an interesting dissonant harmonic background. The piece softens as it moves inexorably towards a whisper at the conclusion.

427

String Quartet No. 7 breaks the mould as it opens with a melodic section. Still quiet and sombre, this is dominated by the cello, for which some wonderful melodies are crafted. Broken up occasionally by brief crescendos, the work drifts between the melodic and chordal styles previously mentioned. There is a hint of an ethnic melody at times, with altered non-scale tones coming to the fore, especially in the crescendos. This introduces a folksy quality to the piece which becomes more obvious toward the end, which is a lonely lilting melody, reminiscent of a shepherd boy's flute.

String Quartet No. 9 opens in a reflective, introspective manner. There is a calm, abstract nature at work here, which is sustained for six minutes before the obligatory crescendo appears. This one is longer than usual but the music eventually finds its way back to new melodic material. As the movement progresses it takes on a serious nature with the cello becoming salient again. The end finally settles into a poignancy, reminiscent of the first quartet. I think it is fair to say that this is the most modern sounding work, slightly dark and with more variation. It may point to a change in the composer's style. This never occurred as he died at 58, two years after completing String Quartet No. 9.

These are marvellous works, gently abstruse, melodious and introspective – my favourite kind of music. Sometimes they sound like a string orchestra and even bring to mind Morton Feldman's *String Quartet and Orchestra*. I would love to hear the unissued quartets just to examine the progression from No. 2 to No. 5.

The review CD, performed by The Tale Quartet on the European BIS label, is available freely on Amazon US and UK. There are also alternative versions available.

This CD is on Spotify, and many quartets are on YouTube. All discussed quartets can be heard on earsense.

Listenability: Pure bliss.

— oo0oo —

Egon Wellesz [1885–1974]

Nationality: Austrian
Quartets: Nine
Style: Early Modern

String Quartet No. 4

Egon Joseph Wellesz was one of Arnold Schoenberg's original students, although history doesn't seemed to have bracketed him with Anton Webern and Alban Berg. The only available CD contains String Quartets Nos. 3, 4 and 6. What a shame – given the state of the classical CD market, I probably won't get a chance to hear all of his other string quartets. For anyone interested in his fascinating life story, there is a very comprehensive internet article, *The Forgotten Modernist*, which can be found here:

https://forbiddenmusic.org/2014/06/04/egon-wellesz-1885-1974-the-forgotten-modernist/

The Fourth Quartet, composed in 1920 is in five movements. Starting with some strong statements, a mood of peace ensues with atonal murmurings supporting a lone violin. The cello is a powerful force briefly, leading the ensemble back into a stasis with all instruments in a low register. Unexpectedly, the passage becomes dance-like, before resuming the previous feeling. A dynamic ensemble sustained phrase leads to an abrupt ending.

The movements seem deemed to be played without pauses as the brief second movement commences immediately. It is a series of sporadic atonal violin lines over another murmuring background. There always seems to be something going on here – the cello is particularly evident, with periodic interjections. Two violins approach the end, which is one pizzicato cello note.

The next movement, again quite short, begins with sparse violins leading into a solo cello passage. There is no apparent tempo as the cello dominates, and the violins add support. Now a scratchy violin introduces a crescendo section which is quickly terminated and a sense of abstraction begins to dominate this piece as we have further dynamic interjections. A solo violin concludes but moves straight into the next movement, seamlessly – it has a small part to play as it hints at a melody. Another loud passage leads to a rhythm being established before the cello is prominent again and some raw violin thrusts lead into a tempo with the violins being interrupted by the cello. A change of tonality leads into a helter-skelter of notes and the cello drives forward, complementing the violins. It soon returns to solo and develops a motif which accelerates to another loud interjection. Solo cello ends the movement.

The finale opens with a raw cello passage. This alternates with violin melodies – again there is no tempo here, it is pure sound. A solo violin is soon joined by a pizzicato cello and this makes for a lamenting mood. One violin supports the other, and the ensemble comes back in, leading to a solo cello statement. Again we have a soundscape with the violins reaching out for something, possibly another cello passage, which is the conclusion of the work.

I must confess to being really taken by this quartet. Conceptually it could be viewed without the movement structure as it constantly returns to several recurring musical spaces. It is mostly tonal, but there are some strange, dissonant passages. It's not profound but I enjoyed its cyclical nature – soundscape upon soundscape.

The performance, by the Artis Quartett Wien is worth mentioning, mostly for the tone of the first violin. It is a fabulous rich sound. Similarly, the cello has a wonderful depth to its tone. Quite remarkable really.

The review CD, *Egon Wellesz, String Quartets Nos 3, 4 & 6,* on the Nimbus label, performed by the Artis Quartett Wien is available on Amazon US and UK

This contents of this disc can be heard on Spotify, earsense and YouTube.

Listenability: Mildly abstract, but very expressive.

[Image courtesy Nimbus Records]

Incidental Images #11

A Most Intimate Medium – Four in a Fiat

[Image courtesy Del Sol Quartet]

Graham Whettam [1927–2007]

Nationality: British
Quartets: Four
Style: Contemporary

String Quartets Nos. 1 & 4

Whettam wrote his four string quartets between 1960 and 2007 and revised his second string quartet in 1997, titling it *Hymnos*. Three quartets are available on CD, Nos. 1, 2 and 4.

The First Quartet is in three movements and opens with a solo cello phrase which is answered by the violins. This process is repeated. The next cello entry brings the violins with it and a longing solo violin melody ensues. The ensemble responds with a melancholy which has both the cello and violin being salient at different times before a rhythmic pizzicato takes over. There is a brief ensemble interlude and the pizzicato returns. The ensemble now leads the music into a mild chaos as the various instruments clash repeatedly. Out of this comes a sustained cello line – the violins meander in but the cello leads the melody. The cello is particularly strong and reaches into its high register where it is joined by a searing violin line, also in the high register. This line concludes the movement.

The next movement opens with a strong flourish, and is energetic as the violins dance and the viola and cello set up a rhythmic phrase – there is also pizzicato in this passage. An energised solo cello line is joined by the violins, but a brief pause drops the tempo and the intensity back to nothing. The cello stays prominent over an introspective passage with the violins going with long melodic lines. A sense of melancholy is achieved as one violin plays long phrases, while the second wanders into a high register, with a sparse feeling. The intensity now increases and a measured rhythmic tempo allows the violins to exchange phrases. Pizzicato returns, but the violins persist with energetic melodies. The movement ends with a strong rhythmic flourish.

The third movement, marked adagietto, begins with a moving solo violin, and the cello enters with a similar feeling in support. This violin and cello duet lasts for some time and moves through several different moods. A pizzicato interlude is followed by a feature for the two violins – sparse but played with great expression. This gradually dissipates and a lone violin in the high register takes us to the end of the work.

The Fourth String Quartet is in four movements and is much more modern than the First. The start is a series of rhythmic thrusts moving into intermittent cello lines, with violins hovering in the background. The ensemble finally enters, but the cello dominates proceedings. As the end approaches, it's all about the cello. Finally the violins have something to add, but the cello persists to the end.

There is no break after the first movement, and the cello continues as it opens the second movement – not for long however. A slight chaos is established as the cello spars with the violins and a pizzicato interlude does nothing to change the emotional atmosphere. The cello and violins carry on their dialogue until the intensity finally drops back. Again the cello dominates with subtle violin interjections. A return to the opening thrusts from the first movement concludes.

The third movement features a solo cello opening, before moving into a chaotic feeling. The cello is again salient – this seems to be a feature of the composer's style. The music now drifts into introspection, which also appears to be familiar territory for the composer. A lonely, lamenting passage gradually builds, and eventually moves into a chaos, with seemingly random musical interjections. This finally gives way to a feeling of peace, with all instruments contributing melodic lines. It finishes with the violin in a high register – very wispy.

The final movement features a skittish opening. The ensemble drifts with no noticeable connection with each other. Slowly a violin dialogue appears leading to a return of the cello, as the violins move into their high register where they play in a rather convoluted manner. Finally we have a moment of peace as a violin creates a high-pitched melody, with the cello making occasional statements. The work closes with a quiet violin playing a handful of random notes.

These two quartets have a sense of modern abstraction about them but they never become noisy or aggressive. I feel a lot of entropy here and I don't believe they resemble any composer I have heard recently.

This CD, by the Carducci Quartet, on the Carducci Classic label also features an evocative *Oboe Quartet*. There is a long oboe solo introduction and various passages with and without strings – sometimes it is just strings. It falls somewhere between the first and fourth quartets in style, with several introspective interludes. It is a fine work.

The disc is available from Amazon US and UK.

It can be found on Spotify and both quartets are on earsense and YouTube.

Listenability: Two quality Contemporary works. The Oboe Quartet is a bonus.

Dag Wiren [1905–1996]

Nationality: Swedish
Quartets: Five
Style: Contemporary

Quartets of Great Substance
String Quartets Nos. 2, 4 & 5

In my view, Dag Wiren is a fine composer and I love the progression from the simple folk harmonies of the early quartets, to the rhythmic and harmonic complexities of the later works. I hope this concept will become clearer in the discussion.

Firstly, String Quartet No. 2 is in three movements, and features a folk purity. It opens in a stately manner with a hint of a melody from the wafting violins. An interplay develops, which moves the music forward, bringing forth a moderate tempo, while retaining the joyful conversation. As it progresses, the violins become busier until a loud flourish settles the piece into a forward propulsion with it almost being chaotic, in a pleasant way. There is a brief pause with a longing feeling taking over. Now the violins converse in a moderate tempo and the emotional intensity begins to rise. Suddenly we are back into a racing tempo mostly of a rhythmic, not melodic, nature. A further change brings the cello to the forefront, leading to a recapitulation of the opening theme – this is most delightful. The violins conclude with a note that hangs in the air.

The next movement opens with a gentle, lilting ambience. It again has a simple nature that is driven by a violin melody with pizzicato accompaniment. A change ensues, bringing the two violins together as a duet before the cello joins in and the mood is again gentle and lilting. After a brief pause we are taken into another idyllic space where the cello serves as a backdrop for some sweeping violin phrases – the rhythm is insistent and the end, slightly surprising.

The final movement begins at a breakneck tempo with much quivering of bows. The tempo drops and a sense of the pastoral is felt. The cello dances and the violins make a series of concise statements and the interplay sets up a joyous texture as the opening tempo is reintroduced. After a playful passage the cello is featured – then follows another surprising end, this time, to the quartet.

String Quartet No. 4, which is in five movements, opens with a solo violin, very beautiful, which is then joined by the viola. The melody is slightly reminiscent of the old French nursery rhyme, *Frère Jaques* – Brother Jack, but in a minor key. The viola plays a harmony to the violin melody and this conversation goes on for a minute or so, with variations being slowly introduced. Suddenly, the violin leaps into life and all instruments play a part in a slight period of chaos. This slowly subsides and the solo violin returns to the opening melody while the ensemble dances around, over and under the violin. The music breaks into a racing tempo with pizzicato effects. It concludes and the opening violin returns with the viola in a call and response moment. An indescribably beautiful melody gives way to a few pizzicato strokes and this magnificent movement is over.

The next movement, which is short, opens with a minimalist motif and the first violin comes in over the top. The motif is constantly changing and increases in intensity. There is now a third layer, with the viola becoming prominent. The cello enters, with its own contribution – now we have excitement with much rhythmic punctuation. It doesn't last and the intensity drops back to a violin melody over a walking cello line, which leads to a tranquil conclusion. It is a small gem in the scheme of things.

The third movement is even shorter. It opens with a repeated, frenetic little passage which is punctuated by various string sound effects and cello statements. It ends on a loud cello note.

The next movement features the viola and a lamenting sound. A violin imparts some colour with sparse phrases as the viola keeps rising in pitch and the violin goes with it until a sustained cello note brings in a variation leading to a return of the opening texture. Again the cello initiates further development – there is some fabulous writing here. I feel like I am invading the composer's personal space by listening in on his musings. The opening returns, which is wonderful, and the viola and violin see the movement out. It ends as it started, peacefully. This is another classic movement – most enchanting.

The beginning of the final movement is completely different from anything else in the piece. It is a brisk, brash statement with the ensemble absolutely pulsating. Eventually the tempo relents and we are left with a musical conversation featuring heavy use of pizzicato. The violins make a statement and the cello responds as a quivering violin appears in the background and gradually increases in volume. A strong cello statement is heard and then the cello walks like a jazz bass as the violins quiver. The intensity rises again and eventually drops back to a solo violin. It's all over.

A contrasting String Quartet No. 5 is in three relatively brief movements. A stark melodic phrase sets the scene for the opening. It's abstract as instruments move in and out, with a lot of action for the bows here. A rhythmic ensemble statement is repeated and modified, and breaks where a solo violin features prominently. A period of call and response is tense and the violins are rhythmically incisive before finishing on a repeat of the opening phrase. I had difficulty describing this movement – it won't settle. Lots of angular melodies and jagged edges can be heard in the accompaniment.

The second movement, the longest of the three, opens with a lamenting phrase, which is developed by all of the instruments. Now the ensemble acts as a canvas upon which a violin meanders and the music is stretched tight until the cello takes over and leads it into a different mood. There is some great writing here with the feeling just how I like it – intangible, abstract, longing. A sudden change introduces an up-tempo pizzicato interlude but the entry of a soulful cello puts an end to this and the music returns to its meditative state, and an end to the movement.

The finale maintains a similar feeling to the previous movement – mournful. The viola carries the load and the music now leaps into life, with rhythmic pizzicato leading the way. The intensity increases and an ascending cello, together with the viola, make for a powerful sound. There is plenty of rhythmic impetus here and the harmonised ascending cello line is repeated while the music gathers energy. After a time the sparsity returns and the violins probe this moment. Nearing the end, the opening is repeated, with perhaps a little more intensity. The energy returns for a time until it eventually concludes peacefully.

I am fond of this CD, titled *String Quartets 2-5* on Daphne Records, by the Lysell Quartet and had to have it for myself. Amazon UK has it for 400 pounds but copies are on Amazon US for a regular price. I was able to obtain a copy from ArkivMusic.

Two different versions are on Spotify, including the Lysell, together with several movements on YouTube. All works can be found on earsense.

Listenability: Absolutely marvellous.

— ooOoo —

Hugo Wolf [1860–1903]

Nationality: Austrian
Quartets: One
Style: Late Romantic

String Quartet No. 1

Hugo Philipp Jacob Wolf's one string quartet was composed between 1878 and 1884. It is considered to be a classic of the Romantic era – I shall attempt to do it justice.

The first movement, which is long, and marked grave, commences in exactly that manner. A deep cello supports some serious violin melodies. There are many violin swoops and a lot of energy before a softer, more uplifting theme is introduced. The music is a bit ambivalent at this stage, modulating between major and minor tonalities, and different intensities. Now we have some forceful violin melodies, with strong cello accompaniment. I hear shades of late Beethoven here, which should give you an idea of some of the textures. A quieter section searches for a melody, upon which it finally settles. A more frantic passage then takes over, as the previously mentioned ambivalence continues. Then for a time, the music consists of one sustained low cello note, before the violins bring some intensity, with much quivering of bows. A wonderfully peaceful solo violin results in a brief lament, and the ensemble eases back in, before gradually raising the intensity again. A pause reintroduces a tempo and the violins resume with another Beethoven inspired theme. A softer tone leads into a dance-like feeling and, the violins reduce the intensity before they move again into a frenzy, and eventually a final flourish.

The following movement opens with a motif taken from Beethoven, which is developed at great length, at a medium intensity. The motif keeps returning until eventually, a very precious violin melody takes over. The accompaniment is complementary and evokes a most attractive passage. Now a change to the minor leads into a brief interlude and, further variations on the motif lead to a conclusion. I find this Beethoven motif to be distracting, it is just so prevalent within the movement.

The third movement is long, and marked langsam, which should make it worthwhile. A lone violin creates a slow melody, and with much subtlety until the other instruments enter, with appropriate respect for the gentle texture. The violin becomes stronger, and it is solo again for a time. The cello interjects with strong lines and the ensemble slowly brings a sense of form to the music, as the violins combine to create a luxuriant atmosphere. A change comes with persistent minor chord thrusts, before returning to the previous feeling. Several violin interjections occur, but the basic emotion is one of deep bliss. Eventually, we have some rhythmic chords in a tempo – the chords don't persist, but the tempo does. Now the violins begin to express optimistic melodies, with occasional rhythmic forays, a bit similar to the earlier ambivalence. A solo violin statement evokes memories of the beginning, and the ensemble gathers around, seeking melodies. With a most graceful ending, this is music from heaven.

The final movement begins in a positive manner, as the violins push hard to create a tempo. A light, airy background allows the first violin to express freely. Now a solo cello statement introduces a propulsive interlude, which eventually gives way to another solo cello statement. The violins become lilting, gathering rhythm as the passage progresses through several mood changes – it seems that ambivalence is an integral part of Wolf's style – tempo changes are in abundance in this movement. A pause brings a busy solo cello phase, which again, builds into a strong tempo that leads to an extended flourish to finish.

This is a major Late Romantic work. My impression is that it owes a heavy debt to Beethoven, particularly in the first two movements. Wolf also arranged it for string orchestra, naming it *Italian Serenade*. This version is not long, so it is probably just one movement. There are only a few orchestral versions that I could find, but it does turn up on various CDs.

My review copy, titled *Wolf – Complete Music for String Quartet*, is on the Brilliant Classics label, performed by the Prometeo String Quartet. This version is available on Amazon US at a nice price. Many other versions exist also.

It is on Spotify, earsense and YouTube.

Listenability: Classic Late Romantic quartet with a stunning slow movement.

Christopher Wright [born 1954]

Nationality: British
Quartets: At least four
Style: Modern Contemporary

Early Works
String Quartets Nos. 1 & 2

The First Quartet opens softly and 40 seconds elapse before you hear any real music. A sombre mood ensues until some dissonant interjections appear – this is heady stuff. A brief pause leads back into the introduction with a harmonised violin melody and more ensemble interjections occur. There seems to be plenty of pauses, and consonant violin melodies become slightly dissonant. Further interjections are followed by a mournful cello melody, before a dancing violin leads into chaos which then transforms into a solo cello statement. The chaos returns for an extended period until a quiet takes over – it's peaceful, featuring violin harmonics. Out of this develops some further, atonal melodies, followed by another pause. The ending is again a little chaotic, finishing on several abrupt chords.

The second movement is marked adagio and features a haunting solo violin. It is joined by a second violin and brings about a special moment. The cello enters and the music slowly edges forward, with a hint of atonality and a slight rise in intensity enhancing this prolonged atmosphere. A pause renews the peace, as the violins are sparse. The sound is soft now as a subtle pizzicato interlude leads the movement to completion. This is a fine movement, very delicate.

The final movement goes straight into chaos but soon diminishes in intensity. Now we have strong, dissonant violin lines, sometimes with a heavy rhythmic emphasis. Another pause creates a new light dancing fragment. Gradually the dissonance and the intensity rise for another extended period, until a chaotic ending takes place. This is quite a noisy movement.

The Second Quartet has an opening with tempo, which makes for a change. It doesn't last for long as a solo violin reaches out over the ensemble with a finely crafted melody, while strings sustain a chord in the background. The violin hints at atonality and a burst of energy leads to a chaotic first violin, together with ensemble interjections. As we move towards the end, pizzicato prevails – this lowers the intensity briefly. A slightly aggressive passage concludes this movement.

A slow walking cello commences the second movement. What a fabulous feeling. Gentle violin notes abound, with some string sound effects in the background – appealing in an abstract way. There is a harmonic shift to a new key and the walking cello ceases. This leads to an increase in dynamics and a salient violin melody with strings quivering underneath. Then there is peace for a time, but all the while tension is in the air. Now the violin and cello converse with much vigour before a pause, and violins add short, discrete statements that

438

cry out. String sound effects dominate as the end comes with shimmering violins, gently fading.

A strong violin statement introduces the finale. Slight chaos follows as the violins play with much conviction, and strong solo violin statements can be heard. When the ensemble enters, there is a lot of musical movement going on, driven by a solid rhythmic impetus. A pause leads to a new mood, with the violins intertwining, swapping and overlapping phrases. Another pause brings on much tension in the violins until the ensemble returns with snippets from the opening, and an interestingly harmonised violin line completes the work.

I would categorise this music as measured Modern. It has plenty of moments of peace, together with some elements of the avant-garde style. These include: great contrast in dynamics; use of silence; atonal melodies; rhythmic complexity; aggressive passages and some just plain noisy music. I still found it interesting, and somewhat different to what I am accustomed to hearing. I expect I make it sound more radical than it really is. Strangely, Quartets Nos. 3 and 4 are more conservative.

These works can be found on a CD titled *Wright: Four String Quartets*, on the Nimbus label by the Fejes Quartet. The disc is freely available on Amazon US and UK.

It is on Spotify – look for the CD with a picture of four coloured sheds on the beach. The whole disc is on earsense and several quartets are on YouTube.

Listenability: Quite confronting sometimes.

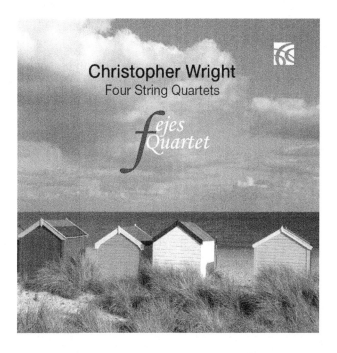

[Image courtesy Nimbus label]

Alexander Zemlinsky [1871–1942]

Nationality: Austrian
Quartets: Four
Style: Early Modern

String Quartet No. 3

Alexander Zemlinsky's life and music are inextricably linked to Arnold Schoenberg. Initially, he was Schoenberg's first and only teacher. It must have been before this time that he wrote his First String Quartet, which is a lush, saccharine, blatantly Romantic work. I hesitate to call it pap, but I don't find it very fulfilling. Eventually, the roles were reversed and Schoenberg began to teach Zemlinsky, whose subsequent output emerged in an Early Modern style, increasing in intensity from No. 2 to No. 4, which is a long and difficult work. Subsequently, Schoenberg married Zemlinsky's sister, Mathilde to complete the cycle of their relationship.

I am going to discuss Zemlinsky's Third Quartet, which is in four movements.

The work commences with a series of atonal melodies and chords, with an open feeling. Now the music becomes more energised, and the ensemble use this new found vigour to construct a short, abstract passage. A change brings forth a gentle dissonance, which is introspective, leading to the violins moving into a more rhythmic mode, before the previous feeling returns. It is extremely sparse as the violins barely lift their heads above water. It does however lead to a fabulous sound, one of deep contemplation. Towards the end, there is a slight flourish from the violins, before the close.

The next movement starts in a sparse manner, with plenty of silences and a few short interjections from the ensemble, before the tension finally breaks and the violins burst into life. This doesn't last and the music returns to a measured sense of abstraction. The mood is static, as things happen slowly before a brief Romantic passage which, strangely enough, doesn't interrupt the abstraction. In fact, it becomes sparser and ends simply on a quiet phrase.

The third movement follows on from the previous atmosphere and violins project tranquil and sparse, slightly atonal melodies. A brief louder phase is fleeting and another inward-looking scene returns. Towards the end, we hear a slight rise in volume, and a lone violin concludes what would have to be one of the most introspective string quartet movements that I have come across.

The finale begins with a lilting violin which receives support from the ensemble. A brief pizzicato interlude leads into a scurrying violin, again at a low volume. The cello enters in a vigorous manner while the violins express themselves in a way that I haven't heard before in this work. There is a slightly burlesque moment and some violin melodies occur before the end comes with two strong chords.

I find this to be a slightly strange work. It is original, but the composer seems to be infatuated with introspection – so be it.

The quartet is freely available on Amazon US and UK. My review copy is a 2-CD complete set on the Chandos label, performed by the Schoenberg Quartet. I also like the sound of a similar set by the LaSalle Quartet. You can obtain various single CD releases.

The Schoenberg set is one of several versions on Spotify and there is a plethora of individual movements and complete quartets on YouTube and earsense.

Listenability: Early Modern, but very easy on the ear.

William Zinn [born 1924]

Nationality: American
Quartets: At least one
Style: Contemporary

Works for String Quartet

As well as String Quartet No. 1, from 1966, there are two single movement works on the review CD. Zinn's music is heavily influenced by Jewish culture and I have decided to discuss these two single movement works – both pieces have a link to the Holocaust.

Elie Wiesel – A Portrait – A low, resonant cello introduces this work with a brief statement, followed by a solo, distant violin, expressing a modal melodic line in the middle register. A response by a stronger violin leads to another instance of the first phrase. The first violin begins another distant melody and the second violin falls in behind it. Now a solo cello expresses a longer passage, until the violins return. The piece continues in the same vein for a time, before the solo cello returns briefly and leads the ensemble into a folk-like melody and a tempo. Cascading violins thrive in this rhythmic passage, with obviously Jewish-inspired modal lines. Again the solo cello has a short solo passage before leading back into a tempo – melodically, it is as important as the violins.

The solo violin returns and a measured ensemble paints a haunting, melodic soundscape before overlapping melodic lines evoke great feeling as the mood oscillates between a dance-like tempo and solo or harmonised melodic statements. There is a great sense of drama as the cello and violins dig into their work. The opening cello and violin statements are constantly repeated, always leading into a dance feeling. Nearing the end, a shrill solo violin and then solo cello reappear, possibly for the last time as the violin follows the cello. More drama is presented, albeit briefly, and a violin duet is joined by the cello. This leads into a short ensemble passage and a considered, consonant solo violin conclusion.

441

Kol Nidre Memorial – This piece, which is based on the theme of the Jewish *Kol Nidre* prayer, begins with a stunning violin duet, again modal, as the ensemble lays down a peaceful harmonic background. Out of this steps a wonderfully pure, aching solo violin line which makes time stand still. Now harmonised lines featuring cello and the two violins are very powerful. The solo violin returns and responds to a moving cello statement, leading to a strong ensemble section. Again, the dynamics are minimal and two violins dialogue before another sweeping solo violin line gives way to ensemble musings – a passage of solo violin, supported by a quivering bow and cello follows. The music is similar to the first piece, in that different feelings are re-presented over the duration. A cello leads into a pulsing section with further strong, harmonised but still modal, melodic lines. Now gathering strength, the ensemble is majestic for a time, before dropping back to the sparsity of two violins. Modal harmony abounds in the louder passages, while Western harmony is present in the quieter moments. The work concludes on one such moment.

These are inherently spiritual works, sometimes akin to John Tavener or Arvo Pärt, perhaps even more powerful at times – not necessarily spiritually, but dynamically.

The review CD is titled *William Zinn - Works for String Quartet*, on the Nimbus label and is performed by the Wihan Quartet. This disc can be found on Spotify, earsense and YouTube.

Listenability: Powerful, moving spiritual works with a Jewish flavour.

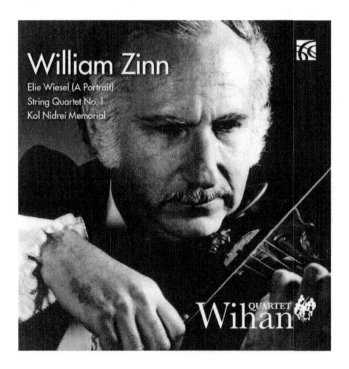

[Image courtesy Nimbus label]
442

APPENDICIES

[handwritten notes, largely illegible]

finale has been arranged for 3. Oral

2. opens with a slow movement
with some *~~~* wonderful
melodies. Second movement is *~~~*
~~~ with an agitated feeling *~~~*
it's quite intense music
combine 2 + 3

3 measured *~~~* keep thinking
it wants to break out into something
fierce

4 *~~~* large but is spiked
with dissonant *~~~* before it
settles into a subdued *~~~*

5 similar to 4 but *~~~* calm
and measured

12 - 35 mins of adagio ( )

~~~ some *~~~* rhythmic *~~~*
similar to No. 8
1. *~~~* Pentatonic
melodies very sparse
some *~~~* but mostly quiet
5 similar diatonic as in 1.
~~~ passage to be performed
in a slow and dignified manner
ADAGIO - slow and graceful

[Scratchings for an early review of Shostakovich SQ No. 15]

Appendix 1 – Glossary

Common Composer Markings

adagietto: slightly faster than adagio

adagio: slowly and gracefully

allegretto: fairly quick – faster than andante and usually slower than allegro

allegro: fast

andante: walking speed – moderately slow

appassionato: with passion

arco: played with the bow – as opposed to plucking the strings

Bartok pizzicato: the strings are to be plucked so hard they hit the fingerboard leading to a harsh sound

battuto: hit – the bow is made to strike the string, not bow it

crescendo: gradually getting louder

espressivo: expressively; may also encourage physical expression by the performer; allows the taking of slight liberties with articulation and dynamics

fortissimo: very loud

grave: very slow – solemn

langsam: slow, slowly, gently

largo: slow and dignified manner

larghetto: rather slow

lento: to be performed slowly

mezzo-forte: moderately loud

moderato: moderate speed

molto: qualifier – very – much – e.g. allegro molto = very fast – molto largo = very slowly

piano: soft

pianissimo: very soft

pizzicato: a technique for stringed instruments where strings are plucked with the right hand

presto: very fast

poco: qualifier – a little – to a small degree – e.g. poco adagio – a little faster than adagio

romanze: played with a song-like character

rubato: played freely, not at a fixed tempo

sarabande: a slow, stately Spanish dance in triple time

vivace: lively

This a just a selection of markings to which I regularly refer – more comprehensive listings can be found all over the internet.

Other Relevant Musical Terms

abstract: music that is not explicitly about anything – in contrast to program music, it is non-representational and often atonal. It could apply to Beethoven's Late Quartets – a complex Bach Fugue or extremely modern works. You can't quite put your finger on it – a bit mysterious.

arpeggio: a chord where notes are played in succession rather than simultaneously. This succession may either be slow, or rapid.

atonal: music that has no tonal centre, and is not in any particular key. Leads to an abstract, often dissonant sounding music. It can also sound very beautiful.

avante-garde: movements or individuals at the forefront of innovation and experimentation in their fields.

canon: a piece of music where one voice repeats the part of another, throughout a section.

chamber music: music for small ensembles, originally played in homes by amateur musicians. Due to this, most of the early chamber music was not technically difficult. Over time, the string quartet has become the most popular chamber ensemble. It is now rarely played in homes.

counterpoint: music consisting of two or more lines that sound simultaneously, each played with a different phrasing.

chromatic: interspersing the seven primary tones of a scale with the five normally unused tones.

Deutsche Grammophon: from Germany, the world's most prolific classical recording company.

entropy: I love this word, for me it's always meant degree of randomness but it has some scientific definition as well.

exposition: the initial presentation of the theme of a composition, movement, or section. The use of the term generally implies that the material will be developed or varied at a later stage.

FOSQC: French One String Quartet Club – the more than a handful of French composers who wrote just one string quartet. Members include: Debussy, Ravel, Faure, Dutilleux and many others, who are scattered throughout this book.

fugue: a short melody or phrase, known as the subject – introduced by one instrument, successively taken up by others and developed by interweaving the parts. For a more detailed definition, please read my *The Art of Fugue* discussion under 'BACH'.

glissando: a glide from one pitch to another – used on stringed instruments. In modern music, the technique of bowing a note, and then sliding the fingers down the fingerboard. This leads to notes that descend in a smeared manner. It, is a very common technique, producing micro-tones, and a whining sound. Plural *glissandi*, but I prefer glissandos.

harmony or harmonic background: the sounding of two or more musical notes at the same time to form chords – used to accompany a melody.

harmonise: the sound of two or more instruments playing consonant notes together, with the same phrasing, leading to a richer texture.

harmonics: the creation of a sound effect on stringed instruments. The player gently touches a string above where a note would normally be fingered, then plucks the string. A bell-like sound ensues.

Impressionism: a movement among various composers in Western classical music, mainly during the late 19th and early 20th centuries, whose music focuses on suggestion and atmosphere, writing about the feeling obtained from some object or event, not about the thing itself – thanks, Wiki.

je ne sais quoi: a pleasant quality that is hard to describe – French.

lyrical: song-like – expressing the composer's emotions in an imaginative and beautiful way.

miniaturism: fitting a lot of musical expression into a small space. I made it up.

minimalism: a hotly debated term. Prominent features of the technique include: consonant harmony; steady pulse; immobile drones; stasis or gradual transformation; and often reiteration of musical phrases or smaller units such as figures, motifs, and cells – thanks, Wiki.

modal: a system of using different scales than the most common major scale. Leads to ethnic or folk-like melodies. Obscure modes are the standard in some middle-eastern countries, leading to the phrase *eastern sounding.*

microtones: intervals smaller than a semitone – the notes between the notes.

Neoclassicism: a twentieth century movement, particularly popular in the period between the two World Wars, in which composers drew inspiration from certain elements of music from the eighteenth century. A reaction against Modernism.

ostinato: a continually repeated, musical phrase or rhythm.

pastoral: having the emotional feeling of a countryside e.g. trees, hills, wide open plains.

pentatonic scales: scales containing only five notes as compared to the seven notes found in a normal scale – commonly used in folk music around the world – leading to an open feel in the melodies.

program music: music intended to convey an impression of a definite series of images, scenes, or events.

recapitulation: repeating a melody that has been played earlier, usually after a development phase.

serial or twelve-tone: although these two terms are technically not identical, I do tend to use them interchangeably for simplicity. The 12 pitches are arranged into a tone-row and the composer then has to follow a series of rules in using the tones. For example, no one tone can be repeated until all of the other eleven have been used. Various manipulations can be made to the basic row, leading to 48 possibilities. Can lead to very difficult music for some listeners.

staccato: a technique where consecutive notes are played sharply and cut off, leaving gaps between the notes

string quartet: a musical ensemble consisting of two violins, a viola and a cello – a piece written for such an ensemble.

syncopated: stressing a normally weak beat.

tonal music/tonality: a musical system that arranges pitches or chords to induce a hierarchy of perceived relations, stabilities, and attractions. The pitch or triadic chord with the greatest stability is called the tonic, and the root of the tonic chord is considered to be the key of a piece or song – as opposed to atonality, which has no key centre. Tonalities may be major or minor, which is a slightly darker version of major.

tone poem: an instrumental composition intended to portray a particular story or poem, scene or mood.

This Glossary, in PDF format can be found at the following address – from here it can be downloaded and/or printed:

www.jhredguitar.com/sq_amim/glossary.pdf

Appendix 2 – Categories and Style Descriptors

I have spent some time thinking about a set of style descriptors for use in discussing string quartets and composers and have come up with seven that seem to suit my needs. Of course this a pretty much an academic exercise – it is just meant to give you some context to the works.

Classical

Usually defined as the period from the death of Bach in 1750 through to Beethoven.

Late Classical

As I only generally discuss quartets from 1800 onwards, with a few exceptions, I consider this category to be quartets written after 1800, until the style disappeared, probably around 1850 – just speculating on that date. Examples would include Arriaga and Cherubini.

Romantic

Quartets written after Beethoven. Examples would include Schumann and Schubert.

Late Romantic

Composers who continued to write Romantic quartets from the late 1800s well into the twentieth century. Examples would include Asasi and Wolf.

Early Modern

Music written in the early to mid-1900s. Examples would include Schoenberg, Bartok and Haba.

Contemporary

An extremely disparate style of current composers, who do not overtly embrace the concept of Modernism to any great degree. Examples would include Tavener and Pärt.

Contemporary Modern

Composers who developed modern styles from the 1950s until now. Examples would include Feldman, and Carter. This style is characterised by immense diversity, with a tendency to varying degrees of difficulty for the listener. Sometimes I'll use **Modern Contemporary** if I feel like it, indicating quite modern.

Of course, styles overlap and my examples may not be the most appropriate, but there you have it. I regularly use **modern** to describe certain traits of quartets written in the twentieth century, where forward looking composers came up with manifold new ways of emotional expression – often of an abstract nature. Some of these styles withered on the vine, but others blossomed and created a significant influence on the genre which remains to this day.

Appendix 3 – String Quartet Blog and Website

My blog, titled *String Quartets – A Most Intimate Medium*, can be found at:

www.sqblog.jhredguitar.com.

I started posting in May 2016, and most of the posts are in this book. I've totally rewritten many posts, especially some of my early efforts, and applied significant changes to others, for various reasons. I would appreciate it if readers would notify me of any typos or errors of fact in this book as I do intend to publish a Third Edition in the future. My direct contact is:

johnhood@iinet.net.au

If you are interested in my other musical life as a composer, blues guitar and harmonica player, I have a site which details my various musical exploits, together with my CDs as free downloads at:

www.jhredguitar.com

I have also written a musical autobiography, *For the Love of Music*, which is available on Amazon Kindle, or as a printed copy on my website.

Best wishes,

John Hood – September, 2018

Printed in Great Britain
by Amazon

18177489R00274